The Economics of Middle East Peace

The Economics of Middle East Peace

Views from the Region

edited by
Stanley Fischer
Dani Rodrik
Elias Tuma

The MIT Press
Cambridge, Massachusetts
London, England

This book was set in Palatino by DEKR Corporation and was printed and bound in the United States of America.

Library of Congress Cataloging-in-Publication Data

The Economics of Middle East peace : views from the region / edited by
Stanley Fischer, Dani Rodrik, Elias Tuma.
p. cm.
"This book is a collection of papers originally presented at a conference at Harvard University on November 14–16, 1991"—P.
Includes bibliographical references and index.
ISBN 0-262-06153-8
1. War—Economic aspects—Middle East—Congresses. 2. Middle East—Defenses—Economic aspects—Congresses. 3. Peace—Economic aspects—Congresses. 4. Middle East—Foreign economic relations—Congresses. 5. Economic stabilization—Middle East—Congresses.
I. Fischer, Stanley. II. Rodrik, Dani. III. Tuma, Elias.
HC415.15.Z9D43 1993
330.956′053—dc20 92-21503
CIP

Contents

Foreword

Joseph A. Califano, Jr.

The Institute for Social and Economic Policy in the Middle East was founded ten years ago on this proposition: politicians sign papers, but people make peace. This volume, the only one of its kind, records two years of extraordinary meetings of Egyptians, Israelis, Jordanians, Lebanese, Palestinians, and Syrians to discuss and develop common economic development plans for the Middle East. The Institute is proud to have this as its first book.

Located at Harvard University's John F. Kennedy School of Government, the Institute's unique mission is to put Middle East Arabs and Israelis together—to study and to work with each other on common problems ranging from economic development and environmental protection to health care and social services. In the process these professionals, Jews and Arabs—the latter either Christian or Moslem—come to appreciate that they share the same dreams for their children and grandchildren, the same concerns for the future, and the same hopes and anxieties. By harnessing their energies and skills, they lay a foundation for peace far more solid and durable than any number of international agreements.

No dream has been more cherished and elusive than the dream of peace for all in the Middle East. Just imagining peace between Israelis and Palestinians, and Israel and its other neighbors, has until recent months seemed an impossible dream. In the winter of 1992–1993, it remains an ideal in which hope takes precedence over experience. But at least, for the first time, something is happening that can fairly be called a peace process. Burdened by history, yet inspired by hope, the participants have turned their energies toward a joint search for peace throughout the Middle East.

Peace is not likely to come as a sudden transformation from the chronic conflict of past decades. It more probably will be achieved in bits and pieces, through laborious and uneven developments and understandings that move the parties along a bumpy, winding road. The search for peace demands courage from the political leaders on all sides, and understanding from their peoples and the rest of the world.

The Institute for Social and Economic Policy in the Middle East seeks to help ease the peace process by shifting attention from past to future, from history to hope. The Institute's focus is on palpable opportunities for economic cooperation among the parties once peace has been achieved—the kind of joint enterprises that can cement a lasting peace.

We are mindful that peace is a product of the parties engaging each other in serious discussion of concrete issues, arguing out disagreements, exploring constructive collaboration. While the initial emphasis of the Institute was on cooperation in the post-peace era, we now are deeply concerned with the economics of transition from conflict to peace. In our view, detailed policy planning for the transition period can accelerate the advent of lasting peace.

That's why the Institute has established the Seminar on Economic Cooperation in the Middle East. The Institute inaugurated the Seminar in 1989 at the John F. Kennedy School of Government. The Seminar brings together economists and business people from the Middle East as well as from Europe, Japan, and North America. Among the Middle East participants are Egyptians, Israelis, Jordanians, Lebanese, Palestinians, and Syrians. Participants from several Gulf States joined the Seminar in the summer of 1992.

This volume is a product of the Seminar, a record of a forum where for the first time in history, Arab and Israeli economists from these places worked together to discuss, assess, and identify opportunities for economic cooperation among all the peoples of the Middle East.

The guiding purpose of the Seminar on Economic Cooperation is to develop a framework for the economic development of the Middle East. To that end, the Seminar focuses on such regional topics as health planning, jobs, economic alliances, data banks, and joint ventures, public or private. In its first year, our Seminar sponsored several large conferences for a general discussion of economic issues. Then the focus shifted to discrete topics, examined in small workshops. At a 1992 workshop on regional health planning, Egyptian, Israeli, Jordanian, and Palestinian participants developed a proposal that called for early concentration on infectious diseases, health information systems, medical and paramedical training, establishing and improving health services and facilities in the West Bank and Gaza, and financing the delivery of health care.

The Institute is greatly indebted to the Seminar's Steering Committee of Harvard and Massachusetts Institute of Technology faculty members. This group includes Professors Thomas Schelling, who acts as chair, Richard Eckaus, Stanley Fischer, Frank Fisher, Richard Freeman, Zvi Griliches, Joseph Newhouse, Dwight Perkins, Henry Rosovsky, and Lester Thurow. They have all participated actively in the Seminar and its workshops.

In addition to the Seminar on Economic Cooperation, The Institute for Social and Economic Policy in the Middle East sponsors the Middle East Educational Fellowship Program, which brings midcareer professionals in the fields of health, human services, and income security from the region to study for one year at the Harvard School of Public Health and the Kennedy School of Government. The Fellows so far have included Egyptians, Israelis (both Arab and Jewish), Jordanians, Lebanese, and Palestinians, and shortly will include Syrians as well as Fellows from the Gulf countries. The Fellows live and work with each other, helping to prepare for shared endeavors in the Middle East, as political circumstances permit. In great measure, this program owes its start and vitality to John Cardinal O'Connor, the Archbishop of New York, the chairman of the Institute's Fellowship Committee.

The Seminar on Economic Cooperation has functioned since September 1989 only through the generous support of far-sighted philanthropists, led by Charles R. Bronfman and Zein A. Mayassi. Important contributors include Malcolm Brachman, Leo Fields, Leo Kahn, Paul Singer, Henry Taub, and Investcorp. I also wish to acknowledge the significant generosity of: Omar Al-Askari, Nicholas Chammas, Max Factor III, Alan Gold, Edwin Jaffe, Raymond Johnson, Melvyn Klein, Leo Nevas, Lyndon Olson, Irving Rabb, and Bernard Rapoport. Most of the above are members of the Institute's unique board, composed as it is of leading Arabs, Palestinians and others, and Jews.

The Institute for Social and Economic Policy in the Middle East hopes that this, its first book publication, will contribute to the quest for peace in the Middle East.

Joseph A. Califano, Jr.
Founding Chairman of the Board
The Institute for Social and Economic Policy in the Middle East
John F. Kennedy School of Government
Harvard University

Acknowledgments

We wish to thank Professors Stanley Fischer, Dani Rodrik, and Elias Tuma for editing the first published volume of The Institute for Social and Economic Policy in the Middle East. Their sustained effort is greatly appreciated. As well, we would like to acknowledge the contributions of the authors of the papers.

The board of this Institute, led by its chairman, Joseph A. Califano, has guided, financed, and defended the Institute through a difficult first decade. On the occasion of the Institute's tenth anniversary, this volume is dedicated to the members of its board.

Leonard J. Hausman
Director

Anna D. Karasik
Associate Director

The Institute for Social and Economic Policy in the Middle East
Kennedy School of Government
Harvard University

1 Introduction

Stanley Fischer,
Dani Rodrick, and
Elias Tuma

This book, a collection of papers originally presented at a conference at Harvard University on November 14–16, 1991, addresses the economic consequences of peace in the Middle East. Our focus is on the economies most directly affected by the Arab-Israeli conflict, those of Egypt, Syria, Jordan, Lebanon, Israel, and the occupied territories. We began these studies about three years ago with a certain mix of idealism, hope, and confidence that whatever investment might be sunk in the cause of peace would pay off in the long run. The complicated logistics involved in putting together the conference and this volume reflect the complexity of Middle Eastern affairs, and of the economics of peace in a region where peaceful relations will come as a shock after decades of conflict. The prospects of a payoff are now much better than when we started, because Arabs and Israelis are finally talking peace with each other.

The following chapters reflect exchanges of ideas and extensive informal consultation among parties with various points of view on the conflict. In that sense the ideas presented are of particular interest as being largely the fruits of joint, though informal, efforts by Arab, Israeli, and other economists in the service of peace. The reader will find here a wide range of perspectives on estimates of the potential economic effects of peace in the region. We will not try to resolve all differences in this introductory chapter, nor try to present a consensus view of any sort. Our purpose in this chapter is twofold: first, to discuss some major themes that have emerged, and second, to provide an overview of the chapters that follow.

Major Themes

Consider that military expenditures in the countries neighboring on the Arab-Israeli conflict exceed on average 15% of national income (compared to 5% in all developing countries). Consider that political instability and the prospect of regional hostilities are the prime deterrent to private investment in the region, both domestic and foreign. Consider that the continuous threat of war has legitimized and entrenched inefficient, inward-looking development strategies, as well as authoritarian political regimes. Consider finally the huge loss of human life, as well as of human and physical capital, in the recurring conflicts of the region. Can anyone seriously doubt that real, durable peace will be an economic boon to the countries of the Middle East?

The answer at the most fundamental level is of course negative. War, or the threat of war, is costly to human life and well-being. The chapters in this volume describe in great detail the detrimental economic consequences of war and the potential benefits of peace for each of the economies in the region. However, one of the important themes that also emerges is that the full benefits of peace, even a comprehensive and durable peace, will not be reaped automatically. Transition costs will have to be paid as armies are demobilized and military factories converted to civilian uses. Governments will have to change the way they manage their economies. They will have to liberalize their economies to unleash entrepreneurial energies in the private sector and balance their budgets to stabilize the macroeconomic environment. Although the transitional costs can be partially offset by external capital inflows, the availability of large amounts of external financing is uncertain and will depend in any case on domestic policy. Hence the benefits of peace will accrue primarily to those countries in which the required changes are undertaken.

What, precisely, are these benefits? As El-Naggar and El-Erian point out in their chapter, peace allows a higher level of national security to be "purchased" at a lower level of spending, and is therefore just like an exogenous improvement in an economy's technology. The resources released can be used to increase present consumption as well as future consumption through productive investments. Because military spending is so high in the Middle East, the potential for such benefits is very large indeed.

Some simple calculations can help quantify these benefits. Suppose that the countries concerned reduce their military spending from the current level of 15% of gross domestic product (GDP) to the developing-country average of 5%. This would release resources worth 10% of GDP. Note that this is a *permanent* increase that would accrue year after year: with a discount rate of 8% (and no growth otherwise), the present value of the savings would be 125% of current GDP. Now suppose further that only half of the resources saved (i.e., 5% of GDP) are invested. At an incremental capital-output ratio (ICOR) of 3, this would yield a permanent increase in the economy's growth rate of $0.05/3 = 1.67\%$. At a higher ICOR of 4, the increase in growth would be $0.05/4 = 1.25\%$.

These increases in growth are as large as any that economists can hope to engineer by their usual advice on policy reform. Moreover, this may not be all. The diminished external threat, we hope, can unleash policy reforms that have been resisted before. The private sector may be given freer rein, regulations and controls eased, and trade liberalized. With the burden of military spending greatly reduced, fiscal deficits and macroeconomic instability may become easier to escape. One effect of these changes in the policy environment would be to channel investments to more productive areas, and to lower the economy's ICOR. This would magnify the effect of the increase in investment. For example, a reduction in ICOR from 4 to 3 on marginal investments would yield an additional increase in growth under the above scenario of just under one-half of a percentage point (0.42%).

In addition, private capital, from both domestic and foreign sources, may be crowded in. As domestic economic management improves and the threat of regional hostilities disappears, investors are likely to perceive the region as a much better investment risk. Although precise figures do not exist, it is widely believed that past capital flight has led to the accumulation of vast resources abroad. If the experience of Latin America is any guide, we can expect a portion of these resources to be repatriated some years after the economic (and political) situation stabilizes.

Finally, peace will make regional economic integration more probable. Looking at regional trade from the perspective of basic customs-union theory, the presumption would be that the economies of the regions are basically competitive with (rather than complementary to) one another and that their natural trade partners are countries *outside* the region, not their neighbors. This would limit benefits from regional trading arrangements such as free trade areas or customs unions. Some integration will take place naturally, however, even in the absence of regional arrangements designed for that purpose: trade flows will become less distorted by the effects of enmities, boycotts, mutual restrictions, et cetera. Arab countries are a natural market for Israeli-manufactured products, as Nadav Halevi argues in his chapter. Egypt's trade with its Arab neighbors is at ridiculously low levels (see the chapter by Heba Handoussa and Nemat Shafik), and this trade can only increase. Moreover, given the small size of the region's economies and the ubiquitous externalities, there is much to be gained by cooperating in areas such as water and infrastructure (e.g., power plants, airports, hotels, tourism projects).

Hence it is not difficult to construct a virtuous-circle scenario under which all of these beneficial consequences feed on one another and enhance the effect of the others. The *indirect* benefits of peace in the form of repatriated private capital and increased incentives for economic reform may turn out to be quantitatively more significant than the direct peace dividend through cuts in military spending.

There is no inherent reason this scenario could not be made a reality. But note the various links in the chain of logic. Peace must be real and durable, and perceived as such. Governments must take advantage of peace to reduce military spending. The resources thereby released must be used—at least in part—for productive investment. Governments must elect to reform their macroeconomic and microeconomic policies. The economies must experience an increase in the efficiency with which resources are utilized, and not get bogged down in transitional adjustment costs.

While one of the central themes in this volume is the large potential for gains, others are more cautionary. Practically all of the chapters stress the need for domestic policy reform in order to reap the peace dividend. They also stress the likely transition costs in the short run, as budgets are adjusted and resources are reallocated. They caution that unless peace is comprehensive there will be little economic gain: the Israeli and Egyptian peace dividends from the Camp David accords were constrained by the continued state of war in the broader Arab-Israeli relationship. They also highlight two important uncertainties in the background. First, how likely is peace to enhance—rather than reduce—the incentives of governments to undertake economic reforms? Second, can external capital inflows be mobilized in adequate quantities to enable the reforms and alleviate short-term costs?

To varying extents, all countries of the region suffer from a complex syndrome of inefficient economic policies and bloated government budgets, a syndrome made possible by external capital inflows and the perceived needs of national security. How are governments likely to respond to changes in the external political environment? On the face of it, the reduction of the external threat should make governments more willing to adopt efficiency-enhancing reforms such as trade liberalization. As noted above, the real gains of peace will be reaped by countries that choose to do so. But as Diwan and Papandreou remind us in their chapter, things need not be that simple. There is considerable latent political instability in many countries of the region due to high levels of urbanization, unemployment, and repressed political activity. The elimination of the external enemy may make it more difficult for these governments to contain the instability. Under the circumstances, economic liberalization, with its short-term costs and dislocations, may be perceived as too dangerous by fragile governments. Paradoxically, this would only delay the economic benefits of peace.

The problems may be eased, and incentives for policy reform enhanced, by making external capital available at generous terms in the wake of peace. But here we face another question mark: what are the likely consequences of peace for the magnitude of external capital inflows? There is some feeling in the region that "good behavior" at the peace talks is likely to be rewarded by the West with financial assistance. However, it is not clear to us from where this assistance would come. Western Europe has its hands tied in the reconstruction of Eastern Europe; the United States has severe budgetary problems; and Japan has so far shown little direct interest in this part of the Middle East. Moreover, much of the Gulf money may dry up as the motivating reason—the state of war against Israel—disappears. This leaves only the multilateral institutions (the International Monetary Fund and the World Bank) and private sources (mainly repatriation of flight capital). Funds from these sources are unlikely to add up to a Marshall Plan for the Middle East. Hence, an extended financial bonanza in the wake of peace is unlikely. This may be too gloomy a picture to draw, but it is intended only to warn against unrealistic expectations, and to focus more intensely on peace as an economic asset in its own right and the potential gains from reduced military spending.

An Overview of the Volume

The contributors of this volume were asked to analyze the potential economic benefits from peace between the Arab countries and Israel, especially those arising from trade and economic cooperation. They did so in their individual capacities, as professional economists. The issues underlying a future Arab-Israeli peace are complex and intensely political, and the participants had different views on the essential elements of a durable peace. Rather than attempt to reach an agreement on this issue, on which we have no comparative advantage, we agreed that each participant should make his or her own assumptions about the political outlines of a future peace. Most of the authors in the volume have assumed there will be a Palestinian state.

The views expressed in these chapters are those of their authors and do not represent the views of the institutions with which they are affiliated, the editors, or of the Institute for Social and Economic Policy in the Middle East. As editors, we have tried to interfere as little as possible with the substance of the papers, except for technical issues that we felt needed clarification. However, we did provide all the authors with comments and suggestions for their consideration in preparing the final version.

In the first of the two regional chapters, Said El-Naggar and Mohamed El-Erian deal with the economic implications of a comprehensive peace in the Middle East. The key word here is comprehensive, which means that peace will be voluntary, durable, and satisfying to all parties, and therefore conducive to free economic interaction among them. In these circumstances, economic and structural reforms deemed necessary would become feasible, though they would not necessarily follow. Commitment to reform by policymakers of each respective country would be necessary to realize the economic benefits of this comprehensive peace. El-Naggar and El-Erian conclude that the benefits of peace would certainly be high because of the reallocation of resources that would follow in favor of productive activities, trade expansion, economic reform, and reduction of risk. These benefits would be enhanced by joint ventures, development of regional infrastructures, and eventual economic integration, all of which would be conducive to expansion of foreign trade and assistance. These potential benefits would of course require special financial institutions to make them possible. Peace would facilitate the establishment of these institutions and bolster the spirit of cooperation.

Ishac Diwan and Nick Papandreou focus on the relationship between peace and economic reform, noting that economic fluctuations in the 1970s and 1980s in the Middle East suggest the need to promote economic stability. Reform has been difficult, however, because the war environment creates rigidities that obstruct change. Furthermore, economic reform, as proposed by international institutions, tends to be perceived as threatening, especially because those types of reform have not always proved to be credible and effective. Finally, economic reform tends to be costly and redistributive and once again forms a threat to those in seats of power. A peace environment, in contrast, could have an impact on the economies of the region in at least three ways: by removing the negative factors generated by war; by giving more freedom and incentives to the private sector; and by increasing the probability of receiving foreign assistance, at least in the period immediately following a peace agreement. Gains may also be realized by potential cooperation in such areas as regional water use and management, labor mobility, and economic stabilization policies. The authors, however, are careful to warn that a peace agreement by itself does not guarantee benefits. In the immediate period following peacemaking, instability and dislocation may occur. Therefore, aid and cooperation from outside the region may be necessary to restore stability and help the respective countries adjust to the peace economy and environment.

In discussing these two chapters, John Waterbury raises some sobering and somewhat pessimistic observations. Both chapters seem to him to be too optimistic because they concentrate on economic variables only, virtually ignoring the unfavorable political structures and the regimes that dominate the Middle East region. Peace and economic cooperation are real possibilities, but unless basic changes in the political structures take place, it is unlikely that many of the potential benefits can be realized.

The next six chapters are case studies of the economic benefits that could accrue to individual countries as a result of peace. Heba Handoussa and Nemat Shafik analyze the economics of peace as applied to Egypt, a country that has had a decade of peaceful relations with Israel. The economic effects of the 1978 settlement with Israel, according to the authors, have been modest. Egypt still spends a high percentage of its GNP on defense, and few economic benefits can be observed. The positive effects have been limited because the peace settlement was partial, neither exhaustive nor applicable to other countries in the region, because of the boycott imposed on Egypt and because of the cut in aid it received from the oil-rich countries.

Nevertheless, the potential economic gains of a comprehensive peace settlement could be great if certain economic reforms are introduced so as to increase incentives, promote Egyptian capital repatriation, and enhance tourism and labor mobility. Economic integration in the region must be viewed with caution, however, given the failure of previous attempts and the limited complementarity among the Arab countries. Whether these trade reforms would permit a higher degree of complementarity to develop through new specialization is not obvious and must be worked on to make it real. Again we are reminded that peace alone will not guarantee prosperity, but peace together with appropriate economic policies should be highly promising.

Rizkallah Hilan looks at the economic consequences of a "just and lasting peace" on Syria, in a mix of philosophical, theoretical, and applied perspectives. For example, he asks whether war can be an engine of growth, or rather a hindrance in the way of growth. In Syria the burden of defense expenditure has been very heavy. Whether peace will bring about a redress of that burden and allow economic gains to be realized will depend on the form of the peace agreement. Will it be based on a balance of forces and thus remove interregional threats, or will it be imposed by the strong on the weak and thus become another source of insecurity and instability? Furthermore, will it be a true and lasting peace arrangement or simply an armistice and a cease-fire agreement? In the latter of each of these two pairs of options the economic consequences can hardly be significant. If there is a genuine and lasting peace, the economic dividend can be great indeed. It could be realized through a reduction of defense expenditures, promotion of trade, joint ventures, resource mobility and reallocation, and eventual regional economic integration. Hilan, however, suggests that the indirect effects of peace on economic development of the country may be more important than the direct effects. Indirect effects could come in the form of reformed economic policies, rational decision making, improved incentives, reduced imbalances, manageable inflation, and higher productivity.

As discussant, William Tyler points out numerous similarities in these two chapters, as Egypt and Syria share several features of their economic structures and policies. Both countries were also beneficiaries of the cold war. Now that it is over, what will happen to aid from the Gulf Economic Cooperation Council, especially when peace comes? Both countries are currently on excellent terms with the Gulf countries following the role they played against Iraq in the Gulf war. But will this last? Tyler estimates that the reduction of military expenditures could increase the growth rate by 1.5% annually as a peace dividend. Such a rate would be considered impressive, especially if it can be sustained over a number of years. Tyler agrees with the authors that realization of the benefits will depend on the resulting economic environment. He is skeptical, however, about the prospects of any global peace dividends.

Nadav Halevi explores the implications of peace from the Israeli perspective. He looks at the current demands on the Israeli economy to absorb immigrants and its need for additional resources. Inasmuch as aid from the outside may be contingent upon progress toward peace, Israel should have an incentive to move in that direction. The dividend of peace will come in different forms, depending on the nature of the peace agreement. First, a major reduction of expenditure on arms in the period immediately following a settlement is unlikely. It takes time to feel secure enough to cut defense expenditure. However, a peace settlement could expedite further aid from the United States, improve relations with the European community, and bring an end to the boycott by multinational corporations. An important impact may result from settlement of the Palestinian-Israeli conflict, depending on whether there will be an economic union between the Palestinian and Israeli economies, normal trade, or total segregation. One thing seems certain, namely that the negative effects of the *intifada* will be removed.

A comprehensive peace agreement could have a great impact on trade relations with the Arab countries, if only by opening up their markets to Israeli products on the same terms as they are open to countries from outside the region. Israel could certainly capture an important segment of that market inasmuch as it can compete successfully with the present exporters. In all these cases, Halevi suggests the benefits would be greatly enhanced if Israel reforms its own economic policies and financial structures to facilitate capital flows and trade movements. Overall, however, he warns that the economic dividends of peace to Israel can be easily exaggerated.

Osama Hamed and Radwan Shaban discuss what they call economic integration between Israel and the occupied territories and its impact on the latter. They focus on the costs suffered by the occupied territories because of seigniorage accruing from the imposed use of the Israeli currency, and because of Israeli tariffs on imports from the rest of the world (with no compensating benefit in the form of tariff revenues). They estimate these costs by assessing the losses incurred by Palestinian holders of Israeli currency as a result of inflation, which represent gains to the Bank of Israel. They also estimate the revenues collected by Israeli authorities through tariffs and customs duties. These losses to the territories are viewed as resource transfers facilitated by the pseudo or imposed integration between the two economies, and from Israeli administrative controls over the economy of the occupied territories. If so, a peace settlement and the creation of a Palestinian state would automatically stop the transfer of resources to Israel and make those resources available to the Palestinian economy. Finally, Hamed and Shaban question the benefits of the presumed integration between Israel and the occupied territories because neither wages nor prices in the two economies have been equalized, as might be expected in genuinely integrated economies.

Gustav Ranis takes issue with authors of both chapters. He questions Halevi's assessment that the peace dividend would be as modest as suggested. He also wonders why Halevi does not put more emphasis on economic reform in Israel, what peace scenarios are being considered, and what lessons can be learned from such economies as those of Singapore and other countries. Turning to Hamed and Shaban's paper, Ranis asks why they dwell so much on the past and on the disadvantages of the relations between Israel and the occupied territories. He also asks whether it is theoretically valid to expect equalization of incomes and prices between the two economies, given the vast differences between them when the so-called integration was initiated. Ranis also questions the methodology and accuracy of the computations applied by Hamed and Shaban. Not only do they ignore any possible benefits realized by the occupied territories under Israeli occupation, but their counterfactual scenario is questionable. For instance, one could hypothesize a scenario based on pre-occupation conditions: would the territories have progressed more than they have under Israeli occupation? Or one could suppose a counterfactual scenario of pre-*intifada*. In either case valuable new insights could be gained.

Amer Bisat and Mohamad Hammour explore the economic prospects of a postwar Lebanon. After surveying the economy of Lebanon prior to the civil war that started in 1975, they illustrate the impact of the war on the economy as reflected in capital destruction, segmentation of markets, economic decline, and loss of human capital because of death, injury, and massive emigration estimated at about 750,000 since 1975. The authors seem optimistic regarding the prospects from reconstruction, depending on the ability of the government to manage the economy efficiently and on the incentives created to attract back expatriate capital, both material and human. They see Lebanon as continuing to occupy a unique position as an intermediary in the economy of the region, with the service sector playing a major role. However, they are less optimistic regarding the manufacturing sector. Although in both the introduction and the conclusion of their chapter the authors suggest a positive impact of the end of the Arab-Israeli conflict, their analysis focuses on the end of the Lebanese civil war, which is more relevant to their topic. Actually Lebanon prospered prior to the civil war in spite of almost three decades of war between the Arab countries and Israel.

Hani Abu-Jubarah addresses the predicament of Jordan, with its high rate of population growth, declining per capita income, returning migrant workers from the Gulf, and loss of remittances. Jordan faces great hardships also because of structural imbalances, trade deficits, and high rates of unemployment, as well as the decline of capital inflows in aid and loans. Although there is an interest in structural reform in Jordan, recent political and economic events have made reform difficult. Abu-Jubarah suggests that Jordan's economic problems cannot be solved on a country basis and should be addressed on a regional basis. Thus a peace settlement will have a major impact on Jordan by opening up channels for trade, resource mobility, and cooperation. Abu-Jubarah does not expect any major capital inflows from outside the region. He sees the solution as emerging primarily within the domestic and regional context.

In his discussion of these two chapters, Howard Pack emphasizes that the Middle East cannot be discussed in isolation of country experiences elsewhere. He is also pessimistic about the prospects for reconstruction of Lebanon if the capital/output ratio in Lebanese industry is about 5, as was suggested. In that case more than capital inflows would be needed. He notes Lebanon's limited agriculture, and its apparent inability to advance manufacturing. Yet, he argues, as for Egypt, Syria, and Israel, it is essential that Lebanon move toward the export of manufactured goods. To do so, liberalization of trade policy and economic stability are necessary, though not sufficient conditions. Difficult political decisions need to be made: will Lebanon or any other country in the region, with the possible exception of Israel, have a government strong and stable enough to make such decisions? Furthermore, contrary to what has been said by most authors regarding reform and liberalization, Pack observes that governments in the newly industrializing countries of Singapore, Taiwan, and Korea have played a major role in the economy. Foreign investment, accompanied by needed skills, may come, if there is economic stability. Furthermore, if there are open borders within the region, with shuttles going back and forth between capitals, business may come; otherwise, the prospects are far from bright.

In an attempt to analyze the economics of transition and to offer advice in making the transition from war to peace economically feasible and beneficial, Ephraim Ahiram explores three stages toward the final settlement, beginning with policies to reverse the deterioration that has followed the *intifada*. The second stage is one of autonomy for the occupied territories, to be followed by the final stage during which the ultimate solution of the territorial conflict will be determined. Accordingly, immediate remedies should be applied now, assuming that goodwill and a desire for settlement exist on both sides of the Israeli-Palestinian conflict. Such remedies would include removal of restrictions on trade and facilitation of economic activity in the territories. Next, a framework should be created to allow the transfer of responsibilities to Palestinian authorities. Ahiram presents almost a blueprint for management of the economy by the Palestinians, but he does not remove Israeli authorities from the economic scene. Quite optimistically, Ahiram visualizes aid from international institutions, cooperation by Israel and Jordan, and smooth sailing for the transition. In the final stage, described in more than half of the chapter, Ahiram presents recommendations on most aspects of the Palestinian economy, from absorbing refugees to export expansion and industrialization. A list of candidate industries is presented for development by the Palestinian economy. Although Ahiram does not discuss how these industries have been selected, and leaves open the question of how his recommendations can be implemented or by whom, his chapter serves an important function by pointing out in a logical sequence the issues that need to be tackled to facilitate the transition and achieve a permanent solution.

Hisham Awartani focuses on the question, Is cooperation possible between the Palestinians and Israelis in economic relations? His answer is a strong affirmative because he sees a wide area of complementarity between the two economies, that of Israel and that of

Palestine, whose boundaries would be those of the occupied territories. Although major obstacles and burdens have been created by the Israeli occupation, Awartani sees cooperation as mutually beneficial in water use and management, trade, tourism, agriculture, and industry. Although the degree of complementarity he visualizes appears too optimistic today, Awartani's views can be very constructive in the long run, because specializations change and complementarities may be created where they currently do not exist. However, removing obstacles and burdens imposed on the Palestinians and freeing the economy to develop on the initiative of the Palestinians themselves are prerequisites for cooperation. Furthermore, cooperation will be possible only when subordination of the Palestinians comes to an end and they are able to deal with Israel on an equal footing. Once the political and military obstacles are removed, Awartani sees an unlimited range of possibilities for cooperation.

Ephraim Kleiman is less optimistic than the other participants in the transition discussion. He focuses on the problems that have emerged during the period of occupation, especially the dependence of the occupied territories on Israel in most aspects of their economies, which may have reached a point of no return at least within the short and medium terms. Kleiman concentrates on economic issues, using national income and balance of payments data as a framework for discussion. A major item of trade is the labor services that are exported daily by commuting to Israel. How will a Palestinian economy be able to absorb this labor, especially when Israel ceases to need it? He notes the obstacles that hinder free flow of trade between the two entities. He then explores the situations should a free trade regime prevail or a regime of protectionism where two autonomous economic entities are created. Kleiman sees better prospects for resolving the economic problems of both entities if they follow the present world movement toward trade liberalization and regional economic cooperation.

In his discussion of these three transition chapters, Sulayman Al-Qudsi expresses appreciation for these works, while taking issue with all of them. Addressing Ahiram's chapter, Al-Qudsi wonders whether the list of suggested industries for the Palestinian economy is exhaustive. A more serious question is what kind of strategy is proposed for this industrialization process in order to establish comparative advantage for the Palestinian economy. How will it be possible to shift from low-quality production to high-quality, export-worthy production? How will the human capital of Palestinians in the diaspora be utilized in this upgrading? Al-Qudsi draws attention to the importance of the Arab market to the Palestinian economy and how joint Israeli-Palestinian cooperation could open that market to Israeli products as well. Finally, Al-Qudsi asks about estimates of costs and benefits of alternative scenarios, the costs of noncooperation between Israel and its neighbors, the incentives that would attract Arab cooperation with Israel and Palestine, a sketch of the institutional changes needed to smooth the transition, and a reasonable timetable for it.

Al-Qudsi sees Awartani's paper as too optimistic. Although he agrees with Awartani regarding potential areas of cooperation, he raises questions about the evidence to support that optimism, given that no cost-benefit estimates are available for any of the proposed areas of potential cooperation. He also raises doubts about the validity of the suggested complementarities between the Israeli and Palestinian economies. Finally, Al-Qudsi suggests that Awartani's paper needs to be set in a broader perspective that includes the potential role of neighboring Arab countries in the Palestinian economy.

In discussing Ephraim Kleiman's chapter Al-Qudsi focuses on Kleiman's argument that the heavy dependence of the occupied territories on the Israeli economy would make it difficult to discontinue that relationship in the future. This argument is untenable, according to Al-Qudsi, because the evident dependence is based on weak foundations: it is imposed, biased against the Palestinians, may be too costly if other alternatives are possible, reinforces the big per capita income gap between the two entities, and it has levied a heavy toll on the infrastructure of the Palestinian economy. Hence, in spite of the costs of discontinuity, the benefits of an alternative may be higher than the costs. Al-Qudsi also questions Kleiman's treatment of labor export to Israel and labor emigration from the occupied territories, inasmuch as both processes are results of imposed conditions that should vanish once peace is established. Finally, Al-Qudsi wonders what positive steps Kleiman would recommend in the way of ameliorating the situation and expediting the transition to a state of peace.

The final session of the conference was devoted to a panel discussion intended to recap and unify the themes of the conference and to invite ideas from the world of business. Zein Mayassi noted the absence of any political discussion, which left a gap in the overall picture. He also wished that the papers presented would come to definite conclusions, rather than leave their findings in the tentative form academicians tend to follow. Finally, he could see no harm if the Palestinian economy were to depend on the Israeli market in the future. As he put it, why not have an open border?

Michael Bruno brought a sobering note to the discussion. First, he was not convinced that peace would bring net economic benefits, given that Israel had grown dramatically in wartime. The problem is chiefly in the structure of economic policy, whether it is in peacetime or wartime. Although Israel would eventually be able to cut its defense expenditures if it withdrew from the occupied territories, those cuts could not be realized very quickly.

Hani Abu Jubarah would have liked to see a model of decision making for the Middle East based on Middle East realities, as well as an agreement on a feasible peace scenario to concentrate on in the chapters. Other issues that deserve attention include the direction of economic development and why it should not move away from agriculture, the free mobility of factors of production, the role of the economies that are not immediate neighbors of Israel and Palestine, the persistent intraregional inequality of wealth and income distribution, and the persistent defective political structures in the region.

These and other missing topics, suggested by participants in the conference, will no doubt receive attention in other contexts. The institute is currently sponsoring studies of labor, health, and water. Other scholars are working on similar projects. Nevertheless, a number of issues remain to be studied carefully. For example, it is important to estimate the economic dislocations that a peace settlement will entail and how to minimize their effects. Another topic is demography and population mobility. Where do the dislocated Palestinians fit into the various peace scenarios under study? We still need to address the issue of Palestinians outside the occupied territories and the role they can play in reaping the economic benefits of peace. How can the heavy emphasis on free trade and liberalization in external advice to the region be reconciled with the traditions of government control and intervention in the market that have prevailed in the region? Another major question to be addressed is, What possible economic benefits would the Arab countries gain from cooperation with Israel that they would not get from dealing with other countries at similar or lower costs? What infrastructural changes are needed to attract foreign capital into the region, whether in the form of loans, grants, or direct investment? What shared economic problems exist within the region that would be resolved by a collaborative approach to internal economic reform? While this volume does not deal with these various issues, we are happy to point to them for further study and analysis. Finally, although there are far better reasons to hope for peace than its economic benefits, we should deploy national economic analysis and decision making to help exploit the benefits that peace will bring within reach—and in so doing, perhaps even hasten that day.

I Case Studies

2 The Economics of Peace: The Egyptian Case

Heba Handoussa and
Nemat Shafik

The Economics of Peace

Egypt is the only Arab country that has attempted to make peace with Israel. Economic motives played an important part in Egypt's decision to sign a peace treaty—the country was facing a severe balance-of-payments crisis, attempts to encourage private investment were floundering, and appeals for more aid were unrequited. Yet the economic benefits of the Camp David accords signed in 1979 have been disappointing for Egypt. Because the peace was not comprehensive, many of the potential gains from regional political stability were never realized. Moreover, Egypt's domestic economic policies were not well tailored to take advantage of the potential gains from peace in the form of increased trade, investment, and productivity.

Once again, the possibility of a peace treaty in the region is on the international agenda. What are the potential economic gains for countries in the region, and how might economic ties reinforce the peace process? In particular, from Egypt's perspective, what makes this peace different from Camp David and how might potential economic and political gains be maximized? This chapter will explore the economic implications of a future peace in the region that is comprehensive in scope. Such a peace would include all parties to the Arab-Israeli conflict and would address the legitimate national aspirations of the Palestinian people. The potential economic consequences of such a peace will be explored in light of Egypt's experience after the Camp David accords.[1] The focus will be on the potential peace dividend associated with reduced military expenditure; the prospects for regional integration including trade, factor flows, and other forms of regional cooperation; and the indirect gains from political stability, particularly investment.

The Economics of War and Peace: A Historical Perspective

Following the creation of the state of Israel in 1948, an era of sustained regional conflict imposed a mobilization of national resources away from development and toward the maintenance of a powerful military establishment and authoritarian state apparatus. Because of Egypt's relatively large population and national income, it has borne the brunt of the Arab defense burden. In the interval 1967 to 1973, military expenditure rose to an average of $1.5 billion per year, or over 25% of Egypt's GDP, wiping out any investment or growth possibilities.[2] During that time, Arab neighbors compensated Egypt for losses of the Suez Canal and Sinai oil revenues ($250 million per year), but these transfers were clearly inadequate, and Egypt's development process stalled.[3]

By the end of 1973, Egypt had been drawn into four wars, which brought it to the brink of economic bankruptcy and political stalemate. The October 1973 war, however, was a breakthrough. The physical recapture of the east bank of the Suez Canal—occupied by Israel since 1967—enabled Egypt to renew its diplomatic ties with the United States and to enter into immediate negotiations for a comprehensive peace settlement of the Arab-Israeli conflict. A second major success of the October war was Egypt's ability to mobilize Arab economic resources. Arab oil producers immediately cut back production; this was followed by Saudi Arabia's unilateral embargo in November 1973 of oil exports to the United States, in response to President Nixon's request to Congress for $2.2 billion in emergency military aid to Israel.[4]

Although the Geneva peace talks did not materialize, Egypt from that point on was determined to signal both to its neighbors and to the international community its commitment to the process of peace rather than war. Indeed, on the economic front Sadat's October Paper, which introduced Egypt's new open door policy (*infitah*) in 1974, was predicated on the achievement of regional stability through a negotiated settlement. The objective of this reorientation of the economy was to link Arab capital with Western technology and Egyptian manpower to revitalize the development process. Egypt also expected its new alliance with the United States to provide sufficient aid flows from the West to rehabilitate, reconstruct, and reinvigorate the economy on the scale of the Marshall Plan for postwar Europe.[5] Domestic public opinion was reoriented to expect that the economic rewards of peace would compensate for the sacrifices made by two generations of Egyptians.

Additionally, six years before Camp David a systematic cutback of Egypt's 900,000-strong army reduced it to half that number.[6] However, cost savings were not significant because most of the demobilized conscripts were immediately recruited by the civil service according to Law 85 of 1973, thereby swelling the government wage bill by 24%.[7] This was one of the first indications of the state's willingness to interfere with the operation of market forces, contrary to the new liberal economic orientation. In fact, the guaranteed employment scheme for graduates of high schools and universities, free education at all levels, and lifelong job security were all perceived as social gains from the Nasser era that the government could not abrogate. Similarly, administered prices for all essential commodities were viewed as a safety net and the public sector continued to bear ever-increasing losses. The open door policy was thus adopted only partially, creating a dual economy: the highly centralized and controlled public sector alongside the more freely operating *infitah* private sector.

In the interval between the October war and the Camp David agreements, economic activity accelerated significantly, particularly as Egypt benefited from the spillovers associated with the oil windfall. Arab aid flows averaged $1.6 billion annually and peaked at 22.6% of GNP in 1975 (table 2.1). U.S. economic aid—suspended since 1965—was resumed in 1975 and reached $672 million in 1978. Aid flows were used to retire Egypt's short-term debt and to start on the massive reconstruction of the war-damaged Suez zone. The Suez Canal was reopened in mid-1975 and a major project to double its capacity was financed by the OECD countries and the World Bank. By 1978, its earnings exceeded $500 million. The petroleum trade balance turned positive in 1976, and petroleum exports reached $1.3 billion in 1978. The oil boom in neighboring Arab countries provided jobs for over one million Egyptians whose remittances rose to $2.0 billion by 1978. Private unrequited transfers reached 13% of Egypt's GNP in 1979 and 1980 and averaged 10% thereafter.

The *infitah*/peace strategy coincided with a boom period. Egypt's terms of trade improved somewhat after the first oil shock in 1973, but there was no significant windfall until after 1975 when petroleum export volumes had increased. Oil production volumes doubled in the late 1970s with new discoveries and the return of the Sinai fields

Table 2.1
Egypt—Selected economic indicators

	1970–75	1975–80	1980–85	1986	1987	1988	1989	1990
Population in millions	34.6	38.9	44.2	47.7	48.8	49.9	51.0	52.1
GNP per capita in current US $	271	426	615	670	690	660	640	600
National accounts			*Millions of 1987 Egyptian Pounds*					
GDP at market prices	15835.8	25785.5	37710.2	44137.0	45249.0	47023.0	48144.0	48766.0
Domestic absorption	20835.6	33446.1	47337.0	52222.0	50427.0	51962.0	52514.0	52759.6
Private consumption, etc.	16615.7	22355.5	31769.8	35823.0	35947.0	36976.0	37538.0	39152.5
General government consumption	3874.0	4344.4	5799.2	6481.0	6330.0	6356.0	6418.0	5134.3
Gross domestic investment	2824.0	6746.2	9768.0	9918.0	8150.0	8630.0	8558.0	8472.8
Government budget			*Millions of Egyptian Pounds at Current Prices*					
Government deficit (−) or surplus	−938.0	−1561.8	−2742.2	−4655.0	−2613.0	−4716.0	−4126.0	NA
Balance of payments			*Millions of current US dollars*					
Exports of goods and services	1535.9	4771.6	7145.0	7028.1	6492.1	8188.5	8612.7	9517.0
Imports of goods and services	2696.4	7866.7	12492.4	13380.1	11378.9	12831.5	14919.0	15821.0
Private current transfers (net)	165.1	1788.5	3006.6	2994.8	3033.2	3406.3	3556.0	3769.0
Workers remittances, received	138.7	1710.8	2971.0	2972.9	3011.9	3383.9	3532.0	3744.0
Official transfers (net)	614.7	290.4	582.3	1209.4	974.0	697.6	756.0	1110.0
of which: official Arab assistance	1534.6	992.2	−39.7	71.8	71.1	NA	NA	NA
Long-term debt (by debtor)	2705.5	10775.8	26766.4	36142.6	42854.0	42963.0	40993.0	NA
Short-term debt	0.0	3000.9	5043.8	6854.8	6267.1	6521.7	7806.0	NA

Table 2.1 (continued)

	1970–75	1975–80	1980–85	1986	1987	1988	1989	1990
Prices			*Annual average, Egyptian Pound per US Dollar*					
Official exchange rate	0.4	0.6	0.9	1.1	1.3	1.8	1.9	2.2
Consumer price index	16.1	27.0	52.4	83.5	100.0	117.7	142.7	166.6
Shares of GDP								
Domestic absorption	131.6%	129.7%	125.5%	118.3%	111.4%	110.5%	109.1%	108.2%
Private consumption, etc.	104.9%	86.7%	84.2%	81.2%	79.4%	78.6%	78.0%	80.3%
General government consumption	24.5%	16.8%	15.4%	14.7%	14.0%	13.5%	13.3%	10.5%
Gross domestic investment	17.8%	26.2%	25.9%	22.5%	18.0%	18.4%	17.8%	17.4%
Government deficit (−) or surplus	−24.4%	−14.4%	−11.1%	−12.1%	−5.8%	−8.6%	−6.4%	NA
Exports of goods and services	16.7%	27.8%	24.8%	19.6%	18.3%	26.4%	25.8%	27.0%
Imports of goods and services	29.4%	45.9%	43.3%	37.3%	32.0%	41.4%	44.7%	44.9%
Private current transfers (net)	1.8%	10.4%	10.4%	8.3%	8.5%	11.0%	10.6%	10.7%
Workers remittances, received	1.5%	10.0%	10.3%	8.3%	8.5%	10.9%	10.6%	10.6%
Official transfers (net)	6.7%	1.7%	2.0%	3.4%	2.7%	2.3%	2.3%	3.1%
of which: official Arab assistance*	16.7%	5.8%	−0.1%	0.2%	0.2%	NA	NA	NA
Long-term debt (by debtor)	29.5%	62.8%	92.8%	100.7%	120.6%	138.7%	122.7%	NA
Short-term debt	NA	17.5%	17.5%	19.1%	17.6%	21.1%	23.4%	NA

Source: World Bank, *World Tables*, 1991.
*Data on official Arab assistance is from van den Boogaerde (1990) and is not necessarily consistent with World Bank data on official transfers.

after the signing of the peace treaty with Israel. Thus the second oil shock in 1979 resulted in a substantial windfall gain to the economy. Real GDP growth rose to almost 10% between 1980–81 and 1982–83—a sharp increase from the 6% rates that prevailed in the late 1970s. Foreign currency earnings rose by 138%, from $2.5 billion in 1974 to $6.0 billion in 1978. Private capital outlays subject to the 1974 investment promotion law (Law 43) brought the cumulative value of employed capital for approved projects to LE 3.8 billion (more than $6 billion at the prevailing exchange rates). However, the combination of a high level of protection, an overvalued exchange rate, and a negative real rate of interest led to strong private sector biases toward import-substituting investments and the production of non-traded goods. Open and suppressed inflation further aggravated the situation, driving a considerable part of private savings into housing and real estate, or to the holding of foreign currency deposits. Nonoil exports declined as relative prices made sectors of comparative advantage unprofitable. The one exception was the tourism sector, which attracted substantial private foreign and domestic investment, achieving a conservative figure of $700 million in balance-of-payments revenues for 1978.[8]

Despite the dramatic gains achieved by the economy after 1973, it was becoming clear that the liberalization and reform package would not achieve sustained economic progress in the absence of regional stability and cooperation. Most of Egypt's new sources of income were either dependent on regional security (for long-term capital flows and the growth in tourism) or tied to the regional petroleum market (remittances, Suez Canal dues, and petroleum exports). Therefore, regional instability was an important negative factor affecting Egypt's domestic stability, which in turn contributed to a deceleration in the scope and pace of economic liberalization.

The Economic Consequences of the Camp David Accords

In 1979, Egypt and Israel signed the U.S.-engineered bilateral peace treaty at Camp David, but "the outcome of the Camp David accords was a far cry from the comprehensive peace that many Egyptians sincerely hoped the Americans would help achieve."[9] On the positive side, it enabled Egypt to regain its Sinai lands with whatever petroleum reserves were left unexploited by Israel. But the costs turned out to be exorbitant: neither the treaty itself was fully implemented, nor were the other parties to the conflict brought to the negotiating table. On the regional front, all other Arab countries broke their diplomatic ties with Egypt, which was isolated both politically and economically for the next eight years. Militarily, Egypt had lost its strike capability in the event of hostilities with Israel, which used its uncontested power to invade Lebanon in 1982. The question of Palestine remained unresolved, Israel having reneged on that part of the Camp David accords that gave autonomy to the Palestinians in the West Bank and Gaza.[10]

Generous U.S. economic aid could hardly compensate for the abrupt cessation of all Arab aid, trade, and capital flows. U.S. economic aid commitments were raised to an annual $1 billion, up from the already high level of $900 million in the previous three years. Moreover, in spite of the unwritten pledge that the United States would match its aid to Egypt with that to Israel, this promise was not kept for long, and the strings attached to aid flows to Egypt rendered their effective value far smaller than the corresponding cash transfers to Israel.[11] Thus economic aid from the United States simply supplanted Arab aid at roughly equivalent levels, although often on less favorable terms.

Moreover, Egypt lost most of the dynamism and momentum that it had built up as part of its peace/*infitah* strategy. Arab aid and private capital immediately dried up, Arab markets were effectively closed to Egyptian-based enterprises, tourist flows from Arab countries dwindled, and large Arab investors pulled out of numerous major joint venture projects in tourism, manufacturing, the free zones, and defense. Regional stability became all the more elusive as political turmoil, armed conflict, and religious extremism turned the entire Middle East into a high-risk region, discouraging the inflow of foreign capital and encouraging domestic capital flight.

There is also little evidence that Egypt reaped a peace dividend after the Camp David accords. Evaluating total military spending is complicated by the fact that some defense-related expenditures appear under other budget categories and official figures do not report arms imports financed by aid or suppliers' credits.[12] Prior to the Camp David accords Egypt's military spending as a share of GNP averaged about 12%, and arms imports were about 2% of GNP during the late 1970s.[13] By 1982, three years after the Camp David accords had been signed, military spending had fallen to 7.2%, but arms imports had increased to 5% of GNP.[14] This large increase in arms imports reflected the new military role in which Egypt was cast and asked to finance. There was a strong need to protect the West's oil interests in an increasingly tense and volatile Middle East region. Contrary to the spirit of the "peace era," and in opposition to the declared policy of allowing the country to shift from "guns to butter," the United States sold Egypt $1 billion worth of arms per year at market rates. Economic development was once again put in jeopardy as the government reallocated its modest savings away from investment and toward defense.

After the Camp David accords, the size of the armed forces was again on the increase, and in 1985 military expenditure was estimated at $124 per capita or 17% of Egypt's per capita income of $720. A study by the Arms Control and Disarmament Agency showed that Egypt ranked 11th out of 144 countries in terms of military expenditure. In the first ten years following Camp David, Egypt purchased $13 billion worth of arms from the United States alone, the United States accounting for 40% of total Egyptian imports of arms.[15] In comparison, the total cost of arms purchases from the socialist block over the 20 years (1954 to 1974) that witnessed three major military confrontations (1956, 1967, and 1973) has been estimated at less than $5 billion.[16] Whereas Egypt accumulated only $2 billion of military debt at the end of the war era (1973), military debt stood at more than $11 billion in 1989.[17]

The military component of the U.S. aid package has in fact offset approximately three-fourths of the gains from its economic grant aid. Although U.S. military aid has been provided (and increased to $1.3 billion per year) on a grant basis since 1985, the interest due on U.S. military debt was put at between $604 million and $720 million in fiscal year 1990, as compared to $927 million obligated in economic grant aid for that year.[18]

Egypt's foreign debt, which peaked at $42 billion in June 1990, has twice been rescheduled at the Paris Club. After the Gulf war, and to enhance Egypt's stabilizing role during the crisis, Arab Gulf countries and the United States agreed to relieve Egypt of a significant proportion of its total debt. Debt forgiveness totaled $13 billion in 1990 (including $6.6 billion of U.S. military debt), reducing Egypt's outstanding debt to $29 billion in 1991. An exceptional grant of $3.6 billion was also disbursed to Egypt in compensation for economic losses sustained during the Gulf crisis. Although the cancellation of debts has relieved Egypt of about $1.3 billion in annual debt service payments, $3.5 billion were still due in 1991–92 alone.[19]

In May 1991 agreement was reached at the Paris Club on further halving Egypt's outstanding debt over the period up to mid-1994, which encompasses the implementation of the IMF standby arrangement and a World Bank structural adjustment loan. The targets of the economic reform program include the reduction of the government budget deficit from 20% of GDP in the last few years to 3.5% by the mid-1990s, a decline in inflation from 30% to 5%, and the elimination of the current account deficit in the balance of payments (excluding interest payments). By mid-1991 the government had implemented the first phase of the reform program—including tariff, exchange rate, interest rate, and price adjustments—as well as introduced a major piece of legislation (Law 203 for Public Business Enterprises) that would give full autonomy to the public sector and allow for privatization.

In July 1991 the Consultative Group Meeting for Egypt was reconvened (after ten years), and representatives of eighteen countries and fourteen national and multinational aid institutions pledged to support Egypt over the medium term, with aid commitments of some $3 billion per year. It is obvious that the magnitude of debt relief and of new aid commitments is directly related to the renewed interest in strengthening Egypt's moderating influence and leverage in regional politics. In the newly emerging world order, industrialized nations cannot tolerate the risk of disruption to the petroleum market, nor the territorial ambitions of some Middle East states that could disrupt the delicate balance of power.

However, it is sobering to remember that for all of the economic assistance that has so far been promised, Egypt's per capita income (which dropped from $720 in 1984 to $640 in 1989) is expected to decline even further as a consequence of the structural adjustment program. With 30% of the population below the poverty line, and with the vulnerable group now including the entire lower echelon of the civil service, the potential for domestic instability is high. Open unemployment stands at two million persons, with poor employment prospects for the additional six million entrants to the labor market by the year 2000. Egypt can no longer be expected to rely on temporary and compensatory flows of aid, and continue to play an effective role in the region. It is clear that a major reason for the failure of Egypt's past efforts at comprehensive economic liberalization has been the configuration of external pressures and internal constraints. A comprehensive peace would reduce the former, while foreign assistance and private capital flows in the context of a full reform effort would remove the latter.

The Economics of a Future Peace: The Peace Dividend

Military Expenditure

Egypt's economic development suffered as a result of the partial implementation of the Camp David accords, which kept regional tensions high, cutting off interregional economic cooperation with other Arab states and discouraging much-needed investment capital from the West. Furthermore, the partial implementation of the liberalization program was in no small part dictated by the need to ensure domestic stability at a time when the economic dividends of peace appeared as elusive as ever given Israel's prevarications over the Palestinian issue.

What can be envisaged for the future, if a comprehensive peace settlement is achieved, is a much more balanced and consistent growth scenario. Three factors would work toward the achievement of a self-sustaining growth path: the transformation of Egypt's military establishment into a peacetime economically viable industry, accountable for its costs and returns; the mobilization of massive aid flows, debt forgiveness, and structural adjustment; and the development of regional economic integration, realizing the full and unexploited potential for free trade, capital, and labor flows.

An essential component of the peace dividend is the reduction in defense expenditure. This can occur either because the size of the military establishment is reduced, or as a result of a cooperative interregional security arrangement whereby the costs are borne by the richer partners to the agreement. Alternatively, the present capital, labor, and technological resources of the military could be redeployed to serve domestic civilian and export needs. In the context of peace, it is most likely that in the short term, Egypt will continue to play the role of regional watchdog, but with a growing share of defense expenditure shouldered by the Gulf countries and the United States. It is also likely that the defense industry will be integrated more closely with its civilian counterpart.

Since the mid-1980s, Egypt's arms industry has been providing some 60% of the military's needs. By 1984 the country was self-sufficient in the production of a wide range of small arms, mortars, rockets, and ammunition. In 1987 a collaborative agreement was signed with the United States for the domestic manufacture of the American MI Abrams tank, the most advanced armored weapons system in the U.S. inventory. Egypt also assembles French Alpha jets and helicopters and manufactures components for MIGs and radar systems. The industry was reported to be exporting between $1 billion and $4 billion in the second half of the 1980s.[20] If true, arms exports represent as much as, and perhaps more than, total civilian manufactured exports. Such high levels of exports, most of which were sold to Iraq, are unlikely to be maintained unless the Arab joint-venture project for military production—established in 1975 and frozen in 1979 as a result of Camp David—is resuscitated.

A comprehensive peace settlement would most probably enable Egypt to achieve a turnaround in its military balance sheet from net loss to gain. A significant number of civilian industries also stand to benefit from the transfer of advanced technology, manpower training, subcontracting, and pooled production capacities. The production of civilian (mainly engineering) products by the military factories has long been institutionalized in Egypt. In 1985–86, these twenty-four factories employed an estimated seventy thousand to one hundred thousand workers and produced civilian output amounting to $300 million.[21] This last figure represents only a small proportion of total manufactured output but could conceivably grow within the framework of specialization for a larger integrated regional market.

Since 1973 the political role of the military has been consistently reduced, with a declining ratio of former officers to civilians in key posts such as the cabinet, governorships, the civil service, and public enterprise. This changing trend has also been accompanied by the reduced political role of the military itself as an institution.[22] The process of democratization, begun under Sadat, has accelerated under President Mubarak. A comprehensive peace settlement would further accelerate the process. At a minimum the state of emergency would be lifted, enhancing the climate for freedom of expression and respect for human rights. The institutions of civil society—parliament, political parties, trade unions, and interest groups—would play a more effective part in the management of social, political, and economic affairs given that a major justification for the dominant and intrusive state apparatus will have been removed.

In the longer term, the outcome of a comprehensive peace in the Middle East should be the gradual reduction in defense expenditure of all the countries in the region. The scaling down of arms purchases and controls on the production of weapons of mass destruction would be stipulated in the peace treaty and monitored by the international community. Total official arms sales to the Middle East were estimated at $16 billion in 1983, excluding military supplies provided on a grant basis. As a percentage of GNP, military spending in the region had subsided in the second half of the 1970s only to rise back to an average of 14% in the first half of the 1980s, as compared to 1.5% for Latin America, 2% for sub-Saharan Africa, and 3.8% for South Asia. In 1984–85 the weight of defense expenditure in GDP for the region ranged from 2%–4% for the countries of North Africa to 17%–19% for Israel, Syria, and Saudi Arabia. The ratio for Iraq was 51%, with a cumulative debt of $85 billion reportedly incurred during its eight-year war with Iran.

For Egypt, if one adds the annual cost of arms imports and debt service on military debt to domestically financed defense expenditure, and adjusts the exchange rate at which imports of arms are calculated, total defense expenditure would have reached 14% of GDP in 1984. This is roughly the same level of military spending relative to national income that prevailed prior to the Camp David accords. The size of Egypt's armed forces, which stabilized at 445,000 over the 1980s, can also be expected to be gradually scaled down. The combined size of the armed forces of the eight Middle East countries closest to the conflict area was 3.3 million in 1984–85, one-and-one-half times that of the United States. The cost savings for Egypt and its neighbors from reduced defense expenditure are thus dramatic.[23]

Aid Assistance

The second major component of the peace dividend that could materialize for Egypt is economic aid from the OECD and the major oil exporting countries. Despite the significant improvements in indicators of human development and social welfare that took place over the past fifteen years, Egypt remains the poorest of the frontline states in the Middle East conflict, with a per capita income of only $640 as compared to $980 for Syria, $1,640 for Jordan, and $9,790 for Israel in 1989. Total aid disbursed to Egypt in the 1980s averaged

$1.6 billion per year, accounting for about 5% of GDP and $35 per capita. In relative terms these levels compare poorly with those achieved in the second half of the 1970s, when aid flows averaged $2.0 billion per year, amounting to 15% of GDP and $55 per capita.[24] Moreover, the burden of debt servicing grew from $1.3 billion in 1981–82 to $4.4 billion in 1986–87, so that aid disbursements were far outweighed by debt repayments.[25]

Regional Integration and Trade

The magnitude of potential gains from regional integration will depend critically on the evolution of Egypt's own domestic incentives, particularly trade policy. The gains from regional investment projects that exploit scale economies or address free rider problems depend more on the existence of a peace treaty than on reform of trade policy. If reforms to the trade regime are not successful, the gains from regional peace will probably be greatest from increased labor migration. This will imply an improvement in foreign exchange revenues, which may be accompanied by increased aid flows from other Arab countries. If domestic reform efforts are successful, however, the gains from increased exports to the region and elsewhere as well as the prospects for substantial private investment by individuals from Arab countries could far outweigh other gains.

Past Regional Integration Attempts

Attempts to promote regional economic integration in the Middle East have been numerous and, as with similar efforts in other parts of the world, fairly unsuccessful. One of the earliest manifestations of this desire for increased integration was a multilateral trading agreement signed in 1953 under the auspices of the Arab League that exempted agricultural commodities from tariff barriers and reduced tariffs on some industrial goods. This was followed in 1956 with the Arab Economic Unity Agreement, which sought full economic union among Egypt, Syria, Iraq, Jordan, and Kuwait. In 1964 this same group of countries, with the exception of Kuwait, formed the Arab Common Market, which sought the gradual elimination of tariff and nontariff barriers over a ten-year period.[26]

In general, the numerous attempts at increasing integration among the Arab states within the region were unsuccessful for similar reasons. Intraregional trade was not important for many of the participants and often bilateral agreements between natural trading partners undermined regional efforts. Moreover, agreements tended to have numerous loopholes that allowed countries to protect certain activities. This was particularly important in sectors where there could have been competition, such as in textiles or food processing. Thus, where the welfare gains from increasing regional trade could have been greatest, protectionist interests at the national level ensured that exemptions from external competition were secured. The success of integration attempts was also affected by political and ideological differences among participants and the continuing conflict with Israel.

Merchandise trade within the Middle East region has always been small in absolute terms and as a relative share of Egypt's total trade. Even prior to the Camp David accords, Egypt traded very little within the region. In the 1970s Egypt's trade was dominated by the industrial countries and the Soviet bloc. More recently, both Egypt's imports and exports are overwhelmingly dominated by the industrial countries, as shown in table 2.2. Regional Arab trade accounted for a mere 1% of Egypt's imports and 5% of Egypt's exports in 1989. Egypt's traditional trading partners in Europe have been somewhat supplanted by the United States, which emerged as a major trading partner because of sourcing requirements associated with U.S. aid flows. Egypt's exports are dominated by minerals and fuels, and its imports consist largely of food and capital goods.

Within the Middle East region, Egypt imported a modest $143 million worth of goods in 1989, consisting largely of chemicals and machinery from Saudi Arabia, crude materials from Iraq, and mineral fuels from Israel (table 2.3). Egypt's exports in the region, which sum to $404 million, are dominated by oil exports to Israel and sales of food and basic manufactures to Saudi Arabia. Egypt's poor export performance to its neighbors stems in part from the current composition of its exports. Egypt's major export, oil, is the last thing its Arab neighbors need (although it is the most important export to Israel). Egypt's manufactures exports deteriorated rapidly in the 1980s as the protected domestic market boomed. Moreover, the demand for many goods from the major oil-exporting countries during the boom years 1973–85 were not met by Egypt, but by the OECD and emerging exporters such as Turkey. Similarly, the composition of Egypt's merchandise imports is also at odds with the current

Table 2.2
Composition of Egypt's world trade, 1989 (current values in thousands of U.S. dollars)

SITC Code	0	1	2	3	4	5	6	7	8	9	All
Category	Food And Live Animals	Beverages And Tobacco	Crude Matls Excl Fuels	Mineral Fuels Etc	Animal, Vegetable Oil, Fat	Chemicals	Basic Manu-factures	Machines, Transport Equip	Misc Manu-factured Goods	Goods Not Classd By Kind	Total Value of Import / Export
Imports											
L. America and Caribbean	26383	3496	49488	0	20843	2793	33259	7801	1344	0	145407
Sub-Saharan Africa	35996	23824	17710	0	0	758	12136	73	113	0	90610
OECD countries	1679953	29376	329502	94812	164634	743905	804013	1307357	205385	1294	5360231
South Asia	81737	554	4619	0	0	4165	16566	22828	1303	0	131772
East Asia	34881	11458	13889	220	54766	25821	114550	107701	40505	0	403791
Middle East	7767	86	25658	29140	113	29717	11232	26107	13067	0	142887
Exports											
L. America and Caribbean	216	76	56	7178	0	81	648	0	3	0	8258
Sub-Saharan Africa	7578	122	460	354	0	3421	11310	1375	3926	8	28554
OECD countries	67893	1081	173712	420443	1401	39030	635322	3755	106859	204	1449700
South Asia	606	1	2788	28504	0	1596	4659	9	41	0	38204
East Asia	2326	36	13988	117352	0	743	10015	238	383	0	145081
Middle East	71122	289	4266	171632	72	23577	98186	4230	29293	862	403529

Note: Middle East include Afghanistan, Bahrain, Iran, Iraq, Israel, Jordan, Kuwait, Lebanon, Libya, Oman, Qatar, Saudi Arabia, United Arab Emirates, and Yemen.
Source: Trade Analysis and Reporting System (TARS), COMTRAD database, United Nations Statistical Office.

Table 2.3
Composition of Egypt's regional trade, 1989 (current values in thousands of U.S. dollars)

SITC Code	0	1	2	3	4	5	6	7	8	9	All
Category	Food And Live Animals	Beverages And Tobacco	Crude Matls Excl Fuels	Mineral Fuels Etc	Animal, Vegetable Oil, Fat	Chemicals	Basic Manu- factures	Machines, Transport Equip	Misc Manu- factured Goods	Goods Not Classd By Kind	Total Value of Import / Export
Imports											
Afghanistan	10	0	0	0	0	0	0	3	0	0	13
Jordan	1031	39	102	1	0	1355	7250	2701	8934	0	21683
Lebanon	1603	3	1643	0	0	2231	1433	5426	964	0	13303
Yemen	110	27	0	0	0	0	0	36	34	0	207
Iran	229	0	0	0	0	0	1	0	0	0	230
Iraq	0	11	22590	0	0	1826	184	115	425	0	25151
Oman	162	0	66	1580	0	18	1510	1755	1191	0	6282
Bahrain	0	0	0	517	0	0	2	81	44	0	644
Israel	881	5	264	20215	0	198	15	815	53	0	22446
Kuwait	107	0	147	1621	0	5	43	2116	718	0	4757
Qatar	0	0	17	579	0	0	0	486	74	0	1156
Saudi Arabia	3634	1	489	4627	113	23272	488	12534	614	0	45772
United Arab	0	0	0	0	0	0	0	0	0	0	0
Libya	0	0	340	0	0	812	36	39	16	0	1243
Middle East	7767	86	25658	29140	113	29717	11232	26107	13067	0	142887

Table 2.3 (continued)

SITC Code	0	1	2	3	4	5	6	7	8	9	All
Category	Food And Live Animals	Beverages And Tobacco	Crude Matls Excl Fuels	Mineral Fuels Etc	Animal, Vegetable Oil, Fat	Chemicals	Basic Manu-factures	Machines, Transport Equip	Misc Manu-factured Goods	Goods Not Classd By Kind	Total Value of Import / Export
Exports											
Afghanistan	0	0	0	0	0	0	17	0	0	0	17
Jordan	4308	5	306	245	1	6032	9733	1553	5482	63	27728
Lebanon	6073	6	484	1063	49	351	2246	80	702	0	11054
Yemen	85	0	245	5296	0	1344	2914	0	1185	11	11080
Iran	0	0	0	0	0	0	1888	0	0	0	1888
Iraq	1113	46	468	0	0	7164	47251	181	8460	72	64755
Oman	4196	31	785	712	14	541	3286	142	1372	203	11282
Bahrain	704	0	13	0	0	86	152	0	233	0	1188
Israel	946	0	235	164170	0	28	2686	7	363	3	168438
Kuwait	9871	45	409	99	2	959	3196	112	2792	64	17549
Qatar	1767	3	80	0	1	1047	1111	7	446	13	4475
Saudi Arabia	40514	133	1209	47	5	5987	21484	1970	6622	433	78404
United Arab	0	0	0	0	0	0	0	0	0	0	0
Libya	1545	20	32	0	0	38	2222	178	1636	0	5671
Middle East	71122	289	4266	171632	72	23577	98186	4230	29293	862	403529

Source: Trade Analysis Reporting System (TARS), COMTRAD database, United Nations Statistical Office.

trading patterns of the region. None of the Arab countries are major exporters of food (particularly grains)[27] or capital goods, which constitute the bulk of Egypt's import needs.

Trade between Israel and Egypt peaked in 1981 at $550 million in Egyptian exports to Israel and $115 million in Israeli exports to Egypt. Israel's exports to Egypt included between forty-two and ninety-two different products, reflecting the fact that it is a more diversified economy. Egypt's exports were in only nine to twenty-two categories, none of which had a value over $1 million except for oil. Trade between the countries' public sectors varied with changing political circumstances and contacts between private individuals were virtually nonexistent.

It is important to note that although the low level of Egypt's trade within the Middle East region is due in part to mismatches in composition, there are many goods that could have been traded within the region that were not because of the absence of domestic incentives to export. Egypt's nonoil export performance suffered as merchandise exports declined steadily in real terms from the early 1970s onward. This decline was offset by the large increase in exogenous resources (oil revenues, remittances, Suez Canal dues, and foreign capital inflows), which rose from 6% of total resources available to the economy (defined as GDP plus net imports) to 45% in 1981.[28] After 1981, oil prices began to fall, but Egypt's export revenues from petroleum continued to increase because of volume increases associated with expanded capacity. Thus exports became increasingly dominated by oil, which completely overshadowed more traditional exports such as cotton, textiles, and food products.

The causes of this sharp decline in nonoil export performance included factors such as the exchange rate, the tariff structure, and institutional obstacles to exporting. In general, these domestic obstacles outweighed the impact of protectionism in potential export markets because they ensured that Egyptian exporters were far from the stage of saturating potential foreign markets. The complex structure of tariffs tended to increase the profitability of domestic sales over exports.[29] Effective protection rates vary substantially across sectors and firms, but in general tariffs have favored sectors in which Egypt has the least actual and potential comparative advantage.[30] There were also a number of institutional obstacles, such as cumbersome import and export control procedures and infrastructural deficiencies, particularly transport, that put exporters at a disadvantage. Cotton exports suffered from the low procurement prices paid to farmers, which benefited public sector textile factories. Public sector industries, which produce the largest share of total exports, were often required to supply the domestic market first and often lacked export marketing capability. Moreover, performance in the one sector where export growth has been rapid, petroleum, could have been substantially higher if domestic subsidies that amounted to about four-fifths of the world price were not in place. Even private sector firms established under Law 43, which was specifically intended to promote export-oriented firms, sold only 6% of their output value abroad between 1974 and 1986.[31] This largely reflected the profitability of sales on the highly protected domestic market when compared to competitive world markets. Thus the growth of merchandise imports in Egypt has outstripped that of exports, resulting in a current account deficit that is estimated at about 10% of GDP in 1991.

Regional trade integration was impaired by Egypt's domestic incentives that were not outward oriented. This was not unique to trade within the region since Egypt's overall nonoil export performance had deteriorated. On the import side, the emergence of the United States as Egypt's major trading partner was clearly a by-product of the sourcing requirements attached to American aid. It seems clear that with appropriate trade policies, regional trade would have played a more important role in the Egyptian economy.

Prospects for Regional Trade

The major obstacle to Egypt increasing regional trade in the past has been the structure of protection both within Egypt and its neighbors. The ongoing reform efforts of the Egyptian government will address many of the domestic obstacles to increasing regional trade, such as the exchange rate and interest rate regimes. The list of banned imports will be reduced to seventy items, and the range of tariffs is expected to narrow from 1%–240% to 5%–100%, and eventually to 10%–80%. The government will attempt to phase out the extensive nontariff barriers over a two-year period as well as to eliminate the few remaining quantitative export restrictions. In addition, the government is attempting to address some of the institutional obstacles that hinder trade, such as the absence of an effective duty drawback system.

As Egypt's own trade policy shifts in favor of the production of tradable goods, there may be growing concern about access to potential foreign markets. This may provide a more strategic rationale for promoting regional trade. Growth of trade within regions has far outstripped world trade growth in recent years; but the Middle East is an exception to this trend.[32] For strategic reasons, it may be preferable to be a part of a regional bloc in order to secure better terms in negotiations with other blocs. For example, fears about protectionism in the European community were an important motive for the Maghreb countries' recent trade agreement. While this may not be the most desirable outcome from a global point of view, it is preferable for any particular country that is not gaining from the current configuration of trading blocs. For Egypt, being part of a regional trade grouping may enhance its bargaining position vis-à-vis other trading blocs and facilitate the transition to a more open and dynamic economy. At this stage, however, the constraints to Egypt's nonoil exports are more domestic than foreign and such strategic concerns are not likely to be important in the short and medium term.

What sorts of goods might Egypt trade with its neighbors? Studies of Egypt's comparative advantage have identified a number of sectors in which domestic resource costs are low and production for the world market is economically viable. These include several light industries such as cotton knit products, some food processing, leather products, and selected engineering goods. There are also some areas where industries are almost competitive at world prices, such as nitrogenous fertilizers, paper, and metal products. Targeted investments in these industries could make production internationally viable. Much of the intermediate and capital goods industry, however, has very high domestic resource costs and would require major restructuring so as to become internationally competitive. These include ceramic and glass products, iron and steel, aluminum, transport equipment, basic chemicals, synthetic fibers, phosphate fertilizers, and basic pulp and paper. Egypt is also a potential exporter of agricultural products in the region with comparative advantage in crops such as onions, oranges, tomatoes, groundnuts, garlic, and potatoes.[33]

A study by Avad, Hirsch, and Tovias focuses on potential trade between Egypt and Israel. The authors identify potential Egyptian exports to Israel as petroleum, textiles, and aluminum. Potential Israeli exports to Egypt are rubber, chemicals and metals, meat, and milk products. However, unless there are relatively substantial transport costs, the potential for increased trade will come from trade expansion rather than from diversion from existing export markets. They estimate the trade diversion potential between the two economies at $496 million for Egypt and $428 million for Israel, but this will only be realized if there are transfer costs to other markets.

How do these potential exports measure up to the export structure and import needs of Egypt's neighbors? The Gulf economies are likely to remain importers of food and manufactured goods for many decades and are an important potential market for an outward-oriented Egyptian economy. Many of the energy-intensive industries that Egypt lacks comparative advantage in—such as fertilizer, aluminum, and other petroleum-based industries—are areas in which the major oil exporting countries of the region are likely to expand. Israel, which is becoming a major producer of the high-technology goods that Egypt will increasingly be importing, could also be a market for Egypt's textiles and light manufactures.

Factor Flows and Regional Integration

While intraregional trade in goods has been very small, factor flows, particularly labor, have been an important integrating force in the region. In effect, factor flows were the mechanism for taking advantage of differential endowments in a context where trade in goods was restricted by protectionism. For Egypt, the inflow of remittance income from migrant labor in the region has become the most important source of foreign exchange revenues for the economy. Both labor and capital flows have increased over time and have often withstood shifting political alliances in the region. This section will focus on labor migration and remittances; regional capital flows will be discussed below in the context of investment.

Egyptian labor had been migrating in small numbers to the Gulf for decades, but the oil boom in the 1970s resulted in a sharp increase in the demand for Egyptian labor. Although no comprehensive figures on the number of migrants from Egypt are available for the recent period, estimates are that the number of migrants rose from one hundred thousand in the early 1970s to over one million in the early 1980s, and to probably double that amount by the late 1980s.[34] The remittances of these regional migrants ranged from 22%–43% of total export earnings between 1974 and 1986. Moreover, because remittances are both in cash and in kind, the officially reported amounts are generally considered underestimates. The growth rate of remittances has fallen in periods of regional political shocks, such as the signing of the Camp David accords in 1979, but has tended to recover fairly quickly thereafter.[35] Egyptian migrants were able to stay in the Gulf throughout the period of the Arab boycott of Egypt, reflecting the existence of structural labor shortages in the Gulf economies.

As a labor-surplus, capital-deficit country, Egypt has benefited from capital inflows from the Gulf, albeit at the cost of some brain drain. Most of Egypt's migrants were unskilled workers employed in the nontradables sectors of the major oil exporting economies, particularly in construction and services.[36] The major exception to this pattern was the almost one million Egyptian agricultural laborers who worked in Iraq during the Iran-Iraq war. But in general, Egypt's migrants tended to be construction workers, teachers, and some skilled professionals. This resulted in labor shortages in certain sectors of the Egyptian economy, such as construction, where Egypt was undergoing its own boom.[37] Egypt's economy, however, is characterized by widespread unemployment and underemployment, so migration of labor was an efficient use of resources from a national perspective.

Remittance income, along with tourism revenues exchanged through the parallel market, supplied the pool of foreign exchange for private sector importers known as the "own exchange" market that existed during the 1980s. Since remittance income represented a temporary windfall for individual migrants, much of it was allocated to expenditure on investments or durable goods. An analysis of rural migrant spending of remitted income based on household survey data in Egypt revealed that 54% was spent on housing and 21% on land.[38] Except for the poorest migrants, the share of remittance income devoted to consumption was fairly low (about 32%). Migrants in the top 20% income quintile devoted over 80% of marginal budget shares to investment. Thus, contrary to the popular perception that migrants consume much of their remittance income, the evidence is that a fairly high proportion went into investment. However, these investments tended to be in nontradable activities, such as land and housing, rather than tradables. This pattern of using income from tradable activities for investments in nontradable sectors is consistent with that which prevailed in the economy as a whole during much of the period.

The prospects for future labor flows could be enhanced if there were peace in the region. Past labor flows have been determined by the substantial wage differentials that exist between labor importing and exporting countries. These wage differentials are likely to persist because labor shortfalls are fairly structural in the major labor importers in the Gulf. What peace may bring about is a shift in the composition of migrant labor to the Gulf economies in a direction that favors Egypt. Many of the Gulf economies have consciously chosen to hire fewer migrants of Arab origin and more from Asia as the result of a perception that Arab migrants, because of their shared language and culture, could more readily become politically active in their host countries. Asian migrants constituted about 35% of total migrants in 1985 compared to about 20% from Egypt.[39] With peace, fears of political unrest spawned by Arab migrants may diminish, and the demand for migrants may increase to the advantage of labor exporters such as Egypt. With about two million Egyptian workers abroad at any point in time and annual recorded remittances of about $3 billion, each migrant remits about $1500 on average per year through official channels (and probably an equivalent amount through unofficial channels and in kind). If Egyptian migrants replaced one-half of Asian migrants to the Gulf, Egypt's total remittance income could rise to about $5.5 billion.[40]

Other Forms of Regional Cooperation

In several other areas there are strong incentives for regional cooperation, such as energy or infrastructure, where there may be economies of scale, or the environment, where there are free rider problems. Water management, of both coastal areas and irrigation water, is one of the most obvious areas where there are substantial potential gains from cooperation. The management of irrigation water in the Nile and Jordan valleys could be made far more efficient with better coordination of use and the introduction of pricing mechanisms for allocating water. Proposals have been made for conveying Nile water eastward, for Israel and Jordan to jointly manage the waters of the Yarmuk, as well as for joint management of common aquifers.[41]

The Mediterranean Sea is one area where countries in the region have been cooperating since the signing of the Barcelona Convention in 1975, well before the signing of the Camp David accords between

Israel and Egypt and before many of the participants had any diplomatic relations with Israel.[42] The Mediterranean coastline is shared by Algeria, Egypt, Israel, Lebanon, Libya, Morocco, Syria, and Tunisia, along with ten other countries. Since 1975 the countries of the Mediterranean have signed a series of protocols to control the emissions of certain pollutants from specific sources.[43] The success of the Mediterranean Action Plan (MAP) stems from the fact that the problem was perceived as one shared by all where coordinated action would be necessary to achieve welfare improvements.[44] In addition, the willingness of the richer countries of the Mediterranean, particularly France, to finance many of the costs associated with the plan encouraged cooperation. In Egypt's case, the desire to participate in the MAP was based on a desire to treat land-based sources of sea pollution and to benefit from aid and technical assistance. In general, the MAP is viewed as a story of successful regional cooperation because scientific evidence shows that the Mediterranean is now much less polluted than it would have been otherwise. The lessons from the MAP experience are that where national interests are being served and financing is available to cover the transition costs, regional cooperation can work, even among nations that have no formal relations.

Cooperation in the energy sectors is another case where scale economies may exist, such as in power transmission grids. Similarly, natural gas use is an area where there are scale economies in the construction of a pipeline and where Egypt currently flares a great deal of gas that could be used to produce energy for Israel or other neighboring countries. Estimated costs and benefits of other such projects—including joint Egyptian-Israeli fertilizer and cement plants—are available, all of which are based on the exploitation of scale economies.[45] The merits of specific projects obviously have to be evaluated in detail, but the lessons from the past are fairly clear—cooperation built on national self-interest and, where possible, supporting finance can work.

Indirect Gains from Political Stability

Indirect gains from political stability in the region stem from increased domestic and foreign confidence in the country's economic prospects. The most important indirect gains from political stability are likely to be higher rates of private investment, both domestic and foreign, and, perhaps more important, increases in the productivity of capital formation in the economy. These productivity gains will depend on the effectiveness of ongoing domestic reforms to increase efficiency and to encourage the production of tradables in the Egyptian economy. In addition, tourism revenues, which have the potential to rise far above current levels and are very sensitive to political developments in the region, may increase with peace.

Private Investment

Egypt has tried to increase private investment since the mid-1960s, after the nationalizations of most medium- and large-scale private enterprises during the early 1960s resulted in a collapse of private capital formation. The passage of Law 43 in 1974, which originally sought to provide incentives for foreign investment, is usually cited as a watershed. Law 43 was actually only a part of a series of legislative changes that came to be known as the *infitah* or "open door policy," and that reflected a changing government perception about the role of the private sector in the economy.[46] The same privileges granted to foreign investors under Law 43 were extended to domestic investors, after much lobbying, in the form of Law 159 in 1981. In 1989 the foreign and domestic investment promotion legislation as consolidated in the form of Law 230. The essential ingredients were the same—tax holidays, repatriation of profits, unrestricted importation of input requirements, and immunity from sequestration.

The level of both domestic and foreign investment in response to the incentives offered by the government was moderate.[47] Private investment in Egypt was starting from a low base given the country's history of nationalizations of private enterprises in the early 1960s. Therefore the growth rates of private investment, particularly during the oil windfall, were high by historical standards. Even so, private investment never exceeded 8% of Egypt's GDP. This compares to a ratio of private investment to GDP of about 10% for all low- and middle-income countries during the late 1980s.[48] Average private investment rates in the high-income countries are approximately double this level, ranging from 18%–22% of GDP.

The General Authority for Investment and Free Zones (GAFI), the organization that administers investment incentives in Egypt, had approved about nine hundred investment projects under Law 43 since 1974, with a cumulative capital value of LE 4604 million in

1989.[49] This represented about 7% of GDP in 1989. The vast majority of these projects, both in terms of numbers and value, were in finance, followed by construction, industry, and services. Despite Law 43's objective of promoting foreign investment, 67% of the investors were Egyptian nationals who chose to invest in foreign exchange so as to have the right to send profits abroad. Investors from Arab countries fell from 24% of total Law 43 investment to only 16% in 1989. Investors from all other countries constituted only 17% of the total. Investment in the free zones, which were intended to be centers of export-oriented manufacturing, tended to be in warehouses for the temporary storage of goods destined for the domestic market. The sectoral distribution of Law 159 investment favored industry and construction, with financial services constituting an important share in terms of equity size and commerce in terms of number of firms.

While the level of private investor response to government incentives was not bad given the low initial position, the composition and productivity of private investments were disappointing. This is because private investors were responding to an incentive structure that induced capital formation in activities with low social returns. For example, subsidized interest rates meant that credit was rationed and allocated according to reputation and contacts rather than on the basis of rates of return. Moreover the structure of interest rate subsidies made it more profitable for banks to lend to commercial activities than to projects in agriculture or industry. Similarly, the availability of protection in many sectors meant that investors focused on activities where tariffs were high or nontariff barriers to competition were in place. Input subsidies for energy and capital goods for some firms, particularly in the public sector but also in the private sector, meant that production was often too energy and capital intensive and did not generate much employment.

Surveys of private investors have identified the instability of the policy regime and the frequency of ad hoc changes as one of the most important constraints to capital formation.[50] This policy uncertainty took the form of changes in regulations concerning duty exemptions, import licenses, and building permits, or the threat of changes in macroeconomic variables such as interest rates and exchange rates. Bureaucratic obstacles often took a number of forms including negative lists prohibiting investment in sectors that were dominated by the public sector and requirements for local content. The possibility of war in the region does not seem to have been the major deterrent to foreign investors in the past. Instead, investors have stated that inadequate infrastructure, bureaucratic obstacles, rigid labor laws, domestic political instability, and the unsustainability of macroeconomic policy were probably more important factors.

The substantial uncertainty in the investment climate was also an important reason why investors focused on activities with quick payback periods and high profits, such as the financial sector. This was also exacerbated by the structure of incentives, such as a tax holiday that encouraged rapid profit making in the early years of the project. Projects in areas such as manufacturing were considered unattractive precisely because they had longer time horizons. All of these features of the incentive structure contributed to reducing the social returns to private investment.[51]

Uncertainty also imposed direct costs on private investors as increasing resources had to be allocated to hedging risks. The most widely perceived risk was the exchange rate, and most medium- and large-scale private investors hedged this risk by holding foreign exchange domestically and abroad and by avoiding debt exposure denominated in foreign exchange. The increase in foreign assets that occurred in Egypt throughout the 1980s was the result of a number of different factors. Private agents were permitted to hold foreign exchange accounts in Egypt after legislative changes that occurred in the early 1970s as part of the open door policy.[52] Combined with the protracted foreign exchange windfall between 1974 and 1986 associated with the oil shocks,[53] the result was that the economy became increasingly "dollarized" as agents sought to allocate the windfall intertemporally. The holding of dollars was in response to the high returns to foreign assets compared to low, often negative, real interest rates on savings held in Egyptian pounds, rising world interest rates, growing domestic inflation, a depreciating parallel market exchange rate, and considerable uncertainty. Econometric evidence shows that the most important determinants of currency substitution in Egypt between 1979 and 1986 were expectations of exchange rate depreciation and political uncertainty.[54]

Private investors also held large stocks of inputs, sometimes equivalent to two years of production needs, in order to hedge against changes in the exchange rate, world inflation, and future permission to import. In addition, diversification of activities, both vertically and multisectorally, was an important mechanism for dealing with uncertainty and risk. Because the stock market is small and not particularly active, diversification had to take the form of direct equity investment in different activities. Many of these hedging strategies imposed substantial costs on the private sector, some of which were passed on to consumers in oligopolistic markets. Moreover, currency diversification implied that the monetary authorities' control over domestic liquidity was reduced, tax revenue capacity was weakened, and the efficacy of exchange rate policy was diminished.

Prospects for Investment

The previous discussion has shown how many of the benefits from private investment in Egypt in the past have been stymied by the domestic incentive structure. The threat of war was not a major direct deterrent to investors, and whatever increase in capital formation that occurred in the late 1970s and early 1980s seems to have been caused more by the foreign exchange windfall experienced by the economy rather than the signing of the Camp David accords in 1979. However, uncertainty about the policy regime played an important role in reducing the social returns to investment, and regional conflict did contribute to the overall unsustainability of the policy regime, particularly fiscal and monetary policy. For example, the high level of military expenditure contributed to a large deficit, which the government financed in part through substantial domestic borrowing. This had the effect of crowding out private investment because administered interest rates resulted in financial markets that were rationed.[55] Similarly, the government's debt overhang may have dissuaded private investors who feared future taxation if the government could no longer service its debt. However, the recent restructuring of Egyptian debt, combined with reforms that altered domestic incentives, could raise the returns to private investment in the future.

One of the most important potential sources of capital inflow is assets held by Egyptian nationals abroad. Reliable estimates of the size of these asset holdings are not available, but a number of different indicators give an approximation. Cross-border bank deposits of Egyptian nonbank residents totaled $4.97 billion in 1989. Assets held by Egyptians in the United States, a small proportion of total foreign assets held by Egyptian nationals, were $713 million in 1986.[56] It seems likely that these amounts are an underestimate of the total of foreign assets held abroad by Egyptians. How likely is it that these foreign assets will return to Egypt? In the case of countries such as Mexico, Chile, and Venezuela, debt reductions combined with structural adjustment efforts contributed to a turnaround of $20 billion in private capital flows over a two-year period, equivalent to about 7.4% of these economies' GDP.[57] A similar result in Egypt would imply capital inflows on the scale of $2.2 billion. But this would require sustained implementation of a comprehensive reform effort.

Regional peace may also have several other indirect benefits, such as promoting Egypt's free trade zones and encouraging tourism. With peace and more dynamic regional trade, the fairly high-skill and low-wage labor force available in Egypt may attract foreign investors into the free zones looking for a base from which to export to the region. Similarly, the potential for tourism, which is a sector particularly vulnerable to regional political instability, remains large. Prior to the Gulf war, tourism had become the second largest foreign exchange earner after remittances. In fiscal year 1989–90, the ministry of tourism estimated earnings of approximately $2.5 billion as the number of tourist nights rose by 10%.[58] However, tourism income in Egypt, even at its peak, remains a fraction of that in other countries. For example, foreign exchange inflows from travel to Turkey were twice as large as those to Egypt in 1989, and those to Spain were thirteen times more.[59]

Economics in the Service of Peace

Peace alone cannot bring about economic prosperity. But peace combined with good economic policies is a powerful force for improving human welfare. Camp David was only a partial peace and the open door policy was only a partial liberalization. Therefore the benefits to the Egyptian economy were small. However, the potential benefits from a comprehensive peace and thorough reform of the economy are substantial and mutually reinforcing. Peace can make it easier for the government to sustain economic reform by reducing pressures on the budget and increasing investor confidence. But both processes, that of peace and that of economic reform, must be comprehensive and successful if the gains are to be realized.

Notes

The views expressed here are those of the authors and do not reflect the views of the institutions with which they are affiliated.

1. Recent data on the Egyptian economy are provided in table 2.1.

2. Waterbury (1978), pp. 6.

3. Handoussa (1991b), p. 206.

4. Waterbury (1978), p. 8.

5. The Sadat Peace Foundation prepared a proposal for a Marshall-type plan to underpin the peace treaty whereby $25 billion would be used to promote intraregional trade through the private sector. External assistance on this scale never materialized, although Egypt and Israel continued to receive the largest portions of the U.S. aid budget.

6. Springborg (1989), p. 95.

7. Handoussa (1988), pp. 21–24.

8. Figures on aid flows and balance-of-payments receipts from Handoussa (1990a) and (1991b), Ikram (1980), p. 351.

9. Quandt (1990), p. 19.

10. Ibrahim (1990), p. 300.

11. Handoussa (1990b), p. 112.

12. Hewitt (1991) explains that the NATO convention is that military aid is reported as defense expenditure by the donor country. Thus countries like Egypt and Israel, which receive substantial military aid, tend to underreport actual military expenditure.

13. U.S. Arms Control and Disarmament Agency (1982).

14. Sivard (1985). Hewitt (1991) reports numbers for military spending as a share of GDP that do indicate a decline in the 1980s relative to the 1970s. But the figures he reports for the 1970s are much higher than those reported in other sources. Also, his adjustment for foreign-financed arms imports to Egypt is too small to take U.S. military aid alone into account. Hewitt notes that his data are constructed on a formula basis and should not be used as concrete estimates for any individual country.

15. Quandt (1990), p. 32–47.

16. Waterbury (1983), p. 397.

17. Handoussa (1990b), p. 114, and Roy (1990), p. 161.

18. Quandt (1990), pp. 47–48, and U.S. Embassy Report (1991), p. 16.

19. World Bank, *World Debt Tables* (1991b).

20. Springborg (1989), pp.107–8, p. 261; Richards and Waterbury (1990), pp 363–64.

21. Richards and Waterbury (1990), p. 364.

22. Springborg (1989), p. 95.

23. Figures on the size of the armed forces and defense expenditure for the Middle East are from Richards and Waterbury (1990), pp. 360–63. Additional figures for Egypt were obtained from Heisbourg (1989), Quandt (1990), and government budget sources.

24. World Bank, *World Development Report* (1984) and (1991c), and Handoussa (1991b) for 1975 to 1977.

25. Handoussa (1991a), p. 4.

26. For a detailed description of past attempts, see Makdisi (1979) and Haseeb and Makdisi (1981). For a more recent description of regional economic institutions, see van den Boogaerde (1990).

27. The exception here is Saudi Arabia, which is able to export wheat because of enormous domestic subsidies.

28. Dervis, Martin, and van Wijnbergen (1984).

29. In a survey of Egyptian private sector firms in 1987, Shafik found that many Egyptian industrialists had export orders but were not interested in filling them, because selling on the domestic market was far more lucrative. Shafik (1989).

30. Lucas and Kheireldin (1981).

31. Shafik (1989).

32. World Bank (1991a).

33. Hassan et al. (1991).

34. The available estimates vary, but all show a clear upward trend over the 1970s and early 1980s. Fergany's estimate based on survey data is that there were no more than 200,000 migrant laborers in 1976. This rose to 1.2 million in 1985. Fergany (1988) cited in Assaad and Commander (1990). Amin and Awney (1985) estimate that as many as 1 million Egyptians were working abroad in the early 1980s, which constituted between 9% and 10% of the labor force. Commander (1987) reports that approximately 5% of the labor force was abroad in the mid-1970s and 9%–10% by 1981–82.

35. In 1976 remittances grew by 106%; then in 1977 the growth rate slowed to 19%. However, by 1978 the growth rate had recovered to 96%. World Bank (1990).

36. For a disaggregation of migrants by occupation, see Serageldin et al. (1983).

37. Between 1981 and 1982 and 1984 and 1985, wages in the construction

sector grew by 73%, a rate that was almost three times greater than the average for all other sectors. However, by 1986–87, construction wages collapsed as oil prices fell sharply. This decline in construction wages reflected both declining demand and the fact that the labor force in the sector had nearly doubled as agricultural workers were increasingly drawn into urban construction. Assad and Commander (1990).

38. Adams (1991).

39. This compares to about 22% from Egypt in 1975 and 23% from Asia. Serageldin et al. (1983), p. 5.

40. This includes official, unofficial, and in-kind remittances on the assumption that the average migrant remits $3,000 in total per year, half of which is through official channels.

41. Kally (1989).

42. Apparently, UNEP averted conflict between the Arab states and Israel by extracting a promise from the Arab states that they would not challenge Israel in exchange for Israeli delegates keeping a low profile. Haas (1990), p. 80.

43. For details on the Mediterranean Action Plan and environmental problems of the sea, see Musu (1991).

44. It is interesting to note that subsequent studies by marine scientists revealed that the currents of the Mediterranean were not sufficiently strong to carry pollutants from the southern to the northern shores. Haas (1990).

45. Fishelson (1989).

46. The centerpiece of the *infitah* was Law 43/1974, which granted foreign investors a five-to-ten-year tax holiday, unrestricted repatriation of profits, and immunity from sequestration. However, a series of subsequent laws (such as Laws 64/1974, 120/1975, 118/1975, 97/1976, 32/1977) achieved partial liberalization of the trade and foreign exchange regime and the banking system.

47. For a summary of investor response to incentives under the open door policy, see Esfahani (1990).

48. Riordan (1990).

49. Esfahani (1990).

50. Ahmed et al. (1984) and Shafik (1989).

51. For an econometric analysis of these conclusions, see Shafik (1991).

52. The relevant laws governing foreign exchange account are Law 64/1974 and Law 97/1976.

53. Although the oil price shocks were in 1973 and 1979, Egypt did not experience a substantial windfall until after 1979 when oil export volumes

increased with new discoveries and the return of the Sinai fields after the signing of the peace treaty with Israel. Shafik (1991).

54. El-Erian (1988).

55. Shafik (1991) found that the quantity of credit available to the private sector was an important explanatory variable for private investment in Egypt.

56. IMF, *International Financial Statistics* (1990).

57. El-Erian (1991).

58. United States Embassy, Cairo (1991).

59. IMF, *Balance of Payments Statistics* (1990).

References

Adams, R. (1991), "The Effects of International Remittances on Poverty, Inequality, and Development in Rural Egypt," International Food Policy Research Institute, Washington D.C.

Ahmed, S., V. Lall, and S. Subramanian (1984), "Fiscal Incentives in Egypt: Their Impact on Private Investment and the Government Budget," processed, World Bank.

Amin, G., and E. Awney (1985), "International Migration of Egyptian Labor," IDRC Report, May.

Assaad, R., and S. Commander (1990), "Egypt: The Labor Market through Boom and Recession," Mimeograph, World Bank, May.

Commander, S. (1987), *The State and Agricultural Development of Egypt Since 1973,* Overseas Development Institute, London.

Dervis, K., R. Martin, and S. van Wijnbergen (1984), "Policy Analysis of Shadow Pricing, Foreign Borrowing and Resource Extraction in Egypt," World Bank Staff Working Paper no. 622.

El-Erian, M. (1988), "Currency Substitution in Egypt and the Yemen Arab Republic: A Comparative Quantitative Analysis," *IMF Staff Papers* 35:1, March.

———.(1991), "The Restoration of Latin America's Access to Voluntary Capital Market Financing," IMF Working Paper, WP/91/74, Washington, D.C.

Esfahani, H. (1990), "The Experience of Foreign Investment in Egypt under Infitah," Bureau of Economic and Business Research Faculty Working Paper no. 90–1710, University of Illinois, Urbana-Champaign, December.

Fergany, N. (1988), "In Pursuit of Livelihood: A Field Study of Egyptian Migration," Center for Arab Unity Studies, Beirut (in Arabic).

Fishelson, G. (1989), "Key Findings of the Middle East Economic Cooperation

Projects," in *Economic Cooperation in the Middle East*, ed. G. Fishelson, Boulder: Westview Press.

Haas, P. (1990), *Saving the Mediterranean: The Politics of International Environmental Cooperation*, New York: Columbia University Press.

Handoussa, H. (1988), "The Burden of Public Service Employment and Remuneration: A Case Study of Egypt," Monograph commissioned by the International Labor Office in Geneva, September.

———. (1990a), "Egypt's Investment Strategy, Policies and Performance Since the Infitah," in *Investment Policies in the Arab Countries*, ed. S. El-Naggar, Washington, International Monetary Fund.

———. (1990b), "Fifteen Years of U.S. Aid to Egypt—A Critical Review," in *The Political Economy of Contemporary Egypt*, ed. I. M. Oweiss, Washington: Center for Contemporary Arab Studies, Georgetown University.

———. (1991a), "Crisis and Challenge: Prospects for the 1990's," in *Employment and Structural Adjustment: Egypt in the 1990's*, in H. Handoussa and G. Potter, International Labor Office, Cairo American University in Cairo Press (forthcoming).

———. (1991b), "The Impact of Foreign Assistance on Egypt's Economic Development: 1952–1986," in *Transitions in Development: The Role of Aid and Commercial Flows*, ed. U. Lele and I. Nabi, San Francisco: International Center for Economic Growth, ICS Press.

Haseeb, K., and S. Makdisi (1981), *Arab Monetary Integration*, London: Croom Helm.

Hassan, R., D. Greenaway, and G. V. Reed (1991), "An Empirical Analysis of Comparative Advantage in Egyptian Agriculture," Mimeograph, University of Nottingham, September.

Heisbourg, Francois (1989), *The Military Balance 1989–1990*, London: International Institute for Strategic Studies.

Hewitt, Daniel (1991), "Military Expenditures: International Comparison of Trends," Working Paper no. 91154, International Monetary Fund, Washington, D.C., May.

Ibrahim, I. (1990), "Egypt, Israel and the Palestinians," in *The Political Economy of Contemporary Egypt*, ed. I. M. Oweiss, Washington: Center for Contemporary Arab Studies, Georgetown University.

Ikram, K. (1980), *Egypt: Economic Management in a Period of Transition*, World Bank Publication, Johns Hopkins University Press, Baltimore.

International Monetary Fund (1990), *Balance of Payments Yearbook*, Washington D.C.

International Monetary Fund (1990), *International Financial Statistics Yearbook*, Washington D.C.

Kally, E. (1989), "The Potential for Cooperation in Water Projects in the Middle East at Peace," in *Economic Cooperation in the Middle East,* ed. G. Fishelson, Boulder: Westview Press.

Lucas, R., and H. Kheireldin (1981), "Comparative Advantage in Egyptian Industry," Report prepared by consultants from Boston University for USAID, Cairo, Egypt, December.

Makdisi, S. (1979), "Arab Economic Cooperation: Implications for the Arab World and World Economies," in R. Albioni, ed., *Arab Industrialization and Economic Integration,* New York: St. Martin's Press.

Musu, I. (1991), "The Interdependence between Environment and Development: Marine Pollution in the Mediterranean Sea," Paper presented at a conference, The Economics of the Transitional Commons, Sienna, Italy, April.

Quandt, W. B. (1990), *The United States and Egypt: An Essay on Policy for the 1990's,* A Brookings Institution Book, Cairo: The American University in Cairo Press.

Richards, A., and J. Waterbury (1990), *A Political Economy of the Middle East,* Boulder: Westview Press.

Riordan, M. (1990), "Estimates of Public and Private Investment," Mimeograph, World Bank, March.

Roy, D. (1990), "Egyptian Debt: Forgive—or Forget?" in *The Political Economy of Contemporary Egypt,* edited by I. M. Oweiss, Washington: Center for Contemporary Arab Studies, Georgetown University.

Serageldin, I., J. Socknat, S. Birks, B. Li, and C. Sinclair (1983), *Manpower and International Labor Migration in the Middle East and North Africa,* Oxford: Oxford University Press.

Shafik, N. (1989), "Private Investment and Public Policy in Egypt," D. Phil thesis, Oxford University.

———. (1991), "Modeling Private Investment in Egypt," *Journal of Development Economics* (forthcoming).

Sivard, Ruth L. (1985), *World Military and Social Expenditures—1985,* Washington, D.C.: World Priorities.

Springborg, R. (1989), *Mubarak's Egypt: Fragmentation of the Political Order,* Boulder: Westview Press.

U.S. Arms Control and Disarmament Agency (1982), *World Military Expenditures and Arms Transfers,* 1970–1979. Washington, D.C.

United States Embassy (1991), "Report for the Arab Republic of Egypt," Foreign Economic Trends and Their Implications for the United States, Mimeograph, April.

van den Boogaerde, P. (1990), "The Composition and Distribution of Financial Assistance from Arab Countries and Arab Regional Institutions," IMF Working Paper, July.

Waterbury, J. (1978), *Egypt: Burdens of the Past, Options for the Future,* Bloomington: Indiana University Press.

———. (1983), *The Egypt of Nasser and Sadat,* New Jersey: Princeton University Press.

World Bank (1990), *World Tables,* Washington, D.C.: Johns Hopkins University Press.

———. (1991a), *Global Economic Prospects,* International Economics Department, Washington, D.C.: World Bank.

———. (1991b), *World Debt Tables,* Washington, D.C.: World Bank.

———. (1989 and 1991c), *World Development Report,* Washington, D.C.: Oxford University Press.

3 The Effects on Economic Development in Syria of a Just and Long-Lasting Peace

Rizkallah Hilan

The major challenge facing Syria since its renaissance in the middle of the nineteenth century has been economic and social development. The Syrian national movement has sought to bring the country into the modern age, regain its former inventive spirit, and reestablish it among the modern nations of the world. In the past the country was part of Greater Syria, a region established since the dawn of history and one that played an eminent role in the development of civilization itself. In more modern times, Syria has aspired to realize its legitimate right to develop; however, this desire has clashed with external forces of Ottoman domination and European colonialism.

From the beginning of the 1920s, the national struggle confronted two new challenges: the occupation of Syrian territory by colonial armies; and its dismantling and submission to the hybrid regime of the mandate, a logical outcome of the old "colonial pact" imposed on the Ottoman Empire and the Zionist plan. This plan, condemned formally by the General Congress of Syria in Paris in July 1919, embodies the Judeo-Arab conflict, which has continually worsened with time. The birth of the state of Israel in 1948 was the definitive blow to historic regional unity, and added a dramatic international dimension to the conflict within the context of the cold war and north-south relations. Newly independent, within frontiers etched by the interests of the Western powers, the new Syria was consequently obliged to provide itself with a rapidly growing armed force to safeguard its national sovereignty and security.

After more than four decades of the arms race, high tensions, and wars, which weigh heavily on the present regional situation and deeply traumatize the national consciousness, a new perspective has appeared on the horizon[1]: as a result of the profound changes happening in the world, the conflict seems to be nearing a political solution. When this undoubtedly inescapable resolution to the conflict has been realized, what will its effects be on the social and economic development of Syria?

This chapter addresses this question in the following way: it attempts a general examination of the impact of militarization on economic growth and development; then it presents a more focused discussion of the effects of the inverse processes of demilitarization and peace. The impact of militarization will be examined at three levels. First, I cover the general concept, based on the experiences of developing countries. Second, I review in more detail the specific case of developing countries; and third I focus on the case of Syria. The second section is dedicated to clarifying the effects of peace on the Syrian economy and will assess the impact of a decrease in military expenditures and reduction in the size of the armed forces. It will also touch on the outcome of peace on trade and will look at the conditions under which substantial and profitable trade can develop for everyone, paving the road to regional integration. In addition to the results mentioned above, the process of creating peace will have other, more general, effects on every aspect of life; these will be the focus of a special study later on.

The first effect concerns tourism, which would be very likely to increase in a climate of regional political stability. The potential impact of peace on the movement of assets, including human capital, will be briefly touched upon. However, the main point will be that, given the qualitative effects that peace will produce within the entire development process, it is likely to have an impact also on the political structure.

The essential question that remains concerns the nature of the peace. This question will lead us briefly to venture far from economics, into the area of political philosophy. This foray could risk blurring our focus; our treatment therefore will of necessity be limited to the introduction of broad hypotheses.

The Relationship between Militarization, Growth, and Development

We start by examining the general issue of the relationship between militarization, growth, and development, drawing on relevant economic literature and concluding with a few remarks that help establish the framework in which to examine the Syrian situation.

Principal Patterns in Economic Thought

A rigorous theoretical analysis of the relationship between militarization and economic growth and, more generally, economic and social development, is still lacking. Economic thought on this issue remains questionable and generally tainted by ideology. It can be summed up in three main categories. For certain authors, militarization, estimated from the relative size of public defense expenditures, plays an important, positive role in economic growth, especially during periods of stagnation and recession, when these expenditures assist the economy to rebound. Expenditures for military R&D, in particular, can play a significant role in technical military innovation, which could then have positive spillover effects on civilian industry. In support of this idea, practical examples are cited, for instance that of the United States and other industrialized countries in the period of the "thirty glorious years" that witnessed the reconstruction of the European and Japanese economies and their exceptional growth.

However, for other authors defense expenditures represent significant burdens slowing down growth and weighing heavily on all levels of the lives of the population. This would be the case especially for the United States and certain other European countries such as France in the 1970s and 1980s compared to Japan and the Federal Republic of Germany. Japan and Germany spend relatively little on defense but perform remarkably well compared to the others who have significant military burdens and experience recurrent economic and social difficulties.

A third line of thought, supported particularly by historians, points out an important relationship between militarization and general long-term decline. This is proposed by Paul Kennedy, who became famous during the war against Iraq (known as Desert Storm), and primarily concerns the historic example of Spain and the present-day United States. The historic example of the Ottoman Empire and the present dramatic example of the former USSR are also evidence for this argument.

Let us conclude this brief resume with the following remarks. The economic impact of militarization remains fairly uncertain. It depends on a number of indeterminate conditions and economic, political, cultural, and psychological factors that vary considerably from one situation to another. Wars and political tensions can be economically profitable to certain countries and social classes, particularly to those that do not participate directly or only partially. These conflicts are undertaken at the expense of others, especially the countries and classes engaged in battle and/or those who bear the costs. However, globally this situation is the same for everyone. Militarization, war, and tension are destructive of productive resources, both material and human as well as on the environment. Therefore, they constitute an unadulterated moral and economic loss.

In a world where danger and aggression are a reality, however, military expenditures remain indispensable for a nation to enjoy an essential element—security. The amount and use of the requisite resources dedicated to this end must therefore be determined in relation to the accomplishments of this function and adhere to economic rationality and democratic authority. Either by nature or by interest, behind the veil of military secrecy, the military/industrial/financial complex tends to abuse rationality and authority, leading to the exaggeration of the importance of the armed forces and an excess of military spending. This type of situation could lead to the militarization of society and to irreparable long-term decline. There are many examples of this in history.

The Case of the Developing World

Countries of the developing world are at a disadvantage compared to the industrialized countries with regard to the effects of militarization on their economies and their societies. These effects are generally much more pernicious for three reasons:

a. These countries are obliged to spend money on imports to build their arms and defense systems. These expenditures use part of the country's meager hard currency resources and waste the beneficial effects that these resources would normally have exercised on industrial and economic growth within these countries. The result is a growing external debt and overall economic decline.

b. The essential needs of the "poor" countries go generally unsatisfied. Any military expense therefore constitutes a heavy burden to support and a kind of useless luxury.

c. Much more so than in advanced countries, the effects of militarization can be particularly dangerous because militarization favors the installation of a political-military authority structure,[2] the effects of which, as we will see later, are precarious for development in general.

In the past the nations of the third world were on the road to militarization for reasons that were not always their own and that did not exactly respond to their real needs. Modern arms and wars have generally served the interests of the countries of the northern hemisphere and weapons manufacturers, as well as the dominant classes of these countries and elsewhere. In addition, a large part of the military hardware of developing countries is financed with foreign aid and especially by foreign loans, which are swiftly transformed into accumulated debt paralyzing their economies and burdening the masses. It is estimated that on average about 40% of developing country debt results from the importation of arms.[3] Also, domestic military expenditures exhaust national budgets, annihilating other public expenditures for development, even for essential needs, resulting in enormous imbalances—both social and economic.

Military Expenditures and Economic Growth in Syria

National security expenditures, broken down between the ministries of defense (90% of the total) and the interior (approximately 10% of the total) make up about 30% of the total of public expenditures (running costs and development costs) in Syria. They amount to approximately 50% of the running costs, which have risen considerably since 1975 (see table 3.1), due undoubtedly to the consequences of the war in 1973 and the increase in public expenditures. It is only since 1987 that these expenditures, including those on security, have decreased as a percentage of various total expenditure measures. National security expenditures are extremely large when compared to other budget items and especially to spending on national education, health and social welfare, and employment. The relative shares of the latter two areas have tended to decrease since 1975 as shown in table 3.1.[4]

Table 3.1 also shows that expenditures for national security constitute a very large burden, which has become increasingly large since 1975, relative to GDP as well as to the product of the goods-producing sectors (agriculture + extractive industries including oil and manufactured goods). However, compared to gross investment (GFCF or gross fixed capital formation), national security expendi-

Table 3.1
National security expenditures in the Syrian economy

	% of current budget expenditures to:				National security expenditures as % of:			Public expenditures as % of GDP	
			National security						
Year	Education (1)	Health & soc. (2)	% (3)	billion S.P. (3a)	GDP (4)	Goods sectors (5)	GFCF (6)	Current budget (7)	Develop. budget (8)
1964	22.1	3.6	53	0.4	10.4	—	58.5	17.6	20.4
1966	23.1	3.5	48	0.4	9.1	—	—	18.4	14.6
1970	16.4	4.2	49	0.7	10.6	23.1	15.7	21.9	21.8
1972	20.7	5.3	50	0.8	9.2	19.2	49.7	18.4	18.4
1975	15.5	2.1	72	3.3	16.3	43.3	64.9	22.8	29.2
1976	—	2.7	68	3.7	15.2	37.8	47.6	24.2	43.7
1978	12.3	2.0	60	4.6	14.8	34.6	51.5	24.8	34.8
1982	13.8	1.9	58	9.8	14.8	38.4	60.1	25.3	25.1
1984	11.9	1.8	57	13.3	18.3	49.6	74.6	32.4	24.6
1988	14.0	1.8	49	14.5	8.1	17.0	56.2	16.5	12.2
1990	15.1	2.5	48	18.1	(8.9)[g]	(19.8)[g]	(61.0)[g]	(19.1)[g]	(12.4)[g]

Source: Central Bureau of Statistics, *Statistical Abstract* (various years). All figures computed in current prices; GDP at factor costs.
(1) including higher education; (2) health, social affairs, and labor.
(3a) billion Syrian pounds (US$ 1 = 3.95 Syrian Pounds up to 1987).
(5) Agriculture and industry (incl. oil and manufacturing) sectors.
(6) total investment (public and private).
(7) + (8) = Total public expenditures as % of GDP.
(g) Provisional figures.

tures have remained at approximately the same high level over the years because investment also climbed strongly (table 3.2), thanks to external financing and also to borrowing from the Central Bank (CBS). These debts have accumulated with time, creating a fundamental imbalance leading to the crisis during the 1980s.

In reality the burden of security expenditures would appear even larger if certain other military costs, dispersed throughout the national budget, were taken into consideration, and especially if a large share of the costs of materials and imported military technology were added to them (assistance without compensation and military loans). Scant information concerning this last category of expenditure is available. Certain well-informed authors cite very high figures concerning the military debt with the USSR (U.S. $15 billion), which we include here without committing ourselves—this would bring the share of security expenditures to about 30% of the GNP.[5]

The question to ask then is how an economy with limited resources, such as that of Syria, could have carried such a burden for so long. The fundamental question must be answered largely from noneconomic considerations, and within a political and cultural context. As is well known, Syria was the birthplace of Arab-Islamic civilization, and since the nineteenth century has been the principal source of Arab nationalism and the anti-imperialist struggle. Because of this, the Syrians see themselves charged with a historic mission of Arab nationalism, which is always expressly evident in their discourse.

In addition, the nation's geostrategic position at the crossroads of the three ancient continents accords it particular international importance as a key country of the region.[6] This historical, cultural, political, and strategic reality has benefited Syria continually with strong, positive support from Arab public opinion, and with support from nonaligned countries as well as from the socialist countries. From this, Syria has consequently received moral support and substantial material benefits that have helped it to avoid suffering from excessively heavy military burdens in its national struggle and with its economic development. In fact, beginning in the middle of the 1950s, the Syrian economy experienced relatively rapid growth rates, after depending primarily on its own resources of accumulated hard currency during the Second World War and subsequently during the Korean War.

Syria was able to provide itself with arms as well as economic and technical assistance as a result of cooperation agreements with the Soviet Union and other countries with planned economies. In turn, this assistance encouraged aid from the West. The average rate of industrial growth attained a level of 12% per year from 1950 to 1956 and 4.8% from 1956 to 1960. From 1960 to 1965, the rate of growth of the GNP was 4.5% and 8% annually in the industrial sector. Total investment was 18.9% of national revenue.[7]

Moral support and external financial assistance after the June 1967 war enabled Syria to reconstruct its economic and political potential. Conversely, Syria gained a significant amount of prestige from the war of October 1973. This marked the beginning of immense financial inflows to the entire region from oil surpluses, from which Syria profited in large measure in various forms: unrequited transfers, estimated at approximately 21 billion Syrian pounds (SP) or approximately $5.4 billion from 1973 to 1979; remittance payments from migrant workers, estimated at $600–$900 million per year; exports of Syrian oil (SP 1.6 billion in 1974, SP 5.2 billion in 1980); and external loans, which contributed to a rapidly accumulating debt (see table 3.2).

This surge of external funds created a general boom. The country was increasingly oriented toward a strongly consumer-based society. Imported luxury items inundated the markets as the commercial deficit increased. Although investment experienced a great rebound, the rate of growth of GNP slowed considerably from the middle of the 1970s. GNP showed no growth between 1981 and 1987, during which time its index oscillated between 96 and 98, except in 1985 when it was at 100 (base 1985 = 100). The GNP index rose to 110 in 1988 but fell back to 99 in 1989.

Industrial production, including the private sector, remained practically stagnant between 1975 and 1986 (table 3.2), a period that included short-term rapid increases (1980–85 and 1987–89), as well as decreases (1976–80 and 1984). Manufacturing industry, which was supposed to be its most dynamic component, followed the same pattern, although with a difference of a few years. The rate of growth of the national manufacturing sector remained moderately positive during the 1970s, attained its maximum between 1980 and 1983, then slumped and became negative from 1986. The production index of this sector (1985 = 100) fell to 93 in 1988 and to 97 in 1980. In 1990 it was back at 100. By the end of the 1980s Syria was in the midst of a grave crisis affecting the entire economy.

Table 3.2
Global figures of Syrian economy, 1961–1989

Years	Average annual growth rate %(a) (a) GDP (1)	(a) industry (2)	(a) mnfctrg. (3)	GFCF as % of GDP (4)	Export import coverage rate (5)	Foreign debt (billion US$) (6)	Internal Debt as % of GDP (7)	Notes (8)
1961–65	4.5	8.0	—	—	80	—	—	—
1966–70	3.6	10.0	2.4	—	58	1790: 0.3[f]	36.5	—
1971–75	13.6	9.3	5.1[b]	20.7	53	1973: 0.7[f]	22.4	—
1976–80	4.5	−3.2*	5.9[b]	29.5	42 (1977–78)	1980: 4.6[f]	36.7	—
1980–85	2.9	5.0	13.5[c]	24.4	44 (1982–85)	2.1[d]	92.8	1987: 65% devaluation of Syrian Pound (1US$=11.25SP)
1984	(−4.0)	(−16.0)	(6.0)			1983: 4.5[f]		
1987–89	4.0	26.0	0.0	17.8 (1986–88)	57.2 (1987–88)	2.3[d]	68.0	
1965–80	9.1[e]	12.0	—		1989: 5.2[e]			
1980–89	1.6[e]	5.2	—					

Source: Central Bureau of Statistics, *Statistical Abstract*, different years
(a) GDP at factor costs excluding (e): at market costs
(b) Industrial development in SAR, AID 1984 (Adjusted values)
(c) five-year Plan for Manufacturing 1981–85, Ministry of Planning, Evaluation Rep of the Fifth Plan (Excl. Milhouse Cie).
(d) The World Bank, World Development Rep 1986 (long-term debt).
(e) Ibidem, 1991 (long- and short-term debt, military debt excluded).
(f) total civil debt including debts to the banks and financing institutions (Arab Econ Unity Review, June 1986 tab pp. 30–170)
*computed from *Statistical Abstract* 1984 Tab. 9/16 p. 526, total industrial product at 1980 constant prices at market costs.

Discoveries of new oil reserves, the relative rebound of the price of crude oil, and the government austerity plan stopped the decline without being able to spark growth. The index of extractive industry increased from 100 in 1985 to 216 and 267 in 1989 and 1990. The production index of the government sector in GNP, at 100 in 1985, fell to 84 in 1989, the same level as in 1981 and 23 points less than the 107 figure for 1984.

Can we conclude then that military expenditures and war weighed heavily on growth and development? What were the principal causes of the crisis of the 1980s? We will respond by the following remarks:

(a) Tension and wars, beginning with the Second World War and the Korean War, the June 1967 war, and especially the October 1973 war, were rather beneficial to the Syrian economy, at least insofar as they were catalysts for financing and aid coming from abroad. The two Gulf wars (Iran-Iraq, then Desert Storm in January 1991) certainly do not contradict this observation!

Certain social sectors, the bourgeoisie of the government and the bourgeoisie of business, prospered and amassed substantial—in some cases, enormous—fortunes, which were direct or indirect results of these wars and the financial flux that occurred during them.

(b) The preceding remarks by no means pertain only to Syria. They can also be applied to other economies of the developing world and elsewhere. Many of these countries have undoubtedly benefited from the dividends of the cold war and the violent wars that accompanied it, without suffering a complete decline of their economies, at least for the time being.

(c) The economic crisis of the 1980s cannot be attributed directly and exclusively to military expenditures even though they were considerable. Rather it was because of inappropriate management of financial, human, and other resources, as well as of the model of growth, which was directly tied to the dominant economic system.

Here again it can be said that this model and this crisis are not specific to Syria. On the contrary, these general effects can be seen in the developing world and other countries, independent of militarization. This becomes apparent when looking at comparative figures produced by the World Bank, compiled in table 3.3. This table, which includes ten third world countries as well as Israel, presents the ranking first of the growth rates of these countries, then the share

Table 3.3
National security expenditures (defense) and average growth rates per annum (in long and medium periods)

	Average annual growth rates						National Secur. Exp. as % of total budget			T. budget as of % of GNP	(8) × (10) / 100	
	GNP/capita		GDP									
Country	1965–87 (1)	rank (2)	1973–84 (3)	rank (4)	1980–87 (5)	rank (6)	1972 (7)	1987 (8)	rank (9)	1983 (10)	% (11)	raw (12)
Korea	6.4	1	7.2	3	8.6	1	25.8	27.3	3	18.3	5.0	5
Egypt	3.5	2	8.5	2	6.3	2	—	19.5	6	39.0	7.7	4
Jordan	—	(3)	9.6	1	4.3	5	33.5	25.9	4	38.4	9.9	3
Tunisia	3.6	4	5.5	5	3.6	6	4.9	5.7	10	37.1	2.1	10
Syria	3.3	5	7.0	4	0.3	11	37.2	32.2[b]	1	54.8[b]	17.6	1
Turkey	2.6	6	4.1	8	5.2	3	15.5	11.4	8	24.3	2.8	9
Mexico	2.5	7	5.1	6	0.5	10	4.5	1.4	11	27.9	0.4	11
Israel	2.5	7	3.1	10	2.2	8	49.9	30.1	2	48.8	14.7	2
Morocco	1.8	9	4.5	7	3.2	7	12.3	14.5	7	33.2	4.8	6
India	1.8	10	4.1	9	4.6	4	26.2	21.5	5	14.9	3.2	8
Chile	0.2	11	2.7	11	1.0	9	6.1	10.7	9	34.8	3.7	7

Source: The World Bank, *World Development Report 1989*, exclusion for (3) and (10) ibid 1986; (a) ibid 1989; (b) *Statistical Abstract 1984*; figures for GDP (Syria).
(7), (8) and (10): Total expenditures (Current & Development budgets) of Central Governments only.
(11) Computed by multiplying (8) × (10) and dividing by 100, which gives figures near to defense expenditures as percentage of GNP.
(2), (4), (6), (9), and (12) ranks of Countries according to the importance of the figures in preceding columns consecutively.

of defense expenditures in total public expenditures, and third, the share of defense expenditures in GNP (note that the numbers in columns 8 and 10 of the table do not correspond to the same year).

Three periods were chosen: 1965–87 represents the long term (column 1), 1973–84 represents the oil boom (column 3), and 1980–87 represents the crisis and austerity programs (column 5). In comparing the data in these columns with those in columns 9 and 12, it would be practically impossible to detect any consistent pattern linking growth rates with the rate of military spending.

What conclusions can we draw? That military expenditures are beneficial to economic growth and social development, or that they only have a negligible influence on them? In my mind, this would oversimplify the matter. To the extent that Syria, as well as other countries that arm themselves, has accomplished this without any particular economic hardship, it is because the military burden has been deferred outside the country or on to future generations. However, this situation, which is strongly connected to the unusual circumstances of the cold war and the recycling of financial surpluses, cannot last indefinitely. Indeed, it seems to have ended with the dramatic changes of recent years in the sense that any further increase in military expenditures will weigh heavier on the economies and populations of the countries concerned.

In reality, the population and especially the middle and poor classes had severe difficulties. The standard of living declined during the 1970s and 1980s, reflecting the rising inflation, the low level of public expenditures on social welfare and the tendency of these expenditures to decrease, while at the same time military expenditures increased beginning in 1975. The budget share devoted to education and social welfare surged from 1988, as is shown in table 3.1, but this is misleading. In fact, spending on education and welfare declined as a share of GNP, as did the national budget. This decrease is certainly the direct result of the crisis, but this is not unusual since military expenditures are always a priority, even when in competition with investment, and even more so with social welfare spending.

We are therefore entitled to assume that a substantial reduction in military expenditures would benefit the accumulation of productive capital as well as the well-being of the society. However, investment is not a panacea. Its very high level during the 1970s and through the middle of the 1980s did not prevent the crisis, in fact it may have even been a cause. We would need to examine how investment spending was managed and more generally, how the economy and even the society in general were managed. How can we interpret the weak economic performance, the low growth rates, and the crisis in spite of the large amounts of investments if not as a result of overall mismanagement? This cannot be tied directly to growing interference and splintering power bases within the dominant authoritative structures and in economic and social activities that resulted in massive corruption with disastrous consequences buttressed by blatant disregard for the law and the mismanagement of institutions.

In summary, can we simply conclude that militarization does not spread freely? The main point is to understand who pays the price for it, when, and how. "To buy more bullets, the Syrians had to bite one," writes an observer.[8] Absolutely, yet what other country wouldn't find itself forced to do the same, unless a new world order capable of ensuring dignity, security, and the legitimate interest of all its members—states, groups, and individuals—were established or at least initiated.

The Economic Effects of Peace

To adequately estimate the effects of peace, it is necessary for us first to look at the nature of the solution, and to formulate some hypotheses.

Hypothetical Elements for a Long-Lasting and Just Peace

First, any settlement of a conflict, as with any other institution, can only be the expression of a balance of power as well as self-interest. According to the classic analysis, it is above all the balance of actual forces that determines the conditions and outcomes of the final agreement. In addition, each of the conflicting parties attempts to place itself in the best power position, hewing to the age-old recipe for tactics, while seeking the maximum possible advantage in the final settlement of the conflict.

Nevertheless, a settlement based purely on the balance of power could never be a just and long-lasting one. Parties whose fundamental interests have not been satisfied will be tempted to break the agreement, calling into question the final or imposed agreement. They will revert to traditionally sinister scenarios of preventative war, wars of revenge and retaliation, and in the worst case, to every sort of terrorist act.

A just and long-lasting peace requires that the deep-rooted and true causes of the conflict be addressed and the certain necessary conditions be met to arrive at a successful solution. The causes of the conflict are in fact imbedded in the dominant culture, namely that of Western society, which according to Jacques Robin, has been founded on a huge illusion of power and on a technological and scientific complex that now functions as an immense dynamo voraciously dominating the industrial, commercial, and military system.[9] The primordial values of this culture—power, manipulation, control, and efficiency—drive the nation, its groups, and individuals to a pitiful end, trampling one another underfoot and propelling them to greed and the most heinous forms of materialism.[10] These values are often justified by acts of the least praiseworthy type as well as cynically tragic. This is obviously Darwinist philosophy, which pits humans against humans, and is at the core of the great evils of history. It is important to understand that this concept could, in principle, produce an armistice, however temporary, but would never guarantee a long-lasting, much less just, peace. Even at best, it cannot ensure the rational development of men and nations.

Rejecting this philosophy as basically defective, Professor Henrick Skolimowski proposes that in the twenty-first century there will be an inspired legal philosophy that will be environmentally based ensuring universal harmony in spite of incredible diversity. These laws would entail interdependence, symbiosis, and respect as well as the values of compassion, responsibility, solidarity, and practicality. According to this world concept, this philosophy proposes a social contract paving the road to a long-lasting and just peace, "the spine of the new world order." The problem, he states, is to underscore our common unity as a human species and as intelligent and sensitive beings desiring and deserving lives imbued with beauty and grace.[11] In the same vein Jacques Robin calls for an economy of service in the development of men, instead of enslaving themselves to their own development, and for everyone to live by an ethic of caring about others and nature.

A key question is whether the time is ripe for this type of solution. Or are such solutions based on a rather simplistic view of human nature? Without a sustainable balance of power, even a great enthusiastic idea would not be viable. For example, *the new world economic order*, a great idea proposed during the 1970s, and *the decade of devel-*

opment during the 1980s, were adopted by the General Assembly of the United Nations but have resulted in no significant change, largely because the great industrialized countries did not support them. So, a utopian solution? Perhaps! But is the only truly realistic option the pursuit of fanciful dreams of grandeur and domination, which have produced such incredible acts of barbarism, gross injustices, and sordid tragedies? If these were the alternative, could we envision a just and long-lasting peace? Would it instead be a kind of appeasement or a constrained peace? An antipeace ushering in the potential for hatred, violence, and future conflagrations?

The fantastic changes that shock our troubled world of today and that surprise even the most astute observers are certainly not gratuitous; they are the results of the crisis in civilization, which the former French president Charles de Gaulle used to explain the great student demonstrations of 1968. And even if the new world order, which these changes herald, remains a vague idea, is it not significant that the leaders of these great countries, and most notably the two superpowers, refer to it? The creation of the new world order is a process that has already begun and that will continue, not because these illustrious people speak of it, or because the masses desire it, but because reality necessitates it to settle the critical problems that face our disturbed world. Accordingly, it seems inescapable that the balance of power will be replaced by a balance of interests, in order to find a solution to these conflicts and to ensure that in the interest of all, collective global security prevails over one-sided, regional, or individual concerns.[12]

What is at the core of the balance of interests? Isn't it the reassertion of ethics in political relations? Can human society remain cohesive, or at least preserve itself, without applying ethical standards of the community of nations that are respected by all? Because morals are at the heart of social reality, science cannot be separated from morality under the pretext of objectivity or realism. Political science would be too shortsighted if it were to ignore this. This is the ethical standard that the human community holds on to, and that inspires innumerable governmental activities, nongovernmental initiatives and global activities, and especially nongovernmental, grass-roots organizations and networks that flourish everywhere in the world.

The most recent example of this is the Stockholm Initiative on Global Security and Governance, which eloquently expresses the idea: "After a decade, which has been largely characterized by selfishness and arrogance, we need to restore global morality . . . a new world order based on justice and peace, democracy and development, the rights of man and international law."[13] This vision is opposite to that found in most writings on the future of international relations. It is even contradicted when the resort to violence remains the preferred means of conflict resolution, to the detriment of collective values and interests.

We adhere to this global vision without pretending that it is the only possible solution. The realist vision is also possible, and at the same time the most catastrophic. Therefore, a hypothesis is introduced, a framework that inspires myriad scenarios. In my mind, it would be futile to read the future as the image of the present. Social science should, without doubt, encourage possibilities for profound change at a ripe historic moment; surprises that burst forth, a new future, whose enlightenment would be buttressed by the lucid actions of men becoming part of social reality. Can the utopia of yesterday be tomorrow's reality? Why not? To sum up, let us say then that we are faced with two possible hypotheses that could inspire the scenarios and processes of a multidimensional peace. The more the solution matches the second, ethical, scenario, the more perceptible, beneficial, stimulating, and workable the economic effects will be.

The Peace Dividends

One of the most direct consequences of peace will be an eventual decrease in national security expenditures. In the first hypothesis of a peace treaty founded on a balance of power unfavorable to the fundamental interests of Syria, the budget for national security will probably be maintained at its present level, or even increased, for three principal reasons: (1) Because the defense budget has already been largely reduced in real value since 1988 (see table 3.1); (2) Given the fundamental changes in international relations and the financial situation of the oil-rich Arab nations, it is very probably that external financial contributions in general and particularly those aimed at the military will be significantly reduced—a reduction that will have to be made up by internal resources; and (3) Syria will be obliged to focus its efforts on obtaining strategic parity, or at least putting together a strike or deterrence force requiring a substantial increase in its real military expenditures.

Consequently, the costs of security may well be more burdensome to the population and especially to the laborer class, whose living conditions are already poor. But it is difficult to conclude that these groups would be ready to accept a general demobilization. On the contrary, they could endure as much privation and sacrifice as would be necessary to preserve national dignity.

This first scenario contradicts the basic theory in this chapter; therefore it will have to be excluded. In the second hypothesis, a global solution based on the present balance of interests, and founded on an active exchange of value-based, ecophilosophical laws opens the possibility of true cooperation and integration in the region. Here the cut in military expenditures could be substantial. One can imagine a gradual reduction of up to 75%, to levels not exceeding 2% to 3% of the GNP by the end of the decade, following the settlement of the conflict. Spending could even continue to decrease, to up to 1% to 2% of GNP thereafter. An additional decrease should be noted; it would come by reducing the enormous hard currency expenditures on imports of arms.

Military spending by the countries of the region is estimated to have been approximately $600 billion during the 1980s, the largest share of which was for the purchase of arms and hardware.[14] If a third dividend, coming from a general disarmament of the industrialized countries, is added to these two, the peace dividend for the present decade would, according to SIPRI, be approximately $1,500 to $2,000 billion.[15] One can only imagine how this kind of miraculous manna could reinforce peace. According to this scenario, Syria could use some $2 billion each year following the conclusion of peace. A substantial dividend, indeed!

These extra funds could be used to consolidate the material base necessary to reinforce the process of peace, which will become irreversible only with the cooperation and integration of the other countries in the region. One of the main problems to which the peace dividend should be applied is the management of the large imbalances of the economy:

- Chronic deficits and increased payments that translate into public debt, both internal and external, as was seen with the devaluation of the pound by 65% in 1987, severely reducing public expenditures (see table 3.2).
- The dramatic decrease in real salaries, especially after 1986. The general price index climbed from 216 to 572 in 1986 and 1989 (base

1980 = 100), while nominal salaries only increased 30% on average in 1987 and 25% in 1989. Therefore the readjustment of salaries is a first priority, especially in the government sector where 75% of the workers earn little more than SP 2000 per month (approximately $45), resulting in a purchasing power well below the required minimum. This increase would be indispensable for enhancing worker productivity and benefiting the vast majority of the population by the peace dividend, thereby gaining its support for the peace process. This increase will benefit trade as well as industry in the country.

• The gradual investment slump will have to be addressed to spark growth in the GNP, which lost 16% between 1981 and 1987.

Effects on Employment

One of the important implications of a settlement will be changes in employment, resulting from the reduction of military service and demobilization of a part of the armed forces. One might think that this reduction would have a negative effect on employment and would increase unemployment. However, it must be taken into consideration that most conscripts generally retain their civilian jobs, and that demobilization could provide the economy and particularly the government with the large number of technical and skilled workers it sorely lacks. In addition, this sector suffers from two well-known phenomena which have a negative effect on the productivity of business and its competitiveness, namely the rapid shuffling of technical and skilled workers and the assigning of several jobs to one worker.[16] The economic recovery in Syria and the reconstruction of the war-torn economies of the region also will absorb some of the workers freed from military service. Altogether, the effects of peace on employment could be rather positive, especially if peace triggers an economic recovery in the region.

Effects on Trade Relations

A quick glance at the structure of foreign trade shows that Syria and other Arab countries principally export raw materials. Israel, on the other hand, exports manufactured goods at the rate of 80% of the total of its exports. In addition, 70% of its exports are sold to the industrialized countries, and only 29% to the developing world.[17] This suggests that trade between the two parties would be characterized by a north-south model. According to our first scenario, important exchanges between the parties currently in conflict would be difficult.

In our second hypothesis all types of exchanges should develop within the framework of a long process of cooperation in the region. At first, a kind of unofficial trade would occur if it is not already happening in some form. But to anticipate the lessening of conflict and tension, and to begin a solid process of cooperation and integration, it would be necessary to anticipate other forms of interaction taking into account the fundamental interests of all the parties involved as well as the process of peace itself.

Are the economies of the region complementary or competitive with one another? For decades, it has constantly been said that the Arab economies are complementary. The factors of production, being unequally divided among Arab nations, would open the road to exchanges and integration of these countries. But in fact this "natural" complementarity has hardly resulted in substantial trade, which remains generally less important than external trade. However, it should be noted that the European economies, which are fundamentally competitive, have from the beginning undertaken a process of integration so that trade developed rapidly, benefiting all the participants. Commerce within the EC has increased from 29% to 30% in 1958, to 50% to 51% in 1978 within the community as a whole. Trade with the rest of the world increased at the same time.[18]

In a world where the factors of production are very mobile and changing, every specialization is possible and economies could be complementary and competitive at the same time. In other words, complementarity and integration, beneficial to all participants, are not natural phenomena. They are the result of a voluntary, organized political process where the competing countries work under equal conditions. The EC, with its multiple organizations and systems, has become through this conscious and organized process a unified community whose economic success is indisputable, and that rests on a peace and collective security previously known. If a clearly focused desire for peace takes hold in the Middle East, which incorporates the interests of all the region's peoples, then the processes of cooperation and integration will culminate in a fundamental development of the region benefiting everyone in the human community.

The concept of competition, perceived and practiced as the greatest form of freedom, uninterested in society as a whole and free from any ethical concerns, would be contrary to the idea of progress. It should be understood in a general sense as ensuring maximum utility (Walras) for all, and therefore be a cardinal instrument of complementarity and progress for society. As Adam Smith wrote in 1776, "Trade, which should naturally be the domain of agreement and friendship for a nation has become the source of hatred and quarrels."[19] A process of complementarity and integration could be undertaken on a cooperative basis, for example, within the framework of mixed commissions, allowing for specialization between companies and between countries, as well as for the transfer of technology and knowledge.

Cooperation could begin at first in certain areas of common interest such as the environment, health, water management, communication and transportation, tourism, scientific and cultural research, crime control, et cetera. "The market is efficient, but it has no heart or brain," writes Paul Samuelson.[20] Therefore, if the people of the region desired a regional community capable of contributing positively to the creation of a new world order founded on high morals and traditional values, they would go beyond purely commercial interests and focus on the balance of interests at regional and global levels.

Effects on Development

One of the most pernicious results of militarization is the ascendancy to power of an authoritative regime. Much more than military expenditures, military/political structures can be responsible for general, long-term decline. Moreover, aren't they responsible in large part for the arms race and the increase in military budgets?

This phenomenon, which is widespread in the developing world, is due above all to the structural weakness of the state in relation to the armed forces, which are relatively better organized and equipped with ultramodern technology including weapons of repression. In joining political power to military might, the military has the tendency to become omnipotent and impose its will on the entire structure of society. A certain number of characteristics is tied to the nature of these regimes. The most general are the obsessive adherence to greatness and prestige; the tendency to use force to solve problems; the hierarchical authority pyramid; the search for immediate efficiency without much consideration to the detail or cost. This culture, which permeates government structures, leads to particularly harmful phenomena, notably the oppression of the civilian population and strict control over criticism, which erodes the innovative spirit, the driving force of all progress.

In addition, economic excesses and the waste of resources—huge expenditures, often badly managed megalomaniacal undertakings, exorbitant public investments, and political control of economic management—are all undertaken to the detriment of the economy. These failures, which affect one another at all levels, lead to enormous costs and serious distortions in the economy, to destructive effects on assets, both material and human, on productivity, and on the competitive capacity of the economy. It may seem paradoxical that the military system, known for its adherence to order and discipline, permits this type of abuse of the law and such slovenly behavior! But, in fact, experience has shown that the hold on political power, without efficient management, opens the way to abuses, if not to extravagances.

The preceding points and others have been noted by a large number of observers who have closely studied these kinds of regimes in developing countries.[21] Professor Elias Tuma points out these same failures and describes them in his important work concerning the countries of the Middle East.[22]

This raises the crucial question: With the conclusion of peace, can we assume that authoritarian systems will disappear and be replaced by normal functioning, democratic institutions and the renaissance of social dynamics, and consequently that economic and cultural performance will attain a high level? This is certainly a critical question; the response to it must be found in the ongoing evolution of the new world order.[24]

A few remarks are necessary, however: It would be difficult to imagine significant political change in the first scenario. An increase in oppression can be imagined, if only to suppress ultranationalistic or fundamentalist opposition. In our second hypothesis, however, which concludes with the framework of a new world order with a heart and a brain (to paraphrase Paul Samuelson), the fundamental political changes that it assumes will have significant widespread repercussions. We can then expect material and moral benefits that are infinitely more important than the immediate economic gain. Thus, a just and long-lasting peace, dynamic and transparent political structures, and overall development can only happen through these long and directly interconnected processes.

I will explain three of the principal effects of such a peace. The tourism sector will certainly be one of the great beneficiaries of such changes, especially since the Syrian government has striven for several years to develop this sector. The major obstacles slowing the expansion of this sector are tied to the political instability and geopolitical fragmentation of the areas directly related to the Arab-Israeli conflict. These obstacles could be quickly removed through a process that includes open borders and the concluding of cooperation agreements on tourism among the countries of the region—a scenario that is unthinkable outside a just and long-lasting peace process.

Let us underscore here that the region as a whole constitutes a complementary area that is extremely significant geographically, historically, culturally, and demographically. Because of its cultural, spiritual, and physical attractions, this region offers an incomparable richness with regard to tourism that could attract millions of visitors from the entire world.

The inflow of hard currency from such a plan could amount to billions of dollars annually and could accelerate growth in every sector of the economy. Also important would be the cultural enrichment and the consolidation of peace resulting from exchanges of every kind among diverse cultures. Let us not forget that such exchanges were among the most important historic factors that made the region the privileged birthplace of civilization, which nourished human history and particularly the culture of the West.

The impact of peace on capital movements remains rather uncertain. The outflow of capital and of manpower has been a continual process that traces its origins to the Ottoman Empire. The phenomenon is tied to factors stemming from the political-military structures and chronic political and economic instability, which have always played a significant and sometimes determining factor in the region. Data about this hemorrhage are very fragmentary, but the phenomenon has expanded enormously in the past two decades, especially with the surplus of oil, the exceptional wealth of certain social classes, and the deterioration of social conditions.

Total flight capital could amount to tens of billions of dollars, and the exodus of managers and technicians in the hundreds of thousands.[24] Can we imagine this pattern stopping and a significant return of this emigrating wealth? Demilitarization and political stability will be positive factors, but it will be the economic recovery to follow that will increase investment and employment opportunities, attracting back the skilled workers and especially flight capital. A substantial increase in public investment will spur the private sector, which will be the principal beneficiary.

It is above all the improvement of the general conditions of the functioning of the economy and society that will exert the most beneficial and most profound influence on development as a whole. The resulting gains will be important in every area. Greater rationality in the management of the economy and society should result in the restoration of respect for the law as well as the rigorous application of the principles of responsibility and democratic authority at every level.

It is important to understand that optimal economic performance is tied to the dense fabric of political and social relations of society, and tied even more tightly to economic factors such as the rate of investment, the rate of profit, and the level of employment. In reality, development is only the overall result of the interrelationship of all these factors. In other words, economic development is only one expression of the development of society or of a nation.

As society functions, produces, and creates surplus, so it develops. It must be free from many impediments that could slow it down or paralyze it, and it must take responsibility for forging its own destiny. This concept is expressed very well in the Report of the South Commission in 1990: "Development is a process which enables human beings to realize their potential. . . . It is a movement away from political, economic or social oppression."[25]

Notes

1. See Maxime Rodinson, *People juif ou problème juif. Sur les visions arabes du conflit israelo-arabe,* Maspero, Paris, 1981, p. 348.

2. G. Chichilniski, R. Falk, and J. Serra, "Authoritarianism and Development," IFA dossier, no. 19, Sept.–Oct. 1980, Nyon, Switzerland; Eqbal Ahmad, "The Neo-Fascist State: Notes on the Pathology of Power in the Third World," IFDA dossier, no. 19, Sept.–Oct. 1980.

3. According to the U.N. Report on the World Social Situation, quoted by I. Thorsson (ref. in note 2 above), p. 99. The figure 40% concerns the twenty countries most indebted in 1983, for the years 1976–80.

4. *Statistical Abstract,* Central Bureau of Statistics, Syrian Arab Republic (SAR).

All figures are taken or computed from this source, unless it is specified to the contrary (different years are used).

5. Elizabet Picard, "Le rôle de la Syrie dans stratégie de paix," *Awrak* 10 (1989), Madrid, p. 225. Elias Tuma reports figures amounting to U.S. $17.6 billion as the amounts of aid credit accorded by all "Socialist countries to the Middle East countries between 1956 and 1978 for military purposes," according to CIA estimations (see for ref. note 24 hereafter), p. 161.

6. Patrick Seale, *The Struggle for Syria,* London: Oxford Univ. Press, 1965.

7. Rizkallah Hilan, *Culture et developpement en Syrie et dans les pays retardes,* Antropos, Paris, 1969, chap. 7–2 and idem, "Emprunts, endettement et développement en Syrie et en Egypte (1946–1989)," Paper presented to the 10th International Congress for Economic History, Leuven, Belgium, 1990. Subsequent figures are drawn from these two sources.

8. Yahya Sadowski, "Cadres, Guns and Money," MERIP Reports no. 134, July–Aug. 1985, p. 5.

9. Jacques Robin, *Charger d'ère,* Seuil, Paris, 1989, pp. 8, 318, and 329.

10. Henrick Skolimowski, "World-Views and Values for the Future," India International Center Quarterly, Futures, Spring 1989, New Delhi, p. 157.

11. Ibid, p. 124. In the same sense Guy Beney, "La citoyenneté au risque de l'ecologie globale," IFSA dossier no. 79 Oct.–Nov. 1990, pp. 71–86, who proposes "un foundement géologique du retournement ethique."

12. Marc Nerfin, "Is Global Civilization Coming?" INDA dossier no. 74, Nov.–Dec. 1989, pp. 63–70; Piotr Gladkow, "International Community; Utopia of Real Prospects?" *Social Sciences,* no. 3, p. 53.

13. Common Responsibility in 1990s, 22 Apr. 1991, p. 6, published by Prime Minister's Office, Stockholm, Sweden.

14. Figures, according to the estimations of the Western Europe Union, quoted by Alain Gresh, in *Le Monde Diplomatique,* Jan. 1990, p. 8.

15. Common Responsiblity, op. cit., p. 16.

16. Ref. in note 9, pp. 39, 52, and 90.

17. World Bank, *World Development Report 1986,* tables 10 and 12.

18. Yves Bernard and J.C. Colli, *Dictionnaire économique et financier,* 4th ed., Seuil, Paris, 1984, p. 355.

19. Quoted by Pierre Droin, *Le Monde,* 23 Oct. 1991.

20. Quoted by Ignacio Ramonet in *Le Monde Diplomatique,* Dec. 1991.

21. Abundant literature, among others: G. Chichilniski and Alias (ref. in note 3); Michael T. Clare, "The International Repression Trade," IFDA dossier no. 10, Argu, 1979, pp. 1–16; for Syria; Raymond Hinnebusch, Y. Sadowski; E. Picard, op. cit. and others.

22. Elias Tuma, *Economic and Political Change in the Middle East*, Pacific Books, California, 1987, pp. 29, 37, 50, 78 and passim.

23. Chichilniski and Alias, op. cit. p. 7.

24. Riskallah Hilan, *Culture et développement en Syrie*, Mayssaloun, Damas, 1981 (in Arabic) pp. 339s.

25. The Report of the South Commission (1990), Preliminary Analysis, IFD dossier no. 79, Oct.–Dec. 1990, p.1.

References

Arnaud, Alain, "La logique d'armement, source de déclin," *Le Monde Diplomatique*, Sept. 1990.

Blagovolin, Sergei, "Military Power: Level, Structure, Purpose," *Social Sciences*, no. 3, 1990, USSR Academy of Science, Moscow.

Cassen, Bernard, "Le vieux continent avide de toucher les dividendes de la paix," *Le Monde Diplomatique*, Aug. 1990.

Gallios, Dominique, "Inconstantes valeurs refuges," *Le Monde*, 15 Jan. 1991.

Gherardi, Sophie, "L'Amerique, la guerre et la prosperité," *Le Monde*, 15 Jan. 1991.

Kennedy, Paul, "Amérique: Les defauts de la cuirasse," interview in *L'Express* no. 2080, 23 May 1991.

Thorsson, Inga, "The Sword Still Hangs," India International Centre, *Quarterly Futures*, Spring 1989, Special Number, New Delhi.

World Bank, *World Development Report*, 1991, p. 140.

Comments

William G. Tyler

Although the two chapters in question endeavor to analyze the economic impact of regional peace on Egypt and Syria, respectively, they are very different in their approaches. The chapter by Rizkallah Hilan on Syria is quite comprehensive in nature; it transcends the boundaries of conventional economics and provocatively ventures into the realms of sociology, philosophy, and political science with discussions of the nature of a just peace, the relevance of a new social contract, and the relationship between military expenditures and authoritarian government. For its part, the chapter by Heba Handoussa and Nemat Shafik is a more straightforward, as well as competently done, piece of economic analysis. For that reason most economists will find it to be the easier chapter to follow.

Despite their differences, both chapters reach quite similar conclusions—that resolution of the regional political conflict would generate considerably economic benefits for both countries. To a large extent, the correspondence in the conclusions reflects the economic parallels between Syria and Egypt, coupled with simple economic logic. Yet, it is important to qualify the general conclusions. In my comments, I would like to focus first on some of these economic similarities and then to comment upon the economic effects of a peace settlement for the two countries.

Economic Similarities between Egypt and Syria

Relevant economic similarities between Egypt and Syria involve their growth patterns, economic policies, compelling need for economic—including fiscal—adjustment and reform, and status as financial beneficiaries of the Cold War and regional rivalries. First, in regard to economic growth, both Egypt and Syria grew rapidly during the 1960s and 1970s, but both experienced declining growth in the 1980s.[1] By the end of the decade both economies were facing economic stagnation. In addition, the nature of the growth was similar; it was public sector led, based on heavy public investment and inward-looking import-substituting industrialization. Both countries benefited from having some modest petroleum reserves that earned foreign exchange, and both were able to obtain significant external financing for their growth, balance of payments, and fiscal deficits through grants and the accumulation of external debt.

Second, economic policies in Egypt and Syria, unlike those for most other Middle Eastern countries, have been quite similar. Those policies have involved heavy-handed, Soviet-style central planning that has led to a predominant state-owned and controlled production apparatus and massive market interventions. Those interventions have included stifling regulations for private sector economic activity. For example, direct controls on prices and trade; multiple and overvalued exchange rates; and credit rationing were used. The results of these policies have been massive resource misallocation, inefficient investment, weak total factoral productivity growth, slowing overall economic growth, and eventual economic stagnation, as external financial support for both countries dissipated.

Third, the reduction of external support has starkly revealed the economic weakness of both countries. It has also revealed the inappropriate nature of their pursued development strategies and the compelling need for economic policy reform. All the problems that characterize the transition from a socialist-style economy to one that is market based exist for Egypt and Syria. Because of the differences in the human resource base, the challenge for Egypt and Syria may be even greater than that faced by the Eastern European countries. Both Egypt and Syria have cautiously begun to reform their economies, with Egypt being somewhat ahead of Syria in pursuing policy reform and structural adjustment.

The need for economic adjustment is most strikingly apparent in its fiscal dimensions. Fiscal imbalances in the past have been financed in a major way by external support, either in the form of grants or loans. Egypt's budget deficit in 1991 totaled about 22% of GDP; Syria's fiscal deficits, while difficult to measure, have also been quite large. With the reduction of external financial support, these deficits have been financed through domestic credit (and money) expansion, resulting in inflation. To avoid increased inflation and economic instability fiscal adjustment is essential, in effect forcing the governments to live more within their means. Necessity is often the handmaiden of reform, but can only be so if the situation is well understood.

Fourth, along with other countries of the region, Egypt and Syria have been in part financial beneficiaries of the Cold War rivalry. Both in the past have been clients of Soviet patronage and advice, with Egypt pulling off a rather dramatic switch of its superpower patron in the mid-1970s. As the Cold War dwindled, and as domestic needs in the superpowers increasingly took precedence, the resource flows from the world powers decreased for both Egypt and Syria. The Cold War rivalry has been overlaid with a regional conflict motivation for aid and other financial flows. In the face of the perceived threat from Israel, Egypt and Syria have parleyed their geographical location and military potential into justifications for receiving substantial financial support from the oil-rich GCC countries. In the years immediately prior to the Gulf war, that aid, like that from the United States and the Soviet Union, was also diminishing.

The Economic Effects of Peace

With all the economic similarities, it should come as no surprise that the economic effects of peace for Egypt and Syria should be similar. As both chapters convincingly argue, there could be substantial peace dividends for both countries. Yet, with all their serious economic problems, peace by itself will be insufficient. What is urgently needed in both Egypt and Syria is economic policy and structural reform, with or without peace. With peace, economic adjustment and reform could take advantage of any peace dividend.

If the overall policy environment is appropriate, there could be a considerable impact of peace stemming from increased growth made possible by the reduction of military expenditures. While the authors do not attempt to undertake any estimation of this effect, some very crude approximations, under heroic assumptions, are possible. The framework for doing so is basically the Harrod-Domar framework, in which growth is a function of capital formation, which in turn is dependent upon the availability of savings. Conservative estimates of military expenditures before the Gulf war for Egypt and Syria are around 10% and 11% of GDP, respectively. If those expenditures, which weigh heavily on the countries' public finances, could be reduced to the average international level of about 5% of GDP, an increase in public and aggregate saving could be effected. (Hilan would prefer to see the peace dividend used to increase wages and consumption.) If the saving resulted in equivalent increased investment, and assuming an incremental capital-output ratio of 3:1 (reflecting a fairly efficient use of resources), annual GDP growth over the medium term could be increased by as much as 1.5% to 2.0% in each country. While this may seem modest, the accumulative effects would be substantial.

Debt reduction and debt service relief could also conceivably be a part of a generalized political and peace settlement for the Middle East. Prior to the May 1991 Paris Club debt rescheduling and relief for Egypt, that country's external debt was equivalent to about 150% of its annual GDP, placing it among the world's most heavily indebted countries. Accrued interest payments, borne through the budget, amounted to nearly 10% of GDP. The Egyptian debt relief—triggered by the Egyptian participation during the Gulf crisis and justified in terms of support for an ambitious, and courageous, economic reform program launched by the Egyptian government—has potentially reduced the present value of future debt service for much of the country's external debt by 50%. In the case of Syria, estimates of the external debt are not well documented but range up to U.S. $18 billion, or about 80% of Syrian GDP. About 80% of the debt is owed to the Soviet Union and is not currently being serviced. The political disintegration of the Soviet Union may well result in some degree of de facto debt relief.

As is the case with a reduction of military expenditures, the reduction of debt service payments results in a first-round increase in public saving (or, to be more precise, a reduction of public dissaving). In the case of Egypt, if those savings made possible by the 1991 debt relief arrangements were channeled into investment, there would be a potential increase in the GDP growth rate of over 1% annually. In both countries, to have this type of beneficial effect, the demand for investment must grow. Since public sector investments are constrained, the increased investment must originate in the private sector. For this to occur there needs to be a stable and attractive economic policy environment, implying the need to pursue economic reform if the grains of any peace settlement are to be channeled into economic growth and development. In their chapter, Handoussa and

Shafik are quite correct in highlighting the indirect effects that peace might have on investment.

Considerable attention is given in both papers to the effects that regional peace might have on regional economic cooperation and trade. It is important not to overstate the benefits of such regional cooperation, bearing in mind that the only new element would be the inclusion of Israel in such possible cooperation. Nothing in the past has precluded greater economic cooperation among the Arab countries. There are in fact considerable flows of labor and capital across national boundaries, as indicated in the papers. Trade flows have been less voluminous, as is well documented by Handoussa and Shafik, and the previous repeated failures of formal cooperation between the Arab countries do not bode well for the future. Israel's potential participation, on the one hand, would appear to complicate reaching any agreement; on the other, such participation might well enhance the possibilities for eventual economic success. In any case, any real benefits would be slow in coming.

With the possible resolution of the regional conflict, there is an optimism regarding the restoration of aid and capital flows to Egypt and Syria. It is important not to overstate these flows. Private flows will depend upon the eventual restoration of credit worthiness for the two countries and the environment for investment, particularly foreign direct investment. The prospect for official aid flows and transfers is not encouraging. The EEC countries have Eastern Europe and the former Soviet republics competing for attention, support, and resources. Japan's interest in the region is closely bound to its self-interest regarding oil, and its generosity may be more focused on other areas in the future. As far as the United States is concerned, domestic concerns and financial constraints have refocused budgetary expenditures and reduced aid flows; the reduction of Cold War tensions has made such reductions more palatable. Peace in the Middle East might well result in less, rather than more, aid to the region. Even the GCC countries, who have been generous supporters of both Egypt and Syria, are facing declining oil prices, increased domestic expenditure demands (including for reconstruction and recovery in Kuwait and Saudi Arabia), and new interests in the Muslim republics of the former Soviet Union. With the elimination of the perceived threat from Israel, it becomes questionable that GCC aid flows to Egypt and Syria would be restored even to previous levels. An underlying, and probably erroneous, assumption in the

Handoussa and Shafik chapter is that the aid flows would be considerable with the introduction of regional peace.

Even more exaggerated is the underlying belief that aid will somehow resolve and remove internal constraints to economic reform and in doing so will promote sustainable growth. The record, certainly for Egypt, is so far a vivid testament to just the opposite. Substantial international support extended to the Egyptian government over the past fifteen years, while having some beneficial effects, has in the main served as a financial means to enable the government to stave off undertaking basic, and politically difficult, steps to reform the economy. Not only are capital flows in the future likely to be less, but they may well be undesirable. Breaking out of the dependence on aid, notwithstanding comparisons of Marshall Plans, would be beneficial for attaining sustainable growth. In the future the challenge for the governments will be to reform the economy; for the institutions providing international financial assistance it will be to support reform without undermining it. Peace may help but will not in itself be sufficient.

Note

1. The experience with real GDP growth, expressed in annual percentage rates, was as follows:

	1965–80	*1980–89*
Egypt	7.3	5.4
Syria	9.1	1.6

Source: World Bank, *World Development Report*, 1991.

4 Economic Implications of Peace: The Israeli Perspective

Nadav Halevi

Peaceful relations between Israel and its Arab neighbors can have far-reaching effects on Israel's economy. The specifics of the economic implications for Israel of peace are of course dependent, to a large extent, upon the type of political solutions achieved; however, a rough picture of the broader possibilities can be considered, with emphasis on issues and directions and not on quantitative predictions.

Two types of effects are considered: those resulting from the fact that the Arab-Israeli conflict is officially resolved, and those relating to possible economic relations between Israel and its neighbors. Resolution of the conflict can improve Israel's relations with non-Arab countries, encourage investment in Israel, and make it easier for Israel to deal with its more immediate economic problems. However, it will be argued below that no substantial peace dividend should be expected in the near future.

Economic relations with the Arab world are harder to predict, because peace does not imply a particular scenario. Some of the alternatives considered suggest that there is room for considerable trade between Israel and its neighbors, which should be mutually beneficial.

The first assumptions that must be made concern time dimensions. At the time of writing (December 1991) there is reason to hope that the recently initiated peace negotiations will result in a peace agreement. Yet it is obvious that the process of negotiation will be protracted, and whatever the successful outcome, it will include a transition period before the ultimate political solutions are imposed. Therefore, a reasonable first assumption is that there will be a substantial interim period before peace is achieved, during at least much of which the Israeli economy will continue to develop in ways little affected by the ultimate peace arrangements. Consequently, the first two sections of this chapter briefly survey the past development and structure of the Israeli economy, and consider the problems and probable developments in the economy during the next few years, ignoring any effects the negotiation process itself may have on developments during, say, the next five years. Also considered are factors resulting from the negotiations that may affect Israel's economic development during this transition period but are unrelated to the ultimate solutions adopted as a result of the negotiations.

Various longer-term implications of peace are also discussed. The term *long* here means a period of a decade or so after the interim period. During this time the peace will be tested, with measures dependent on greater trust being attempted slowly. It is here assumed that this process will be a long one; it is unrealistic to expect an overnight transition to relations similar to countries which have a less protracted history of hostility. Consequently, the possible economic effects of far-reaching cooperation, of the kind that requires considerable mutual dependence and the forfeiting of economic sovereignty, among the present belligerents are not considered here. There may be great advantages for Israel in being part of an economic union of the Middle East, but that possibility seems remote at this time.

This chapter also addresses the often-raised issue of an important peace dividend: whether peace can be expected to reduce the level of defense expenditures, thus releasing resources to more productive uses. A look at potential relations with the Arab countries reveals that the economic policies adopted may range from ostracism to substantial cooperation, thus providing alternative scenarios. Relations between Israel and the territories now occupied by Israel, which are here assumed to be granted some form of sovereignty in the future,[1] and possible trade relations with other Arab countries are explored as well.

An Overview of Israel's Economic Development

During the period of the British control of Palestine from 1918 until 1948, the Jewish and Arab sectors developed in large part as separate entities. From 1922 there were periodic calls by Palestinian Arab leaders for a boycott on "Zionist goods," but it was not until the mid-1930s that the Arab boycott and general strike led to virtual complete separation of the two economies. The Jewish sector bought land from Arabs, paid rent for housing, employed Arab workers, and bought some goods, mainly agricultural commodities and building materials. The total net payment for factor services by the Jewish sector to the Arab sector gradually decreased from a high of around 10% of its domestic product in the early 1920s to around 3% in the late 1930s.[2] Total purchases of products by the Jewish sector from the Arab sector in 1936 were estimated at about 3% of the Jewish domestic product, and sales to the Arab sector were a bit over 4% of the Jewish domestic product and 5% of the Arab domestic product.[3]

During the years of World War II, the Arab boycott was suspended. In this period the Jewish economy of Palestine diverted its exports from the traditional markets (mainly Great Britain) to the surrounding countries of the Middle East. As a result of the demand by the Middle East Supply Centre (located in Cairo), which supervised the economic war effort in the region, industry received a major stimulus. But a total boycott on Zionist goods was declared by the newly formed Arab League in 1945, and came into effect in the beginning of 1946. The War of Independence and its aftermath—the emergence of the state of Israel and the de facto annexation of the Gaza Strip by Egypt and of the West Bank by Jordan—led to a complete separation of Israel economically from both its Arab neighbors in the parts of Palestine not incorporated into the Jewish state, and all other Arab territories. Israel's economic development until 1967 therefore took place as if it was an island separated by seas from its nearest trading partners.

Israel was faced with severe economic problems in the early years of its independence: it had to conduct a war of survival, absorb mass immigration from the displaced-person camps of Europe and the Arab countries (some 700,000 between 1948 and 1952, a number larger than the Jewish population at the beginning of the period), and create a modern economic structure. During the following twenty years Israel successfully absorbed this immigration, created a modern agriculture, industry, and infrastructure, and achieved a very high average rate of growth of real national income: over 10% and some 6% per capita.[4] These achievements were greatly facilitated by generous inflows of foreign capital: unilateral contributions from Jews living in the Diaspora and from the U.S. government, German reparations and restitutions, and loans (mainly from the United States) and private investment.

Table 4.1
Economic indicators for Israel (average for subperiods)

	1977–1980	1981–1984	1985–1987	1988–1990
Population ('000)	3,742	4,053	4,300	4,540
Civilian labor force ('000)	1,264	1,390	1,471	1,602
Migration balance ('000)	18.4	4.6	−1.3	65.9
Import surplus ($ millions)	2,517	4,624	4,413	4,675
Net unilateral transfers ($ millions)	2,517	2,937	5,049	5,056
Growth of business-sector GNP (%)	3.7	2.9	6.1	3.6
Business-sector factor productivity (%)	0.6	0.5	3.8	1.9
Inflation rate (%)	80	193	21	18
Unemployment rate (%)	3.8	5.1	6.6	8.3
Current account balance (% of GNP)	−1.0	−1.5	0.2[a]	0.4
Government budget deficit (% of GNP)	13.1	10.3	1.6	2.3

a. Excluding $1.5 billion in emergency aid.
Sources: Computed from Central Bureau of Statistics, *Statistical Abstract of Israel*, and Bank of Israel, *Annual Reports*.

From 1973 until the present time, Israel's economic development has been much more modest. There have been periods of stagnation and slow growth—averaging less than half of those of the first twenty-five years—rampant inflation (1983–85), worsening balance-of-payments deficits, and relatively high unemployment. Table 4.1 presents some indicators for Israel's economic performance since 1977.

Because of its small size and the paucity of natural resources, Israel has been very reliant on foreign trade. Cut off from its Arab neighbors, this trade has been mainly with the industrial world of Western Europe and the United States. Though Israel still has a persistent deficit in the goods-and-services account of the balance of payments, it has developed a large and varied volume of exports, with sophisticated products, such as electronics, replacing in importance the traditional exports of citrus fruit and simpler industrial goods, such as foodstuffs, plywood, and textiles. In addition to the protection from competing products from the neighboring countries, because of political hostility, Israel employed extensive protectionist measures to help foster its own agricultural and industrial development. However, from the early 1960s it was realized that Israel must be able to compete with the modern world if it wishes to continue to prosper;

consequently, protectionism was gradually reduced, at least for most industrial goods. This process has been aided by trade arrangements: a free trade area agreement in industrial goods with the EC (from 1975) and a free trade area agreement with the United States (from 1985).

Problems and Prospects of the Near Future

As the 1980s were coming to a close, Israel was facing problems that required major reforms in the economy. Though the rampant inflation of the first half of the decade had been brought under control, Israel had not yet found a way to reduce the inflation rate to the one digit level. More critical was the fact that growth was sporadic, and nowhere near that of earlier periods, or of the rates achieved by other newly industrial economies after the crises of the 1970s. Unemployment was at a higher level (close to 9% in 1989) than Israel's social and political structure used to consider acceptable. The persistent balance-of-payments problems were not decreasing. Moreover, some of Israel's proudest achievements—the cooperative agricultural settlements and the industrial complex of the Histadrut (Israel's all-inclusive labor union)—were in dire economic straits as a result of mismanagement and reckless expansion during the inflationary period.

These problems led to a widely held belief that major reforms, if not restructuring, of the economy were necessary. Chief among these was a reduction of the role of government in the economy. Even after some decrease from the high levels of government expenditures attained in the inflationary first half of the 1980s, total public expenditures were equal to some 58% of national product in 1988 and 1989.[5] These figures reflect not only high defense expenditures (to be discussed in greater detail below) but also the high level of civilian consumption and transfer payments attained during the period of prosperity. Moreover, government nonbudgetary interference in the economy was still strong: the capital market was still dominated by the government, and there remained (in fact reintroduced) elements of domestic protectionism in the foreign trade regime.

The year 1990 witnessed a change that will have profound effects on Israel's social, political, and economic structure. This was the renewal, on a large scale, of immigration from the Soviet Union. In 1990 the total number of arriving immigrants was 200,000, more than ten times the annual averages during the previous decade. Renewed immigration toward the end of 1989 led to forecasts of much larger numbers in the following years. At first the estimates for 1990 were some 40,000; these were later raised to 100,000; the actual doubling of that estimate meant that Israel's initial planning and budgeting for absorption of immigration was woefully inadequate.

Studies carried out by the research department of the Bank of Israel in 1990 on the economic requirements for absorption of 100,000 immigrants annually for a period of five years were fairly optimistic. This level of immigration is far smaller in absolute terms, and much more so in relative terms, than that of the earliest years of statehood, and more closely resembles the situation in the 1960s. The Israeli economy in the 1990s is much more developed and sophisticated than that of the 1960s. It is starting from a less satisfactory macroeconomic environment, however, with inflation still not completely under control and unemployment at a high level. The studies conclude that there is to be expected a time lag between the immediate financial requirements for housing, interim consumption, and investments, both public and private, for the integration into productive employment of these immigrants and their ultimate contributions to economic product (and through taxation of their product on the balancing of budgetary expenditure).[6] However, it is shown that streamlining of housing activity, cutting of other budgetary expenditures, and reforms of the capital and labor markets in order to stimulate private investment could minimize the immediate inflationary effects of immigration absorption and speed the attainment of its expected stimulation of economic growth.

In actuality, the arrival of a much larger number of immigrants in 1990 than expected, and the failure to adopt many of the reforms suggested, meant that ad hoc measures were taken, leading to considerable inefficiency and lack of coordination between housing and employment requirements. Whereas the housing needs were met, by and large, the problems of employment are still to be solved, and are not yet fully felt because of the lag between arrival of immigrants and their entry into the labor force. The flow of immigrants in 1990 led to expectations of even larger flows in the immediate future: an additional 1 million immigrants from the Soviet Union were predicted, with as many as 400,000 arriving in 1991.

Obviously, a much larger influx of immigrants changes the dynamics of the economy. Another study carried out at the Bank of Israel examined the interim effects on the economy of this larger immigration.[7] While it was still expected that the long-range effects of the mass immigration would greatly benefit the economy, especially in view of the fact that these immigrants brought with them an unusually high level of skills and education, the transitional problems would be formidable, and would essentially result from the lag between the arrival of immigrants and their contribution to output. The transition period could last as long as eight to ten years, during which there would be a much higher than normal level of unemployment. The severity of unemployment and the contribution of the new immigrants will depend primarily on the level of capital inflow and on the possible wage flexibility in the economy. With no limit on borrowing potential—specifically, the possibility of increasing the foreign debt by as much as $40 billion over a five-year period—and with wage flexibility (the most optimistic combination), the problems of transition would be manageable. However, even a limitation of foreign borrowing potential to the still substantial sum of $25 billion, and insufficiently flexible labor markets, could lead to an unemployment level as high as 20% before new investments would add sufficient new employment positions to restore unemployment to more acceptable levels.[8] This analysis is intended to point out possibilities and areas of concern for policy consideration; it is not intended to be an actual prediction. However, it does suggest that the economy will face extremely stormy weather before the beneficial effects of new mass immigration will be felt.

Despite these rather worrying scenarios, the Bank of Israel was still optimistic in its presentation of a plan for immigrant absorption:[9] with the appropriate economic policy and foreign capital inflow, a million immigrants could be absorbed over five years, with national product growing annually at no less than 7% during the period.

Naturally, the problems of absorption depend on the pace of immigration; the more prolonged the process, that is, the smaller the number of immigrants arriving annually, the easier it will be for the economy to handle them. In fact, during the first nine months of 1991 the total number of immigrants was about 140,000. Changes in Soviet policy on issuance of passports, problems of absorption in Israel reported back to the Soviet Union by relatives in Israel, and changing expectations about developments in the Soviet Union itself and their effects on the life of Jews there all combined to slow the rate of immigration. Ironically, immediate problems of absorption reduce the overall problems by causing some Soviet Jews to postpone their immigration.

The dramatic upheavals in the second half of 1991, culminating in the dissolution of the Soviet Union, have substantially increased the uncertainty about the total number and timing of Soviet Jewish emigration to Israel. In the opinion of those most closely concerned with this immigration the forecast of 1 million immigrants is still considered to be realistic; there is less unanimity about the pace of immigration. Consequently, as a working hypothesis for this chapter, it is assumed that the population of Israel, which reached 5 million toward the end of 1991, will grow in keeping with such a level of immigration before the long-range peace implications are relevant, and the economy that will face the new situation will be one that has already absorbed these immigrants. Clearly, the slower the pace of immigration, the easier is the absorption problem and the less reliant on foreign capital inflow Israel must be. Conversely, if the present turbulence in the former Soviet Union continues, the number of immigrants that may be expected to arrive in the near future will far exceed Israel's capacity to absorb them in a short period of time: thus, Israel will face a much more difficult economic period before their absorption is completed.

The absorption of 1 million immigrants, with the addition to the population from natural increase, will entail the creation of about 600,000 new places of employment; this addition is equal to 37% of the average labor force in 1990. Such an increase in the labor force (and on the assumption that it will be actively employed) implies a substantial strengthening of the economy but also considerable structural change. The immigrants from the Soviet Union bring with them a level of human capital, as measured by education and work experience, above the existing national average. It has been estimated that once these immigrants are absorbed productively Israel will have an extremely high proportion of persons with academic degrees in the labor force.[10]

Not all of this human capital can be used to maximum effect: the expected number of medical personnel and musicians, for example, is far larger than such a small country can absorb. Even with imaginative efforts to make use of this talent it is clear that many of the specialized skills will not be applicable, and people will have to change their professions. This will be true as well for many of the engineers, who may find that their specific specialties are not suited for application in the Israeli economy, or that their relatively high age may make it impossible for them to find suitable jobs. Based on studies of the absorption of the Soviet immigrants who came in the 1970s, when some 40% had to change their profession, almost always by moving down in the formal skill scale, a similar phenomenon is expected in the 1990s. Thus, many engineers may find themselves working as technicians. However, unlike the developments of recent years, when most of the additions to the labor force were absorbed in services, public and private, it is expected that 30% to 40% of the immigrants will be absorbed in manufacturing, in the still-intensive industries that have been the fastest-growing manufacturing sectors.

The absorption of the highly skilled new immigrants will entail a reversal of the trend in recent years toward relative expansion of services, and will shift Israel's economic development to manufacturing. But to do so Israel will have to intensify its trade liberalizations efforts, that is, adhere to its recently announced goal of forcing its manufacturing to be competitive not only with that of Western Europe and the United States but also with that of the newly industrialized countries. If this challenge is successfully met, Israel will be able to concentrate on export-led growth, and in this way tackle its perennial balance-of-payments problems, which of necessity will be intensified in the interim period.

Israel has been extremely fortunate in being able to mobilize very large sums of foreign inflows to augment its own national product, thus making its possible to allocate large sums to defense, investment, and public services without the need to drastically curtail private consumption. Much of this inflow came in the form of unilateral transfers: from Jewish philanthropy; from Germany, in the form of reparations and restitutions; and from the U.S. government, in civilian and military aid. The growth of U.S. aid after 1972 significantly reduced the relative importance of the other sources. Most years the total of unilateral transfers was not sufficient to cover the deficit in the goods-and-services account of the balance of payments (i.e., the import surplus), and long term and short term capital flows, were needed to make up the difference. Here, too, the major source has been loans from the U.S. government. The latter were drastically reduced from 1986, and eliminated from 1989, when U.S. aid was given entirely in the form of grants. By the end of 1990 Israel had built up a gross foreign debt of some $32 billion, about half of which was covered by assets held abroad by Israeli banks.

The increases in the import surplus from 1991 to 1995, as a result of the needs of immigrant absorption, have been estimated at no less than $25 billion over and above the expected inflow of unilateral transfers. This implies that Israel will have an external debt of $40 billion at that time. Even the most optimistic assumptions about Israel's ability to attract private investments inescapably lead to the conclusion that such large sums must come from governments and banks, the latter with governmental loan guarantees. Thus, at the end of the interim period, Israel will be so heavily indebted that further development will in all likelihood have to be based on much less reliance on new foreign borrowing.

In summary, we are making the more optimistic assumption that the Israeli economy that will be facing the new peace opportunities is one that has already been successful in absorbing a substantial inflow of Soviet Jews. It will have attained, by the close of the interim period, an income per capita level comparable to the less affluent of the industrialized countries, will have an unusually skilled labor force, and will be an economy more heavily concentrated in modern, high-tech industry.[11] However, it will still have formidable balance-of-payments problems and a heavy debt burden. These problems will require Israel to rely on export-led growth, if it wishes to resume and maintain a respectable rate of welfare improvement.

Some Possible Interim Effects

The mere entry into a process that is intended to lead, or gives promise of leading, to a resolution of the Arab-Israeli conflict, can have a number of effects on the economic development of Israel. Here we consider two such effects: the response of foreign governments and investors to the peace process, and the possible decrease in activities associated with the *intifada*.

The response of foreign governments may be felt first of all in readiness to lend Israel funds needed for immigrant absorption. Whether or not loans and loan guarantees are formally tied to Israel's readiness to push forward the peace process, there is no doubt that such progress will do much to loosen purse strings in the United States and Europe. Thus, Israel may benefit in being able to absorb the immigrants in line with the predictions of the more optimistic forecasts, mentioned above, regarding the availability of foreign loans.

Of perhaps no less importance in this respect is the possible influence of the peace process on foreign private investment. Israel's record in attracting foreign private investment has been mixed, and on the whole, disappointing. During the 1960s many in Israel believed that private investment inflows would grow to be more important than philanthropic funds or intergovernmental flows. Though many hundreds of foreign companies have found it profitable to invest in Israel, the net inflows from private investment never reached large numbers: in recent years, foreign direct investment in Israel did not exceed $200 million annually.[12]

Many reasons have been advanced for this disappointing record. One is the Israeli bureaucracy: despite many liberal terms in the tax and foreign exchange systems designed to encourage and facilitate foreign investment, the bureaucratic maze that must be navigated has remained formidable and discouraging. But it is probable that two other factors must be given greater weight. The first is the political unrest in the region: the frequency of outright war, and the always present possibility that political instability may have adverse effects on economic conditions and on economic freedom. This risk cannot but deter many potential investors. The expected returns on investments in Israel must be very high relative to competing locations to compensate for the additional risk. Peace in the region, if it is expected to be lasting, will surely reduce significantly this risk factor and will give much greater prominence to purely economic calculations in estimating profitability of investment in Israel. Although this more far-reaching effect will necessarily have to await an actual peace agreement, the mere prospects of peace may elicit some greater readiness to invest in Israel.

The second and probably more immediate factor is the Arab secondary boycott, whereby foreign firms have been threatened with loss of Arab business if they do more than "normal" business with Israel, especially investing in Israel. Some countries have passed antiboycott legislation. Among these, the United States takes the most drastic action, whereas some European countries are less active. Some countries (e.g., Great Britain) do not take any antiboycott action. The most extreme cases are Japan and Korea: they have tended to bend over backward, avoiding economic ties with Israel that could antagonize Arab countries even if not specifically banned. There is no reliable estimate of the deterring effects of these boycotts on investment in Israel.[13] As mentioned, many hundreds of companies have not been deterred; however, the fact that many of the major multinational corporations are noticeably absent from the list of companies investing in Israel suggests that the effects of the boycott are significant. It is to be expected that the earliest stages of peace negotiations will lead to (perhaps be contingent upon) official cancellation of the boycott and threat of boycott of foreign companies (though probably not of the primary boycott, that is, direct Arab trade with Israel).

The Israeli economy will have much to offer foreign investors, who will be relieved of the fear of Arab boycott. Its wealth of scientific and engineering expertise should encourage the inflow of investment, particularly of companies wishing to take advantage of Israel's preferential trade arrangements both with the United States and the EC. No attempt is made here to give a quantitative estimate of these investments. Though it would probably be overoptimistic to expect that such flows will be of a magnitude resembling the governmental transfers of earlier years, their impact on capital formation, improved productivity, growth, and export creation should be much greater than equivalent unilateral foreign transfers or government loans.[14]

The EC has indicated that Israel's requests for special arrangements to negate the possible detrimental effects on Israel's trade with the community resulting from the expected reforms of 1992, perhaps the same status accorded the EFTA countries, will receive favorable response once there is significant movement toward peace. If such movement does indeed lead to more favorable arrangements with the EC, for example, easier acceptance of Israeli standards as compatible with the new European ones, Israel's exports will benefit, and the stimulation to foreign investment mentioned above will be more pronounced.

It is possible that progress in the peace negotiations will reduce the militancy of the *intifada,* and thus mitigate its economic effects on Israel. The economic costs to Israel of the *intifada* arise from four sources: loss of income from reduced exports to the territories, dislocations in the economy because of the absence of part of the Arab labor working in Israel, additional direct and indirect military expenditures, and loss of tourist revenue.

Israel's exports to the territories decreased by an estimated $322 million (28%) in 1988, and by an additional $83 million in 1989; it has been estimated that more than half of these decreases were recouped in 1990.[15] These decreases reflect both voluntary boycott of Israeli products and reduced spending capacity resulting from reduced income. Whereas GDP in the territories is believed not to have decreased substantially in 1988 and in 1989, income from employment outside the territories (from work in Israel and elsewhere) is estimated to have decreased by more, after substantial growth in the previous period.[16]

Employment of workers in Israel in 1988 fell considerably from restrictions on the supply side, increased slightly in 1989.[17] It decreased drastically again in 1990 and the first half of 1991 to perhaps less than half the pre-*intifada* level because of restrictions from the demand side as a result of fears generated by acts of violence and the Gulf war. Disruptions of output and inefficiencies arising from sudden decreases in employment from the territories have been severe in some industries, particularly in construction. Additional defense expenditures have not been large—they have been estimated for 1988 at no more than 0.2% of GNP and have probably not risen in the more recent period.[18]

The effects on tourism have been more significant. After a record year in 1987 the number of tourists dropped by 15% in 1988. Although there was no decrease in foreign exchange receipts from tourists, the expected increase would have been about $200 million more; considering that the value added in tourism is higher than in exports of goods, this implies that the loss from the fall in tourism was greater than from the decreased exports to the territories. Tourist receipts picked up in 1989 but fell in 1990 as the tourist industry was severely hit by the Gulf crisis; there seems to have been a substantial recovery in 1991.

Various estimates have been made of the total income loss from all these factors. One estimate is that the loss of exports and tourist receipts alone reduced GNP by about 1% in 1988.[19] A more comprehensive estimate for 1988, based on partial data and projections but taking into account all the indirect effects of reduced exports and imports, arrived at a new loss to Israel of 1.7% of GNP.[20]

It is possible that dissident groups seeking to sabotage the peace efforts will try to keep the *intifada* active during the interim period; but in any event its economic costs have decreased significantly in the past two years. Over time the economy has adjusted to the decrease in Arab labor; ore Israelis and foreign workers from other countries have replaced workers from the territories, and in some industries, such as housing construction, more capital-intensive (labor-saving) methods are being employed. Tourism will probably increase at a faster pace if violence is reduced, but exports to the territories will not expand substantially until the income in the territories resumes rapid growth. A reasonable estimate of the net gain resulting from a complete end to the *intifada* cannot be more than 1% of GNP.

Defense Burden and Possible Peace Dividend

Israel has always had to devote a very large part of its resources to defense; in the truest sense, it is the inability to allocate these resources to other uses—investment and private and nondefense public consumption—that constitutes a defense burden. Examples often cited—Germany and Japan—suggest that much higher rates of growth of income and well-being could have been achieved had the defense burden been smaller. The importance attached to the role of the high cost of the arms race in the deterioration of the Soviet economy has led to foreboding about the economic dangers Israel may face if the defense burden cannot be reduced. In fact, the potential peace dividend from reduced defense expenditures is frequently cited as *the* major economic benefit of peace.

In order to make any appraisal of the possible magnitudes of such a peace dividend, it is necessary to consider (1) what is included in defense spending; (2) in what ways the defense burden should be defined; that is, consider different assumptions regarding the availability of foreign resources and their allocation; (3) what are the factors that determine whether defense spending is likely to change; and (4) what these changes can mean in terms of a defense burden.

Published estimates of defense spending refer to expenditures made in accordance with the defense budget, and usually distinguish between domestic expenditures and expenditures in foreign exchange for imports of military equipment. However, the budgeted expenditures do not include all the costs to the economy. Among the major additional costs are the true alternative costs of reserve duty, future pensions, stockpiling, construction of civilian shelters, and land set aside for use by the military. These additional expenditures, not included in official statistics, have been estimated as equal to no less than half the official domestic expenditures.[21] Table 4.2 presents various measures of the defense burden, defined as defense expenditures as a percent of some relevant magnitude. The figures are

Table 4.2
Measures of the defense burden

	Budgeted	Inflated[a]
1. Defense expenditure, as % of GNP	14.7	19.9
2. Defense expenditure, as % of GNP *plus* all unilateral transfers	13.6	18.4
3. Defense expenditures, as % of GNP *plus* unilateral transfers *minus* U.S. military grants[b]	14.0	18.9
4. Defense expenditures, as % of GNP *plus* all non–U.S. unilateral transfers[c]	14.3	19.3
5. Defense expenditures *minus* U.S. military grants, as % of GNP	11.8	17.0
6. Defense expenditures *minus* all U.S. grants, as % of GNP	9.8	15.0
7. Defense expenditures *minus* U.S. grants, as % of GNP *plus* all non–U.S. unilateral transfers	9.5	14.5

a. Based on figures "inflated" by assuming real domestic costs 50% higher than budgeted items.
b. Unilateral transfers in source tables converted to domestic currency by use of effective exchange rates.
c. Unilateral transfers in domestic currency allocated between U.S. military grants, total U.S. aid, and others by dollar ratios of these items in balance-of-payments data.
Sources: Computed from data in Bank of Israel (1991) pp. 174, 221, and 239.

arithmetic averages for the 1988–90 period. The second column of the table, presented for illustrative purposes only, arbitrarily adds 50% to the official domestic expenditures; these inflated estimates of domestic expenditures are then added to the imports to arrive at total defense expenditures (the numerator in the computed percentages).

After a prolonged trend of rising to new plateaus after each war, the defense burden was substantially reduced in the 1980s. But as shown by line 1 of table 4.2 defense expenditures as a percent of GNP averaged close to 15 in recent years; adding the unofficial components raises the percentage to about 20. Even the smaller figure is extremely high by any international comparison.[22]

It has been argued that these figures exaggerate the true burden on the Israeli economy, because Israel has been fortunate in having at its disposal large annual sums of unilateral transfers, which added to its national income have given it total resources for allocation among alternative uses, including defense, larger than its product alone. Line 2 shows that measuring the defense burden in terms of expenditures as a percent of GNP plus net unilateral transfers reduces the estimates somewhat; but they remain extremely high.

Since the Yom Kippur War, Israel has been the recipient of generous U.S. military aid and additional economic aid.[23] Ignoring the fact that tied aid is not exactly equivalent to aid given with no restrictions on its use, one can argue that the U.S. military aid shifts part of the burden of defense from the Israeli to the United States taxpayer. Line 5 therefore deducts this aid from total defense expenditures; as a percent of GNP, the budgeted expenditures are close to 12, a level still twice as high as that of the United States. Even if one adopts the position that *all* U.S. aid is intended to reduce Israel's defense burden, and would not otherwise be given—surely an indefensible assertion—and deducts all U.S. unilateral transfers from the defense expenditures, the ratio to GNP (line 6) is close to 10%. Using GNP plus non-U.S. unilateral transfers in the denominator (line 7) does not lead to a low burden: the budgeted defense burden, at 9.5%, is still high compared to the industrial countries; adding the arbitrary amount for nonbudgeted items gives a ratio extremely high by any international comparison.

To what extent will Israel reduce its defense expenditures if there is a peace agreement? Only some ideas on the subject can be suggested. As already mentioned, an end to or substantial reduction in hostile activity in the territories may reduce defense-related expenditures somewhat in the interim period. Whether further reductions in this area are forthcoming depends on what is done with the territories: if Israel withdraws from the territories, it may be able to save all the expenses associated with maintaining order there—but not if Jewish settlements remain there, and Israel retains some responsibility for their defense. Removal of any existing settlements—in fact the realization by settlers in the territories that they may find themselves under foreign control—would involve substantial costs for the relocation of settlers.[24]

Immediate costs will be associated with the construction of military installations to replace those that exist in any territory relinquished. The more substantial expenditures relate to building and maintaining a military shield. To what extent this can be reduced depends on Israel's perception of the dangers to its security that remain after a peace accord is signed. As in any investment decision involving risk, one must take into account both probability and payoff. The most widely held belief in Israel is that there is an asymmetry between victory and defeat in war: whereas Israel can hope to defeat any single Arab attack, it cannot win a decisive, permanent, military victory over the Arab world; but Israel cannot afford to lose even one war, for that could end its existence. After the peace treaty with Egypt, then viewed as Israel's potentially most dangerous enemy, the probability of war declined, and also the potential danger to Israel's existence from any foreseeable war. This does much to explain the declining trend in defense expenditures during the 1980s. However, the Gulf war changed perceptions dramatically. The possible devastating effects of use of weapons of mass destruction, combined with the possibility that their use may come from hostile countries not immediately adjacent to Israel (e.g., Iraq, Iran, or Libya) have raised the estimated cost of war even while the probability of its breaking out may have declined. Whereas the signing of a peace agreement with Syria, until recently considered to be Israel's most implacable foe, may reduce tensions substantially, the possible support that dissident Palestinian groups may garner, particularly among groups contending for power in the (until now) far-from-united Arab world, will inevitably force Israel to be very cautious for many years after the peace accords are signed. Considering the extremely high and relatively rising costs of defense against weapons of mass destruction, such as early warning systems and antimissile missiles, not to mention replacing the entire network of air-raid shelters, it now appears highly unlikely that Israel will make any further substantial cutbacks in its defense expenditures in the foreseeable future. At best, a peace accord will prevent an escalation in these expenditures.

But defense expenditures are only half of the equation for defense burden. What about the financing of these expenditures? Even assuming that expenditures do not rise relative to national income, one must consider unilateral transfers. It is here assumed that Israel will continue to get the same level of financial support it now receives from the Jewish Diaspora. However, in recent years these amounts have been overshadowed by U.S. aid. Whatever Israel's perceptions concerning the dangers to its security following a peace accord, there is little doubt that the United States will consider these dangers to be substantially reduced. If so, it is likely that U.S. military aid will be drastically curtailed, even if other economic aid is not.[25] If Israel continues to spend the same relative amounts of GNP on defense while U.S. aid is curtailed, the effective burden of defense will be much higher, not lower, for at least a substantial period of time. (Rough indicators are shown in lines 3 and 4 of Table 4.2). Only after a relatively long period of time, during which relations with the Arab countries have developed in such a way that Israel will no longer feel threatened by the possibility that the peace will collapse, can one realistically hope for any significant peace dividend in terms of reduced burden of defense. This pessimistic conclusion regarding the financial peace dividend in no way diminishes optimism regarding the more important peace dividend: the reduced threat of war and its costs, mainly in human lives.

Economic Relations with the Territories

The effects on the Israeli economy of relations with the Arab world can vary from negligible to significant, depending on the economic policies adopted by the parties to the peace accords. There is a basic difference between relations with the territories and with external Arab states: the latter relate to possible relations between areas until now officially completely isolated, that is, the creation of trade between previously belligerent states, whereas the territories have been part of a nonvoluntary economic union, entirely subject to Israel's desires.

A major consequence of Israel's political control has been the settlement of Jews in the territories. Any relocation will involve costs, and even with limited relocation the peace arrangements will probably entail reallocation of land and water resources in the territories. However, the importance of land and water use by Jews in the territories is primarily political; the economic significance is not large. In fact, contrary to a belief frequently voiced, the territories are not an economic asset for Israel of a magnitude to have any significant bearing on Israel's willingness to divest itself of them.

The development of economic relations between Israel and the territories prior to the *intifada* is discussed in detail and documented in Kleiman's chapter in this volume; consequently only the salient points are repeated here. Israel was the major source of imports to the territories, but the share of the territories in Israel's exports was not very large: 11.3% of goods, and only 8.6% of goods and services in 1987, and only 5% in 1990.[26] Some of this trade was border trade, that is, trade in goods for which transaction costs (mainly transportation) are so high that they do not enter significantly into international trade except to very close neighbors. However, much of the trade was what is called trade diversion: goods that would have been bought from other countries had not Israeli products been given special protection by tariffs or other measures. As mentioned above, as a result of the *intifada* exports to the territories fell at first, and even after resuming growth reached only 5% of total exports. Capital investments have been negligible, in fact perhaps negative, with the main netting item being pension commitments by Israel to workers from the territories. As far as the territories are concerned, a most significant economic factor has been labor employed in Israel. Here, too, the significance for Israel was slight in the overall, only some 7% of total employment in Israel before the *intifada,* though in particular industries the percentages were much higher, reaching 45.6% in construction, 18.1% in manufacturing, and 14.5% in agriculture in 1987.[27] As a result of the *intifada,* these figures fell drastically, as discussed above.

What future relations can be expected? Three alternatives are considered: an economic union,[28] normal trade, and complete segregation of the two economies.

For the territories purely economic consideration would dictate enhanced relations. A voluntary economic union (whatever its legal structure) between Israel and the territories that provides for generally unrestricted access to both goods and factors of production would clearly be to their benefit; the smaller economic entity in such a union is usually the main beneficiary, and given the major role of Israel in the territories' employment and income, the closing of Israel's borders completely to workers from the territories would have severe economic consequences; it would take many years of development to provide alternative sources of employment.[29] Of course, a voluntary union would differ from the present arrangement in that provisions would probably be made to provide some selective infant industry protection from competitive Israeli industries, and Israel would have to abolish its present restrictions on imports from the territories. As far as Israel is concerned such an arrangement would retain Israel's preferential status vis à vis other countries, thereby encouraging trade diversion in the sense that a relatively higher share of new trade, generated by growing economies, will come from Israel. This factor is not of major importance, though a return to the pre-*intifada* level of exports to the territories is not inconsequential.

Israel itself is undergoing a process of trade liberalization, at least as far as industrial products are concerned, that will be well advanced, if not completed, by the end of the interim period. Consequently Israel will not have significant protection, and in a union with the territories, a highly protective external tariff wall cannot be expected. Only if the territories have a high protective wall exclusive of Israel will the latter enjoy enhanced trade diversion.

A union means that Israel will have to open its borders to competition from the territories: this would be felt immediately in agricultural products and in some labor-intensive industries, which can be expected to expand in the territories. Thus, the balance of trade with the territories resulting from an economic union will not be of great importance, though the Israeli consumer will certainly benefit from cheaper imports.

Israel will be unlikely to greatly expand its employment of workers from the territories in the near future, recently having been burned by the necessity for quick adjustment; but in the longer run employment of workers from the territories may increase: given Israel's relatively large and growing proportion of highly educated workers, there will be a demand for both unskilled and specialized skilled labor. The geographic proximity to the territories makes possible commuting to work; thus these workers would be much cheaper than migrant workers from other countries who have to be housed. Availability of such a labor force would make the development of Israel's industry more efficient.

Capital flows between Israel and the territories have not been large: most of Israel's public investment expenditures there have been covered by taxes, total private investment by Israelis in the territories (exclusive of Jewish settlements) has been slight, and there has been some net accumulation of pension rights in Israel by workers from the territories.[30] An economic union would make investments by Israelis in the territories less risky, and surely there will be many cases where it would be more economic to move capital to the territories rather than have labor commute to Israel; however, the economic benefits of this must outweigh the subsidy element that Israelis now get, and presumably may continue to get, when investing in Israel. A return to larger volumes of employment of workers from the territories in Israel will increase pension deductions. All in all, the net capital flows with a complete union would not be of significant size relative to the Israeli economy.

Taking all the factors into account, it is reasonable to conclude that though particular Israeli industries would be hurt and therefore strongly lobby against a mutually beneficial economic union, the net economic benefits for Israel of such a union would be positive, though probably not of major magnitude.

Political and emotional considerations are likely to play a dominant role in determining economic relations with Israel on the part of the territories. Lingering hostility will surely engender pressure to restrict relations to a minimum and strengthen the position of those who will argue that a growing economy must have a high protective wall against more-developed neighbors. In the extreme this would mean complete separation of the economies, as existed before 1967. For Israel this would mean loss of the future benefits that could be attained by union, but not very large losses compared to the existing situation. Exports to the territories would stop, but as already stated they have not been large in recent years. The process of adjustment to decreased labor from the territories, carried out in 1990–91, would be taken to its ultimate conclusion; again, the net additional cost to the economy would not be substantial, even allowing for the costs of transferring accumulated pension rights.

Because the cost to the territories would be so great, this extreme scenario would be least likely. It would be more realistic to expect some arrangement whereby the territories would not give Israel preferential treatment but would accord it the same trade policy as applied to other countries. This would give the territories more freedom to protect what they will consider to be deserving industries, but would not necessarily have to preclude free movement of labor from the territories to Israel.[31] With such an arrangement Israel would lose any advantages it now has regarding trade diversion. As mentioned, these may decline in any event. But Israel would still have the advantages of economic proximity, not only in the geographic sense but also in the sense that familiarity cuts costs. These advantages will be partly offset by hostility—engendered private discrimination—but business motivations may be expected to overcome much of this. Thus, Israel's share of the territories' imports will be smaller than at present, but any possible fall in Israel's exports cannot be very substantial. On the other hand, restrictions are a two-participant game: exports from the territories to Israel will fall, even if there need be no fall in factor receipts; therefore the balance of trade would not change to Israel's disadvantage.

Though it is possible that this scenario would not alter employment of workers from the territories in Israel, it will restrict the flow of capital from Israel to the territories (compared to the union scenario). Even if restrictions on such flows are not placed, and in this scenario they probably would be, the inducement to investment in the territories by Israelis for production to be shipped to Israel would be diminished.

Economic nationalism will also surely limit the extent to which the territories will be willing to forego economic independence for the sake of economic savings obtainable from reliance on Israeli infrastructure. Thus, while a case can be made for the saving in resources that the territories can achieve by using Israeli port facilities, electricity, and communication networks, and the advantages of joint ventures in industries with scale economies, at present it is not reasonable to assume, given the record of hostility, that the territories will accept such reliance on Israel.[32] There will, of course, have to be some cooperation in areas such as use of water resources, but the possible effects of ambitious joint enterprises are not considered here.

Relations with Neighboring Arab Countries

Although there may be some indirect trade with Arab countries via the territories, Israel's trade with its neighbors is negligible. Even Egypt, with which Israel has a peace agreement, has restricted its trade with Israel to virtually only the export of oil and tourist services; the widely predicted trade benefits of peace simply did not materialize. It is reasonable to expect that peace negotiations that will result in the official cancellation of the Arab primary boycott against Israel will create a new situation in this respect. There will still remain the heritage of hostility, which may deter business relationships, but without public sanctions against trade with Israel such trade will surely develop, if only gradually.

It is here assumed that the first and most important trade relations that develop will be under a policy that gives Israel the same conditions as are accorded other countries, neither preferential treatment nor official special obstacles. What kind of trade can be expected? Surely there is room for border trade, that is, trade in goods whose transportation and other geographically affected costs are so high that in general only trade with close neighbors is economic. Many agricultural goods, particularly perishables, are included in this category, but a careful product-by-product study would point out many industrial commodities (e.g., cement) for which transportation costs are relatively high and consequently reduce their trade-to-product ratio to much less than the average for industrial products.[33] Thus, for items that can be transported very cheaply by land, Israel may find markets in neighboring countries. These are goods that at present Israel produces only for domestic (and the territories') consumption.

A second category of goods includes trade diversion: goods that are now bought by its neighbors from other countries but that Israeli exports may replace. The main benefit to Israel will come from expanded trade.[34] Table 4.3 presents some data on Israeli industrial exports and on the imports by selected Arab countries. It is clear that the Arab countries import large volumes of goods that belong in the same classes as major Israeli exports. Why should one expect trade diversion to take place? For some items there may be substantial savings in transportation costs, but for most of these goods the transportation costs are not of major importance; therefore Israel would have to show some competitive edge to replace imports now coming from other industrial exporters. There are benefits from proximity other than transportation cost savings. The more specialized and sophisticated the product, the more difficult it is to penetrate new markets and to convince potential buyers that one's product matches their requirements (such products form a growing part of Israel's industrial output). Close geographic proximity, and the common cultural backgrounds of neighboring Arabs with Israeli Arabs and Israelis from Arab countries, can facilitate the business contacts necessary to match product specifications to requirements.

Even if Israeli exports do not replace existing imports from other countries, being allowed to participate in the trade of such an important market, whose total imports will surely expand with growth, cannot but give Israel new export opportunities. The potential for trade expansion is not restricted to categories where production and consumption patterns of prospective partners are complementary in the sense that one country is a net exporter and the other a net importer. Recent studies of trade patterns have emphasized the importance of intraindustry trade, that is, where both countries export and import the same product categories. Thus, even in such cases there may be complementarity within categories, which can be best exploited for mutual benefit by sectorial cooperative arrange-

Table 4.3
Trade in industrial commodities

	Israeli exports		Imports by Arab countries						
	$ mill.	% of industrial exports[a] 1985–88	Egypt 1985–88	Jordan 1985–88	Syria 1984–87	Saudi Arabia 1984–87	Kuwait 1981–84	United Arab Emirates 1972–82	Total
Organic chemicals	297	5.7	232	14	17	85	99	68	514
Inorganic chemicals	203	3.9	148	36	30	96	—	—	309
Fertilizer	183	3.5	72	12	16	90	—	—	190
Plastic materials, etc.	137	2.6	458	57	75	280	28	69	966
Chemical materials n.e.s.	239	4.6	343	37	47	244	30	80	781
Textile yarn, fabrics, etc.	181	3.5	226	84	132	1,361	370	457	2,629
Tools	79	1.5	50	7	15	—	—	33	105
Base metal mfrs n.e.s.	474	9.1	158	18	19	194	—	33	421
Power-generating equipment	91	1.8	231	311	78	551	811	1,455	3,436
Machines for special industry	95	1.8	932	72	153	575	1,038	841	3,609
Metalworking machinery	44	0.8	67	—	10	—	—	690	767
General industrial machinery n.e.s.	227	4.4	813	78	160	1,779	—	—	2,829
Office equipment	165	3.2	103	11	0	275	—	—	389
Telecom and sound equipment	353	6.8	369	51	27	695	—	210	1,351
Electric machinery	335	6.4	709	63	88	1,487	—	117	2,463
Clothing & accessories	305	5.9	—	52	—	832	325	227	1,435
Precision instruments	151	2.9	169	40	—	330	191	0	729
Precious jewelry, gold-silverware	172	3.3	—	36	—	327	—	37	401
Total	3,728	71.8	5,078	977	864	9,198	2,890	4,316	28,321

a. Excluding diamonds.
Source: U.N., *International Trade Statistics Yearbook 1988*, vols. 1 and 2.

ments. For example, a study of the Egyptian and Israeli textile industries has shown such mutual benefits. There sectoral cooperation can lead to development of trade between the two countries in inputs for the production of final products that can be profitably exported to third countries.[35] Other studies have shown similar prospects in other manufacturing industries.[36]

Another area of great trade potential is services. Tourism comes first to mind, as it is a widely acclaimed growth industry. However, the growth of world trade in computer services and contract construction has been no less dramatic. There is no reason to believe that Israel will not find substantial markets in the neighboring countries for its expertise in these areas, if not excluded for political reasons. Similarly, Israel's experience in water planning may be exploited in a regional context. Israel will surely find it easier to employ productively its newly acquired human capital if the neighboring markets are open to it.

The trade potentials of course are two sided: Israel can export but it must also import. Imports will be both of the border trade variety and trade diversion and expansion. The Israeli consumer can only benefit from such imports.

How much and how fast such trade potentials with its neighbors can be realized is a political speculation, but it is not too optimistic to believe that, given a peace accord acceptable to all parties, there can be substantial benefits to Israel from such trade (and of course to the partners as well), much of which is realizable even before the utopian long-term. In this timeframe, it appears that these trade potentials are the main economic benefits that Israel can expect from a peace accord. As mentioned above, Israel will have to rely on export-led growth if it is to continue to prosper.

Notes

1. To minimize the extent of political controversy that a paper of this kind unavoidably entails, the nature of the Palestinian entity that will emerge from the peace negotiations is not speculated about; however, it is assumed that entity will have economic sovereignty. Again, to minimize irrelevant controversy, a neutral term—the territories—will be used throughout to designate areas occupied by Israel as a result of the 1967 war.

2. Metzer and Kaplan (1990), p. 140.

3. The computation is based on Gaathon's data on intersectoral trade (1978),

p. 19, and Metzer and Kaplan's data on domestic products of each sector (1990), pp. 138–39.

4. For detailed surveys of Israel's economic development until the mid-1960s and from then to the mid-1980s, see Halevi and Klinov-Malul (1968) and Ben-Porath (1986), respectively.

5. All figures on national aggregates in the late 1980s are taken from the Bank of Israel (1991).

6. Bank of Israel (1990).

7. Herkovic and Meridor (1991).

8. These illustrative figures are based on the estimates appearing in Herkovic and Meridor (op. cit.) and Bank of Israel (1991).

9. Bank of Israel (1991).

10. Of 800,000 immigrants, the number with academic degrees is estimated as 100,000: this will raise the percent in the labor force to 14%, as compared with 9% in Israel prior to this immigration. (Ofer, Flug, and Kassir 1991).

11. Agriculture, of great importance ideologically, has been a declining sector (accounting for less than 4% of national income in recent years). Even with the most optimistic forecasts about regional water arrangements, water resources will not be sufficient to permit Israel to put under cultivation all its arable land before the day when desalinization becomes relevant. Existing agriculture will be hard pressed to compete for water with other sectors.

12. Central Bureau of Statistics (1990), table 7.1.

13. For a survey of Arab boycott activity and Israel's response, see Rolef (1989).

14. A given balance-of-payments deficit financed by private investment from abroad tends to go more to capital formation and less to increasing consumption, private and public, than unilateral transfers and government loans (see Halevi 1976). Moreover, Israel will need to develop close contact with firms in the United States and in the EC to compete there; foreign investment will create these contacts.

15. Bank of Israel (1991), p. 220.

16. Central Bureau of Statistics (1991), p. 8.

17. The average number of hours worked in Israel is estimated to have fallen by 24% in 1988, and to have risen by 2% in 1989 (ibid., p. 84).

18. The estimate for 1988 is by Baudot-Trajtenberg (1988); the assumption that there were no significant later increases is based on estimates in Bank of Israel (1991), p. 174, showing that the share in total wages of the defense budget, which had risen from 8.7% in 1987 to 9.3% in 1988 dropped slightly (to 9.2%) in 1989 and 1990.

19. Bank of Israel (1989), p. 153; its estimate as a percent of business GNP is converted to total GNP.

20. Baudot-Trajtenberg (1988).

21. The most comprehensive analysis and estimates of the burden of defense have been made by Berglas (1986).

22. See Daniel P. Hewitt, "Military Expenditures: International Comparison of Trends," IMF Working Paper, Fiscal Affairs Department, 1991.

23. The military aid is mostly tied to purchases in the United States. Though there have been years when total direct military imports have exceeded this aid, the totals of both components are roughly similar.

24. Clawson and Rosen (1991), p. 40, consider the possibility of relocating all the Jewish settlers in lands occupied in 1967, giving figures ranging from 50,000 to 200,000, three-fourths of the larger figure being settlers in Jerusalem. It is probable that the total number of relocated people will not be large; however, past experience suggests that their relocation will involve costs above the mere cost of alternative homes.

25. Except for special equipment given as a result of the Gulf war, Israel has been getting an amount fixed in nominal dollars; thus, in real purchasing power, and even more in terms of GNP, U.S. military aid has been on a declining trend.

26. Computed from data in Bank of Israel (1991).

27. Kleiman, this volume, table 12.2 and 12.3. It should be noted that the Israeli statistics always include all of Jerusalem in Israel; adding East Jerusalem the territories would not lead to any change in conclusions about relative magnitudes.

28. Logically one should consider a customs union before a complete economic union; however, it seems reasonable to assume that restrictions on trade in goods would be more likely than curtailment of labor movements.

29. The problem of employment of residents of the territories has grown as a result of the Gulf war, and would be much more extreme if a peace accord would result in substantial repatriation of Palestinians now living abroad; difficult economic conditions may keep out the more skilled labor force that could more easily find alternative places of employment, but not the poorest segments living in refugee camps.

30. See Kleiman's chapter in this volume.

31. This would be an interesting exception to the common practice of customs unions preceding free movement of factors.

32. For a thorough analysis of the economic dependence and its relevance for economic relations among recent belligerents, see Arad, Hirsch, and Tovias (1983).

33. An interesting attempt to identify such products, using trade statistics of several European countries, is presented in Arad, Hirsch, and Tovias (1983).

34. Of course, to the extent that Israel itself diverts exports now going to other countries to the neighbors, the only net benefit may come from saving in transportation costs.

35. Arad et al., 1983.

36. Ben-Shahar, Fishelson, and Hirsch (1989).

References

Arad, R., S. Hirsch, and A. Tovias (1983), *The Economics of Peacemaking*. Trade Policy Research Center. London.

Bank of Israel (1988), *Annual Report 1987* (Hebrew). Jerusalem.

Bank of Israel (1989), *Annual Report 1988* (Hebrew). Jerusalem.

Bank of Israel (1990), *Annual Report 1989* (Hebrew). Jerusalem.

Bank of Israel (1991), *Annual Report 1990* (Hebrew). Jerusalem.

Bank of Israel Research Department (1990), *Economic Policy during a Period of Immigration* (Hebrew). Jerusalem.

Bank of Israel Research Department (1991), *A Program for the Absorption of One Million Immigrants* (Hebrew). Jerusalem.

Baudot-Trajtenberg, Nadine (1988), *Impact on the Israel Economy of the Uprising in the Territories.* Department of Economics Bank Hapoalim, Tel Aviv.

Ben-Porath, Y., ed. (1986), *The Israel Economy: Maturing through Crisis*. Harvard University Press. Cambridge, Ma.

Ben-Shahar, H., G. Fishelson, and S. Hirsch (1989), *Economic Cooperation and Middle East Peace*. Weidenfeld and Nicolson. London.

Berglas, E. (1986), "Defense and the Economy," in Ben-Porath (1986).

Central Bureau of Statistics (1990), *Statistical Abstract of Israel 1989*. Jerusalem.

Clawson, P., and H. Rosen (1991), *The Economic Consequences of Peace for Israel, the Palestinians and Jordan*. Policy Paper 25. The Washington Institute. Washington, D.C.

Gaathon, A. L. (1978). *National Income and Outlay in Palestine, 1936* (2nd, enlarged ed.). Bank of Israel. Jerusalem.

Halevi, N. (1976), "The Effects on Investment and Consumption of Import Surpluses of Developing Countries," *Economic Journal* 86.

Halevi, H., and R. Klinov-Malul (1968), *The Economic Development of Israel*. Praeger. New York.

Herkovic, T., and L. (Rubin) Meridor (1991), *The Macroeconomic Effects of Mass Immigration to Israel*. Bank of Israel Research Department. Jerusalem.

Metzer, J., and O. Kaplan (1990), *The Jewish and Arab Economies in Mandatory Palestine: Product, Employment and Growth* (Hebrew). Maurice Falk Institute for Economic Research in Israel. Jerusalem.

Ofer, G., K. Flug, and N. (Kaliner) Kassir (1991), *Absorption in Employment in 1990 and Thereafter: Aspects of Retention and Change of Profession* (Hebrew). Bank of Israel Research Department. Jerusalem.

Rolef, S. H. (1989), *Israel's Anti-Boycott Policy*. The Leonard David Institute. Jerusalem.

5

One-Sided Customs and Monetary Union: The Case of the West Bank and Gaza Strip under Israeli Occupation

Osama A. Hamed and
Radwan A. Shaban

This chapter focuses on certain economic implications of Israeli occupation of the Palestinian territories of the West Bank and Gaza Strip. We also provide a partial assessment of some economic benefits to the Palestinians if and when the Palestinian-Israeli conflict is peacefully resolved. While the fundamental need for resolving the Palestinian question is not economic, we maintain that such resolution is essential for reaping any economic benefit that may flow from a peaceful settlement of the Middle East conflict, as frustrated national aspirations will continue to form a basis for regional conflict. We assume in our analysis that an independent Palestinian state will emerge as a cornerstone of any peaceful, comprehensive, and durable settlement of the Middle East conflict, if such settlement ever takes place.

The economic implications of a peaceful settlement are largely drawn from analyzing the economic development of the West Bank and Gaza Strip during the period under Israeli occupation. Such conclusions will clearly have limited relevance for an independent Palestinian state since such a state would have a radically different set of resources, constraints, and objectives from the current occupation authority. Yet the starting point for the economic policy of a Palestinian state will be the inherited mix of occupation economic policies and the economic structure that has developed under occupation.

Whereas the experiences of various international economic units in economic integration are based on negotiations that lead to mutually beneficial arrangements, the economic integration of Israel and the occupied territories has been conducted in the context of occupation where the Palestinians have had very little say in the design of economic policies that affect their economic welfare. We focus the current analysis on the implications of one-sided integration in the sphere of macroeconomic variables like monetary integration and output and price fluctuations, and in the sphere of commercial policy.

By focusing on these two sets of issues, we intentionally ignore others that have important implications for the potential benefits and costs of peace. The issues not analyzed here include the following:

1. The public finance aspect of the occupation authority: The UNCTAD (1989b) report briefly assesses the budget situation of the occupation authority. While such authority attempts to run a balanced budget, its "revenues" may fall slightly short of its expenditures in some years and it would then be "subsidized" by the Israeli treasury. However, substantial payments by the Palestinians are not counted as a revenue item, such as the social security tax on Palestinians working in Israel, who are required to pay but are not eligible for the benefits of the social security system. Other examples of off-budget revenue items include the value-added taxes on imports and the substantial resource transfers that are quantified in this chapter. An *economic* analysis of the public finances of occupation authority is much needed to evaluate the overall economic implications of the occupation.

2. Labor mobility of the Palestinian labor force: Of particular interest is to analyze the economic and political forces that lead to an export of almost exclusively unskilled workers to Israel while skilled workers are exported to the Arab Gulf countries. It would also be interesting to quantify the implications of restrictive government policy in limiting the expansion of domestic Palestinian employment.

3. Financial and human capital resources of the Diaspora Palestinians: These resources are substantial and could play an important role in developing the postoccupation Palestinian economy. It would be important to quantify these resources and to think of appropriate mechanisms of tapping them.

4. The impact of occupation on tourism and the potential role of this sector in a future Palestinian state should be studied. Tourism is an important sector in the West Bank economy, but there has been a leakage in the benefits flowing from tourism under occupation

because the Palestinian tourist infrastructure has not been allowed to develop and compete with the Israeli tourist infrastructure. With a comprehensive peaceful settlement, an independent Palestine would benefit from tourism not only because of the increased volume due to stability, but could also benefit from constructing an airport, hotels, and a tourist infrastructure.

5. Efficiency and growth implications of the absence of the financial intermediation sector in Occupied Palestine: While there have been descriptive analyses of the extremely restricted operation of the financial intermediation sector under Israeli occupation, there is a need for the more difficult task of quantifying the forgone output and growth that could have been achieved if this sector were freely operating. The role of the banking institutions and the monetary authority of an independent Palestine in an interdependent economic atmosphere with neighboring countries should also be addressed.

6. Economic cost of land expropriation and the Jewish settlement activity should also be evaluated.

7. The political economy of water resource usage and its implications for Palestinian agriculture under occupation and the potential of agriculture as a source of economic growth in an independent Palestinian state should be analyzed. What is the Palestinian forgone agricultural and total output that resulted from restrictions on Palestinian use of their water resources while Israeli farmers and Jewish settlers were allowed a much freer access to the water resources? In a context of "fair" access to water within a peaceful settlement, what is the optimal pricing strategy of water in an independent Palestine?

8. Technology transfer and its implications for the Palestinian agricultural sector, which has been the main recipient of such transfer especially in the area of intensive cultivation, should also be studied.

There is a definite need for analyzing these issues in order to gain a comprehensive understanding of Palestinian economic development under Israeli occupation. However, the proper detailed study of these issues is beyond the scope of this chapter.[1]

In approaching the economic issues of the West Bank and Gaza under occupation, the researcher is immediately faced with serious data limitations. With the exception of few localized and scattered surveys that have been carried out by some Palestinian economists, the researcher would ultimately have to rely on the only data source for the whole period, which is the official statistical publication of the Israeli government. The absence of alternative data sources makes it impossible to check the accuracy of the official statistics or to obtain additional information over and above the official statistics. Related to this point is the unavailability of detailed microeconomic data at the level of the household or worker, which would be essential to measure and test models of household behavior under occupation. Official data are published at a highly aggregated level; for example, the composition of trade between Israel and the West Bank and Gaza is aggregated into agricultural and industrial commodities, with no further breakdown of the commodity types. Data on the West Bank and Gaza are usually published on an annual basis, without monthly or quarterly details for some of the data. Moreover, the Israeli Central Bureau of Statistics warns of the larger sampling errors inherent in the data on the occupied territories in comparison, say, to the data on Israel proper. Indeed, the Israeli statistical publications stopped providing some basic information on the West Bank and Gaza after the Palestinian *intifada* started in late 1987 because of difficulties in data collection and the greater unreliability of the collected data. An important additional shortcoming of the published data of the West Bank and Gaza is the inadequate coverage of the Palestinian population under occupation, since such data purposely exclude the Arab population of East Jerusalem on political grounds.

The next section assesses the overall economic performance of the West Bank and Gaza under Israeli occupation. We discuss the macroeconomic shocks that lead to output and price fluctuations, and we emphasize the absence of fiscal or monetary stabilization policies under occupation. In addition we estimate the inflation tax that the Palestinians pay as a result of the monetary integration of the West Bank and Gaza with the inflationary Israeli economy. A simple trade-theoretic model that captures the economic implications of forcing the Palestinian economy into a customs union with Israel where the tariffs are collected by the Israeli government is also presented. We measure the forgone tariff revenues that a Palestinian state could have collected in the absence of occupation, and we summarize the findings of this chapter by providing a partial assessment of the cost of statelessness for the Palestinians, and conjecture on some future challenges for the Palestinian state.

Macroeconomic Performance under Occupation

Output Level and Growth under Occupation

In a global perspective, the Palestinian economy of the West Bank and Gaza is relatively small. In 1987, the year of the outbreak of the *intifada* against Israeli occupation, official estimates put the population at 868,000 and 565,000 people in the West Bank and Gaza, respectively. The combined population of 1.4 million people, excluding that of East Jerusalem, had a gross national product (GNP) of U.S. $2.49 billion. With a combined per capita GNP of $1717 in 1987, the West Bank and Gaza would be comparable to the middle-income economies, using the World Bank's classification.[2] Using that classification, the Palestinian economy would marginally have a higher per capita GNP than that of Syria ($1640) or Jordan ($1560), but would have a lower per capita GNP than that of Malaysia ($1810) or Mexico ($1830) in 1987. The evolution of the Palestinian GNP and the gross domestic product (GDP) from 1970 to 1987 is presented in table 5.1.[3]

The record appears to be a commendable level of development, especially in comparison with neighboring Jordan and Syria. Moreover, the Palestinian per capita GDP and per capita GNP are much higher in 1987 than they were in 1966, a year before the Israeli occupation, as indicated by table 5.1. It is also interesting to note that growth rates of real GDP were quite high in the period immediately following the occupation.

Such indicators have been considered by Bregman and Lerner as an evidence that the Palestinian economic integration with Israel under occupation has benefited the Palestinians economically.[4] The justification of this argument is that the removal of tariff barriers between the occupied territories and Israel should theoretically be beneficial for both economies, with the poorer and smaller Palestinian economy reaping a disproportionate share of the benefits. The case of Bregman and Lerner is based on the rapid growth rate of the GDP in the occupied territories between 1968 and 1973. One should not, however, be surprised that the Palestinian GDP grew at very high rates during that period as it was coming out of the shock of the 1967 war and Israeli occupation. As table 5.1 demonstrates, this growth was not sustained. More recently, the argument on economic benefits of the Israeli occupation is summarized in terms of the Palestinian labor flows into Israel and the relative increase in the importance of

Table 5.1
Basic indicators of population and mational accounts, the West Bank and Gaza Strip 1970–1987

	West Bank			Gaza Strip			West Bank and Gaza Strip		
							% Growth rate		Government expenditure as % of GNP
Year	Population (1)	GDP (2)	GNP (3)	Population (4)	GDP (5)	GNP (6)	Population (7)	Real GDP (8)	(9)
1966	843	159	180	350	40	52	—	—	—
1970	608	123	137	370	52	59	1.7	9.6	14.4
1971	623	155	188	379	71	81	2.4	13.8	12.6
1972	634	206	262	387	87	115	1.9	17.5	10.5
1973	652	248	311	402	114	160	3.3	−4.1	11.1
1974	670	415	502	414	157	217	2.8	23.2	9.5
1975	675	394	512	426	166	230	1.6	−2.0	9.0
1976	683	472	593	437	199	273	1.8	16.3	8.2
1977	696	477	601	451	219	295	2.3	−1.8	8.4
1978	708	522	650	463	204	288	2.1	16.1	7.4
1979	719	595	772	445	263	395	−0.7	−2.0	7.4

Table 5.1 (continued)

	West Bank			Gaza Strip			West Bank and Gaza Strip		
							% Growth rate		Government expenditure as % of GNP
Year	Population (1)	GDP (2)	GNP (3)	Population (4)	GDP (5)	GNP (6)	Population (7)	Real GDP (8)	(9)
1966	843	159	180	350	40	52	—	—	—
1970	608	123	137	370	52	59	1.7	9.6	14.4
1971	623	155	188	379	71	81	2.4	13.8	12.6
1972	634	206	262	387	87	115	1.9	17.5	10.5
1973	652	248	311	402	114	160	3.3	−4.1	11.1
1974	670	415	502	414	157	217	2.8	23.2	9.5
1975	675	394	512	426	166	230	1.6	−2.0	9.0
1976	683	472	593	437	199	273	1.8	16.3	8.2
1977	696	477	601	451	219	295	2.3	−1.8	8.4
1978	708	522	650	463	204	288	2.1	16.1	7.4
1979	719	595	772	445	263	395	−0.7	−2.0	7.4

exports in GDP.[5] This argument is partial as it does not relate to overall welfare measures.

The above arguments about the economic benefits of Israeli occupation to the Palestinian economy assume implicitly or explicitly a two-way integration between the Palestinian and Israeli economies. If that were the case, this should have equalized the returns to the factors of production in the two economies. However, two decades after the Israeli occupation, the Palestinian per capita GNP is only one-fourth of Israeli per capita GNP. Moreover, the growth rate of the Palestinian per capita GNP under Israeli occupation is not higher than the comparably endowed Jordan.[6] For the period 1970–87, the average annual real growth rates of per capita GDP were 4.26% for the West Bank and 1.31% for Gaza Strip. The combined average annual growth rate of per capita GDP for the West Bank and Gaza for the same period was 3.46%. In comparison, the rate of growth of Jordanian per capita GDP in the same period was 4.23%.

Furthermore, since Israeli occupation there has been a substantial increase in the portion of the Palestinian income earned in economic activity outside the occupied territories, either from transfers or worker remittances, and it therefore cannot be attributed to improved domestic economic conditions. The increasing importance of the non-domestic portion of income can be seen in figure 5.1, where gross domestic product as a ratio of gross national product is less than 100%, and the ratio seems to secularly decline under occupation. Even in comparison with Jordan, an economy that is highly dependent on nondomestic income, the West Bank and Gaza are clearly more dependent on foreign transfers and worker remittances. By the end of the period under consideration, about one-fourth of the income of the West Bank and about one-third of that of the Gaza Strip originated outside their boundaries. The sharp decline in the importance of domestic economic activity in generating national income may be partly attributed to the increased demand for Palestinian labor in the Gulf region and in Israel. But the limited job opportunities at home were probably more significant in pushing Palestinian workers outside their economy.[7] The stagnation in job opportunities in the West Bank and Gaza is attributable to the Israeli occupation in various ways. The factors involved are direct Israeli restrictions, which inhibit investment and production activity,[8] political uncertainty concerning the future of the area, economic uncertainty that results from large output and price fluctuation and from

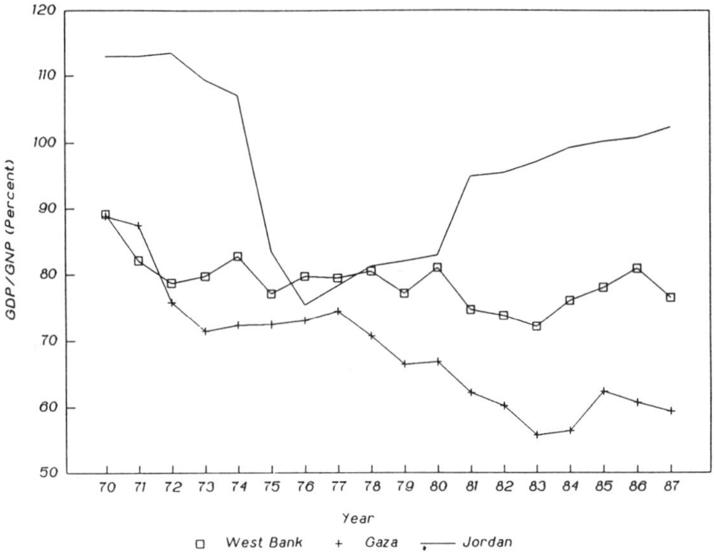

Figure 5.1
Gross domestic product as a percent of gross national product

the practices of the occupation authorities, and the underdeveloped financial intermediation sector.

Finally, domestic economic activity in the occupied territories that could be attributed to the government expenditure is quite limited. Indeed, the ratio of government expenditure to GNP has steadily declined under occupation. The relative contribution of the government expenditure to GNP was approximately halved from 14.4% in 1970 to 6.9% in 1987 (see table 5.1).

Based on all this, one can hardly then make a case that the occupied territories have benefited in some overall sense from their integration with the Israeli economy.

Output Fluctuations

The sizable portion of the nondomestically earned income in the Palestinian GNP implies that the Palestinian economy is subjected to external shocks that are amplified into large output and price fluctuations. The growth pattern of the Palestinian economy has been uneven. The real per capita GDP of the occupied territories grew at

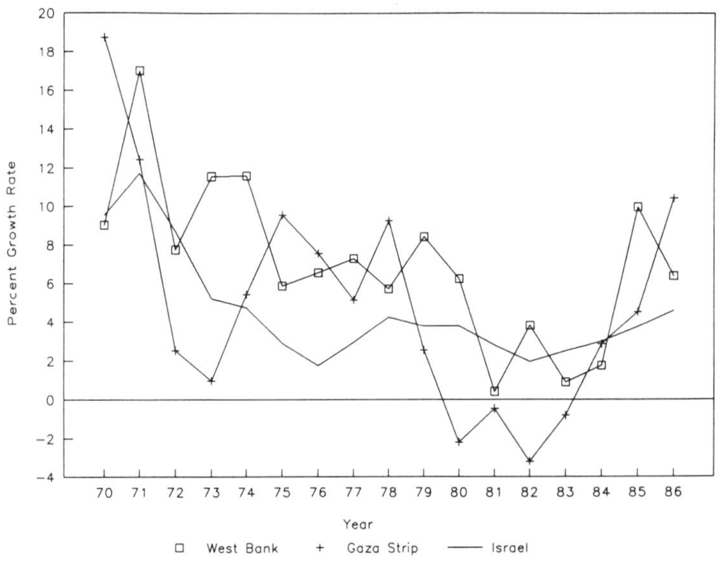

Figure 5.2
Growth rates of real GDP, two-year moving average

an annual average of 5.85% in the period 1970–79, while it barely grew at an average rate of 0.01% in the period 1980–87. If we consider the two Palestinian occupied regions separately, the average annual growth rates of per capita GDP in the period 1970–79 were 6.74% and 3.79% in the West Bank and Gaza Strip, while the comparable rates for the 1980–87 period were 0.38% and –1.00% for the West Bank and Gaza Strip, respectively.

Figure 5.2 illustrates the two-year moving averages of real GDP growth rates for the West Bank, Gaza Strip, and Israel.[9] The variations in the growth rates of the occupied territories are obviously greater than those of Israel. A simple regression of such growth rates on their lagged values and an intercept yields a coefficient of 0.37, 0.50, and 0.75 for the West Bank, Gaza Strip, and Israel, respectively; the *t* statistics associated with these coefficients are 1.5, 2.9, and 5.9 for the West Bank, Gaza Strip, and Israel, respectively. If the Palestinian economy was truly integrated with the Israeli economy, such integration along with the general macrostabilization policies should have reduced the gap in output fluctuations between Israel and the occupied territories. The greater output fluctuations of the Palestinian economy than those of Israel are indicative of the one-sided economic integration between Israel and the occupied territories.

Palestinian domestic product fluctuates much more widely than the Israeli economy for various reasons. First, the Palestinian economy is subjected to more shocks than the Israeli economy. The Palestinian economy is affected by the usual shocks of the Israeli economy—weather, international prices of imported goods, and variations in Israeli money supply, to name a few. In addition, the Palestinian economy is influenced by fluctuations in the demand for its labor by the Gulf Arab countries and Israel, and it is constantly disrupted by curfews, strikes, and arbitrary administrative restrictions. Second, when subjected to comparable external shocks, the impact of such events on the Palestinian economy tends to be more severe because of its higher degree of openness. Third, unlike the Israeli economy, shocks experienced by the Palestinian economy are not mitigated by automatic fiscal stabilizers or by active countercyclical fiscal and monetary policies.

Automatic fiscal stabilizers in the West Bank and Gaza are very weak. Unemployment benefits are not available even for Palestinians working in Israel, and there is no national welfare system. There is no countercyclical fiscal policy because the occupation authority limits its expenditure to certain forms of collected government revenues. In fact, the importance of public expenditure has declined steadily since Israeli occupation, as we have previously argued (see table 5.1).

The occupied territories do not control their own money supply, which rules out monetary policy as a stabilization policy instrument. They have no currency of their own and no banking system to speak of. Consequently, they have no domestically created money. All available money is injected through foreign trade, remittances, or transfers. The stability of money supply is therefore contingent on the stability of the balance of payment. Knowing that wages and transfers, which tended to fluctuate considerably over the period under study, account for a substantial share of current account, the growth of money supply in this period is expected to be destabilizing.

Price Fluctuations

Given the de facto economic and monetary union that has occurred between Israel and the occupied territories, it should be expected that the law of one price would prevail and that there would be no

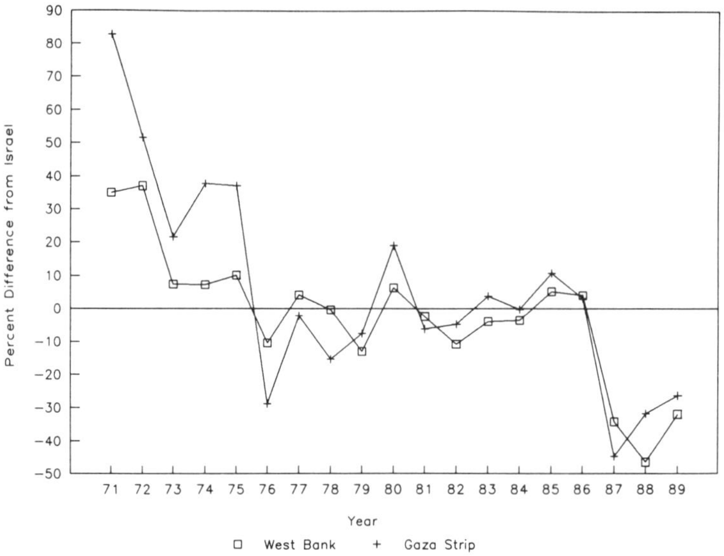

Figure 5.3
Percent difference in inflation rates between Israel and occupied territories (as a percent of Israeli inflation)

systematic differences in the inflation rates between Israel and the occupied territories. The occupied territories do not have a separate monetary authority, and the Israeli currency has been the legal tender there since the 1967 occupation. Assuming the removal of trade barriers between Israel and the territories, and given the very short distances between the regions, one would expect the movement of goods and services to equalize any price differential that may arise between Israel and the West Bank and Gaza.

Yet, figure 5.3 demonstrates systematic differences in the inflation rates, based on the consumer price indexes, between Israel on the one hand and the West Bank and Gaza Strip on the other. This figure shows the difference between Palestinian and Israeli inflation rates as a percent of the Israeli inflation rate. It is apparent from the figure that the inflation rates in the West Bank and Gaza were relatively close to the Israeli rates during the period 1976–86, when the inflation rates were high and exceeded 50% per annum for most of the years. In this period the whole price structure seemed to be driven by the rapidly expanding money supply. But the relative difference in the inflation rates between the occupied territories and Israel was systematic during the period of moderate inflation prior to 1976 and post-1986; inflation rates were higher in the occupied territories in the period prior to 1976 and lower in the post-1986 period in comparison with Israeli inflation rates.

The systematic differences between the inflation rates contradict what one would expect from a truly integrated economic structure. Such a difference may be explained by the Israeli restrictions on the movement of goods and factors of production, and by the money supply shocks that the occupied territories are subjected to because of their dependence on foreign trade as a source of money supply.

The Israeli authorities allow free mobility of goods and labor between Israel and the occupied territories, but important classes of Palestinian exports are restricted from entry into the Israeli markets. Whereas Israeli farmers have free access to Palestinian markets, the export of agricultural products from the West Bank and Gaza to Israel is allowed only if Israeli production fails to satisfy domestic demand (Kahan 1987; UNCTAD 1989a). Some Palestinian goods, like pharmaceutical products, are kept out of Israel because their potential markets are dominated by government or quasi-government agencies, which tend to give preferential treatment to Israeli-made products (UNCTAD 1989a). In the labor market, the restrictions on Palestinian access to the Israeli market are more subtle. There are no formal restrictions on Palestinian employment in Israel. Permits for such employment are required but the enforcement is not always effective. Nevertheless, despite the abundance of Palestinian college graduates and holders of professional and technical degrees, Palestinian employment in Israel is limited almost exclusively to low-skilled jobs, mostly in construction, agriculture, and services.

Restrictions on Palestinian exports to Israel create a price difference between the occupied territories and Israel for a significant category of goods and services, referred to here as restricted goods to differentiate them from tradables, whose prices are the same on both markets. Differences in the prices of restricted goods in the Palestinian and Israeli markets lead in turn to differences in the inflation rates.

The price of restricted goods in the occupied territories is a function of demand for these goods in Israel and abroad, which in turn depends on changes in Israeli restrictions. It is also a function of Palestinian money supply, which tends to be unstable because it is determined by the Palestinian current account balance, which fluctuates considerably.[10] Between 1970 and 1975, the Palestinian inflation rate was higher than Israel's. This may be explained by the large increases in foreign transfers and remittances as a result of the surge of Palestinian employment in Israel and the Gulf. Similarly, the large reduction in transfers and remittances in the post-1986 period must have accounted for negative current account and money supply shocks, leading to lower inflation rates than was the case in Israel.

Involuntary Monetary Union and the Seigniorage Tax

Even though Israeli currency was made legal tender in the West Bank and Gaza Strip soon after their occupation by Israel, other currencies continued to circulate, particularly in the West Bank. In view of the steady depreciation of the Israeli currency in the period under study, the Palestinians in the occupied territories did not use the Israeli currency as a store of value. This function of money was served mostly by the Jordanian dinar and, to a lesser extent, by the U.S. dollar. The Israeli currency, however, was used for daily transactions almost exclusively.[11]

This Palestinian use of the Israeli currency provides a mechanism of resource transfer from the Palestinians to the Israeli Central Bank. If the Palestinians utilize a currency that is printed by a Palestinian government, such a transfer would be used to fund the Palestinian government's expenditure, which would presumably increase the welfare of the Palestinian population. This mechanism of resource transfer has hardly been recognized in the literature on the costs and benefits of occupation. The seigniorage tax arises from inflation, which erodes the value of outstanding balances leading to a reduction in the real liability of the Israeli Central Bank, and from the increased demand for real balances because of economic growth in the Palestinian economy.

To quantify the magnitude of resource transfer, we need to estimate Israeli currency in circulation in the occupied territories, a quantity that is not provided in official statistics. One way of making such an estimate is to assume that the ratio of Israeli currency in circulation in the occupied territories is the same as in Israel. Based on this assumption, we estimate the Israeli currency in circulation in the Palestinian economy by the following:

$$C_{plt} = C_{ipt} * [Y_{pt}/(Y_{it} + Y_{pt})] \quad (5.1)$$

where,

C_{plt} = Total Israeli currency in circulation in the occupied territories at midyear.
C_{ipt} = Total Israeli currency in circulation in both Israel and the occupied territories,
Y_{it} = Israeli GNP in year t, and
Y_{pt} = Palestinian GNP in year t.

Such estimate of Israeli currency held by Palestinians in the occupied territories is unrealistically low because it ignores the fact that cash is used more widely as a medium of exchange in the occupied territories than in Israel. Unlike Israelis, Palestinians hardly ever use personal checks, traveler's checks, or credit cards as a means of payment because the banking system in the occupied territories is extremely limited in its operations. Therefore, to be more realistic, we provide the following alternative estimate of currency held by the Palestinians at midyear:

$$C_{plt} = (C_{ipt} + D_{it}) * [Y_{pt}/(Y_{it} + Y_{pt})], \qquad (5.2)$$

where D_{it} denotes total Israeli demand deposits.

Equation (5.2) assumes that Palestinians hold currency as means of payment to the same extent that Israelis hold currency and demand deposits. In using equation (5.2) to estimate Palestinian holding of Israeli currency, we should note that this equation does not account for the use of non-Israeli currencies in some large purchases, like houses. Such use, however, represents only a small portion of Palestinian transaction demand for money. Moreover, the upward bias caused by it is probably more than offset by ignoring the Israeli use of credit cards and traveler's checks as means of payment.

Using equation (5.1) would then provide a low estimate of the currency held by Palestinians at midyear, while the alternative use of equation (5.2) would give the high estimate of this currency. To estimate the holdings of currency at the end of any given year, we use the geometric average of the holdings at midyear of that year and the following year:

$$C_{p2t} = (C_{plt} * C_{pl(t+1)})^{1/2} \qquad (5.3)$$

where C_{p2t} is the total Israeli currency in circulation in the occupied territories at end of year t. C_{plt} is either the low or the high estimate of currency at midyear *t*. The revenues collected by Israel's Central Bank in a given year would then equal the change in the real value of holdings of this currency in a given year.

Table 5.2 provides two different end year estimates of currency in circulation in the occupied territories. The low estimate is presented in column (1) of the table and is based on equations (5.1) and (5.3), while the high estimate in column (2) is based on equations (5.1) and (5.3). Columns (5) and (6) of the same table provide lower- and upper-bound estimates for annual seigniorage revenues collected from the occupied territories, computed by dividing the annual change in the Palestinian monetary base—columns (3) and (4)—by the Palestinian GNP.

It is clear from table 5.2 that the seigniorage revenues collected by the Israeli Central Bank represent a significant fraction of Palestinian GNP. The average low and high estimates of seigniorage revenues for the period 1970–87 were 1.6% and 4.2% of Palestinian GNP, respectively. In 1990 U.S. dollars, this resource transfer ranges from a low estimate of 0.7 billion to a high estimate of 1.8 billion, with compounding at a real interest rate of 3% per annum. In comparison, the Israeli government collected very little seigniorage revenue from Israel proper in this period due to substantial credit subsidies enjoyed by the different sectors of the Israeli economy and the payment of interest on bank reserves, which account for more than one-half of the monetary base (Sokoler 1987; Liviatan and Piterman 1986).

Commercial Policy and Involuntary Customs Union

The second major focus of this paper is the analysis of the implications of commercial policy under occupation. Trade between Israel and the occupied territories is not subject to tariffs, and imports to both economies are subjected to the same tariff schedule. Unlike the traditional customs union discussed in economic literature, the present Israeli-Palestinian union is involuntary. All policies on external tariff structure and on the commodities that can flow in a given direction and the timing of this movement are unilaterally designed and implemented by Israel with only its interests in mind. The Israeli government collects all the tariff revenues for itself, regardless of the border across which commodities are imported. This implies a substantial resource transfer in the presence of high levels of protection given to the Israeli industry, as we shall argue below. Even though

Table 5.2
Seigniorage revenues

Year	End year[a] monetary base in million IL		Change in monetary base in million IL		Seigniorage revenues			
					as % of GNP[b]		Amount (mil. $)	
	low (1)	high (2)	low (3)	high (4)	low (5)	high (6)	low (7)	high (8)
1969	41	107						
1970	51	133	9	25	1.4	3.7	2.7	7.2
1971	74	198	23	66	2.3	6.6	6.1	17.6
1972	119	296	46	98	2.9	6.2	10.9	23.3
1973	159	386	39	90	2.0	4.5	9.4	21.4
1974	190	504	31	118	1.0	3.7	6.9	26.2
1975	260	714	70	210	1.5	4.4	11.0	32.9
1976	332	961	72	246	1.0	3.6	9.0	30.9
1977	450	1362	118	402	1.3	4.3	11.3	38.4
1978	637	1922	187	559	1.1	3.4	10.7	32.0
1979	1012	3149	375	1228	1.3	4.1	14.7	48.3
1980	1885	5769	872	2619	1.2	3.5	17.0	51.1
1981	3557	10629	1672	4861	1.1	3.1	14.6	42.5
1982	8328	23633	4770	13004	1.3	3.6	19.7	53.6
1983	31798	76499	23471	52866	2.5	5.7	41.8	94.0
1984	139755	300964	107956	224465	2.4	4.9	36.8	76.6
1985	426401	914940	286647	613976	1.8	3.8	24.3	52.1
1986	792766	1837357	366365	922417	1.2	2.9	24.6	62.0
1987	900688	2080653	107922	243296	0.2	0.6	6.7	15.6

Note: IL is Israeli lira, which is Israel's old currency.

a. Calculated as the geometric mean of Palestinian holdings of Israeli currency at midyear. The low estimate of midyear holdings is calculated by multiplying total Israeli currency in circulation by the ratio of Palestinian GNP to the combined sum of Palestinian and Israeli GNP, see eq. (5.1) in text. The high estimate of midyear holdings is calculated by multiplying the sum of total Israeli currency in circulation and Israeli current accounts multiplied by the ratio Palestinian GNP to combined sum of Palestinian and Israeli GNP, see eq. (5.2).

b. Calculated by dividing the change in end-year monetary base by Palestinian GNP.

the average tariff rate charged on consumer goods has declined in the past two decades, it is still high. In 1987 it was close to 50% (see table 5.3).

The rest of this section utilizes the basic static trade-theoretic model to analyze the present customs union between Israel and the occupied territories and its implications for future economic relations between Israel and Palestine. The current analysis ignores such issues as economies of scale and the dynamic comparative advantage. Distributional issues within a given population will be ignored in order to focus on the aggregate benefits and costs of the customs union arrangement to the Palestinians and Israelis.

In such a framework the counterfactual situation, against which the actual situation is compared, is characterized by a Palestinian state with jurisdiction over its commercial policy. Since it is difficult to compare two second-best situations against each other, we assume that the Palestinian state would have imposed the same structure of Israeli tariffs on all commodities imported into Palestine, including the goods imported from Israel. It is also assumed that Israel would impose its tariff structure on imported goods from Palestine. The difference between the actual and hypothetical situations would not be in the levels of production, consumption, and deadweight losses, but it would be in the government tariff revenue collection. With occupation the tariff revenues are appropriated by the Israeli government, whereas an independent Palestinian state would utilize the tariff revenues to cover public expenditure, which would ultimately benefit the Palestinian public.

Theoretical Framework

For notational purposes, let Q_d and Q_s represent the domestic demand and supply curves for a tradable good. Superscripts i and p refer to variables that are specific to the Israeli and Palestinian markets, respectively. Let t represent the Israeli tariff rate that is currently applied to imports into the customs union. The international price of the tradable good is denoted by p^*. M stands for the quantity imported and is equal to $Q_d - Q_s$.

The economic implications of the customs union for the occupied territories are presented in figure 5.4. It is clear from the top panel of this figure that producers in the occupied territories benefit from their access to the Israeli protected market with its higher prices than

Table 5.3
Forgone tariff revenues of occupied Palestine

Year	Tariff rate[a] %		Occupied territories				West Bank	Gaza
			Low estimate		High estimate		High estimate	
	Low[b] (1)	High[c] (2)	(Mil. \$) Amount[d] (3)	% of GNP (4)	(Mil. \$) Amount[d] (5)	% of GNP (6)	% of GNP (7)	% of GNP (8)
1970	40.0	75.1	31.4	16.0	59.0	30.1	26.6	38.3
1971	45.4	79.7	42.9	15.9	75.4	28.0	23.2	39.0
1972	41.9	67.7	51.1	13.6	82.7	21.9	18.8	29.0
1973	41.0	69.4	61.2	13.0	103.5	22.0	20.3	25.4
1974	51.3	86.6	114.7	16.0	193.7	27.0	22.3	37.7
1975	42.3	74.0	120.1	16.2	210.0	28.3	23.2	39.8
1976	45.9	83.0	133.5	15.4	241.2	27.9	23.9	36.4
1977	39.0	71.2	137.7	15.4	251.5	28.1	22.9	38.7
1978	29.5	57.6	88.1	9.4	171.6	18.3	15.3	25.0
1979	27.7	53.6	110.6	9.5	213.7	18.3	18.0	18.9
1980	26.9	49.0	118.4	8.1	215.7	14.7	14.0	16.1
1981	25.1	47.4	112.7	8.1	212.8	15.3	15.5	14.9
1982	29.0	54.8	136.5	9.1	257.9	17.1	16.7	18.0
1983	30.6	59.1	152.9	9.2	295.5	17.8	17.0	19.4
1984	24.2	46.3	121.3	7.8	232.1	14.9	13.4	18.2
1985	23.6	44.6	114.7	8.4	216.8	15.8	13.5	21.3
1986	30.3	56.6	186.7	8.7	348.4	16.3	13.1	24.4
1987	30.1	53.3	224.8	9.0	398.7	16.0	14.9	18.6

Sources: The annual issues of the *Statistical Abstract of Israel* published by Israel's Central Bureau of Statistics, no. 23–no. 41, years 1972–1990, and authors' computation.

a. The tariff rate is computed as the sum of purchase tax, surcharges, and customs duty divided by the value of imports. Annual average exchange rates were obtained from the International Monetary Fund's *International Financial Statistics* to make the numerator and denominator in comparable currency for the years prior to 1976.

b. The low estimate of the tariff rate assumes that the composition of Palestinian imports is 40% consumer goods, 40% intermediate goods, and 20% investment goods.

c. The high estimate of the tariff rate assumes that 100% of Palestinian imports are consumer goods.

d. Measured in million current U.S. dollars. This is measured as the total Palestinian imports multiplied by the relevant tariff rate minus Palestinian exports to Israel times the same tariff rate.

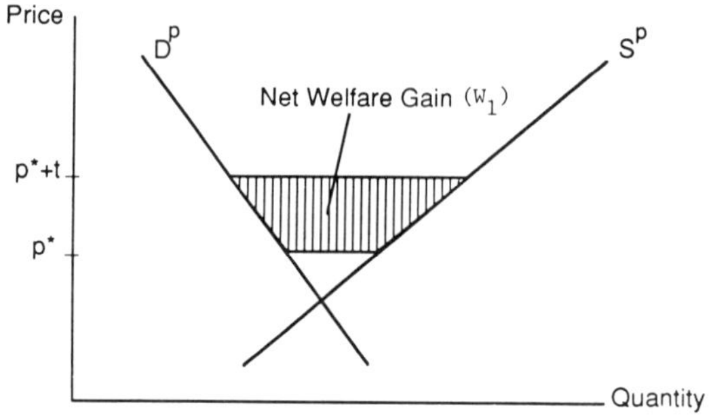

A. The Market for a Palestinian Exportable

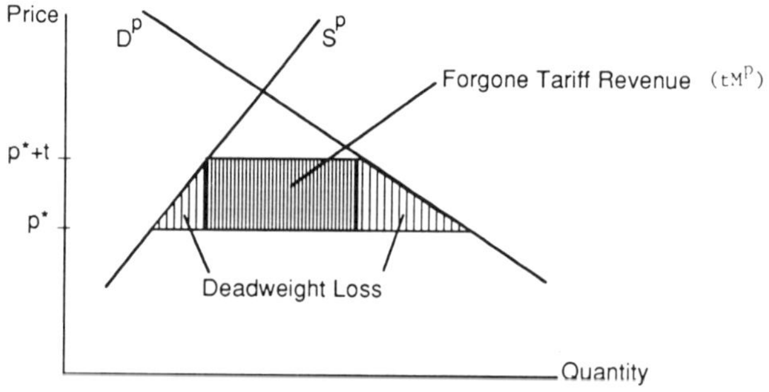

B. The Market for a Palestinian Importable

Figure 5.4
The impact of Israeli tariffs on Palestinian markets

would be the case in the absence of the customs union. Such access makes the price of Palestinian exportables rise above the international price by the tariff on this commodity, hurting consumers but benefiting the Palestinian producers to a greater extent. The combined welfare effect is beneficial to the Palestinians in this case and is measured by the shaded area in this figure. The net welfare *increase* in the Palestinian exportable market is measured by W_i, which is approximated by

$$W_i = tX - \tfrac{1}{2}\,(t^2/p^*)\,(Q_d^p\,\epsilon_d^p + Q_s^p\,\epsilon_s^p), \tag{5.4}$$

where X is the Palestinian exports to the *Israeli market* and ϵ_d^p and ϵ_s^p are the (absolute values of the) price elasticities of the demand and supply curves of the Palestinian exportables, respectively. In other words, the overall benefit to the Palestinians from access to the protected Israeli market is equal to the forgone tariff revenues that the Israeli government would have collected in the presence of tariff barriers between Israel and Palestine, minus terms that are analogous to the deadweight loss in demand and supply that arise from tariffs.

However, the increase in domestic prices as a result of joining the customs union generates a welfare loss in the market for importables. The lower panel of figure 5.4 illustrates the outcome of the Israeli tariff imposed on Palestinian imports. The analysis of the welfare implication of a tariff is a standard textbook case where consumers lose to a greater extent than the combined gain of the producers' profit and the government's revenues. However, the net welfare loss from a tariff in this case is greater than the standard deadweight loss because the tariff revenues are collected by the Israeli government and not by the Palestinians. Therefore, the total welfare *loss* of the Palestinians is given by W_2, where

$$W_2 = tM^p + \tfrac{1}{2}\,(t^2/p^*)\,(Q_d^p\,\epsilon_d^p + Q_s^p\,\epsilon_s^p). \tag{5.5}$$

In principle, whether the Palestinians benefit from the customs union with Israel depends on whether the sum of benefits for all exportable markets, as given in equation (5.4), outweighs the sum of losses generated by tariff rate increases on importables, as given by equation (5.5). Since the available trade data of the West Bank and Gaza are aggregated, we should think of equations (5.4) and (5.5) as applying to the aggregate Palestinian exports and imports. Then, the *net welfare loss* of the Palestinians is the difference between W_2 and W_1 , denoted by W_3:

$$W_3 = W_2 - W_1 = t(M^p - X) + (t^2/p^*)\,(Q_d^p\,\epsilon_d^p + Q_s^p\,\epsilon_s^p). \qquad (5.6)$$

The first term in the expression is equal to the tariff revenue collected on *net* imports from Israel in addition to the total Palestinian imports from other countries. In this formula X represents the Palestinian exports to Israel only, while M stands for the overall imports into occupied Palestine—whether they originate in Israel, Jordan, or other countries. The second term is the usual sum of deadweight losses arising from deviations from international prices.

Cost of Commercial Policy to the Palestinian Economy

Figure 5.5 illustrates broad indicators of external trade of the occupied territories for the period 1970–87.[12] Given the severe Israeli restrictions on direct Palestinian imports whether from Jordan or from countries other than Israel, Palestinian imports from Israel constitute about 90% of their total imports over the whole period. Israel is also the major destination of Palestinian exports. In assessing these trends, one has to realize that much of the Palestinian trade with Israel is merely in the form of reexports; Israeli traders act as intermediaries between the Palestinians and the outside world. This intermediation adds to the cost of Palestinian imports. Unfortunately, the unavailability of detailed data makes it impossible to disentangle the extent to which Palestinian trade with Israel is merely a reflection of reexports in order to get around Israeli restrictions on direct Palestinian imports, and the extent to which such trade represents genuine trade between the two economies.[13]

When considering the total exports and imports of the occupied territories as a percentage of their gross national product, two clear results emerge. First, the Palestinian economy is very open; from 1970 to 1987 imports averaged around 41% of GNP in the West Bank and 62% of Gaza's GNP. The differences between the two regions are probably a reflection of limited diversity of production activity in Gaza in comparison to the West Bank. Given Gaza's reliance on the export of labor services to Israel, it seems that Gaza Strip has become a model of a "dormitory region," where Palestinians work during the day in Israel and return at night to their homes, where they spend their earned income on imported consumer goods. The second important aspect that emerges from figure 5.5 is the persistence of the trade deficit in goods between the West Bank and Gaza on the

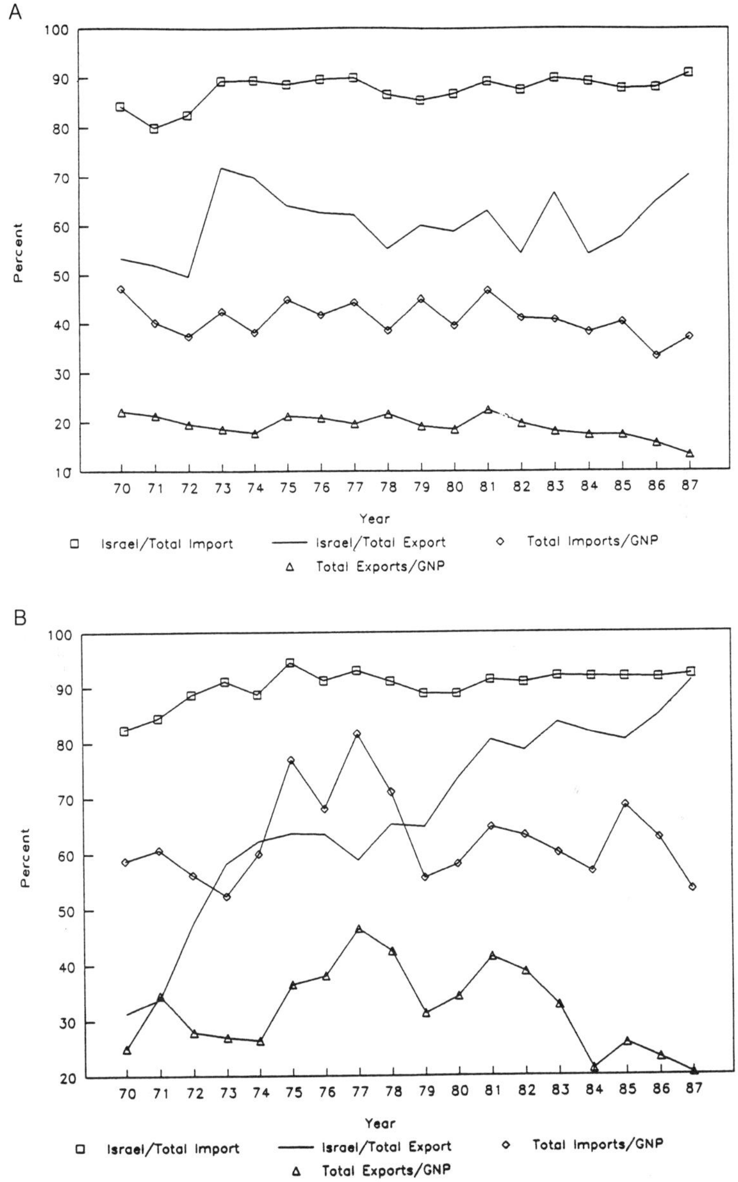

Figure 5.5
Trade indicators: A. West Bank, 1970–1987; B. Gaza Strip, 1970–1987

one hand, and the rest of the world (mostly Israel) on the other. The average trade deficit in goods from 1970 to 1987 equals 22% of GNP in the West Bank and 31% of GNP in Gaza Strip. Given the importance of trade to the Palestinian economy, and given the substantial merchandise trade deficit, one would expect to find a substantial impact of Israel's commercial policy and the customs union on the welfare of the Palestinians and on the transfer of resources between Israel and the occupied territories.

In the general discussion of the fiscal burden of occupation, the tariff revenues based on commodities imported across the Jordan River or from other countries via Israeli ports for the specific use of Palestinians are assumed to reflect the income of the Israeli government from Palestinian imports. We argue that imports from and exports to Israel by Palestinian firms have to be accounted for as well. While no tariffs are levied on these goods, it is clear that a sizable portion of Israeli exports to the occupied territories consists of reexports by Israeli traders who face better and quicker treatment in clearing their imports than the Palestinians would. In any case the appropriate economic analysis of occupation (or one-sided customs union) is to compare the welfare of consumers, producers, and the government in the actual situation with a situation where Palestinians assume sovereignty over trade policy.

In addition to data on Palestinian exports to Israel and total Palestinian imports, the computation of the forgone Palestinian revenues requires an assessment of the Israeli tariff rates during the period under consideration. Since the current analysis focuses on the resource transfer (and not on the extent of protection given to the Israeli or Palestinian industry), we need to compute the nominal rates of protection. The absence of detail on the structure of Palestinian trade with Israel forces us to compute aggregate rates of tariff protection on Palestinian imports. The annual tariff rates applied to Israeli imports are computed as the sum of purchase tax, surcharges, and custom duty that are applied to the imports divided by their CIF value. The value-added tax, which has been imposed since the mid-1970s, is not included in the computation of import taxes because it is equally applied to imports and domestically produced goods, even though it represents an additional resource transfer to the Israeli treasury that should be quantified.

Given the radical difference in the structures of economic activity between Israel on the one hand and the West Bank and Gaza on the other, it is unreasonable to assume that the structure of the imports of the two economies is similar. Given the limited development of the Palestinian industrial activity, one would expect the Palestinian economy to be an importer of consumer goods to a much greater extent than the Israeli economy. Therefore, the computation of a general tariff rate based on the Israeli composition of overall imports is misleading. We present two alternative methods of estimating the tariff rate applied to Palestinian imports. The high estimate of the tariff rate, presented in column (2) of table 5.3, assumes that all Palestinian imports are consumer goods, and are subject to the general Israeli tariff on consumer goods. The low estimate of the tariff rate applied to Palestinian goods is presented in column (1) of table 5.3 and is based on the assumption that the composition of Palestinian imports is similar to that of Jordanian imports. Analysis of Jordan's composition of imports reveals the following rough composition of its imports: 40% are consumer goods, 40% are intermediate goods, and the remaining 20% are investment goods.[14] The low tariff rate in table 5.3 is then computed as the weighted average of Israel's aggregate tariff rate on consumer goods, intermediate goods, and investment goods, where these categories have the weights of 0.4, 0.4, and 0.2, respectively.[15]

There are several reasons that lead us to argue that the low estimate of tariff rates seriously underestimates the tariff rate applied to Palestinian imports. One would expect Palestinian imports to have a higher fraction of consumer goods than Jordanian imports for two reasons. First, Palestinian industry and economic activity have been restrained by Israeli regulation, whereas Jordanian economic policy has encouraged the development of enterprises and domestic economic activity. Second, the gap between GNP and GDP is much larger in the Palestinian economy than in the Jordanian economy (see fig. 5.1), which implies that a higher fraction of Palestinian income is spent on consumer goods that are not produced domestically. Even if the Palestinian composition of imports is similar to the Jordanian one, the low tariff rate in table 5.3 underestimates the true tariff rate applied to Palestinian imports. A substantial fraction of Israel's intermediate goods, such as unworked diamonds and fodder, is of no relevance to the Palestinian economy; these goods are generally imported duty free, thus making Israel's overall tariff rate on intermediate goods much lower than what would apply to Palestinian imports of intermediate goods.

Table 5.3 illustrates an overall decline in the degree of protectionism in Israel; the average tariff rate on consumer goods declined from around 75 to 80% in the early 1970s to close to 50% in the 1980s.[16] There was a parallel decline in the tariff rates on intermediate and investment goods over the same period, as reflected in the pattern of the low estimate of the tariff rate. Such an overall decline seemed to have occurred mostly between 1977 and 1979.[17]

According to equation (5.6), the forgone tariff revenues equal the tariff rate multiplied by the total value of Palestinian imports minus the Palestinian exports to Israel, to a first-order approximation. Columns (3)–(6) of table 5.3 present the magnitude of forgone Palestinian tariff revenues that are collected by Israel, using both the low and high estimates of the tariff rates. The importance of tariff revenue appropriation differs in the occupied regions. Given the greater significance of imports and the larger merchandise trade deficit in Gaza, it is reasonable to expect the forgone tariff revenues to be greater in Gaza than in the West Bank, as is confirmed by comparing columns (7) and (8) of table 5.3.

While the nominal value of forgone tariff revenue has increased during the years 1970 to 1987, table 5.3 demonstrates that the relative importance of forgone tariff revenues in relation to Palestinian GNP has declined over this period as a result of the trend of declining Israeli protectionism.

However, the stark conclusion based on this table is that the magnitude of forgone Palestinian tariff revenues is substantial. The low estimate of Israel's appropriation of tariff revenues is equal to 12% of Palestinian GNP on average from 1970 to 1987, while the high estimate of such appropriation is close to 21% of Palestinian GNP over the same period. Converting the resource transfer into real dollars and compounding at a real interest rate of 3%,[18] the forgone tariff revenues collected from Palestinian imports minus the benefits from exporting to Israel amount to U.S. $5.2 and $9.4 billion (1990), according to the low and high estimates, respectively.

Another way of appreciating the magnitude of this resource transfer is to compare it to the government expenditure that is reported in table 5.1. The forgone tariff revenue is greater than the total expenditure of the occupation authority in the West Bank and Gaza in every single year even according to the low estimate of resource transfer, and it is generally greater than twice the government expenditure according to the high estimate. Yet the tariff appropriation is not generally considered a revenue item in the budget of the occupation authority, which aims to be a "balanced budget."

Concluding Remarks

Although we have not attempted a comprehensive accounting of the economic benefits and costs of the Israeli occupation of the West Bank and Gaza, the evidence provided in our chapter indicates that its overall impact is not positive. The average growth rate for Palestinian GNP per capita in the period under study was not higher than the comparably endowed Jordan. Meanwhile, the greater dependence on nondomestically generated income, the economic and political shocks of the occupation, and the loss of stabilization tools resulted in greater output and price fluctuation in this period.

We also identify important mechanisms of resource transfer from the occupied territories to the Israeli government. The monetary integration of the West Bank and Gaza Strip with Israel, and the use of Israeli currency as legal tender, lead to a transfer of resources because of the erosion of balances resulting from inflation and because of the increased demand for money due to growth. Israel's highly protective commercial policy coupled with the one-sided customs union on the West Bank and Gaza has also led to appropriating significant tariff revenues by the Israeli treasury. The combined impact of the resource transfer resulting from the commercial and monetary integration is substantial. Averaged over the period 1970–87, a lower bound estimate for this resource transfer is about 13% (or one-eighth) of the Palestinian GNP, while the high estimate puts it close to 25% (or one-fourth) of Palestinian GNP. In terms of 1990 U.S. dollars, the total sum of this compounded resource transfer (at a 3% real interest rate) would range between a low estimate of about 6 billion to a high estimate of about 11 billion. It is significant to realize that both mechanisms of resource transfer have not been discussed in the literature. It is also significant that the Israeli occupation authority attempts to run an annually balanced budget, but without counting the transfers that we quantify as income sources. Therefore, these substantial resource transfers are over and above other revenues that are collected to cover the expenditure of the administration of the occupation authority.

With a political settlement, one would expect the Palestinians to regain these substantial resource transfers. Yet a future Palestinian state should not expect the current resource transfer to materialize in the form of future government revenues, since the extent to which this takes place would depend on its future policies. A highly protectionist strategy, like Israel's, may generate substantial tariff revenues but could be disastrous for the long-run development potential of Palestinian agriculture and industry.

A peaceful settlement is expected to have other economic benefits for the Palestinians and for the region. It can lead to major changes in investment and trade patterns in the Middle East. For these changes to take place, however, the settlement needs to be comprehensive and permanent. It also needs to involve the Palestinians in the occupied territories as well as the Diaspora Palestinians. The Diaspora Palestinians would gain the security and protection of the Palestinian state, and they could be a major source of the investment funds that will be needed to rebuild the Palestinian economy. These investment funds will be essential in the first few years of the settlement, as foreign investors are expected to be cautious in the early period. In such an environment, investment by the Diaspora Palestinians will not only help revive the Palestinian economy but may also encourage foreign investment by influencing expectations about economic and political risk as well. The involvement of the Palestinians in the Diaspora will also make it possible for the Palestinian economy to reclaim some of its accumulated investment in human capital. This will in turn provide the technical skills needed to revitalize the industrial sector, if it is to become the engine of growth in an independent Palestinian state.

If the peaceful settlement includes a transition period, some benefits could still be realized in this period. However, these benefits would be much more limited than those discussed above. On the one hand, it is unrealistic to expect significant foreign investment in the transition period because of uncertainty about future political and economic arrangements. Yet arrangements could and should be made in this period to put an end to the transfer of seigniorage and tariff revenues from the Palestinian economy to Israel. Moreover, if the Palestinians have control over immigration in this period, the Palestinian economy may also be able to attract some of the accumulated human and physical capital of the Palestinians in the Diaspora. In the absence of Palestinian control over immigration and compensation schemes for reclaiming Palestinian resources transferred to

Israel, we do not think that the Palestinian economy would survive the transition period without a substantial infusion of foreign aid.

Interim political arrangements should recognize the substantial resource transfer from the occupied territories to Israel, and appropriate compensatory schemes should be devised to nullify the resource flow from the occupied territories to Israel. Such schemes should also serve the purpose of allowing Palestinian economic institutions to mature to a level that would serve the needs of an independent Palestine.

Notes

The chapter has greatly benefited from detailed comments by Stanley Fischer and from the questions and comments of the participants in the conference.

1. These issues have been tackled to some extent in Abed (1988) and Benvenisti (1990).

2. See the World Bank (1989), table 1, pp. 164–165.

3. The system of data collection in the occupied territories has collapsed since the outbreak of the *intifada*, and there are no available data on the Palestinian national accounts since 1987. We ignore data regarding the first two years of occupation because of their transitional nature.

4. Bregman's argument is published in Hebrew and is discussed in Van Arkadie (1977); Lerner's argument is developed in Lerner and Ben-Sahar (1975).

5. See Kleiman (1990, and the chapter in this book) for a summary of these arguments. Kleiman's argument concerning increased trade creation is weak because it rests on comparing trade indicators of the West Bank after Israeli occupation with similar indicators of 1966; the "data" for 1966 are really "guesstimates" because they were constructed *after* 1967 and are known to be quite unreliable.

6. The comparable average annual growth rates of real per capita GNP during the period 1970–87 are 4.8% for Jordan, 4.84% for the West Bank, and 3.66% for Gaza Strip.

7. While it may not be possible to find the appropriate data set to test this hypothesis, the argument is supported by the discrepancy in the ratios of GDP/GNP between Jordan and the occupied territories (see fig. 5.1).

8. All investment projects have to be approved by the Israeli authorities. In some cases, like a proposed cement plant in Hebron, the investment application is rejected outright. In others, potential investors are discouraged by the costly and lengthy approval process.

9. The two-year moving average is used to neutralize the impact of the West

Bank's olive output fluctuation, which tends to have a two-year cycle. This would also overcome any statistical artifact that may result from the quality of the data; the practice of using a two-year moving average is strongly recommended by Israel's Central Bureau of Statistics in the computation of growth rates of national output.

10. In the absence of significant foreign investment and domestically created money, the change in money supply is basically equal to the current account. Theoretically we should be able to reconstruct the money supply of the West Bank and Gaza by estimating the amount of currency in circulation there in 1966 and adjusting it for their annual current account balances since then. All the components of the Palestinian account, however, are measured with error, including the trade balance with Israel. The absolute value of the current account is therefore not reliable. This became obvious when we attempted to reconstruct Palestinian money supply by using balance-of-payments data.

11. Large purchases like land and used automobile are sometimes priced in Jordanian dinars or US dollars.

12. We ignore the period prior to 1970 because it is a transitional period when the occupied economies were still suffering from the occupation shock. Official Israeli sources provide no trade data for the post-*intifada* period.

13. Kleiman (1992) refers to "anecdotal evidence" to argue that a "considerable amount" of imports from third countries is indeed purchased through Israeli importers. Similar observations are also made by others; see UNCTAD (1989a), for example.

14. The analysis is carried out by mapping the detailed list of Jordan's ninety-nine imported categories of goods into Israel's list of twenty-eight categories of goods, and then aggregating Jordan's imports into consumer, intermediate, and investment goods. The mapping was done from table no. 98 in Jordan's *Statistical Yearbook* for 1985 to table VIII/11 in the *Statistical Abstract of Israel*, no. 38. This cumbersome process is carried out because Israel's published tables on tariffs do not use the same categories as Jordan's list of imports.

15. Israel's average tariff rate is highest on consumer goods and lowest on intermediate goods, with investment goods subjected to an intermediate tariff rate.

16. These tariff rates are consistent with the estimates of Michaely (1975), p. 71.

17. The reported aggregate tariff rates mask the fact that the customs duties have declined faster than the reported tariff rates, as there has been an opposing increase in the importance of purchase tax component of the overall tariff rate.

18. The amount of tariff revenues is converted into 1990 U.S. dollars using

the U.S. consumer price index (CPI). The CPI values are taken from the *Economic Report of the President 1991*, table 113.

References

Abed, George, ed. *The Palestinian Economy: Studies in Development under Prolonged Occupation*. London: Routledge, 1988.

Benvenisti, Meron. *1987 Report: Demographic, Economic, Legal, Social, and Political Development in the West Bank*. Jerusalem: Jerusalem Post, 1987.

Central Bureau of Statistics. *Statistical Abstract of Israel*, Annual publications, nos. 23–41, 1972–90.

Council of Economic Advisors. *Economic Report of the President 1991*. Washington, D.C., 1991.

Department of Statistics, the Hashemite Kingdom of Jordan. *Statistical Yearbook 1985*, no. 36, 1985.

International Monetary Fund. *International Financial Statistics*. various issues.

Gharaibeh, Fawzi A. *The Economies of the West Bank and Gaza Strip*. Boulder: Westview Press, 1985.

Kahan, David. *Agriculture and Water Resources in the West Bank and Gaza*. Jerusalem: Jerusalem Post, 1987.

Kleiman, Ephraim. "The Future of Palestinian-Arab and Israeli Economic Relationships." Mimeograph, Hebrew University of Jerusalem, June 1990.

Kleiman, Ephraim. "Some Basic Problems of the Economic Relationships between Israel and the West Bank and Gaza." Delivered at the Conference on the The Economics of Middle East Peace and appearing in this volume, 1992.

Lerner, Abba, and Haim. Ben-Sahar. *The Economics of Efficiency and Growth: Lessons from Israel and the West Bank*. Cambridge, Mass.: Ballinger, 1975.

Liviatan, Nissan, and Sylvia Piterman. "Accelerating Inflation and the Balance of Payments Crises, 1973–1984," in *The Israeli Economy*, ed. Yoram Ben-Porath. Cambridge, Mass., Harvard University Press [1986].

Michaely, Michael. *Foreign Trade Regimes and Economic Development*. Vol. 3, *Israel*. New York: National Bureau of Economic Research, 1975.

Sokoler, Meir. "The Inflation Tax on Real Balances, the Inflation Subsidy on Credit, and the Inflationary Process in Israel." *Bank of Israel Review* 59 (1987).

United Nations Conference on Trade and Development. *Palestinian External Trade under Israeli Occupation*. New York: United Nations, UNCTAD/RDP/SEU/1, 1989a.

———. *Palestinian Financial Sector under Israeli Occupation*. New York: United Nations, 1989b.

Van Arkadie, Brian. *Benefits and Burdens: A Report on the West Bank and Gaza Strip Economies Since 1967*. New York: Carnegie Endowment for International Peace, 1977.

World Bank. *World Development Report 1989*. O‹ford University Press, 1989.

Comments

Gustav Ranis

Let me first emphasize that I consider myself a "new boy on this block," without prior research experience in the Middle East. Although it may be of some advantage to have a completely open and relatively clear mind on this complicated and emotional subject, I am nevertheless keenly aware of the fact that I am suffering from a lack of specific local knowledge in commenting on these two very interesting chapters.

On the other hand, this made it relatively easy for me to try to assume the role of a man from Mars for this commentary. As such—although we all carry some baggage—I frankly expected these two chapters to deal more with the economics of a future Middle East peace, one focused on Israel, the other on the territories, that is, specifically on what might be feasible, within reason and over time, given the condition of a peaceful settlement. Thus, while the past and the initial specific conditions attending that peace would be important considerations to fill in any such panorama, I am afraid that both chapters do not quite come up to the presumed charge. While they are useful, highly competent, and informative, both somehow find it difficult to analyze a potentially very different future. The most important reason for this is the general difficulty of sweeping away the heavy hand of history, even on the part of non-politicians, that is, economists.

Let me discuss the two chapters in order. Nadav Halevi's piece attempts to examine the Israeli economic landscape, understandably mostly in a qualitative rather than quantitative fashion. In terms of the kind of peace, gradual, grudging, that he envisions as most likely, he expounds in some detail why he does not expect there to be a large peace dividend and spends a lot of time focusing on the expected wave of Soviet immigrants under alternative push and pull assumptions. He also indicates that foreign capital flows will continue to be very important, probably shifting from aid to private foreign investment over time, and discusses the impact of the *intifada* on Israel's GNP growth. (Incidentally, I found it a bit surprising that, while the territories are viewed as not very important to Israel before the *intifada*, the acknowledged losses in tourism receipts and foreign private investment would not be expected to continue to have a substantial impact on Israel's future growth.)

What I found most lacking in this otherwise highly competent chapter, however, is the need for greater emphasis on the still outstanding agenda of domestic macro- and micropolicy reforms. Perhaps these are handled elsewhere and therefore need not be treated in this particular chapter, but I would argue that any discussion of the benefits of peace needs to be tied to domestic policy reforms in all areas of the region, including Israel, regardless of the size of the impact of various exogenous factors such as immigration pressures. For example, we know, or are told, that protectionism is still strong; that Histadrut subsidies and other interventions remain formidable; the management incentives are lacking and other problems abound in the kibbutzim; that much of the foreign capital flowing into Israel today is highly dependent on the goodwill of the United States officially and American Jewry privately.

Such a situation begs for an analysis of what the combination of peace and reforms could do in changing the performance of the economy. For example, the question of how to respond to future Soviet immigration waves, at whatever level, is immediately placed in a very different context when we deal with more flexible labor markets than are currently in vogue. Indeed, the "immigration threat" may well serve as a catalyst for much-needed structural change. But it is all too clear that the Likud government, which originally came in on the promise of substantial policy reform, has by general agreement only gone a small way in the direction of the reforms needed under almost any scenario. We all know, as the paper points out, that exports are going to be an ever-increasing necessity for Israel, but we surely also realize that they have to be increasingly competitive and cannot be directly or indirectly subsidized on a substantial scale.

If we accept the reasonable assumption that future U.S. aid levels will decline, as our attention wanders in the aftermath of a peace settlement, Israel can only hope that hardheaded, unsentimental DFI, probably largely export oriented, will increase substantially. If one development model makes sense for Israel to consider, it is probably that of Singapore, given its large endowment of high-talent workforce, its relatively inefficient agricultural sector, and its potentially good access to multinational capital. Incidentally, it is not very clear to me why an increase in Israel's skill levels, especially pronounced as a consequence of the future wave of immigration, necessarily means that industry would increase relative to trade and services. As I see the Singapore model, banking, insurance, as well as high tech could loom important in Israel's future. Under such circumstances, export processing zones may constitute a valuable steppingstone to an increased overall openness of the economy as Israel increases its exports—and not only to the traditional European and North American markets but increasingly also to the rest of the Middle East and to Africa, where Israel had a strong foothold prior to 1973.

One way of examining the potential here might be to take another look at World War II experience, that is, during the period of the Middle East Supply Center when there was no Arab boycott and an economics-dominated division of labor was in play, at least within the region.

Turning to the Hamed/Shaban chapter, this very informative piece dwells all too heavily on the real or perceived injustices of the past instead of on the future and thus demonstrates the understandable difficulties encountered, even by academics, in being able to contemplate real peace and its consequences. This chapter focuses heavily on the disadvantages and losses inflicted on the territories by their incomplete integration with Israel, the imposition of the seigniorage tax, and the loss of tariff revenue to which they would be entitled under statehood. It points to the fact that the territories are more subject to shocks, given fluctuations in the current account with Israel, and that per capita income after many years of annexation is still four times higher in Israel.

Let me first comment on that "bottom line" remark. Would anyone really expect, even in a less asymmetric common market that now exists between Israel and the territories, that there would be convergence in per capita incomes over such a relatively short period of time? If one looks at the United States, say, Mississippi and Connecticut, or even two contiguous states, we find a perseverance of relatively large per capita income differentials over much longer periods of time, even in the presence of full common market integration.

As far as monetary policy is concerned, it seems to me that the chapter here objected to too much integration, calling for a separate monetary authority for the territories in place of being the unwilling victims of Israel's inflation. While the chapter does not explicitly say so, it comes close to implying that the seigniorage tax was really almost intentionally levied on the territories, though we know that a substantial effort was made by the Bank of Israel after 1985 to stabilize that inflation. Frankly, I think of the seigniorage tax and the issue of how large it turns out to be as largely a function of changes in velocity that are not referred to in the chapter. Velocity is the result of a struggle between the government and private claimants for resources, rather than the result of a struggle between Israel and the territories. In any case, I would think that the seigniorage tax would be *de minimis* and should not play as large a role in any discussion of past injustices as it does in this chapter. I was also not very clear about the analytical basis for the claim that differential prices of so-called restricted goods, as opposed to traded goods, cause inflation when it is generally understood that the phenomenon is largely a monetary, not a "cost-push," phenomenon.

Turning to the argument concerning the forgone tariff revenue, it is very clear here that the chapter needs somehow to close the system, that is, to at least make the admission that it contains only a very partial analysis. Here I would suggest having a look at the analysis of undivided Pakistan when East Pakistani (now Bangladeshi) economists analyzed the flow of taxes and expenditures, along with the sources and allocations of foreign exchange receipts, as a way of establishing how and to what extent the territories were discriminated against or benefited by their forced partial union with Israel. I recall that Penelope Hartland did a similar study on interregional flows within the United States.

In summary, what I found lacking in both these chapters is more discussion of the potential for both Israel and the territories in case peace does break out and policies are adjusted on both sides, under different assumptions about the ultimate political solution that emerges. I would view such an exercise not as pie in the sky but as an effort to reach a realistic assessment of what the play of dynamic comparative advantage is likely to yield, as between Israel and the territories and the rest of the world.

Putting flesh on the potential for positive-sum games as well as on how such gains are likely to be distributed would include focusing on the potential for Smithian as well as Schumpeterian types of technology change that can be anticipated in the absence of boycotts and other interventions in the normal functioning of commodity and input markets, the free movement of capital, and perhaps of labor. One could attempt to paint a scenario under which Israel would be taking on high-tech industrial and service exports, the territories initially agricultural and service exports, increasingly food processing, shoes, leather, furniture, all for local as well as international markets, and exploring the possibilities for subcontracting with Israel and participating in her increased export orientation. It is possible that the territories will continue to have a deficit with Israel and a surplus with the rest of the world, especially Jordan, as part of a multilateral trading system. Whether or not the above scenario is indeed realistic in the eyes of those more knowledgeable about the region than I am is less relevant than that some such forward-looking dynamic analysis is needed, with special emphasis on the relationship between Israel and the territories, probably under alternative assumptions on the nature of any interim and final political settlement.

6 Economic Prospects for a Postwar Lebanon

Amer Bisat and
Mohamad L. Hammour

In the past sixteen years Lebanon has suffered a tragic history of intense internal warfare and large-scale economic destruction. An eventual Arab-Israeli peace agreement, or any such major political change in the Middle East, will affect the Lebanese economy mainly through its consequences on the country's political stability and on future prospects for reconstruction.

Lebanon has been chronically sensitive to its regional environment. The Palestinian and Syrian involvement in its internal conflicts, Israel's invasions in 1978 and 1982 and its continuing occupation in the South, the Iranian influence after the revolution, and Iraq's support for General Aoun's movement provide overwhelming evidence of this. The most recent example of such regional sensitivity was the repercussion of the Gulf war on Syria's role in Lebanon and on the improved prospects for state reconstruction.

It is thus clear that Lebanon's internal political situation can be strongly affected by an Arab-Israeli peace agreement. But the implications for Lebanon depend crucially on the nature of such an agreement. Experience has shown that such partial peace agreements as the Camp David accords or the 1983 Lebanese-Israeli treaty, which relegated the Palestinian question to a secondary position, accomplished little in terms of internal or regional stability. Real stability requires a comprehensive approach that directly addresses the central issue of the Arab-Israeli conflict, namely the occupation of and continuing settlement on Palestinian land. Only a just resolution of this question that gives Palestinians sovereignty over their homeland is likely to put the region on a new path of political stability and growth. It is the economic implications of this kind of scenario on Lebanon that we will be considering in this chapter.

The regional stability resulting from a resolution of the Arab-Israeli conflict would no doubt strengthen the political settlement in Lebanon and improve the prospects for economic reconstruction. Our working hypothesis is that Lebanon has reached a credible and durable internal political arrangement, and that reconstruction will take place in a stable and prospering regional economic environment.

Analyzing the economic implications of this scenario is a hazardous exercise. Not only has Lebanon gone through a sixteen-year transformation about which we have only fragmentary information, but to this we must add the uncertainties concerning future internal and regional arrangements and the impact of a peace agreement on both. This forces us to limit ourselves to a general, structural type of analysis.

Our starting point is a review of the Lebanese economy before the war, and the central regional intermediation role its predominant service sector used to perform. We next turn to the internal and external changes that have affected Lebanon since 1975. The simple view that the Lebanese economy will quickly recover its original shape once peace is achieved is undermined by the irreversible nature of many of these transformations. We argue that the new Lebanese economy is likely to be more of a peripheral one, and that its service sector will be less dominant, both domestically and regionally. The path of reconstruction itself will be a difficult one, and may be constrained by disorganized policy-making and by a shortage of capital and skills.[1]

The Prewar Economy

Prior to 1975 Lebanon was in many ways an economic success story. The country experienced a real growth rate averaging 6.9% yearly for the period 1960–74,[2] generally low inflation, continuous balance-of-payment surpluses averaging 5.8% of GDP for the period 1964–74, and a highly stable and convertible currency. It is estimated that in 1972 GDP was $2.1 billion for a population of 2.2 million. Table 6.1 gives a summary of main economic indicators for this period.[3]

Three major features characterized the function and structure of the economy: Lebanon's function as an economic intermediary between the industrialized West and its Middle Eastern neighbors; its laissez-faire system that allowed the unimpeded development of this role; and the predominance of the service sector that resulted from it.

Table 6.1
Lebanon—Macroeconomic data (1964–74)

	Avg. 1964–66	Avg. 1967–69	Avg. 1970–72	Avg. 1973–74
Gross domestic product				
In millions of £	3530	4220	5544	—
In millions of US[1]	1141	1317	1749	—
National income (in percent of GDP)				
Private Consumption	88.43	86.11	86.52	—
Gross investment	22.87	19.22	19.59	—
Government consumption	10.03	10.57	9.84	—
Net exports	−21.34	−15.90	−15.95	—
Exports	19.04	22.20	25.23	—
Import (−)	40.37	38.10	41.18	—
Balance of payments (in percent of GDP)				
Current account	−9.50	−4.25	−2.58	—
Capital account	11.92	6.15	15.58	—
Balance of payments	2.42	1.90	13.00	—
Inflation and exchange rate				
CPI inflation (in percent)	—		3.26	8.53
WPI inflation (in percent)	1.96	2.43	3.00	0.00
Exchange rate (£/$; Avg.)	3.09	3.20	3.18	2.47

1. Using average exchange rate.

Source: International Financial Statistics; International Monetary Fund, Yearbook (various issues); Washington, D.C.
1964–69 Balance of Payments: Le Balance de Paiemonts du Liban 1960–1969; Ministry of Planning.
1970–74 Balance of Payments: Banque Du Liban Annual Report (1974) (as cited By Mallat [1988], table 22C, pp. 77–78).

Intermediation

Lebanese economic intermediation[4] can be traced back at least to the second half of the nineteenth century, when Levantine ports (Tripoli, Beirut, Sidon, etc.) served as the junction between European-dominated Mediterranean trade and Syrian-Lebanese interior trade.[5] It was the time when French and other European companies started constructing the modern harbor of Beirut, roads, and railroads linking it to Damascus and other Syrian cities. This infrastructure was later expanded, and financial institutions were developed to service trading and construction activities.

The local intermediating bourgeoisie that developed out of this history, including a majority of Christians with special ties to Europe,[6] had close business relationships with the West and had nurtured the linguistic, educational, and commercial skills that best served its position. A highly developed Western-style private education system produced graduates fluent in Western languages and in possession of a variety of professional skills that were scarce in the region. The best known institution of this kind is the American University of Beirut, the first university on the Western model in the region, which educated many Lebanese and Arab professionals and policymakers. Even though private education was not accessible to the many poor, and public education left little to be desired, Lebanon had the highest adult literacy rate of all Arab countries (73.5% in 1980).[7] In terms of foreign language skills, as many as 43% of residents aged ten to sixty in 1970 could speak French.[8]

The scope of Lebanese intermediation was greatly expanded with the growth of the Arab oil-producing economies starting in the 1950s. The country was well positioned to play a central role in servicing the professional, financial, and commercial needs of the modernizing Gulf states. Lebanese traders, engineers, technicians, physicians, lawyers, and teachers offered their services in that region, while many of its surpluses were channeled into Lebanon's banking, real estate, commercial, and tourism sectors.

Laissez-Faire

Lebanon's economic vitality was greatly enhanced by the very liberal economic stance of its government, at a time when activist policies were followed by many of its neighbors. Business could be conducted under few restrictions, and whatever regulations existed were often ignored. The tax burden was low, labor organization was weak, capital could move freely, and bank supervision was limited and coupled with a Swiss-style bank secrecy law.[9] The economy was very open, with imports equivalent to 43% of GDP in 1972.

The size of the government was kept moderate. Its expenditures amounted to an average of 10.2% of GDP between 1964 and 1972 and were financed mainly through indirect taxes.[10] Public investment was geared toward the needs of the private business sector. Income redistribution and social welfare programs were limited. The latest study of income distribution, which unfortunately dates from 1959, found great disparities with 4% of the population earning 32% of total income.[11] This state of affairs may not have changed much by the early 1970s and, arguably, exacerbated the tensions that led to internal conflict.

While they lasted, Lebanon's relative stability and openness were an advantage at a time when political turmoil and increased state control were sweeping the region. The elimination of competition from the Haifa port in 1948 and the closing of the Suez Canal in 1967 strengthened Beirut in its function as the region's entrepôt. The creation of the state of Israel in 1948, the Egyptian and Iraqi revolutions of 1952 and 1958, a series of coups d'état in Syria, and the ensuing nationalizations and restrictions on capital movements allowed Lebanon to attract the financial and human capital as well as the commercial contacts of the Levant's trading class. A large number of Arab immigrants actively participated in the financing and development of the Lebanese economy.

A Service Economy

The orientation of the Lebanese economy led to the dominance of the service sector, which was performing most of the country's regional intermediation role. A look at table 6.2 reveals that services accounted for 56% of employment[12] and 73% of GDP in 1970, much higher than the 1965 average of 46% of GDP in middle-income economies.[13] The country's specialization in services allowed it to take advantage of its unique position in the region, but was achieved at the expense of development in the industrial and agricultural sectors. In 1970, value added per employee in manufacturing and agriculture was 69% and 41% of the same measure in the service sector.[14]

Table 6.2
Lebanon—GDP and employment by sector (1970) (in percent)

	Share of GDP	Share of employment
Agriculture	9.2	18.9
Manufacturing and mining	13.6	17.8
Construction	4.5	6.5
Services	72.7	56.3
Transportation and utilities	10.5	8.1
Trade	31.4	17
Financial services	3.4	3.4
Real estate	8.8	—
Other services	9.9	20.3
Public administration	8.7	7.5
Undetermined	—	0.4
Total	100	100

Sources: GDP Shares: Lebanon, Ministry of Planning (as quoted by Makdisi [1979], p. 141). Employment Shares: Lebanon, Ministry of Planning (1972).

The regional function of the Lebanese service sector is best seen from the balance-of-payments estimates in table 6.1. Although the country had a trade deficit that averaged 25.4% of GDP over the period 1964–72, its current account deficit averaged only 5.5%. The difference, equivalent to an average 19.9% of GDP, was mostly because of a surplus in the net provision of services to nonresidents (other factors accounted for only a quarter of this amount).[15] Foreign travelers, many of whom came not only as tourists but also as businesspeople, medical patients, or students, were an important source of income. Their number grew with the infrastructure that was developed to receive them, and reached an estimated 2.3 million in 1972 who spent the equivalent of 9.8% of GDP.[16] Another substantial source of income was transit trade, transport, and insurance. Lebanon functioned as a depot through which goods transited between the Mediterranean and the Arab hinterland, as well as an intermediary for the export of Saudi and Iraqi oil. This function was reinvigorated by the closure of the Suez Canal in 1967, after it appeared to be losing steam.[17]

Although its direct contribution to GDP may not have been large (it was estimated at 3.4% in 1970), the financial sector should be added to this list as the sector through which large flows of foreign capital were channeled into the country. Between 1964 and 1972, net capital inflows were equivalent to an average 11.2% of GDP and indirectly financed more than half of domestic investment.[18] Funds originated from the region's oil economies, from Lebanon's politically unstable neighbors, and from Lebanese emigrants and were placed both in Lebanon and in international capital markets. The financial sector that performed this function was the most developed in the region,[19] with bank deposits equal to 98% of GDP in 1972.[20]

Manufacturing and agriculture, on the other hand, were much less developed than services. Both sectors had evolved with little government intervention and were geared toward a regional market that absorbed 54% of Lebanese exports in 1974. The agricultural sector had experienced a significant transformation from silk-related and cereal production to fruit growing, almost entirely at the initiative of the private sector.[21] In 1971 three-fourths of the fruit produced was exported to the regional market.[22]

Manufacturing had also developed privately under the government's nonprotective low tariff policy. In stark contrast with the state-controlled heavy industries found in such countries as Algeria and Egypt, Lebanese industry was dominated by very small firms. The 1971 industrial census found that of the country's 11,000 industrial firms, 10,700 had fewer than twenty-five workers. They accounted for 55% of industrial employment and 40% of value added.[23] The sector specialized in low-skill light manufacturing, mostly in the areas of food processing, clothing, and construction materials.[24] There were many signs of accelerating manufacturing growth in the early 1970s and especially following the 1973–74 oil boom, as demand from the region's oil economies expanded. The share of industrial products in total exports grew from 73% in 1970 to 86% in 1974.[25] But this mini-boom was aborted at the outbreak of internal strife in 1975.

Internal and External Changes since 1975

Although the prewar period provides us with the only well-documented, firm basis we have to predict the future of a peacetime Lebanese economy, it can be quite misleading if we ignore the many structural and irreversible changes that have affected Lebanon since the start of the internal conflict in 1975. The sixteen years of war resulted in large-scale economic destruction and decay, and the disruption of Lebanon's regional intermediation role. The private sector responded through a contraction and reorientation of most of its activities, as well as a massive emigration of large segments of the domestic economy. Lebanon's regional economic environment has also been transformed. As it enters its reconstruction phase, Lebanon will find that its services are much less unique and needed than they used to be, and that its neighbors have developed substitutes for them. However, this loss of competitive advantage may be offset by the sheer increase in size of the Gulf economies since the oil boom of the 1970s.

Ravages of War

If Lebanese macroeconomic data were unreliable before the war, they became often simply unavailable thereafter. Table 6.3 gives a number of the more reliable statistics for this period.[26] An indication of the general collapse in standards of living that resulted from the war can be found in the evolution of the official minimum wage. In terms of 1990 U.S. dollars, the minimum monthly wage fell from $279 in 1975 to $65 in 1990, thus losing three-quarters of its dollar purchasing power. No statistics on other wages are available, but a 1989 study concluded that deterioration in other wages was even greater, as wage dispersion narrowed.[27]

One can distinguish two main phases in the evolution of the wartime economy, separated by the 1982 Israeli invasion (Hamdan 1989, Nasr 1990). The first phase was one of apparent prosperity despite the war. In addition to the considerable economic reserves—both public and private—that were accumulated before 1975, the country benefited from the oil boom that expanded demand for its output and emigrant workers. It also received large transfers of political money that financed different factions, including the large Palestinian economy.[28] All of these factors were reversed in the second phase, which saw no less than an economic collapse. Israeli-inflicted destruction was followed by a failed attempt at state reconstruction and a breakdown of expectations concerning a near resolution of the conflict. Economic reserves were by then thoroughly depleted or destroyed, oil-led growth in the region had subsided, and the flow of political money had become much more timid. It is in this phase that our minimum wage index experienced its major fall, having lost only 5% of its purchasing power as measured in 1990 U.S. dollars in the 1975–82 period.

The cumulative effect on infrastructure of sixteen years of destruction and decay is tragic. Most adversely affected were housing, industrial plants, transportation, telecommunication, water supply, and irrigation facilities.[29] It is estimated that the Israeli invasion alone caused $2 billion of damage in physical property.[30] The country's educational institutions and its ability to maintain its human capital also deteriorated seriously.[31]

The Wartime Economy

The destruction of economic infrastructure was accompanied by a disruption of Lebanon's regional economic function. The economy's response to this disruption exhibited two principal characteristics. First, domestic economic activity showed a remarkable adaptability to the new circumstances. Second, large segments of the domestic economy relocated abroad.

The adaptability of the domestic private sector took a multiplicity of forms.[32] Most of the traditionally dominant service sector activities—transit trade, financial services, transportation, tourism—either experienced severe contraction or had to reorient their activity in new directions. The financial sector can be taken as an example.[33] In the first seven years of the war, this sector did not seem to be adversely affected and sustained its previous growth rate. But, in fact, its main domain of activity had been redirected from channeling investment funds to channeling political money and remittances. After 1982, the considerable reduction in these flows and other financial strains caused a gradual contraction in most banks and resulted in a financial crisis.[34]

The industrial and agricultural sectors, less directly tied to regional intermediation, were able to absorb the shock in a first phase and return, before the 1982 invasion, to estimated output levels often comparable to what they were before the war.[35] However, both sectors had to yield in a second phase to the accumulating burden of destruction, lack of investment, shortage of skills, and to the uncertainty and costs of channeling goods in a politically fragmented space. Nevertheless, the resilience exhibited by manufacturing against many odds, its adaptation to capital shortage by relying even further on small-scale labor-intensive enterprise,[36] its taking advan-

Table 6.3
Lebanon—Macroeconomic data (1975–90)
(millions of U.S. dollars unless otherwise indicated/1)

	1975	1976	1977	1978	1979	1980	1981	1982	1983	1984	1985	1986	1987	1988	1989	1990
Fiscal variables																
Budget deficit/2	96	169	185	211	306	522	548	1346	1756	1435	1267	762	336	626	933	—
Interest payment on public debt	20	8	15	24	34	60	114	240	365	371	356	280	71	193	305	—
Total public debt	—	—	—	—	322	1125	2069	4326	4570	3980	3420	1398	922	1484	2465	—
External	—	—	—	—	93	491	580	643	610	448	416	458	496	500	520	—
Internal/3	—	—	—	—	229	634	1489	3683	3960	3532	3004	940	426	984	1945	—
From bdl	—	—	—	—	—	—	428	460	967	1422	885	423	288	211	439	—
Non-bdl/4	—	—	—	—	—	—	1060	3223	2994	2109	2119	518	137	773	1506	—
Monetary variables																
M2 growth rt. (%)	11.5	4.7	28.6	19.4	27.3	31.5	40.3	20.3	27.0	23.7	56.1	172.0	354.2	47.8	13.4	55.1
Net foreign assets	2125	3576	2617	2797	3189	3661	4231	4530	3781	2238	2619	2494	2635	3276	3012	—
With bdl/s	1199	2990	1547	1810	1509	1565	1492	2591	2083	670	1073	487	368	978	928	—
With comm. banks	926	586	1071	987	1679	2096	2739	1940	1698	1568	1546	2008	2267	2299	2083	—

Table 6.3 (continued)

	1975	1976	1977	1978	1979	1980	1981	1982	1983	1984	1985	1986	1987	1988	1989	1990
Trade																
Net exports	−775	−71	−734	−1026	−1727	−2359	−2895	−2666	−3027	−2476	−1654	−1582	−1340	−1732	−1734	−1886
Exports	1121	496	691	755	773	841	815	719	572	431	376	412	468	601	502	499
Imports	1896	567	1425	1780	2500	3200	3710	3385	3598	2907	2030	1994	1807	2333	2236	2385
Registered ind'l exports/6	—	—	—	—	—	529	526	405	286	140	136	126	187	271	175	—
Prices fx. rates & wages																
Inflation rate/7	9.9	28.9	19.3	10.2	23.8	23.7	16	13.8	7.2	14.8	64	105	403	155	70	142
Nominal fx. rate (LL/$) (LL/$; pd. averag	2.3	2.87	3.07	2.96	3.24	3.44	4.31	4.74	4.53	6.51	16.42	38.37	224.60	409.23	496.70	695.10
Real fx. rate/8	—	—	—	—	—	100	119	122	112	147	234	272	328	244	182	147
Min. month. wage/9	115	115	136	136	168	196	186	195	243	192	90	70	28	49	70	65

1/ End-of-year exchange rate used for stock variables and average exchange rate used for flow variables.
2/ Defined as the sum of the changes in net borrowing from Banque De Liban (BDL), T.Bills in circulation, and external debt.
3/ Defined as sum of cumulative loans loans from BDL, and outstanding amount of T.Bills.
4/ The sum of outstanding treasury bills (excluding those held by BDL) and commercial banks' lending to public institutions.
5/ Excludes holding of 9.2 millions ounces of gold.
6/ Industrial exports that were registered with the Ministry of Petroleum and Industry.
7/ Figure for 1990 is the change in price index from October 1989 to October 1990.
8/ Defined as nominal $ exchange rate multiplied by U.S. price index divided by Lebanese price index.
9/ For 1986–1989, values are the averages of the two minimum wages that were legislated in the year.
10/ Figure for May 1991.

Sources: Except for what follows all data derived from Banque De Liban "Annual Report" (various issues). Net Exports, exports, imports, nominal exchange rate, U. index: "International Financial Statistics," International Monetary Fund; Registered Industrial Exports: Ministry of Petroleum and Industry (as quoted by and BDL Yearbook (1989): Minimum wages: Institute of Industrial Studies, "Developments of Minimum Wages and Cost of Living Adjustments" (in Arabic).

tage of falling real wages to increase output vigorously between 1984 and 1988,[37] are encouraging signs for the future of this sector.

In the absence of central political authority, one unfortunate way in which economic activity was reoriented is the various forms of illegal activity that formed the parallel economy—smuggling, extortion, drug cultivation and trade, arms and ammunition trade, etc.[38] There is a danger that vested interest in such activities is such that they may persist beyond any political settlement unless the government has the will, power, and dedication to eradicate them.

Emigration

The second way in which the Lebanese economy adapted to the war situation is through a massive emigration of large segments of the domestic economy, both in the form of worker emigration and of the relocation abroad of service sector concerns. Though no exact figures exist, Labaki (1989, 1990) estimates that net emigration reached a total of 740,000 between 1975 and 1988, followed by another 240,000 who fled the escalation of hostilities in 1989.[39] The scale of this phenomenon is astounding for a country of about 3 million inhabitants. Early emigration was biased toward active participants in the labor force, who represented 50% of emigrants to Arab countries in 1975.[40] This share was reduced to 25%–30% by 1985, as emigrant workers settled and were followed by their families. Another characteristic of emigration is its bias toward skilled workers. Eighty percent of emigrant workers to Arab oil-producing countries in the 1975–82 period had technical qualifications of some kind. Thus emigration has been a major drain on the country's skilled labor resources and seems to be increasingly permanent. It has, however, provided a large flow of remittances that have helped cover the country's trade deficit.

The emigration of workers was accompanied by an emigration of businesses. Before the war a large number of multinational companies active in the Middle East had their headquarters in Beirut.[41] Moreover, Lebanese businesses were increasing their scope of operations to the Arab world. The war severed the first type of presence and expedited the second, as most internationally active firms relocated abroad. Labaki (1990) illustrates this phenomenon with a 1979 list of sixteen Lebanese insurance companies that were operating in the Gulf region as well as in Cyprus, Greece, and Jordan.

Regional Transformation

In addition to the changes that have affected its domestic economy, Lebanon has seen its regional environment undergo dramatic transformations. As it enters its reconstruction phase, the country will find that its traditional intermediation role is less essential than it used to be, and that the services it can offer are less unique. To its advantage, however, it will find a much larger regional market.

Lebanon has to a large extent been replaced in the services it used to provide to the region's economies. The Gulf economies have developed their own banking, insurance, transportation, medical, and educational facilities. International concerns, once based in Beirut, have consolidated their presence in other countries—the Gulf states, Bahrain, Cyprus, et cetera. The Gulf countries' capital surpluses, for example, are now to a large extent managed directly by the West's capital markets, with no need for Lebanese institutions. To take another example, Lebanon is no longer important for the transit trade between the Mediterranean and the Arab hinterland. Besides the reopening of the Suez Canal, many of the region's economies have developed and modernized their own harbor facilities to fill their needs or compete in transit trade (Saudi Arabia's Jiddah and Dammam, Syria's Latakia and Tartous, Jordan's Aqaba, etc.).[42]

Neither can Lebanon be expected to resume its original role as an enclave of free enterprise and stability in the region. Given the country's legacy of political instability, as well as the *infitah* movement toward liberalization in a number of the region's economies, Lebanon cannot be expected to regain its unique edge in attracting foreign investments.

However, we must keep in mind that most of Lebanon's prewar economic successes were achieved before the fourfold oil price increase of 1973–74. One particularly relevant measure of the oil economies' tremendous growth in the 1970s is Saudi Arabia's trade deficit in nonfactor services, which grew from $90 million in 1970 to $24,283 million in 1980.[43] Lebanon may not need to recover its previously dominant role in exporting services or attracting capital to prosper in this environment. The question is to what extent this larger market will compensate for its loss of competitive and historical advantage.

Table 6.4
Lebanon—Central Government Revenues, 1970–72 (in percent)

	1970	1971	1972
Total tax revenue/GDP	10.4	11.2	11.2
Share of tax revenue			
Indirect taxes	57	61	65
Customs duties	15	14	18
Fees and dues	14	15	15
Direct taxes	29	24	20
Income taxes	15	14	18
Total	100	100	100

Source: Lebanon, Ministry of Finance (as quoted in Makdisi [1979], table 2, p. 140).

Economic Prospects for a Postwar Lebanon

From the history of Lebanon's economy we can now turn to its economic reconstruction prospects under a peace scenario. We identify two critical factors for the pace of reconstruction. The first is the government, and its ability to manage the difficult fiscal situation it will be facing. The second is the willingness of capital and skills to return to Lebanon. Where reconstruction will be taking the Lebanese economy is difficult to ascertain, but it is unlikely that Lebanon's service sector will recover its previously central position in the region. This may lead to greater domestic sectoral balance, with a more important role for the light manufacturing sector.

Government Finances

Legacies
To understand the future fiscal and monetary policy challenges the Lebanese government will face, we must start with a quick overview of the history of public finance in Lebanon.[44] We have seen that, consistent with its economic liberalism, prewar Lebanon had a moderately sized government. As indicated in table 6.4, the central government relied mostly on indirect taxes, fees, and dues, which provided 80% of total tax revenue in 1972. The contribution of direct taxes was limited, accounting for only 20% in the same year. Although Lebanon had a full legal income taxation system, in practice

tax collection was lax, and tax evasion was widespread and difficult to track because of bank secrecy.[45] Nevertheless the government managed to maintain moderate budget deficits in the 1957–67 period, followed by surpluses until 1974.[46] In 1975 public debt was very small, and the Bank of Lebanon had accumulated $1.2 billion in foreign currency and 9.2 million ounces of gold.

This state of financial soundness started deteriorating following the outbreak of hostilities in 1975, as tax revenue suffered and an increasing gap appeared in the government's finances. But the real difficulties came after the 1982 Israeli invasion. As the Gemayel government was using up foreign currency reserves to reequip the national army, its attempt at state reconstruction was collapsing with the gradual encroaching of militias into state territory. In subsequent years the government had to bear the burden of paying its unproductive employees, providing unpaid-for electricity and telephone service, and subsidizing fuel, bread, and credit for various sectors of the economy, while its capacity to raise revenue was breaking down. Militia-controlled harbors, smuggling, and the mere incapacity to tax stripped the state of its major sources of revenue.[47] Estimated tax revenue decreased from 39% of expenditures in 1980 to 9% in 1986 and 2% in 1989.

The resulting budget deficits were such that between 1982 and 1984 public debt increased from $3.6 to $5.3 billion, and the Central Bank's sale of foreign exchange reserves to the treasury reduced their amount from $2.6 to $0.7 billion. In 1985 the Bank of Lebanon, under a new leadership, tried to reaccumulate reserves and started heavily monetizing the deficit. Inflation accelerated and reached an estimated 1987 peak of 403%, while real public debt decreased to $1.4 billion. High inflation was accompanied by a collapse in the nominal exchange rate, which overshot and led to a temporary real depreciation, and dollarization of the economy.[48] Although debt inflation and the suspension of fuel subsidies gave some relief, the gap in the government's finances could not be closed. In dollar terms public debt increased to $2.5 billion in 1989, and inflation seemed to be accelerating again, reaching an estimated October-to-October rate of 142% in 1990.

The Future

Even with the return to full central government authority and capacity to tax, the fiscal situation will be very difficult in the future. In addition to its ordinary expenditures, the government will have to finance a large public reconstruction program. Moreover, given the polarization in the distribution of income that resulted from the war, the government will face political pressures for social welfare programs, especially in the area of housing for the *muhajjarin* (displaced populations). The official Council for Development and Reconstruction estimates that the government will need to spend $4.5 billion over the next five years, including $3 billion over the next three years, for the emergency rehabilitation of basic services and for priority programs.[49]

The government would be lucky if it could manage to balance even its *current* budget. Considering that the budget deficit was $918 million in 1989, current spending will be *at least* $1 billion per year. Iskandar (1991) estimates that indirect taxes, fees, and dues can cover less than half this amount. If they account for the same share of total revenue as in the prewar days, direct taxes may not add more than $100 million. A sound reinvestment of the Central Bank's 9.2 million ounces of gold reserves—which the government may be reluctant to do—could probably return an additional $300–$400 million per year and close the gap. Even under this very optimistic scenario, we are left with the much-needed public investment program.

How will the government finance its deficits? In a December 1991 Paris conference, Lebanon received a commitment for $700 million in aid for the next three years from various industrialized and oil-exporting countries.[50] As far as debt finance is concerned, the government's indebtedness in 1989 was already $2.5 billion, although external debt was only $520 million. Thus Lebanon is likely to receive foreign loans from the World Bank and other parties, but the amount is uncertain. In any case, a substantial part of the budget deficit will have to be financed internally. Finally, the government is well advised not to return to inflationary finance to close its budget gap, and perhaps slow down the reconstruction program if needed. The exchange rate appreciation accompanying the resurgence of capital inflows provides an opportunity to stop runaway inflation. Returning to inflationary finance would be putting the cart before the horse. An unstable currency may undermine the capital inflows that help finance the very reconstruction program (private and public) the government seeks to accelerate.

In practice there is a real danger that a weak Lebanese government may find its borrowing capacity insufficient to finance the expenditures it is under pressure to make, and may automatically monetize its deficits. This is a classic recipe for runaway inflation. Conditioning international lending on fiscal discipline will help reduce this risk. In any case a fiscal reform is urgently needed. Its object should be to improve the government's capacity to raise revenue in the least distorting way possible. It should improve the way taxes are collected, while avoiding the high tax rates that would jeopardize the return of capital and skills. A well-executed reform would help reduce current deficits, improve the confidence of lenders, and provide future revenue to service the government's accumulating debt.

Capital Inflows and Return Migration

With the destruction that has afflicted the economy's infrastructure in the past sixteen years and the emigration that has drained Lebanon's human resources, the pace of economic reconstruction will depend mostly on the resurgence of capital inflows and return migration. These are likely to place a limiting constraint on growth.

Lebanon's total reconstruction needs for capital are very large.[51] An interesting example of the scale of needed resources is the Downtown Beirut Reconstruction Project, a plan to reconstruct from scratch an area of 1.4 million square meters. The project would be owned jointly by the government, holders of land titles, tenants, and investors who would put perhaps $1 billion.[52] With the current levels of income the contribution of domestic saving to reconstruction can only be minor, and the economy will have to rely on capital inflows from abroad. This may lead to an appreciation of the real exchange rate, which would hurt the export sector.

Private investment funds may come to a large extent from Lebanese fortunes abroad. An encouraging indication is the $610 million combined balance-of-payments surplus of the Central Bank and commercial banks in the first six months of 1991, a time when the political situation was improving but still uncertain.[53] Arab capital other than Lebanese may constitute another important source of funds. Naturally, Lebanon cannot recover the lion's share it used to receive of Arab foreign investments, estimated at 58% of the cumulative $1.2 billion Arab capital invested abroad between 1945 and 1968.[54] But the drastic reduction in this share may be offset by the large increase in Arab assets abroad, and the apparent willingness to invest them in developing countries (Sherbiny 1986 estimates that $53 billion of the cumulative $474 billion OPEC surpluses in 1984 were invested in developing countries).[55]

Whatever its source, investment will depend on perceptions of the country's political stability, as well as on the productive prospects of the economy. This is where a peaceful settlement of the Middle East conflict would be most beneficial. It may both reduce the country's political risks and guarantee a favorable regional market in which its economy can prosper. The government's ability to finance its share of reconstruction also will depend on such factors. This is not only true of private lending, but also to a large extent of grants and loans from international agencies. In the past the Lebanese government has been repeatedly denied promised funds because of the unsettled political situation.

In addition to capital, returning skilled labor will also be necessary for reconstruction. Before the war Lebanon distinguished itself with skills that were scarce in the region. The fact that Lebanese emigration was biased toward skilled workers, and that the region's other economies have been improving the quality of their work force, will considerably reduce Lebanon's advantage. It is difficult to predict the magnitude of return migration. A good portion of the large emigration fleeing the hostilities of 1989–90 was probably temporary. But the estimated 750,000 emigrants who left before then may not return so easily. To the previously mentioned signs of permanent settling, we may add the fact that an estimated one-third of this emigration took place more than ten years ago (Labaki 1990). Lebanese businesses operating in the Gulf will also find it disadvantageous to relocate away from their customers. But even if it does not return, this emigrant worker and business community will nevertheless benefit the country through its wide international commercial network, as well as through its remittances.

Return of the Service Economy?

The Lebanese economy must be reconstructed from scratch. The question is whether it will return to the same service-led regional intermediation function it used to perform, or whether it will grow in new directions. Our guess is that, although they will remain the main sector in the economy, Lebanese services are likely to be less dominant both domestically and regionally. On the other hand, the light manufacturing sector should account for an increased share of GDP.

In terms of comparative advantage, one has to conclude that human capital intensive exports, in particular services, will still play a major role in the economy. The country is so small that it must remain very open. Except for its adequate agricultural potential, it has a very limited physical resource base to rely on. Its physical capital stock has been destroyed, and its human resources, however much eroded, will remain its primary asset.

But, as has been emphasized in recent trade theory,[56] history can play as determinant a role as comparative advantage. When the existing infrastructure, institutions, networks, and qualified work force are important for the decision to locate new service activities in a country, then a successful history can have a snowballing effect. This phenomenon worked to Lebanon's advantage in the past, but it may now work to its disadvantage. The disruption of Lebanon's service exports for sixteen years, the fact that they have been supplanted by others, the emigration of skills, the destruction of infrastructure will likely prevent the country from recovering its central position in the Middle East. Even if its service sector prospers again, it will remain a peripheral one.

One should not be overly pessimistic, however. The scale of the regional economy compared to what it was before 1973 is such that, for all we know, a small peripheral Lebanese economy may do as well in the future as it did before the war as the regional economic hub. Lebanon still benefits from some advantages. It has a broad international business network provided by its emigrant labor force and businesses. Its currently very weak financial sector will probably be reviewed in the process of financing reconstruction, and it may be able to take advantage of bank secrecy to expand its operations further. The tourism sector, which will take long before it can rebuild its image and infrastructure, will meanwhile benefit from the large emigrant Lebanese community.

Nevertheless Lebanon's loss of comparative and historical advantage in the export of services is likely to lead to greater sectoral balance. It does not take much insight to predict that the construction sector and its related industries will thrive. More interestingly, there are good reasons to believe that light manufacturing will account for a bigger share of GDP than before the war. In the early 1970s, a structural tilt in the domestic economy toward more manufacturing in response to regional growth was already apparent, as the provision of services was shifting closer to the customer. Writing right before the war, Dubar and Nasr (1976, p. 77) could predict "a substantial increase in the share of industry in GDP, that would exceed twenty percent in 1980." During the war, manufacturing showed remarkable resilience despite severe handicaps. It shifted toward smaller labor-intensive units to substitute for disappearing capital and take advantage of reduced real wages. An important development during this period was the flow of refugees and rural migrants, who formed a large urban pool of cheap labor, particularly in the southern suburbs of the capital, of which industry now can take advantage. However, manufacturers will have to face the problems associated with a poor public infrastructure, the scarcity of capital and skills, and the higher real exchange rate that may accompany capital inflows.

These problems will also affect agriculture, which will have to compete with other sectors for capital. But if capital is available, Lebanese agriculture could take advantage of an important irrigation potential (estimated at 215,000 hectares of irrigated land, compared to 86,000 hectares currently irrigated)[57] and adopt advanced intensive agricultural techniques to meet the growing needs of the regional market. However, as is typical of the development process, one would still expect to see the share of agriculture in domestic employment and output decline over time.

Conclusion

This chapter examined the possible economic effects on Lebanon of Arab-Israeli peace. Because of Lebanon's sixteen years of internal strife, the most important contribution of a peace scenario would be on the settlement of the Lebanese political crisis and the prospects for economic reconstruction. Although Arab-Israeli peace may not be a necessary condition for such a settlement, it would probably reinforce it.

The country is very fragile economically and will have to walk a tightrope in the transition toward recovery. Although a vigorous reconstruction phase is not impossible, its pace may be constrained by disorganized policy-making and a slow return of capital and skills. At the end, even if this trial is passed, the permanent changes of the past sixteen years may lead to a very different Lebanese economy from what it was before the war. It may be more of a peripheral economy in the region, and its service sector may be less dominant.

Notes

1. We are grateful to Stanley Fischer and Elias Tuma for helpful comments. This paper was written while Amer Bisat was at Columbia University. The views expressed here are those of the authors; they do not represent the views of the International Monetary Fund, its staff, or its executive board.

2. Estimate based on Mallat (1988), table 7, p. 38.

3. Most of the available data on the Lebanese economy are highly unreliable and should be interpreted with care.

4. For a further analysis of Lebanon's regional intermediation role, see Nasr (1978).

5. For an analysis of the economy of Mount Lebanon and Syria between 1880 and 1914, see Owen (1981), chap. 10.

6. For an account of the economic role of minorities in the Middle East during this period, see Issawi (1982), pp. 89–92.

7. Richards and Waterbury (1990), table 5.5, p. 113.

8. Ministry of Planning (1972), p. 98.

9. Between independence and 1964, central banking responsibilities were given to the private *Banque de Syrie et du Liban,* and prudential regulations and supervision were virtually nonexistent. The Bank Secrecy Law was promulgated in 1956. The Lebanese Central Bank (Bank of Lebanon) began operations in 1964, but commercial banking was left practically unregulated until the failure of Intra Bank in 1966, and the establishment of the Banking Control Commission in 1967 (see Makdisi [1979], pp. 48–53).

10. Public finance during this period is discussed in more detail later in this chapter.

11. Study done by the IRFED Mission and quoted by Aly and Abdun-Nur (1975), pp. 160–63.

12. Employment shares may be somewhat distorted by the fact that they do not account for the employment of Palestinians who reside in refugee camps (Ministry of Planning [1972], p. 6).

13. World Bank (1990), pp. 182–83.

14. See Aly and Abdun-Nur (1975), p. 162. For reference, the corresponding ratios for the United States were 79% and 104% in 1970.

15. See Mallat (1988), table 22b, pp. 75–76.

16. See Mallat (1988), table 21, p. 70; Badre (1972), pp. 170–73.

17. See Mallat (1988), table 20, p. 68.

18. Gross private domestic investment accounted for an average 20.6% of GDP during this period.

19. As an indicator, Lebanon had 70.6 bank branches per million inhabitants in 1970s, compared to 45.6 in Turkey, 40.2 in Iran, 24.6 in Jordan, and 6.1 in Syria (Makdisi [1979], p. 176). For a description of the Lebanese financial sector during this period, see Makdisi (1979), pp. 39–48.

20. Mallat (1988), p. 218.

21. See Dubar and Nasr (1976), pp. 93–97.

22. Ibid., p. 94.

23. Ibid., tables II.7–II.8, pp. 77–78.

24. Ibid., p. 80.

25. Maroun (1984), table 3, p. 31.

26. Because of the unreliability of inflation figures in this period, we had to translate data into U.S. dollars to get some notion of their variation in "real" terms.

27. See Hamdan (1989), p. 27.

28. See Khalidi (1984).

29. See Council for Development and Reconstruction (1983).

30. Ibid., p. I.5.

31. See Al-Amine (1989).

32. See Hamdan (1989).

33. For a detailed survey of financial sector developments during the war, see Chaib (1985) and Bisat (1990).

34. In 1990 alone the Central Bank had to inject $127 million into fifteen banks on the verge of failing, and force another five banks to resort to its funds and raise their capital to acceptable levels.

35. Nawam (1988) estimates the value of industrial exports at $726 million in 1974 and $1,317 million in 1981, which amounts to roughly equal values in real terms. Similarly, fruit exports were estimated at 338,000 tons in 1974 and 333,000 in 1980 (Maroun [1984], table 5, p. 33).

36. The share of small industrial firms with five to nine workers increased from 20% of industrial employment in 1971 to 36% in 1985 (Hamdan [1989], p. 35).

37. Nawam (1988) estimates industrial exports to have increased from $320 to $728 million (first nine months) over this period.

38. See Zagorin (1982) and Nasr (1990).

39. This last figure is for the first eight months of the year.

40. All statistics in this paragraph are from Labaki (1990).

41. Of the 772 service sector corporations operating in Beirut in 1970, 248 were subsidiaries of foreign corporations and 152 were mixed-capital corporations (Dubar and Nasr [1976], p. 68).

42. See Maroun (1984), chap. 6.

43. See Katouzian (1989), p. 55.

44. For a discussion of Lebanese public finance before 1975 see Makdisi (1979), pp. 35–38, and Mallat (1988), pp. 261–81 and 351–86.

45. Torbey (1987) gives a detailed discussion of Lebanon's income tax system.

46. See Mallat (1988), table 5, pp. 272–73.

47. Abu Sakr (1988) gives a detailed discussion of state finances during this period.

48. For a further analysis of this episode, see Saba (1987) and Saidi (1989).

49. The funds are to be allocated as follows: 58% for infrastructure; 27% for social services (including 21% for housing); 13% for the productive sector; and 2% for management and technical assistance (*al-Nahar* 13 December 1991, p. 1).

50. *Al-Nahar,* 14 Dec. 1991, p. 1.

51. According to a recent U.N. report presented to the Council for Development and Reconstruction, Lebanon requires $18 billion as a prerequisite for a return to "the normal cycle of growth," including $5 billion for public infrastructure (*Al-Hayat,* 27 August 1991, p. 9). Although this number appears excessively large, it reflects the country's extreme needs for capital.

52. *Al-Hayat,* 3 Oct. 1991, p. 9.

53. *Al-Hayat,* 17 Aug. 1991.

54. Study by the Lebanese Ministry of Planning, quoted in Maroun (1984), p. 9. The original Lebanese pound figures (L£ 2.2 billion of the cumulative L£ 3.8 billion Arab foreign investments went to Lebanon) were converted at an average exchange rate of 3.2 L£/$ for this period.

55. See Sherbiny (1986), table 1, p. 7.

56. See, e.g., Helpman and Krugman (1985), and Krugman (1991a, 1991b).

57. See Baalbaki and Mahfouz (1985), pp. 25–26.

References

Abu Sakr, Habib (1988): "The Economic and Financial Situation and its Possible Remedies," *Proche-Orient Etudes Economiques* 40 (in Arabic).

Al-Amine, Adnan (1989): "L'Institution scolaire et la desarticulation de l'etat," *Maghreb Machrek* 125, July–Sept., 117–25.

Aly, Hamdi F., and Nabil Abdun-Nur (1975); "An Appraisal of the Six Year Plan of Lebanon (1972–1977)," *Middle East Journal* 29–2, 151–64.

Baalbaki, Ahmad, and Farajallah Mahfouz (1985): *The Agricultural Sector in Lebanon: Major Changes during the Civil War (al qita' al zira'i fi lubnan),* Beirut: Dar al-Farabi (in Arabic).

Badre, Albert Y. (1972): "Economic Development of Lebanon" Charles A. Cooper and Sidney S. Alexander, eds., *Economic Development and Population Growth in the Middle East,* N.Y.: American Elsevier.

Bisat, Hisham (1990): "The Solvency of the Lebanese Banking System 1982–1989: Causes and Lessons," Union of Arab Banks, Manuscript (in Arabic).

Chaib, André (1985): "The Solvency of the Lebanese Banking System during the Crisis," Banque du Liban, *Bulletin Trimestriel,* 24–27, 85–93 (in Arabic).

Council for Development and Reconstruction (1983): "The Reconstruction Project," Manuscript, April.

Dubar, Claude, and Salim Nasr (1976): *Les Classes sociales au Liban,* Presses de La Fondation Nationale des Sciences Politiques.

Hamdan, Kamal (1989): "Les Libanais face à la crise economique et sociale: Etendue et limites des prodessus d'adaptation," *Maghreb Machrek* 125, July–Sept., 19–39.

Helpman, Elhanan, and Paul R. Krugman (1985): *Market Structure and Foreign Trade,* Cambridge: MIT Press.

Iskandar, Marwan (1991): "The Lebanese Economy: Program for Action," Manuscript.

Issawi, Charles (1982): *An Economic History of the Middle East and North Africa,* New York: Columbia University Press.

Katouzian, Homa (1989): "Oil and Economic Development in the Middle East," in Georges Sabbagh, ed., *The Modern Economic and Social History of the Middle East in its World Context,* New York: Cambridge University Press.

Khalidi, Rashid (1984): "The Palestinians in Lebanon," *Middle East Journal,* Spring.

Krugman, Paul (1991a): "History versus Expectations," *Quarterly Journal of Economics* 106, 651–67.

Krugman, Paul (1991b): "Increasing Returns and Economic Geography," *Journal of Political Economy* 99, 483–99.

Labaki, Boutros (1989): "L'Emigration externe," *Maghreb Machrek* 125, July–Sept., 40–52.

Labaki, Boutros (1990): "Lebanese Emigration during the War (1979–1989)," Manuscript.

Makdisi, Samir A. (1977): "An Appraisal of Lebanon's Political Economic Development," *Middle East Journal,* Summer, 267–80.

Makdisi, Samir A. (1979): *Financial Policy and Economic Growth: The Lebanese Experience,* New York: Columbia University Press.

Mallat, Raymond A. (1988): *The Economic Challenge,* Beirut: Notre Dame University Press.

Maroun, Ibrahim (1984): *L'Economie libanaise, le marché arabe et la concurrence israélienne,* Beirut: Publishing and Marketing House.

Ministry of Planning (1972): *L'Enquête par sondage sur la population active au Liban,* vol. 2, République Libanaise, Ministère du Plan, Direction Centrale de la Statistique, July.

Nasr, Salim (1978): "The Crisis of Lebanese Capitalism," *MERIP Reports,* 73.

Nasr, Salim (1990): "Lebanon's War: Is the End in Sight?" *Middle East Report,* Jan.–Feb., 5–8.

Nawam, Imad (1988): "Manufacturing in Lebanon in the Years 1982–1988," Banque du Liban, *Bulletin Trimestriel,* nos. 36–37, 42–45 (in Arabic).

Owen, Roger (1981): *The Middle East in the World Economy: 1800–1914,* New York: Methuen.

Richards, Alan, and John Waterbury (1990): *A Political Economy of the Middle East,* Boulder: Westview Press.

Saba, Elias (1987): "The Lebanese Central Bank and the Value of the Lebanese Pound," in Muhyiddin al-Qaisi, ed., *The National Currency, Security and Development (al naqd al watani wal amn wal inma'),* Beirut.

Saidi, Nasser (1989): "Deficits, Inflation, and Depreciation: Lebanon's Experience, 1964–1988."

Sherbiny, Naiem A. (1986): "Arab Financial Institutions and Developing Countries," World Bank Staff Working Papers, no. 794.

Torbey, Joseph (1987): *Income Taxes in Lebanon: The New System (al dara'ib 'alal dakhl fi lubnan: an nidham al jadid),* Beirut: Dar-an-Nahar (in Arabic).

World Bank (1990): *World Development Report,* New York: Oxford University Press.

Zagorin, A. (1982): "A House Divided," *Foreign Policy,* Fall, 111–21.

7 The Economics of Peace: Jordan

Hani Abu-Jabarah

Prelude

It has been said that no people in the Middle East received the news of the convening of the fall 1991 peace conference in Madrid with more optimism than the Jordanians. And understandably so; few students of Middle East history would contest the fact that on the Arab side, no nation—besides the Palestinians themselves—is more deeply affected by the Arab-Israeli conflict than Jordan. The conflict has placed severe hardships on all aspects of Jordanian life, especially economic affairs. The drain on the country's very limited economic factor endowment has made the already scarce resources devoted to development still scarcer. That is why Jordan is keen to pursue a just, honorable, and durable state of peace in the Middle East.

Objective of the Chapter

The purpose of this chapter is to expose the current economic conditions under which Jordanians live. The present status of the economy is described with the aim of showing the negative impact of the state of instability. This would lead us to reflect on the economic consequences of peace on Jordan in both the short and long run.

The Economic Facts

Jordan is poorly endowed with natural resources. So far no minerals, other than phosphates, have been discovered and exploited on a commercial basis. The country's water resources are extremely scarce, and it has only one outlet to the sea, with very narrow shores. No raw materials are domestically available to support heavy industrial-

Table 7.1
Jordan's macroeconomic indicators

	1986	1987	1988	1989	1990
GDP at market prices in US$ mn (a)	5,828	6,180	5,840	4,410	3,870
GDP at constant prices $mn (a)	5,900	6,333	5,756	3,560	2,900
Population mn (b)	2.796	2.897	3.001	3.111	3.453
Per capita incomes $ (at constant prices)	2,110	2,186	1,918	1,145	840
Exports FOB $ mn (c)	742	932	1,016	1,110	900
Imports CIF $ mn	2,422	2,696	2,716	2,399	2,250
Current account $ mn	−40	−352	−294	−82	−600
Reserves excluding gold $ mn (a)	437	425	110	471	849
Exchange rate (average) (a)					
Jordanian dinar per US $	0.350	0.339	0.372	0.570	0.664
Consumer price inflation	—	0.2	6.6	25.8	16.1

(a) Central Bank of Jordan figures.
(b) Department of Statistics figures.
(c) Ministry of Finance figures, on a balance of payment basis.

ization. From the extremely salty waters of the Dead Sea Jordan mines potash, which together with phosphates accounts for 40% of export earnings.[1]

These natural constraints, coupled with the fact that Jordan has had to devote a major proportion of its available resources to the military establishment, made Jordan dependent on foreign aid to survive.[2] Jordan received funds to supplement the central government's budget from the United Kingdom during the 1940s and 1950s, from the United States during the 1960s, and from the Arab oil-producing Gulf states during the 1970s and 1980s. Without such financial aid, Jordan would not have been able to bridge the gap between its needs and its resources.

Let us briefly look into the economic facts of recent years. Table 7.1 gives some macroeconomic indicators. If converted from Jordanian dinars (JD) to U.S. dollars, the gross domestic product (GDP) grew by 7% in 1987, and then it declined by 9%, 38%, and 18% for the years 1988, 1989, and 1990, respectively. The significant decrease in GDP in 1989 is due to the dramatic fall of the JD in the fourth quarter of 1988.[3] The sudden depreciation of the exchange rate of the JD introduced instability in almost all sectors of the economy. Valued in JD, the GDP witnesses negative growth rates of 2.1%, 3.9%, and

Table 7.2
Funds inflow to Jordan

	1986	1987	1988	1989	1990
Expatriates' transfers in $ mn (a)	1,204	954	910	610	610
Foreign aid received in $ mn (a)	700	620	655	645	625
Total external debt in $ mn (b)	5,026	6,373	6,564	7,418	8,900
Debt service ratio (%) (b)	21.0	25.5	29.8	19.5	35.0

(a) Central Bank of Jordan figures.
(b) The Economist Intelligence Unit figures.

8.2% in 1988, 1989, and 1990, respectively. Naturally, this fact was reflected in the decline of the standard of living of Jordanian citizens, whose per capita incomes have consistently fallen since 1987, to the alarming level of $840 in 1990, compared with $2,110 in 1986.

As table 7.1 shows, the gap separating imports from exports is abnormally wide. In 1990, for instance, Jordan imported $2.5 million worth of goods for each $1 million worth it exported. This is a typical year for the state of Jordan's international trade. To bridge the gap separating imports from exports, Jordan has traditionally depended on three external sources of funds. First, Jordanians working abroad constitute the second most important source of foreign exchange earnings. The expatriates' transfers are superseded only by export earnings. Second, foreign aid is an indispensable source of foreign exchange for Jordan. Without foreign aid, the country would not be able to meet the badly needed financing of imports. Third, Jordan has resorted to external lenders—both private institutions and governments—to secure the foreign exchange it needs to supplement its own earnings. Table 7.2 shows that the total value of foreign debt has persistently grown over the years. Therefore the debt service ratio has also grown to a crippling magnitude.[4] No wonder Jordan has not been able to completely service its debt for the past five years.

The Structure of the Economy

Jordan's economy can be described as more of a service economy than a goods-producing economy. Table 7.3 shows that only about

Table 7.3
The relative importance of the contribution of the economic sectors to the gross domestic product at constant factor cost (in percentages)

Sector	1986	1987	1988	1989	1990
Agriculture	5.2	6.4	7.7	6.8	7.7
Manufacturing	14.6	14.5	15.0	16.3	16.9
Electricity and water	3.5	3.6	3.5	3.7	4.2
Construction	9.2	8.2	7.5	7.4	8.1
Total goods-producing sectors	32.5	32.7	33.7	34.2	36.9
Trade	15.7	15.5	12.8	13.0	11.5
Transportation and communication	14.0	13.9	13.5	12.6	8.3
Finance and other services	16.8	16.5	17.0	18.2	19.8
Government	19.7	20.1	20.1	20.7	22.2
Other services	1.3	1.3	1.9	1.3	1.3
Total services sectors	67.5	67.3	66.3	65.8	63.1
Gross domestic product	100.0	100.0	100.0	100.0	100.0

Source: Jordan Central Bank, *The 27th Annual Report* (Amman: Dept. of Research, 1990), p. 12.

one third of GDP is produced by the goods-producing sectors of agriculture, manufacturing, electricity, water, and construction. Within the goods-producing sectors, the agricultural sector did not contribute on average, more than 7.5% to GDP. This explains why Jordanians import most of the food they consume. And in spite of the manufacturing sector's larger contribution to GDP (about 17%), it is still modest in relative importance. Hence it is not surprising that exports are only 40% of the value of imports.

Public Finance

Jordan has never had a balanced budget. The government's domestic revenues from taxes and other sources have consistently fallen short of expenditures. With only the current portion of the military expenditures included, Jordan experienced a budget deficit year in and year out.[5] As shown in table 7.4, the relative magnitude of the deficit as a percentage of GDP had reached its maximum in 1987 and 1988,

Table 7.4
Jordan's budget deficit

Year	Deficit in $ mn	As a percent of GDP
1986	440.0	7.5
1987	595.0	9.5
1988	552.0	9.3
1989	233.0	5.4
1990	143.0	3.7

Source: Central Bank of Jordan, *The 27th Annual Report, 1990*, p. 51.

then started to fall in absolute and relative terms. Despite this fact, it seems that Jordan has a chronic deficit, which points out to the urgent need for structural adjustment throughout the economy.

To rectify this situation, the government has recently adopted a policy aimed at promoting domestic revenues and containing expenditures. Table 7.5 shows that during the five-year period the growth rate of public expenditures dropped from 8.6% to 4.1%. Simultaneously, the growth rate of domestic public revenues has almost doubled during the five-year period under study, rising from 16.7% to 32.0%. As a percentage of GDP, expenditures remained at about 40%, while revenues have grown from 25.2% to about 29%. This should explain the reduction in the government deficit, as reflected in table 7.4.

Public Capital Expenditures

Theoretically speaking, Jordan has adopted a policy of a free economy. Ownership and management of factors of production are supposed to be held by the private sector. Therefore saving, investment, and management of producing units are mainly undertaken by the private sector. The government, however, plays a moderately active role. For example, the sole airliner, the postal service, telecommunications, water services, and electricity generation are all owned and operated by the public sector. Further, the government is a shareholder in several corporations in the country.[6]

Capital formation therefore is accomplished by investment initiated by both the public and the private sectors. The negative growth rates of GDP seen in table 7.1 reflect the near absence of investment by

Table 7.5
Growth rates of public expenditures and domestic revenues

Year	Growth rates of expenditures (percent)	Expenditures as a percent of GDP	Growth rate of revenue (percent)	Revenues as a percent of GDP
1986	8.6	40.4	16.7	25.2
1987	6.2	41.9	3.3	25.4
1988	5.8	42.1	2.4	24.7
1989	7.2	39.1	3.9	22.3
1990	4.1	40.3	32.0	29.1

Source: Central Bank of Jordan, *The 27th Annual Report, 1990*, pp. 48 and 52.

the private sector. Saving and consequently investment by the private sector declined to zero for 1989 and 1990. Likewise, public capital expenditures witnessed negative growth rates for the period 1988–1990. As exhibited by table 7.6, public capital expenditure declined as a percentage of both total public expenditures and GDP. No wonder therefore that unemployment averaged around 25% for 1991.[7] There were no new projects to absorb the growth in the labor force.

To summarize, the economic conditions of Jordan in the non-peace era in general—and in the turbulent two years (1990 and 1991) of the Gulf crisis and the war that followed it, in particular—have suffered and are still suffering from the instability of the region. GDP and, consequently, the standards of living of the Jordanians have appreciably deteriorated. Unemployment has soared to the alarming level of over 25%. Inflation has shot up to almost 26% in 1989 as a result of the sudden fall in value of the dinar against all major foreign currencies in the fourth quarter of 1988.[8] Further, as Jordan's foreign currency earnings have declined, the country could not finance its imports without resorting to external borrowing. The result was a crippling loan burden that added yet another problem to Jordan's multiple economic difficulties, namely the inability to service foreign debt. This fact called for a corrective economic program. Let us now consider how the status quo of no peace and the resulting lack of stability in the Middle East negatively affects Jordan, from a purely economic viewpoint.

Table 7.6
Growth rates of public capital expenditures relative to public expenditures and gross domestic product

Year	Growth rates (percent)	As a percentage of public expenditures	As a percentage of GDP
1986	17.2	30.8	12.4
1987	7.4	31.1	13.0
1988	−5.9	27.7	11.6
1989	−5.2	24.5	9.6
1990	−22.5	18.2	7.3

Source: Central Bank of Jordan, *The 27th Annual Report, 1990*, p. 54.

The Non-Peace Economy

Jordan has suffered from the state of instability in the Middle East since the inception of the the Arab-Israeli conflict in the 1940s. Because it is poorly endowed with natural resources, Jordan tried to meet the needs of its people by formulating economic plans whereby the private sector plays the dominant role, with the public sector being a helper.[9] Unfortunately, every time Jordan formulated a plan, it was interrupted by the disturbing consequences of the Middle East conflict.

In 1948 Jordan received the first wave of Palestinian refugees, estimated at 350,000 people. Although the United Nations initiated a relief program, the assistance fell short of achieving its objectives. Therefore Jordan had to allocate part of its scarce resources to accommodate the refugees.

Jordan adapted itself to the reality of almost doubling its population between 1948 and 1967. The economic growth of those years was modest but assuring.[10] As a result of the Six Day War of 1967, again Jordan received 400,000 refugees in the second wave of Palestinian refugees.[11] The country had to halt its economic development plans to attend to the newly created human problems associated with the influx of the refugees. The standard of living of the Jordanians deteriorated; further, the country allocated part of its resources to rebuild its armed forces.

In the aftermath of the 1967 war, Jordan resumed its economic development, to be interrupted again by the 1973 war between Egypt and Syria on one side, and Israel on the other. In 1973, Jordanian planners devised a three-year plan covering the period 1973–1975, followed by another five-year economic plan extending from 1976 to 1981. During the eight-year period of 1973 to 1981, Jordan achieved an impressive real growth rate of 11% per annum in its gross national product.[12] Inflation averaged about 11.5% during the same period.[13] Between 1982 and 1988, Jordan experienced a relative slowdown in economic growth, though growth remained healthy. The average real growth rate of GDP for the seven-year period was 5.1%.[14] In 1988, the economy received a very severe shock when Jordan's currency lost about 50% of its value against the U.S. dollar and other foreign currencies. The depreciation in the dinar came about when the Arab oil-producing states discontinued their financial aid to Jordan. Jordan therefore lost an important source of foreign exchange, and due to the depletion of foreign exchange reserves, the depreciation of the dinar became inevitable. The impact on the economy was severe: GDP experienced a negative growth rate of 9% in 1988.[15]

Jordan's economic problems continued into 1989, with a deeper recession and a further decline in real growth rate of GDP of 38%.[16] When Iraq occupied Kuwait in August 1990, the setback to Jordan's economy climaxed with a further drop in GDP of 18.2%.[17] The unemployment level was estimated by some Jordanian economists to be 25%.[18] It was literally an economic disaster for Jordan.

The Economic Implications of the State of No Peace

Given this background on Jordan's economy, we must ask the following important question: What impact does the state of no peace between Israel and Jordan have on Jordan's economy? In answering the question, we will avoid addressing the historical, emotional, and legal aspects of the conflict. I believe that Jordan has supported a just cause in the Palestinian's quest for a national identity in their homeland, Palestine. I think that the people and government of Jordan have taken a political stance of this issue with the full awareness of its economic consequences. Nevertheless, the question is still valid: What are the economic implications of the Middle East conflict?

The answer to this question is of paramount importance in light of the fact that Jordan is participating in the peace process, and all parties concerned should be aware of the economic consequences for Jordan. In trying to find some answers, we will try to identify the economic costs that Jordan had to pay as a result of its involvement in Middle East politics.

Military Costs

The first economic sacrifice that comes to mind is the cost of the resources devoted to Jordan's military establishment. Since this is so obvious, and since there are no reliable statistics published on military spending, we will not seriously tackle this issue. However, it is sufficient to note that, with Jordan's very limited resources, the burden of keeping more than 100,000 men in the army is definitely heavy.[19] One could argue that Jordan received foreign military aid to build up its army; therefore, the country did not use its own resources and, consequently, it did not bear a heavy military cost. The answer to such a contention is crystal clear: the benefits of foreign aid would have been far-reaching had the funds been invested in the goods-producing sectors. As small as it is, Jordan's economy would have grown at faster rates had the funds been diverted away from the military.

Another opinion would criticize our assertion by claiming that had Jordan not been in conflict with Israel, it would still have had to maintain an army to defend itself against other potential enemies. I do not believe that Jordan would have invested in its armed forces the funds it did invest between 1948 and 1992, had the Arab-Israeli conflict never existed.

As stated earlier, the economic sacrifices of the state of no peace are many. No one limited study can exhaust them all. Therefore, I chose to discuss the impact of the Middle East conflict on the labor market, Jordan's earning of foreign exchange, and the standard of living in Jordan.

The Impact on the Labor Market

A comprehensive study on Jordanians working abroad estimated that 35% of the work force are employed outside of Jordan.[20] Further, 86% of the expatriates work in the Arab Gulf states.[21] Of the Jordanians working in the Gulf, 85% were hosted by Saudi Arabia and Kuwait just before the Gulf crisis erupted in August 1990.[22] Although the Jordanians who were working in Kuwait returned home in 1990, the majority of the expatriates are still working in the Gulf states.

A number of benefits accrue to the economy of Jordan as a result of having about 350,000 Jordanians working abroad. First, the absorption of about one third of the labor force by foreign markets reduces unemployment figures to a tolerable level. Normally, the unemployment level in Jordan is estimated to be about 10%.[23] Just prior to the Gulf war in 1990, and because Jordan was passing through a recession that started in 1988, the unemployment level was put at 16.8%.[24]

Second, the expatriates are an essential source of foreign exchange. As noted earlier, exports cannot finance more than 40% of Jordan's imports. Therefore remittances from expatriates enable Jordanians to have a standard of living higher than they could afford had such remittances not materialized.[25]

The third advantage of having one third of the labor force working abroad is the relative strength that the national currency enjoys as a result of the expatriates' transfers. Since Jordanians abroad earn their incomes in foreign currencies, they raise the aggregate demand on the dinar and supply the Jordan market with foreign exchange. The effect is that the price of the dinar is higher than it would have been had such a demand not been created. One can conclude, therefore, that the inflow of foreign exchange transferred by the expatriates operates as a stabilizing factor for the rate at which the national currency unit is exchanged for foreign currencies.

The fourth advantage of having about 350,000 Jordanians working abroad is the savings in national resources that Jordan realizes. The average Jordanian family consists of six people; if we assume that 50% of those working abroad live with their families, we then have about 1 million Jordanians living outside Jordan. One can imagine what kind of a pressure they could exert on Jordan's infrastructure had they resided in Jordan. The funds needed to offer them basic services such as education, health care, housing, etc., would be beyond Jordan's financial capacity. No doubt, the government's budget deficit reported in table 7.4 would have been much larger. If, for one reason or another, a foreign country that hosts a significant number of Jordanian workers asks them to go home for good, they will be a source of instability in the domestic labor market.

When Iraq took over Kuwait on August 2, 1990, the government of Jordan did not take a strong stand against Iraq, though it made it clear that Jordan does not condone any occupation. Instead, Jordan strived very actively to find a peaceful solution to the conflict and tried to bring in other Arab states to mediate between Kuwait and Iraq. The Kuwaiti government opposed Jordan's position very strongly. When the government of Kuwait returned after the war was over in March 1991, it ordered Jordanians working in Kuwait to leave. As a matter of fact, many Jordanians left Kuwait and returned home before hostilities commenced, to escape the horrors of the imminent war. The result was that more than 300,000 returnees had to reside in Jordan in a matter of weeks, if not days.[26] One can imagine the economic consequences of such an influx of people on a rich economy, not to mention its effects on a poor and small economy like that of Jordan. It is not easy for any nation to increase its population by 10% almost overnight. The returnees made an already bad labor market even worse. Unemployment jumped suddenly from 16% to about 25%. Jordan lost part of the badly needed foreign exchange it used to earn. The pressure on domestic resources and facilities has been intensified. A state of chaos prevailed in the housing sector, bringing with it the consequences of the imbalance between supply and demand in residential housing. An observer might ask: How is the occupation of Kuwait by Iraq linked with the Arab-Israeli conflict? Iraq claimed that its army went to Kuwait because Kuwait and Saudi Arabia brought down the price of oil in the world market. Since Iraq earns about 90% of its foreign exchange from oil exports, the lower prices would not enable Iraq to earn enough resources to confront Israel, the occupier of Arab lands since 1967. Moreover, Iraq maintained that the United States—the main ally of Kuwait and Saudi Arabia—applies double standards to Iraq and Israel. Although it demanded the unconditional withdrawal of Iraq from Kuwait, the United States does not correspondingly demand the unconditional withdrawal of Israel from the Arab land. The point here is that the conflict between Israel and the Arab countries often fuels of conflict among the Arab countries of the region. Once the Arab-Israeli conflict is resolved in a just manner, an important source of potential explosion is defused.

The Impact on Jordan's Earnings of Foreign Exchange

Jordan's foreign exchange earnings come from four sources: expatriates remittances, exports of goods and services, foreign financial aid, and tourism. We have already discussed the relationship between the state of no peace and the remittances of Jordanians working abroad. Exports are significantly affected by the stability of the region. Table 7.7 summarizes the main destination of exports for 1990. About 42.3% of Jordan's export earnings in 1990 came from Iraq and the rest of the Arab world. Again, let us use the Gulf war

Table 7.7
Main destinations of exports in the year 1990 (percent)

Iraq	23.2
Other Arab countries	19.1
India	21.1
Eastern Europe and the republics of the former Soviet Union	6.9
European Community	3.6
Other countries	26.1

Source: Central Bank of Jordan, *The 27th Annual Report, 1990*, p. 68.

of 1990–91 as just one example of what we mean by the sensitivity of exports to stability (or the lack of it). For two different reasons, Jordan lost most of its exports to both Iraq (23.1% of total exports) and Saudi Arabia (8.9%). Jordan's earnings of foreign exchange were negatively affected by its loss of exports to those two main markets. No prudent observer of Middle East economics would argue that international trade in any other region of the world is more heavily influenced by political factors.

Moreover, we know that the domestic Jordanian market is limited due to the small population (less than 4 million people) and low capacity of aggregate demand because of low per capita income (less than $900). Many factories cannot take full advantage of economies of scale. They are torn by two conflicting variables: if they build small industries with limited capacities, their cost per unit becomes high and consequently they cannot compete in foreign markets. If, on the other hand, Jordanian industrialists build big plants with large capacities, part of the capacities may sit idle should they lose their foreign markets due to political and military instabilities. In 1990–91, the leading manufacturer of pharmaceuticals lost about 73% of its sales because it lost the Iraqi and Saudi markets. The company sells only 27% of its production in the domestic market.[27] The prices of its pharmaceuticals are competitive because it took advantage of economies of scale.

As for foreign financial aid, it is as sensitive to instability as both expatriates' transfers and exports. The Arab Gulf oil-producing states discontinued financial aid to Jordan in the aftermath of the Gulf crisis. Further, the United States suspended financial air—about 60 million—to Jordan. Of course, the importance of U.S. financial aid stems not from its magnitude, but from the political implications attached to it.

The effect of political instability on tourism and its earnings of foreign exchange needs no elaboration. The correlation between the number of foreigners who visit Jordan as tourists and the state of unrest in the Middle East must be clear. For example, it is estimated that Jordan lost $403 million from its tourism income in 1990 as a result of the Gulf crisis and war.[28]

The Impact on the Standard of Living

The effect of the allocation of resources to the military or the loss of income in the years of no peace in the Middle East will be reflected in a lower standard of living for Jordanians. Let us substantiate this statement by reviewing the lessons of the Gulf war.

A United Nations fund, Unicef, published a report in March 1991 that summarized the social conditions of the Jordanians in general and children in particular. According to the report, nearly one third of the Jordanian population now lives beneath the poverty line.[29] (The poverty line is measured on the basis of family income, with $130 per month being used as the gauge.) The report points out that the Jordanian people were ill-prepared for the Gulf crisis, the proportion of the population below the poverty line having risen from 15% to 23% in the two years before Iraq entered Kuwait. It estimates that as many as 250,000 children under the age of twelve are threatened with malnutrition, and that their access to adequate education and health care has been reduced.[30]

As noted earlier, per capita income in Jordan fell from the peak of $2,180 in 1986 to $843 in 1990, a drop of 61%, or an average annual decline of 15.25%.[31] These facts lead us to the conclusion that the social cost attached to a nonpeaceful Middle East is very high indeed.

The Peace Dividends: A Jordanian Perspective

National Rights Supersede Economics

There is no doubt that Jordan has been adversely affected by the prevailing conditions of instability in Middle East. Therefore, essential economic benefits will result from a peaceful settlement. But most Jordanians believe that the Arab-Israeli confrontation is in essence a national and political conflict. Jordan believes that the Palestinians have the right to live freely on the soil upon which they have lived for thousands of years. Hence Jordan's prime concern is not to attain economic advantages from peace; rather, Jordan's main objective is to trade peace for land. This is the necessary condition for peace. It is the withdrawal of Israel from the Arab lands occupied in 1967 that will allow the Palestinians to assume their natural and legitimate rights to their own soil.

Having stated this fact clearly, let us consider the benefits of peace from a Jordanian perspective.

Economic Dividends to Peace

This chapter attempts to show that the lack of peace in the Middle East had its repercussions on the economy. Therefore, if peace is planted in the area, Jordan will harvest several economic crops. Although many advantages will materialize only after a number of years elapse, some will appear in the short run.

Reallocation of Resources

Again, one obvious positive outcome of peace is the savings realized by reducing military expenditure. Some analysts maintain that Jordan might not reduce its military outlays right after peace arrives. Instead, it will wait and see if the state of peace will grant the country the security it needs, as a precondition for significantly reducing its military spending. No sensible analyst, however, would argue against the fact that, whether in the short or long run, Jordan will realize that it must spend less on the military and more on economic development.

Stabilizing the Submarkets

It is expected that when peace prevails, the submarkets of the economy will be more stabilized. We have seen that as a result of the region's several wars, Jordan had to absorb wave after wave of refugees. This automatically brings with it a disequilibrium between the market forces of supply and demand. Many crises usually take place in housing, education, health care, food availability, and almost every other sector. On top of that, prices tend to run upward.

An important dividend to peace is the anticipated stability of the labor market. Jordanian workers would not be threatened with deportation from their host countries on political grounds. Hence unemployment would be much lower in an era of peace.

Further, Jordan will enjoy more stable markets for its exports. As we have seen in table 7.7, Jordan's main trade partners are countries in the region. Experience has taught us that borders close to Jordan's exports whenever a conflict in the region arises. Therefore, once peace comes, the international trade of the region will flow in a smoother manner.

Moreover, once a state of peace prevails, this will probably bring about agreements on all critical issues. One important issue is the allocation of water. If given its fair share of water, Jordan's agricultural production will be better planned and developed, reducing the problem of fluctuating agricultural output.

Foreign Capital Inflow

Jordan will urgently need both foreign financial aid and foreign investment to restructure its economy. Both sources of foreign capital inflow are highly sensitive to instability in the area.

Since the outbreak of the Gulf crisis in 1990, Jordan could not service its debt. It continues to accumulate arrears of interest and principal, which amounted to about \$1.3 billion by the middle of 1992.[32] Before rescheduling Jordan's foreign debt (about \$8.9 billion), the International Monetary Fund reached an agreement with Jordan on readjusting its economy. The program is dependent on reducing the growth rate of consumption and increasing the growth rate of investment. The plan has no chance of success without an inflow of external capital. The readjustment program extends over the years 1992 to 1998.

One cannot imagine the complete success of the plan without the existence of a state of peace in the Middle East. Both foreign direct financial aid and investment capital are highly sensitive to the stability of the region. Only peace would give Jordan's efforts at restructuring its economy an opportunity to succeed. In the past, Jordan lost foreign financial aid as a result of its involvement, whether direct or indirect, in the region's conflicts. Moreover, it is probably that Jordan's creditors will be more inclined to grant debt relief in times of peace.

Economic Integration of the Region

Perhaps one of the most positive consequences of peace in the Middle East would be the removal of obstacles to economic integration of some economies in the area. To be realistic, this possible outcome would be attainable only in the long run.

The world realized several years ago that there is no future for small, fragmented, and disintegrating economies. To compete on a more equal footing with both the huge economy of the United States and the efficient economy of Japan, Western European countries began to coordinate their economic policies in some selected sectors as much as three decades ago. A few years later, they moved toward greater economic integration. Those countries are working now toward economic unity.

The Middle Eastern countries will soon discover that they too can compete more efficiently in the global market if they join economic forces. The countries of the region will realize that there are several advantages for all countries in such an integration.

First, there would be a utilization of the concept of complementary economies. Some countries are rich with natural resources (e.g., oil). Other countries are endowed with minerals. A third group of countries have water resources; and a fourth group are suppliers of inexpensive human resources. A few other countries have a reasonably developed base of technology. Small but producing economies, like that of Jordan, will have easier access to the regional markets. Hence Jordan, for example, can take advantage of economies of scale. Erecting relatively large plants would lower the fixed cost per unit. Jordanian products, therefore, will become more competitive.

The second advantage of economic integration is better utilization of resources. When each economy concentrates on what it can produce best, every country of the region benefits by selling at profitable margins and buying at competitive prices.

A third benefit of economic integration would be the achievement of the much-needed stability in the subsectors. When there is free movement of factors of production, especially labor and capital, the automatic adjustment of the market forces operate more efficiently. Unemployment would be at normal levels. No abrupt mass movement of labor, as that of 1967 and 1990, would take place.

Likewise, capital will flow from the economies that have it in abundance to those economies that need it most. Financial institutions will develop their capacities as efficient mediators between suppliers of capital and those who demand it. These financial institutions will operate on regional and global scales, rather than only a country scale, as the case is now.

An economist cannot cite all benefits that might accrue from an integrated Middle East. Once peace prevails, economic policymakers cannot escape the rational conclusion that survivors must seek larger integrated economies. They will realize that economic cooperation will benefit all individual countries of the region. Each country could maximize its economic benefits by joining the larger economic entity.

To be sure, such an economic integration will not be accomplished in a few years; it is, rather, a long-term dividend to peace. Moreover, the mere arrival of peace will not automatically bring with it economic integration. But peace will provide a necessary condition for any form of economic cooperation among the countries of the region. Peace is a necessary condition, but not a sufficient one. Peace and goodwill are the two necessary and sufficient conditions for the improved economic well-being of the Middle East, including Jordan.

Notes

1. Central Bank of Jordan, *Monthly Statistical Bulletin, Vol. 28, No 1,* January 1992, p. 66.

2. Business International Limited, *The Economist Intelligence Unit Jordan Country Report No. 21991* (London: the E1V), 1991, p. 5.

3. As shown in table 7.1, the Jordanian dinar lost about 54% of its value against the U.S. dollar in 1989.

4. The debt service ratio is calculated by dividing the value of exports by the sum of interest accrued plus the loan installments falling due.

5. No statistics are available on Jordan's annual expenditures on military equipment and arms. But it is widely assumed that it is relatively high since Jordan has to equip about 100,000 men under military service.

6. Examples are phosphates, potash, oil refining, cement, and a host of corporations whose shares are publicly traded and have mixed ownership and management between the private and public sectors.

7. Fahed Fanek, *The Readjustment Economic Plan, 1992–1998* (F. Fanek Association: Amman, 1992) p. 32.

8. Consumer price inflation for the past three years of 1989, 1990, and 1991 was as follows: 25.8%, 16.1%, and 9%, respectively. For further details look at The Economic Intelligence Unit, *Jordan Country Report No. 21991,* published by Business International Limited (London: 40 Duke Street W1A 1DW, May 7, 1991), p. 3.

9. Jordan started to formulate a series of economic development plans in the 1960s. The latest plan was put forth in 1986 by the Ministry of Planning.

10. Annual Report of Jordan Central Bank, 1984, p. 3.

11. I. Asfour, p. 4.

12. I. Asfour, p. 99.

13. I. Asfour, p. 98.

14. Central Bank of Jordan, *Monthly Statistical Bulletin, July 1988* (Amman: Department of Research, 1988), p. 71.

15. Central Bank of Jordan, *The 25th Annual Report, 1988* (Amman: Department of Research), p. 7.

16. The Economist Intelligence Unit, p. 3.

17. Jordan Economic Monitor (Amman: Published by Fahed Al Fanek, Issue No. 10/91), p. 7.

18. International Labor Office, *Yearbook of Labor Statistics* (Geneva: ILO, 1990), p. 109.

19. The London-based International Institute for Strategic Studies issued a report entitled, *Military Balance, 1991.* In this report, the Institute said that Jordan's armed forces have 90,000 men in the army, 11,000 in the air force, 500 in the navy, and 35,000 in reserves.

20. I. Asfour, p. 11.

21. I. Asfour, p. 16.

22. International Labor Office, p. 110.

23. Jordan Department of Labor, *The Annual Report, 1990* (Amman: Dept of Labor, 1991), p. 17.

24. Jordan Department of Labor, p. 3.

25. To appreciate this point, the reader should review table 7.2.

26. The workers returned from Kuwait along with them their families, which is why the number of returnees exceeded 300,000 people.

27. The Arab Pharmaceutical Corporation, *Annual Report,* 1991, p. 3.

28. Jordan Central Bank, *27th Annual Report,* p. 85.

29. UNICEF, *The Social Life of the Children in Jordan* (New York: United Nations Press, 1991).

30. UNICEF, p. 16.

31. Jordan Central Bank, *27th Annual Report,* p. 9.

32. Jordan Central Bank, *27th Annual Report, 1990,* p. 59.

References

Asfour, I. (1984), *Expatriates Capital Transfers and Their Impact on the Economy of Jordan,* Amman: Central Bank's Dept. of Research.

Business International Limited (1991), *The Economist Intelligence Unit, Jordan Country Report No. 21991*, London: 40 Duke St.W1A.

Central Bank of Jordan (1992), *Monthly Statistical Bulletin*, Amman: Dept. of Research.

Central Bank of Jordan (1990), *The 27th Annual Report*, Amman: Dept. of Research.

Fanek, Fahed (1992), *The Readjustment Economic Plan, 1992–1998*, Amman: Fanek Association.

Fanek, Fahed, *Jordan Economic Monitor*, Amman: Fahed Fanek, Issue No 10/91.

International Labor Office (1990), *Yearbook of Labor Statistics*, Geneva: ILO.

International Institute for Strategic Studies (1991), *Military Balance*, London.

Jordan Ministry of Finance (1992), *Annual Budget*, Amman: Government Press.

Jordan Ministry of Labor (1991), *Annual Report*, Amman: Government Press.

Jordan Department of Statistics (1990), *Statistical Yearbook*.

UNICEF (1991), *The Social Life of Jordan's Children*, New York: United Nations Press.

Comments

Howard Pack

The Bisat and Hammour (BH) chapter contains a largely dismal forecast for the Lebanese economy without fully considering potentially optimistic options offered by a peace. On the other hand, the authors omit two critical issues, namely the role of Syria in Lebanon's future and the importance of income distribution in any reconstruction plans.

Consider first the omissions. Quite surprisingly, except for elliptical references, the de facto annexation of Lebanon by Syria is not discussed though it poses critical questions. Will the Lebanese be allowed to implement policies that improve Lebanon's growth prospects, or will policies be subordinated to Syria's needs? One need not be a congenital pessimist to view the second outcome as the more probable, in which case much of the authors' discussion is beside the point. While it is likely that Lebanese entrepreneurs will be imaginative in exploiting individual profit opportunities, they may function in a hostile economic environment.

A second major political issue ignored by the authors is the role of income distribution. As they briefly note, the pre–1975 income distribution contributed to the atmosphere conducive to the civil war. Any growth program that does not explicitly attempt to ameliorate these perceived grievances will be vulnerable to domestic opposition and to exploitation by external forces.

The following comments assume that the country can be guided largely in the interest of the Lebanese. In looking forward, much of the BH chapter seeks a growth pole for the reconstruction of the economy. The authors are correct in their view that it will be difficult to revive the service sectors. Since the disruptions began in 1975, services in the rest of the world have experienced an extraordinary technological leap in hardware and software. Given past instability and the technical gaps between Lebanon and OECD service firms, it seems unlikely that the Lebanese can achieve much growth in this sector, even allowing for the larger size of the Gulf countries' transactions.

Currently, agriculture and manufacturing are still relatively unimportant but as in Jordan, the West Bank, and the Gaza Strip, a greater allocation of complementary resources and improved productivity is likely to be the only development strategy available. Growth in these sectors, given the shortage of capital, will have to rely on labor-intensive, small-scale industrial firms and farms. Such an approach is also desirable if current economic grievances of the poor are to be addressed and their allegiance to the government secured. Assuming that the reported decline in real wages is correct, one of the major variables conducive to such development already exists. Maintaining other relative prices, particularly interest rates and the price of imported equipment, at scarcity levels will encourage the use of labor-intensive technologies in both agriculture and manufacturing. But other policies are needed as well, particularly in light of the limited experience in manufacturing and agriculture as a result of the concentration on services in the pre–1975 economy.

Agricultural extension and research, credit facilities for exporters, and technological help for small-scale enterprises were critical for successful small-scale development in other countries, such as Taiwan. If improving the status of the poor Shia in the rural areas is taken to be an important component of a politically robust program of reconstruction, a substantial proportion of such efforts needs to occur in the south of the country, though there will undoubtedly be pressure to concentrate resources in the major urban areas, particularly Beirut.

Ideally, Lebanon could take advantage of its proximity to the large Middle East market and orient some of its initial production to exports. The exchange rate regime and tariff structure will need to be neutral as between exports and domestic sales. Even if all the required policies are initiated by Lebanese authorities, they will have to meet Syrian approval and may conflict with Syria's objectives.

Moving away from the concentration on Lebanon, peace—between Arabs and Israelis and Arabs and Arabs—offers considerable potential, particularly in manufacturing. One of the lessons that can be drawn from the success of the Asian countries is the importance of regional spillover effects. The factories of individual small countries in the Middle East are not likely to offer sufficient diversity to justify extensive attention from potential purchasers. It is common for American and European wholesalers and retailers to stop in several countries for different products in one trip to Asia. Intercountry accessibility will also have an impact on direct foreign investment, a potential source of investment that could reduce the domestic saving required to rebuild the country.

Open borders, transportation links, regional shuttle flights, and open communication are necessary to appeal to purchasers of exports. The possibility of establishing commercial relations with a Lebanese producer of blouses, an Israeli manufacturer of high-fashion bathing suits, and an Egyptian supplier of designer linen, conserves commuting and supervision time for purchasers who can obtain scale economies from one regional office. The absence of communications between Beirut, Tel Aviv, and Amman is likely to be more important to a potential buyer for Galeries Lafayette than the historical causes of the absent facility.

While the historical legacy of dislike and distrust militates against the development of the prerequisites for being regionally competitive, the rapid development of many alternative suppliers leaves the entire Middle East vulnerable to slow development while other regions dedicated to economic growth succeed. International competition for a limited market comes not only from the relatively well-known Asian exporters but also from the newly resurgent Latin American economies and many of the East European countries.

If there are to be economic gains in addition to the more important benefit of saved lives and limbs, they are more likely to be found in the regional spillover effects sketched above rather than in interregional trade.

II Regional Issues

8

The Economic Implications of a Comprehensive Peace in the Middle East

Said El-Naggar and
Mohamed El-Erian

The protracted Arab-Israeli conflict has adversely affected the economic, social, and political development of countries in the Middle Eastern region. In the economic field, concerns about armed hostilities and border instability have been reflected in large military outlays, with consequent pressures on public sector resources. Moreover, uncertainty as to the prospects for a peaceful settlement of the conflict, together with the absence of the sustained implementation of sound economic and financial policies, have inhibited long-term investments in productive activities. As a result, the economies of the Middle East have failed to exploit their considerable economic potential at both the national and regional level.

The economic cost of the conflict is likely to increase over the next few years. Rapid technological change has accelerated the incidence of product obsolescence, especially in military hardware, thereby intensifying the push toward constant renewal and modernization. Several countries are experiencing high natural population growth rates, increasing pressures on an already limited economic base. This, compounded by the recent heavy migration to Israel, will place additional competing claims on the natural resource foundation of the region (including its increasingly fragile water supply). Externally, investors' attention continues to shift to the opportunities offered by the economic and structural reform programs being implemented, to various degrees, in countries of Eastern Europe and the former USSR, Latin America, and Asia. In this context, the Middle Eastern countries increasingly risk being the laggards in a process of greater global competition for development finance resources—all the more so if account is taken of the emergence and consolidation of regional trading arrangements in Latin America (including the North American free trade agreement currently under negotiation) and Europe.

Against this background the present chapter provides an overview discussion of the economic costs of the Arab-Israeli conflict and the possible longer-term impact on the region's economies of a comprehensive and durable peace—thereby establishing an analytical framework for the country-specific companion chapters in the volume. While most of the analysis is directly relevant for the so-called front-line participants in the conflict, it also has implications for other countries in the region given the potential positive externalities of greater regional economic and financial cooperation.

The chapter is organized as follows: After the introduction, the second section specifies two key parameters of the analysis—the nature of the peace process and the enabling economic, financial, and structural reform policy environment. The third section provides summary indicators of the economic costs of the protracted conflict, focusing both on national and regional factors. This provides the basis for an analysis of the channels through which a possible peace in the region can favorably affect economic welfare. While this analysis is accompanied by some discussion of the potential sequencing and timing of the incidence of the peace benefits, it focuses essentially on the longer-term impact of peace rather than on the issues that arise in the transition to peace. The final section summarizes the key findings of the chapter.

Key Parameters for Analyzing the Implications of Peace

At the outset it is important to emphasize two key parameters of any analysis of the possible impact of peace on the economies of the Middle East. First, to have a lasting economic impact the resolution of the conflict must entail a real, durable, and comprehensive peace. This is by no means an easy task. It is assumed herein that the peace would be real in the sense that all parties would make the decision not to resort to arms in the settlement of their disputes. It would be durable in the sense that an effective security arrangement, acceptable to all parties concerned, would make it very difficult for any single one of them, or a combination of them, to break the peace compact. Finally, it is assumed that peace would be comprehensive in that it settles all outstanding problems in a manner that addresses the legitimate aspirations of all parties to the conflict—notably the Palestinian people, as well as border issues between Israel on the one hand and Lebanon, Jordan, and Syria on the other.

The second key parameter relates to the stance of economic, financial, and structural reform policies. The resolution of the conflict constitutes a necessary but not sufficient condition for full exploitation of the region's development potential. Past repeated attempts at achieving continued economic growth have also been frustrated by inappropriate policies in individual countries, as well as by adverse exogenous shocks (e.g., sharp fluctuations in oil prices, other adverse terms of trade developments, protectionism in industrial countries, etc.). Accordingly, for the potential economic benefits of peace to be fully realized the resolution of the conflict would need to be supported by the sustained implementation of policies aimed at eliminating domestic financial imbalances, improving the pricing structure of the economies, and enhancing their supply responsiveness through fundamental structural reforms in the areas of, inter alia, trade liberalization, divestiture of public sector enterprises, financial liberalization, and deregulation of domestic economic activities. At the same time the incentive for policy reforms may increase with the advent of peace, reflecting the scope for a shift in policy emphasis away from resolving a long-standing source of regional instability.

The Economic Costs of the Arab-Israeli Conflict

In addition to its considerable human losses, the conflict has entailed significant economic costs for countries in the Middle East region. Most evident is the opportunity cost of devoting scarce resources to military expenditures. Other significant costs at the country level include disincentive effects on foreign direct and portfolio investment inflows, the failure to exploit fully the countries' production and tourism potential, and the significant risk premia facing external lenders with adverse implications for the countries' access to financial markets. Overall, therefore, the conflict has imposed significant resource requirements on those countries while limiting their potential for mobilizing such resources. This has been compounded by regionwide inefficiencies including inappropriate specialization among factors of production, welfare losses in terms of inefficient trade and financial arrangements, and the slow development of important infrastructure programs.

The following sections discuss in greater detail these interrelated factors, which as noted earlier also reflect the failure to sustain the implementation of sound economic and financial policies. Given the overview nature of this chapter, no attempt is made to quantify in a comprehensive manner the costs of the conflict—nor, in the next section that discusses the benefits of its resolution—at the level of the individual parties to the conflict.

Direct Resource Costs of Military Expenditures

A significant portion of the resources allocated to the military may be viewed as the main direct, but by no means sole, cost of providing defense in a conflict-ridden region. Accordingly, a discussion of the cost of the Arab-Israeli conflict must start with a quantitative analysis of military expenditures by the countries in the region—albeit a partial analysis given the difficulties faced in reliably identifying all components of military expenditures.[1]

The amount of resources that Middle Eastern countries have devoted to military expenditures is, by any measure, substantial. The region as a whole has been shown to account for the highest relative allocation of resources to military expenditures among all developing-country regions.[2] For the period 1972–88, military expenditures (excluding expenditures funded by foreign assistance),[3] accounted for 10.1% of GDP, almost twice the average of 5.3% for developing countries as a group.[4] Moreover, the share of the region's military outlays in total world military expenditures has increased from an average of 5.9% in 1972–79 to 8.0% in 1980–88, the latter accounting for 40% of the developing-country share.[5]

By excluding military purchases financed by foreign aid—a particularly important factor in Egypt and Israel—the above estimates provide only a partial picture of the total resources devoted to military outlays. Thus, when account is taken of foreign-funded equipment purchases, the share of the region's outlays in total world military expenditures increases to an estimated 9.1% (43% of the developing country share). At the individual country level, Middle Eastern countries represent ten of the eleven countries accounting for the highest military expenditures relative to GDP in 1972–88. Military expenditures also account for a substantial share of the Middle East's total imports and budgetary outlays. Arms and related products represented 15.4% of the region's total imports in 1980–88 (up from 13.3% in 1972–79) and 40% of total world military imports.[6] Although the ratio has declined somewhat in recent years, budgetary military outlays (excluding aid-funded expenditures) accounted for 21.0% of total central government expenditures in 1980–88, compared to a world average of 15.6%. Some Middle Eastern countries have been shown to spend more on the military than on civilian capital formation, food, or housing.[7]

These documented expenditures represent substantial claims on the region's resources.[8] Several countries in the region—including Egypt, Israel, Jordan, and Syria—have experienced difficult budgetary situations, with the central government fiscal deficits for the region as a whole averaging some 8% of GDP in the last decade; this constitutes the highest of any developing-country region and is some 4% above the average for all developing countries.[9] While the magnitudes differ in specific country cases, the financing of these deficits has been associated with a sharp increase in the region's external indebtedness, with total debt increasing from 35% of exports of goods and services in 1981 to an estimated 113% in 1991. Consequently, debt servicing burdens have increased significantly, as reflected in a doubling of the debt service ratio. At the same time, with relatively narrow domestic capital markets, the domestic financing of the budget has often exacerbated inflationary and foreign exchange pressures in some of the countries.

Indirect Costs of the Conflict

Domestic Investment

The public sector's financing requirements have also adversely affected the productive investment activities of the private sector. Increased effective taxation—either directly or through the inflation mechanism—has lowered expected returns on domestic investments. Attempts by some countries to impose below-market domestic interest rates, partly as a means of lowering the cost of budgetary financing, have tended to discourage domestic savings in local currency-denominated instruments, and to exacerbate resource misallocation. This has aggravated the impact of high-risk premia associated with regional tension because of the conflict. The overall result has been a low domestic savings effort. Moreover, the growing share of domestic savings held internally in foreign-exchange instruments in some of the region's economies[10] has been accompanied by large amounts of private sector resources being devoted to capital flight and consumption.

The heightened perceptions of risks, although not the sole cause, have also adversely affected the region's ability to attract external savings on a voluntary basis. Recent aggregate estimates suggest that foreign direct investment inflows for Egypt, Jordan, Israel, and Syria averaged only 1% of their combined GDP in the 1980s.[11] Moreover, such inflows have fallen quickly in response to an intensification of tensions in the region. Thus, the significant increase in inflows (to some 2.5% of GDP) immediately after the Camp David accords between Egypt and Israel was not sustained, with the deterioration in risk perceptions following the Israeli invasion of Lebanon in 1982 associated with a sharp decline (to 0.5% of GDP). The subsequent gradual recovery over the next four years was reversed in the context of concern about regional instability associated with the series of hijackings and security threats.

Perceptions of substantial risk premia have also adversely affected the countries' ability to mobilize other forms of private external financing on reasonable terms. Thus, unlike other developing-country regions, the sharp increase in the region's indebtedness primarily reflected borrowing from official bilateral creditors. Most frontline states have had limited, if any, access to voluntary medium-term private external credits. In the specific case of Israel, geopolitical risks were cited by Standard and Poor's as the main factor in the affirmation in June 1989 of a low-investment grade rating (BBB–) to the country's sovereign debt.

Foreign-Exchange Earnings

The regional instability has also undermined several countries' foreign exchange receipts from current external transactions. Thus, some questions have arisen about the stability of long-term trade contracts. This has been compounded by the debt service requirements on loans used to finance military imports.[12] More evident is the volatility in tourism-related receipts as a result of their sensitivity to regional political instability.

Travel receipts for Egypt, Israel, Jordan, and Syria have been extremely sensitive to variations in the level of regional tension. As was the case for inflows of foreign direct investment, the 8% real increase in travel earnings following the Camp David accords was not sustained, with a sharp fall occurring in 1982 (14% in real terms), concurrent with Israel's invasion of Lebanon.[13] The subsequent recovery was also halted by the heightened regional uncertainties associated with the intensification of hijacking activities. Finally, the Iraqi invasion of Kuwait in August 1990 and associated concerns about an enlargement of hostilities were reflected in a sharp decline in earnings, which is estimated at some 22% in real terms for the year as a whole relative to the 1989 level.

Trade and Other Regional Relations

Despite obvious resource complementarities among countries in the region, intraregional trade accounts for a small portion of their external trading activity. Thus, such flows accounted for only 6% of the region's total trade in 1984–89, declining to under 5% in 1990; the latter represents the lowest ratio of intraregional trade among all regions, including Africa.[14] Moreover, a significant portion of the limited intraregional trade that has taken place consists of crude oil. These findings are valid also for the trade conducted between Egypt and Israel following the signing of the Camp David accords.

Limitations on intraregional trade are but one reflection of the welfare-diminishing elements related to the conflict in the Middle East. They have been accompanied by efficiency losses stemming from the inappropriate allocation of factors of production at the regional level. Moreover, the conflict has contributed to slowing, if not halting, progress on important regional infrastructure projects such as management of scarce water resources, electricity, and energy grid networking and in integrating financial relations. More generally, even moderate attempts at multilateral integration among Arab countries in the region have been largely ineffective.[15] This reflects not only political circumstances in the region but also the fact that the prospects for effective economic integration have been undermined by a lack of harmonization of macroeconomic policies and structures among countries.

Potential Gains from a Comprehensive Peace

In addition to permitting a simultaneous cross-country reduction in military expenditures, a comprehensive and durable Arab-Israeli peace would involve significant externality-related gains. The key factors determining the economic gains from peace will be the pattern of reallocation of military expenditures; the supportive impact of larger private sector investment and other growth-inducing activities;

the response of external savings; and progress toward the regional harmonization of growth-oriented economic, financial, and structural policies. As noted earlier, critical enabling factors include the sustained implementation of sound economic and financial policies in individual countries, as well as the equitable sharing of peace dividends among the affected parties.[16] Indeed, these factors themselves constitute important challenges for policymakers, with differing importance among countries in the region. While the subsequent analysis addresses the longer-term benefits of peace, this should not detract attention from the important issues that arise in the process of transition to peace. As is the case for any fundamental structural change, the transition to peace will entail domestic economic costs for some segments of population in countries in the region. Accordingly, consideration would need to be given as how best to alleviate these costs, lest they serve to frustrate the achievement of the substantial longer-term benefits of a comprehensive peace.

Some Aggregate Indicators

Several analyses have been undertaken seeking to quantify the potential impact of peace in the Middle East. The results of a research program on economic cooperation in the Middle East, for example, suggest that had peace been implemented in the early 1980s, GNP ten years later would be considerably higher—some 24% for Egypt, Jordan, Lebanon, and Syria, and 22% higher for Israel—as compared to a situation of continued conflict.[17] This would be reflected in higher per capita private consumptions levels (15%–18%) and investment levels (52%–55%).

Caution is required in interpreting the results of such studies, however. The resolution of the conflict through a durable and comprehensive peace will involve important and fundamental changes in the region's structural relationships. Projections based on historical relationships provide only a limited insight into actual prospects. Moreover, the detailed aspects of the peace process itself, including its implementation format and timetable, are subject to considerable uncertainty. Accordingly, given the perspective of the companion chapters in this volume, the following sections focus on the channels through which peace may lead to substantial economic gains, rather than attempt a quantification of these gains.

The Economic Impact of Reallocating a Share of the Resources Devoted to Military Expenditures

Peace can be viewed as a form of "technological progress" that would enable the countries in the Middle East to produce the same quantity of output (in this case, national security) with fewer resources. For example, it may be estimated that Middle Eastern countries would save in the range of some U.S. $30 billion per year were their military expenditures (relative to GDP) reduced to the world average. The realization of such savings will depend in part on developing an effective mechanism for measuring military expenditures and determining the magnitude and timing of a regionally coordinated expenditure reduction effort.[18] While savings from this source would support increased public sector spending on key infrastructural and social activities, the bulk of the freed resources would also allow for larger private sector investment in productive capital. Under appropriately designed macroeconomic and structural reform programs, this would be achieved concurrent with a reduction in inflationary and foreign exchange pressures.

The growth impact of reallocating military expenditures would increase to the extent that countries in the Middle East have access, on appropriate terms, to external financial assistance previously tied to military expenditures. Such assistance, if made available by creditor countries and if allocated to productive uses, would relax binding foreign-exchange constraints while generating returns well in excess of their debt servicing costs. Appropriately designed mechanisms for foreign assistance would also facilitate the implementation of economic and financial reform policies. As yet, major creditor countries to the region have not indicated their intentions to continue providing the same level of external assistance outside military programs.[19] Indeed, the question on the reallocation of aid among nonmilitary uses in the Middle East also concerns the extent to which the previously tied resources would be channeled to different groups of recipients, including in other developing countries and within the creditor countries themselves.

An analysis of the gains from a reallocation of military expenditures must also take into account the elimination of possible beneficial spillover effects associated with such expenditures. Some countries in the region, notably Egypt and Israel, have built up a significant arms manufacturing industry with the aim of reducing external dependency, particularly in the event of emergencies, and of exploiting external markets. In addition to the employment opportunities, this industry is thus an important source of foreign-exchange earnings.

The literature identifies four main growth-inducing elements of military expenditures:[20] (1) increased aggregate demand for locally produced military components; (2) the potential for increased civilian productivity as a result of the provision of public infrastructure by the military; (3) enhancing civilian output through military training; and (4) the civilian application of research and development activities of the military.[21]

In assessing these factors it must be recognized that, through an appropriate reallocation of resources devoted to military expenditures, the majority of the growth benefits (including through employment and larger foreign-exchange receipts) attributed to the military may be achieved more efficiently with a program that directly sets out to do so. This is particularly the case for outlays on public infrastructure and civilian training. This consideration is reinforced by the limited growth-inducing externalities that result from the pattern of expenditures in the Middle East. As documented earlier, imports account for a significant share of military purchases.[22] This reduces the positive impact of domestic military expenditures on component production. Moreover, since the major portion of the research and development activities is conducted outside the region, the beneficial impact on civilian activities would be quite limited, even if direct applicability is assumed.

Other Potential Benefits at the Country Level

In the previous section the benefits of peace resulted from the potential reduction in the cost of providing national security. Although the most obvious form of benefit, it may not be the most important. More significant is the impact in terms of new opportunities for trade, financial, and labor flows that did not exist prior to the advent of peace. These changes augment the amount of resources available to the countries concerned, as distinct from a simple reallocation. In particular, the resolution of the conflict has the potential to enhance these countries' ability to expand domestic production supported by the repatriation of residents' flight capital, attracting foreign direct and portfolio investment, and strengthening the earning stream from exports of goods and services. There would nevertheless be dislocations in some areas of the economy closely linked to military activities, but their costs would be small when compared to the potential benefits accruing from peace.

A comprehensive and durable peace would contribute to a major reduction in private sector perceptions of credit and country transfer risks. Together with the sustained implementation of sound economic and financial policies, this would result in higher expected returns on domestic investment activities, which in turn would stimulate inflows of foreign direct and portfolio investment. It should be noted, however, that consistent with the experience of other developing countries, the magnitude of such inflows is unlikely to be large relative to receipts of external financial assistance, particularly in the early phases of economic and financial reform.[23] The reduction in transfer risk would also, ceteris paribus, reduce the constraints faced by several countries in mobilizing significant amounts of unsecured credits on international capital markets (i.e., international bond and bank loan financing). Accordingly, these countries would face lower financing costs concurrent with the improvement in their ability to generate satisfactory returns on debt-financed activities.

The improved prospects for the capital account of the balance of payments would be accompanied by a more favorable outlook for the current account. This would result primarily from higher sustained receipts from travel and other tourism-related activities, as well as from larger unrequited transfers, accompanied by prospects for larger exports of goods and other services over the medium term.[24] In effect, the higher domestic investment would enhance the region's production of tradables, allowing for a reversal in the chronic deterioration in the nonoil trade balance of most countries in the Middle East. The prospects for such a reversal would be enhanced by a more efficient allocation of existing factors of production.

Regional Dimension

As noted earlier, the Middle East is characterized by significant complementarities in factor endowments. These relate not only to the relative importance of capital and labor but also to differences within these resource groupings—thereby providing, along with the size of the area's market, a large potential for welfare gains from a greater degree of regional integration.

On the Arab side, some countries are well advanced on the path of industrialization. Others are at earlier levels, while the oil-exporting countries of the Gulf constitute a unique category. Israel stands at a higher level of industrialization. Despite the obvious potential for intraregional activities, the present pattern of regional factor allocation has evolved over the years on the reality of virtually no trade or financial links between the Arab countries and Israel. A major contribution of peace would thus be to allow countries to reap efficiency gains through greater economies of scale, specialization, and competition—with more effective regional harmonization of economic relations supporting, rather than substituting for, greater integration with the international economy.

Joint Production and Trade

The impact of a general improvement in the environment for investment activities would be reinforced by opportunities for joint production, particularly in the areas of agriculture, agro-industries, and manufacturing industry. The scope for sectoral cooperation between parties to the conflict has been the subject of a number of studies.[25] Such cooperation may take the form initially of subcontracting arrangements, to be followed by joint ventures and direct investments. In the case of Israel and Egypt, for example, studies have pointed to significant production complementarities in the clothing industry. Taking advantage of these complementarities would lower production costs, allowing producers to capture a larger market share both within and outside the Middle East. One aim, for example, would be to capitalize on the competitive advantage of Egypt (cotton, yarn, sewing, and other labor-intensive processes) and Israel (design, printing, and marketing).[26] Other identified industries providing scope for welfare-gaining cooperation include fertilizers and cement.

With regard to trade, the early stages of a peace era would be dominated by those products and services in which each side enjoys an overwhelming comparative advantage. On the Israeli side this may include high value-added agricultural and relatively capital-intensive light manufacturing products, while on the Arab side the emphasis would be on food products, oil and other raw materials, and labor-intensive manufacturing goods.

The above considerations are reinforced by the proximity factor. Geographical distances between parties to the conflict are small, especially when compared to the extraregional suppliers and markets. This reduces transport costs in both joint production and trade, enhancing the prospects for welfare gains from greater regional integration.

Regional Infrastructure

The development of countries in the Middle East would also benefit from the implementation of key regional infrastructure projects, including water management programs, electric power grids, networks of gas and petroleum pipelines, improved road port, and rail access, and regional tourism activities. Such projects could be financed to a significant extent by intraregional foreign direct investment flows. The issue that has attracted the most attention in this regard is that of water management programs, namely the importance of an agreement on how to enhance and share currently dwindling water resources. Competing claims on limited water supplies are considered by many observers as a major destabilizing factor in a traditionally arid/semiarid area. In this context, regional projects provide a channel for alleviating associated pressures, with the key being the development of an appropriately designed multiparty exchange of water.[27]

With regard to energy, pooling mechanisms (e.g., power transmission grids) linking the individual networks of parties to the conflict would allow those countries to meet their electricity requirements more efficiently while exploiting variations in peak demand periods among these countries. The establishment of peace would also allow for the expansion of the region's oil pipeline network, providing, for example, greater conveyance systems to the Mediterranean for those countries with no direct access. At the same time other forms of land transportation—which would become possible as border tensions decline—would lower transportation costs for several products. Finally, the region would be in a position to attract larger tourist inflows as a result of possibilities to "package" several countries in one tour.

Sequencing of Integration

Notwithstanding the considerable potential for dynamic intraregional benefits, it should be recognized that the associated economic and structural transformation would not occur overnight. It is more realistic to envisage a scenario of gradual growth of commercial and financial ties over a period of time during which the two sides will learn to know each other better, become familiar with existing institutional structures and regulations, and more important, overcome long years of hostility, suspicion, and violence. For this reason the benefits of peace at the intraregional level might pass through three successive stages.

In the first stage after the establishment of a comprehensive peace, economic relations are likely to consist primarily of ad hoc commercial transactions. At the beginning they would be exploratory, tentative, and perhaps intermittent. But they will pave the way for more intensive and sustained interactions. The second stage would witness the emergence of normal and systematic trade relations together with institutionalized financial links. The third and final stage would see significant progress in the harmonization of institutional structures in support of a normal and full system of commercial, financial, and technological relations. The length of time required to reach this third stage is difficult to determine, because there are many imponderables that come into play. On the assumptions that peace would take root quickly and that goodwill gestures from both sides would not be rare and far between, peace could come to fruition within a relatively short period of time. Indeed, the process may be strengthened in its initial phases by efforts to implement regional projects, also supported by countries outside the region.

Role of Foreign Financial Assistance

A significant portion of the region's military expenditures has been financed through foreign aid. As noted earlier, the reallocation of such aid to productive uses within the Middle East could contribute to the economic and social development of countries in the region, including by encouraging the implementation of far-reaching structural reform policies. As in other cases, financial assistance to countries in the Middle East should seek not to substitute for, but rather to facilitate, the sustained implementation of sound economic policies. Moreover, it should be consistent with a gradual replacement of official assistance by private sector capital inflows, primarily in the form of foreign direct and portfolio investments and capital repatriation. The specification of the terms on official financial assistance would involve crafting a careful balance between project, sector, and general balance-of-payments loans. All loans would be provided on terms consistent both with the financing requirements for high-yielding investments and with the debt servicing capacity of the recipients. The amounts and terms of financial support would need to be tailored to the diverse circumstances of individual recipient countries and be supplemented by the provision of technical assistance, as needed.[28]

In addition to the magnitude and terms of such assistance, a key issue relates to the most effective institutional mechanisms for mobilizing and allocating external flows in support of a comprehensive economic and structural transformation process; as well as the extent to which these mechanisms may be used for improved regional harmonization of economic, structural reform, and financial policies. There has been a wide range of proposals in this area including the establishment of a Middle Eastern "Marshall Plan,"[29] the creation of a regional development bank (similar to the recently created European Bank for Reconstruction and Development),[30] and the strengthening of existing regional institutions (such as the Arab Fund for Economic and Social Development and the Arab Monetary Fund). Each of these proposals has its benefits as well as its limitations, and would need to be considered in-depth in light, inter alia, of the evolution of political considerations. Accordingly, this section is limited to identifying the main factors to be evaluated.

Reliance on existing regional institutions provides a readily available vehicle for intermediating financial assistance, while drawing on the considerable accumulated regional expertise within these institutions. At the same time, however, the structure of these institutions would need to be modified to encompass a larger group of donors and recipients, as well as to strengthen the operational procedures. The creation of a new regional institution—a Middle East Bank for Reconstruction and Development (MEBRD)—would allow for a fresh specification of membership and operational procedures in line with the new conditions in the region. Indeed, the Middle East is currently the only developing-country region without a multilateral development bank able to mobilize substantial resources and channel them to productive use through project and program lending. The Arab Fund for Economic and Social Development is the nearest approximation to this concept. But there are a number of important differences, including the limited membership and the fact that this institution does not act as a financial intermediary between international capital markets and productive investment opportunities in the region. It would also provide an important early basis for mechanisms for countries in the region to work together, as well as for broader multilateral support for regional projects. A new institution with such intermediation ability would facilitate the mobilization of private capital in support of the development of the region.

While offering benefits, the establishment of an MEBRD would likely be a protracted process. It would involve substantial overhead costs and political maneuvering, and come at a time of increasing constraints on the budgets of the potential large shareholders of such an institution. The establishment and operation of the MEBRD would also require close coordination with existing institutions to avoid undue duplication. Therefore, interim and more flexible instruments may be needed pending the clarification, inter alia, of the political and institutional conditions. Such an interim mechanism would allow for immediate visible support for the peace process from outside the region, while leaving the option open for the establishment of more formal mechanisms over time, as appropriate.

One possible option would be the establishment of a mechanism under which major creditors would coordinate their provision of financial assistance in support of the region's economic reform efforts. Such a mechanism—which could draw upon the lessons from the experiences of the Special Program of Assistance for Africa—would allow for the monitoring of the mobilization and allocation of aid through periodic creditor/recipient meetings and a more regular comprehensive reporting system. It would complement assistance available through existing international financial institutions (e.g., the International Monetary Fund and the World Bank). These institutions provide a readily available multilateral framework with well-established practices and procedures, including a wide and flexible set of financing instruments in support of economic reforms in the region.

Concluding Remarks

The protracted Arab-Israeli conflict has imposed enormous human, economic, and political costs on the countries in the Middle East. Its resolution—through a real, durable, and comprehensive peace—constitutes a necessary, though not sufficient, condition for exploiting the considerable economic potential of countries in the region. This chapter has argued that the potential benefits of peace stem from an array of factors of both national and regional dimensions. The most obvious and direct benefit would accrue from the possibility of reallocating some of the resources currently devoted to national security. Perhaps more important, however, are the dynamic benefits emanating from the improved sociopolitical environment. Within the participants' borders this would allow for increased investment opportunities, financed through greater domestic and external savings. Given the obvious complementarities in the factor endowment of these participants, as well as the size of an integrated market, the resulting benefits would be reinforced by the realization of a more appropriate allocation of factors of production at the regional level, together with more efficient trade and financial arrangements. The latter would include strengthening the intermediation process that allows funding from international capital markets to be channeled to productive investment opportunities in the Middle East.

While the potential benefits of peace are substantial, their realization constitutes a difficult challenge given the array of obstacles to overcome. The nature of peace is critical in that it must meet the legitimate aspirations of all parties to the conflict and be supported by effective enforcement mechanisms acceptable to these parties. Moreover, as is the case for any fundamental structural change, the transition to peace will entail costs to some segments of population in Middle Eastern countries, the alleviation of which is an important element in facilitating the achievement of a comprehensive and durable peace. To translate into and be reinforced by an enduring economic improvement, peace must be accompanied by the sustained implementation of sound economic, financial, and structural reform policies. Finally, given the long years of hostility, suspicion, and mistrust, the associated economic transformation induced by the resolution of the conflict will take some time before it comes to full fruition.

Notes

The views expressed in the chapter are those of the authors and do not necessarily represent those of the institutions with which they are affiliated.

1. The estimation of the budgetary, trade, and external debt implications of military spending is hampered by a lack of transparency and comprehensiveness in the data reported by individual countries. For example, Berglas (1986) points to factors that result in a true cost of Israeli military spending that is 50% above the budget level.

2. Estimates reported in Hewitt (1991b), based on data compiled by the Stockholm International Peace Research Institute (SIPRI).

3. As noted in Hewitt (1991b), SIPRI follows the NATO convention of including military aid to other nations in the military outlays of the creditor/donor country. Accordingly, the data reported for developing countries do not include expenditures financed by foreign aid.

4. These reported military expenditures cover total government outlays and, in addition to excluding military aid receipts from other nations, also omit, to the extent possible, items that are civilian in nature.

5. A discussion of intertemporal trends is contained in Sheffer (1989).

6. A recent study by Brzoska (1990) shows that reductions in military imports have tended to lag a decline in other imports induced by financing constraints. Other studies analyzing the sensitivity of military spending in developing countries to overall budgetary and foreign-exchange constraints include De Masi and Lorie (1989) and Hewitt (1991a). A more general analysis of the high-priority designation attributed by developing countries to military outlays is contained in McKinley (1989).

7. Hewitt (1991b).

8. In addition to data limitations, several considerations suggest that the overall cost of the military establishment, as measured by the opportunity cost of the resources, would be greater than indicated by direct budgetary estimates.

9. Based on data contained in IMF (1991a). The median estimate for the Middle East averaged 11% during this period, compared to 5% for all developing countries.

10. Quantitative indicators of the growth in currency substitution in Egypt may be found in El-Erian (1988).

11. Estimates derived on the basis of data contained in IMF (1990, 1991a).

12. Recently, the United States forgave almost U.S. $7 billion of Egypt's military debt.

13. Annual estimates derived on the basis of data contained in IMF (1990). As documented in Meital (1989), this is also true for tourist activity between Egypt and Israel. Thus, the number of visitors in 1981 between the two countries (principally, Israeli nationals visiting Egypt) was double that of the preceding year. It rose further in the first half of 1982 but declined thereafter in the context of increased tensions associated with the Israeli invasion of Lebanon.

14. Estimates derived from IMF (1991b). It should be noted that the aggregate estimates conceal a great deal of variations at the country level.

15. See papers in Gueciqueur (1984), as well as Benchenane (1983), El-Mallakh et al. (1977), and Weiss (1985).

16. The latter issue is developed further in Arad, Hirsch, and Tovias (1983), who introduce the concept of "vested interest in peace" (VIUP). They argue

that the economic underpinning of a viable peace would involve improving the economic welfare of all participants in the process, while at the same time increasing (or leaving unchanged) VIP *within* the individual groups. At the country level there is likely to be a certain asymmetry in the benefits that would accrue to Israel on the one hand and to the Arab countries on the other. In economic terms a real, durable, and comprehensive peace would appear to carry greater benefits for Israel: it would provide it with access to the large Arab market, as well as consolidate the removal of the boycott, which adversely affects the operations in Arab countries of third-party companies with large Israeli-related activities.

17. Ben-Shahar (1989). Additional information on the comparative quantitative analysis of the impact of peace on Egypt, Israel, Jordan, Lebanon, Syria, and the economy of the West Bank is contained in chapter 3 of Ben-Shahar et al. (1989).

18. As noted earlier the extent of the reduction in military expenditures will depend in part on the nature of the peace, including the extent to which it is supported by an effective security arrangement. Other determinants include the prospects for a reduction in other sources of regional tension and the pressure imposed by industrial countries for reducing military expenditures.

19. There have been several suggestions to tie aid to the Middle East to a reduction in military expenditures. See, for example, McNamara (1991).

20. See, for example, Deger and Smith (1983), Frederiksen and Looney (1982), and McKenley (1989). The issue of military spillovers among alliance countries is discussed in Gonzalez and Mehay (1990), who also assess the scope for economies of scale to national defense.

21. This argument was cited by European countries in justifying subsidies to the Airbus project to compensate for benefits accruing to competing U.S. manufacturers on account of defense-related activities.

22. It has been estimated by Sheffer (1989), for example, that 36% of Israel's total defense outlays in 1984 were spent abroad.

23. For developing countries as a whole, inflows of foreign direct investment were equivalent to around a quarter of these countries' receipt of official transfers and net external loans in 1988–90 (IMF [1991a]).

24. Within this overall tendency, there may be some decline in certain types of foreign exchange inflows including, for example, transfers made by the Jewish Diaspora because of security threats.

25. See, for example, Arad, Hirsch, and Tovias (1983) and Hirsch (1989). An overview is provided in Fishelson (1989).

26. See Hirsch (1989).

27. The scope for cooperative water projects is discussed in Kally (1989) and Rossant (1989). See also chapter 3 in Ben-Shahar et al. (1989).

28. In addition to financial support and facilitating the transfer of technology to the Middle East, countries outside the region may contribute to the process by providing improved and nondiscriminatory access to their markets.

29. See, for example, Starr (1989).

30. Including the recent proposal by U.S. secretary of state Baker. An earlier proposal for a Middle East Development Fund is set out in Gafny (1989).

References

Arad, Ruth, Seev Hirsch, and Alfred Tovias (1983), *The Economics of Peace-Making: Focus on the Egyptian-Israeli Situation,* Macmillan Press, London.

Benchenane, Mustapha (1983), "L'Integration economique arabe," *Revue Tiers Monde,* Oct.–Dec.

Ben-Porath, Yoram (ed.) (1986), *The Israeli Economy,* Harvard University Press, Cambridge.

Ben-Shahar, Haim (1989), "Economic Cooperation in the Middle East: From Dream to Reality," in Fishelson (ed.).

Ben-Shahar, Haim et al. (ed.) (1989), *Economic Cooperation and Middle East Peace,* Weidenfeld and Nicolson, London.

Berglas, Eitan (1986), "Defense and the Economy," in Ben Porath (ed.).

Brzoska, M. (1990), "Military Trade, Aid and Developing Country Debt," Mimeograph.

Deger, Saadat, and Ron Smith (1983), Military Expenditure and Growth in Less Developed Countries," *Journal of Conflict Resolution,* vol. 27, no.2, June.

Deger, Saadat, and Somnath Sen (1990), *Military Expenditures: The Political Economy of National Security,* Oxford University Press, Oxford.

De Masi, Paula, and Henri Lorie (1989), "How Resilient Are Military Expenditures," *Staff Papers,* vol. 36, no. 1.

El-Erian, Mohamed A. (1988), "Currency Substitution in Egypt and the Yemen Arab Republic," *Staff Papers,* vol. 35, no. 1.

El-Mallakh, Ragaei et al. (1977), *Capital Investment in the Middle East: The Use of Surplus Funds for Regional Development,* Praeger Publishers, New York, New York.

Fishelson, Gideon (ed.) (1989), *Economic Cooperation in the Middle East,* Westview Press, Boulder, Colorado.

Fishelson, Gideon (1989), "Key Findings of the Middle East Economic Cooperation Projects," in Fishelson (ed.).

Frederiksen, Peter, and Robert Looney (1982), "Defense Expenditures and

Economic Growth in Developing Countries: Some Further Empirical Evidence," *Journal of Economic Development*, July.

Gafney, Arnon (1989), "The Middle East Development Fund," in Fishelson (ed.).

Gonzalez, Rondolfo, and Stephen Mehay (1990). "Publicness, Scale, and Spillover Effects in Defense Spending," *Public Finance Quarterly*, July.

Guecìqueur, Adda (ed.) (1984), *The Problems of Arab Economic Development and Integration*, Westview Press, Boulder, Colorado.

Hewitt, Daniel P. (1991a), "Military Expenditure: Econometric Testing of Economic and Political Influences," *IMF Working Paper*, WP/91/53, May.

Hewitt, Daniel P. (1991b), "Military Expenditure: International Comparison of Trends," *IMF Working Paper*, WP/91/54, May.

Hirsch, Seev (1989), "Trade Regimes in the Middle East," in Fishelson (ed.).

International Monetary Fund (1990), *Balance of Payments Yearbook*, IMF, Washington, D.C.

International Monetary Fund (1991a), *World Economic Outlook*, IMF, Washington, D.C.

International Monetary Fund (1991b), *Direction of Trade Yearbook 1991*, IMF, Washington, D.C.

Kally, Elisha (1989), "The Potential for Cooperation in Water Projects in the Middle East at Peace," in Fishelson (ed.).

McKinley, R. D. (1989), *Third World Military Expenditure*, Pinter Publishers, London.

McNamara, Robert S. (1991), "The Post-Cold War World and its Implications for Military Expenditures in Developing Countries," Paper prepared for the World Bank's Annual Conference on Development Economics, Washington, D.C., April 25–26.

Meital, Yoram (1989), "The Economic Relations between Israel and Egypt: Tourism, 1979–84," in Fishelson (ed.).

Rossant, John (1989), "A Proposal for a Cooperative Water Project: The Aqaba-Eilat Canal," in Fishelson (ed.).

Sheffer, Eliezer (1989), "The Economic Burden of the Arms Race in the Middle East," in Fishelson (ed.).

Starr, Joyce R. (1989), "A Marshall Plan for the Middle East," in Fishelson (ed.).

Weiss, Dieter (1985), "European Economic Integration: A Relevant Experience for an Arab Common Market?" *L'Egypte Contemporaine*, July.

9

The Peace Process and Economic Reforms in the Middle East

Ishac Diwan and
Nick Papandreou

The establishment of a Palestinian state, the recognition of Israel by its Arab neighbors and the ending of their economic boycott, and the development of peaceful relations among the countries of the region would mark the end of an era in modern history, an event no less significant than the end of the cold war. That true peace is in the long-run interests of the region and of the world as a whole cannot be doubted: in addition to the tragedy of the Palestinian people, Arab-Israeli wars in 1948, 1967, 1973, and 1982 have led to massive destruction and casualties, and have threatened the world with nuclear warfare on several occasions. Emerging from centuries of Ottoman occupation and European interference, the situation created by the occupation of Arab land—at a time when the rest of the third world was busy decolonizing—has had a profound effect on the formation and organization of the young Arab states, and on their political aspirations. Israeli society has also paid a high price, since one consequence of continued instability in the region is in the militarization of its culture and the emergence of what could be characterized as a war economy, with a large share of output accounted for by defense-related activity.

Large economic benefits could potentially be reaped by all countries of the region in a postpeace environment. These advantages would stem from the reductions of military expenditure, reduction in investment risk increased cooperation in the areas of trade, labor mobility, water management, and tourism, and from the dynamic gains of an enlarged sphere of economic activity that a decrease in regional instability would promote. A virtuous circle may come about, as stability will generally reinforce economic integration within the region as much as it will itself be reinforced by increased intra-regional economic relations.

While peace will create an environment that is conducive to substantial long-term benefits, only countries that are able to adjust their policies to the new realities will partake of these benefits. In the short term, however, the needed adjustment measures will be costly, and the benefits will come gradually. For example, the reduced security need calls for a redirecting of resources away from the military and toward more productive sectors. However, demobilizing large armies is likely to create unemployment and disturb economic activity in the short term.

In this chapter we ask whether the countries of the region are likely to rapidly undertake the needed adjustment measures. Such an examination is useful for assessing the impact of peace on future growth prospects, because the potential economic benefits will in most cases arise only in the aftermath of specific policy actions. We proceed by looking at past experiences with economic reforms, trying to understand their main characteristics as they relate to the economic and political environment of the time, and attempt to project this experience onto the likely postpeace environment. What emerges from this analysis is that (1) the aid and capital inflows of the past have led to policy preferences that ignored development goals; (2) growth prospects have been severely dampened by the economic crisis unfolding in the region since the mid-1980s and exacerbated by the recent Gulf war, and by the unwillingness of governments to implement much-needed economic adjustments and reforms; (3) the peace process will affect in many ways the old socioeconomic tradeoffs, creating new challenges and new growth opportunities for the countries that can adjust their policies to the new realities. In particular, a reduction in geopolitical instability is expected to (i) improve the supply response to economic incentives, (ii) improve governments' ability to undertake serious reform, since governments will now be able to afford a greater level of domestic instability as compared to what would be feasible within an unstable regional environment, (iii) make possible greater regional cooperation, and (iv) make lending for reform on a conditional basis viable. Finally (4), there are two major sources of risk to serious reform and regional peace. The first is unemployment in the region, a problem compounded by the return of expatriate labor and, in Israel's case, the expected wave of emigrants from the former Soviet Union. The second is the impact of domestic instability resulting from reforms. This instability could be lessened and smoothed through conditional financing, something that is more possible in the postpeace world or even during the ongoing peace process. But overall, it is not possible to tell at the time of this writing (January 1992) whether the postpeace environment will encourage the adoption of adjustment measures.

Over the long term, prosperity, economic growth, and regional integration are at the same time an important vehicle to deepening the peace process and a valuable guarantee of a lasting solution. Given the great need for adjustment finance to smooth the cost of reform and reconstruction over time and make it more attractive, we conclude by stressing the need for the creation of a regional development bank.

From Growth to Crisis

One of the region's outstanding characteristics during the 1970s and early 1980s was the high level of capital inflows, which in turn sustained strong economic growth. A second characteristic was that these inflows were severely reduced in the 1980s, especially after 1985, creating large external and fiscal imbalances that ultimately led to a sharp contraction in economic activity. This section briefly chronicles the expansion of the state as economic agent in the 1970s and the increased macroeconomic disequilibria of the 1980s. We then describe the economic reforms attempted to date and examine the reasons behind the extreme gradualism that has characterized them. While the quality of the data for all the frontline states is dubious, the main focus is on Egypt, Jordan, and Syria; Lebanon's statistics are extremely spotty, and the case of Israel is somewhat different.

Growth in the 1970s

After the Arab-Israeli war of 1967, the frontline Arab states received pledges from the Gulf states for economic aid to support the Arab cause.[1] With the dramatic oil price increase of 1973, the alliance blossomed and economic aid increased dramatically (table 9.1). Arab aid fluctuated with oil revenues as well as other considerations, mostly political. Until the Camp David agreement in 1979, Egypt was the largest recipient of that aid, receiving on average 15% of its GNP during the period 1973–76 (with a peak of \$1.9 billion, or about 23% of GNP in 1975). In 1979 Arab aid to Egypt was completely cut off, but this was amply compensated with bilateral, multilateral, and private loans from the West and especially the United States. Aid to Syria and Jordan steadily increased with Syria and Jordan receiving

Table 9.1
External financing 1973–89 by sources (current $ U.S. billion and percentages)

	1973–76	1977–81	1982–85	1986–89
Total Arab assistance (net loans plus grants, cumulative)				
Egypt	6.1	3.2	−0.1	0.3
Jordan	1.0	4.0	2.6	1.5
Syria	2.0	6.2	2.8	1.4
Lebanon	0.2	0.8	0.1	0
Other official transfers (net loans plus grants, cumulative)				
Egypt	0.9	5.0	6.1	6.4
Jordan	0.4	0.6	0.3	0.6
Syria	0.1	0.3	0.2	0.4
Lebanon	0	0.2	0.2	0.3
Net multilaterals (cumulative) loans (non-Arab sources)				
Egypt	0.3	1.6	1.6	1.4
Jordan	0.1	0.2	0.1	0.4
Syria	0.1	0.4	0.3	0.2
Lebanon	0.1	0.1	0.2	0.1
Private net flows (cumulative)				
Egypt	0.2	2.2	3.0	1.6
Jordan	0.0	0.3	0.9	1.4
Syria	0.2	0.1	0.2	0.1
Lebanon	0	0	0	0
Total financing (cumulative) from all sources (net)				
Egypt	7.5	12.0	10.6	9.8
Jordan	1.5	5.0	3.9	3.9
Syria	2.3	7.0	3.5	2.1
Lebanon	0.2	1.2	0.5	0.4
Total (net) average financing to GNP (in percent)				
Egypt	17.5	13.5	9.6	7.9
Jordan	39.8	38.7	25.7	20.5
Syria	10.1	12.7	5.4	2.4
Lebanon	2.0	6.8	4.1	4.9

Sources: WDT: various issues, van den Boogaerde 1990, and Nowels, Larry, and Jonathan Sandford 1991.
Note: Flows are netted out of principal repayments.

Table 9.2
Growth rates for selected periods, 1973–89

	1960–1973		1973–1980		1980–1988	
	GDP	GDP/POP	GDP	GDP/POP	GDP	GDP/POP
Egypt	5.9	3.5	11.1	8.4	4.3	1.5
Israel	9.2	5.6	3.2	0.8	3.0	1.3
Jordan	4.5	1.4	9.4	6.9	2.8	1.0
Syria	6.9	3.5	13.0	9.2	0.7	−2.8

Source: Summers and Heston, 1991.

Arab assistance averaging about 9% and 30% respectively of their GNP during 1973–79. Jordan was also able to increase its disbursements from these sources. At the same time Arab aid to Syria and Jordan tripled in absolute terms, with Syria receiving about $1.6 billion (about 16% of GNP at the official exchange rate), and Jordan $1.2 billion (about 47% of GNP) in 1979. During the 1970s, U.S. assistance to Israel was also high, fluctuating around $2 billion a year (with the exception of 1979, where it reached $4.9 billion).

The boom period of the 1970s was marked by a large dose of regional instability that to some extent motivated the massive official capital inflow, which in turn allowed for relative stability at home. This period was marked by a rapid growth of the economy, and of the state, because much of the external assistance was channeled directly through the government's budget. During the period 1973–80, real per capita GDP growth averaged 8% in Egypt, 7% in Jordan, over 9% in Syria (table 9.2), and just under 1% in Israel. Lebanon, however, was left behind as its drama unfolded, and output in the early 1980s was lower in real terms than in 1975.

An indication of the government's dependence on external sources of support are these countries' reliance on non-tax revenues for government expenditures. For the frontline states, table 9.3 shows that nontax revenues represented 33% of total current revenue in 1972 and 31% in 1989, while for the less subsidized states of the region (Morocco, Tunisia, and Turkey) the figures are 15% in 1972 and 16% in 1989. These inflows gave governments enormous leeway in economic policy and permitted the evasion of hard development choices. Rather than the emergence of states possessing the "normal" functions of extraction, regulation, and oversight, the period of the 1970s

Table 9.3
Central government current revenue (percentages)

	Income tax revenue		Indirect tax revenue		Nontax revenues		Total revenue to GDP		Other tax revenues	
	1972	1989	1972	1989	1972	1989	1972	1989	1972	1989
Egypt	15	11	36	36	38					
Syria	7	25	10	9	53	47	25	24	29	19
Jordan	9	9	16	16	36	32	23	39	43	
Israel	40	38	20	31	10	15	31	40	30	16
Average	19	24	15	19	33	31	28	29	33	26
Comparators										
Morocco	16	19	46	46	13	8	19	22		
Tunisia	16	13	32	20	16	23	24	32	37	44
Turkey	31	43	31	30	18	18	21	19		
Average	21	25	36	32	15	16	21	24	37	44

Source: World bank: WDR (1991), Table 12 (Central Government Revenue), and van de Boogaerde, 1990 (Table 32).

and early 1980s witnessed the evolution of states based mostly on the distribution of wealth.[2] Yet, unlike their East Asian counterparts and possibly because of a number of other factors (for example, different security needs and larger income and wealth disparities), Middle Eastern governments were not able to align their distributive function to economic performance very effectively. While the regulatory environments did not manage to create an environment conducive to the creation and generation of wealth, the inflow of external aid also must have reduced the domestic demand for economic reforms, both by governments that did not need to rely on taxation to generate income,[3] and by civil society, whose consumption level increased markedly relative to the 1960s.[4] Observers generally agree that, although difficult to quantify, the most important economic impact on the Middle East of the confrontation years has been a marked decline of economic efficiency.

Crisis in the 1980s

The current economic crisis in the region started in the mid and late 1980s, coming hard on the heels of the boom years. By 1985 economic growth had decelerated markedly and income was barely keeping up with population growth. For the whole period 1980–88, real per capita growth averaged only 1.5% in Egypt (turning negative by 1986), 1% in Jordan (turning negative by 1988), and −3% in Syria (table 9.2).

Growth in the 1980s was adversely affected by three main problems. First, there were several adverse developments in the international and regional environment. Starting in 1982, but especially after 1985, the decline of oil revenues had devastating effects throughout the region. To give a sense of the magnitudes involved, note that total Arab oil revenues declined from a high of $213 billion in 1980 to a low of $53 billion in 1986. Egypt and Syria were directly affected as the revenues of their oil export were halved, and Syria and Jordan were indirectly hit by sharp reductions in Arab aid, which by 1986 had dwindled to about 20% of their 1980 levels (table 9.1). Workers' remittances were also reduced, but not by as much.[5] The *intifada* also affected both Jordan and Israel. In Jordan, because of increased tensions, the authorities took steps to sever the country's legal and administrative ties with the West Bank. This led to anxiety among the Palestinians as to their status, and by the end of 1988 capital flight had exhausted Jordan's foreign-exchange reserves. The *intifada* also affected Israel, which has just emerged from a tough stabilization program. Amid increasing uncertainty and depressed tourism, growth remained elusive. In Lebanon the economic decline was deepened after the 1982 Israeli invasion and the ensuing events. By 1989 it was estimated that real GDP was at about one-fifth of its 1975 level. Second, expansionary domestic policies, in particular large budget deficits, led to prolonged and significant excesses of aggregate demand for resources relative to resources available internally or obtainable from abroad on a sustainable basis. In Egypt the government deficit remained at around 20% of GNP throughout the 1980s, in Jordan the deficit shot up to 19% of GNP by 1985 and to 23% in 1987, and in Syria it hovered around 18%–20% of GDP in 1984–85.

Third, as foreign net resources dwindled, governments turned increasingly to financial repression, monetization, and import restrictions. This added to the inefficiencies in resource allocation attributable to an inappropriate system of government incentives and controls inherited from the 1960s and 1970s, and reduced productivity and potential growth further. In these countries the incentive system has become highly distorted with a multitude of price, foreign-exchange, and trade controls. Factors and goods markets have been subject to heavy state intervention with competition restricted. In Egypt, for example, agriculture was until recently strictly regulated and in spite of the emergence of a private sector in the mid-1970s, rigidly controlled public enterprises still produce 75% of manufacturing, 75% of nonagricultural GDP, and half of GDP.

Needed Adjustment and Reforms

Development economists call "adjustment" the desirable economic change in response to a new set of circumstances. Its goal is to raise output toward its potential level after the occurrence of a shock that disturbs the rationality of old economic choices.

On the macroeconomic side the combination of overexpansionary domestic policies and a deteriorating international environment required policies designed to reduce overall expenditure and in particular fiscal deficits, as well as switching policies to encourage the production of tradable goods.[6] But the economies of the region exhibited a high degree of inflexibility in adjusting to external shocks, preferring instead to accumulate external debt as long as loans were available. Macroeconomic adjustment programs were initiated generally when the external imbalances simply could not be sustained for lack of financing, often under the aegis of the IMF in the context of standby agreements. Between 1981 and 1985 Egypt borrowed (on a net basis) between $2 and $3 billion a year, mostly from official sources, and by 1985 its debt-to-export ratio stood at over 300% (tables 9.1 and 9.4). By 1986 debt service due exceeded what could be borrowed, net transfers turned negative, and arrears exceeded $2 billion. The situation could not be sustained, and a Paris Club rescheduling was arranged in 1987 in the context of an IMF program (which was discontinued after the first drawing). Jordan borrowed on average about $500 million between 1986 and 1989, mostly from private sources, and by 1989 its debt-to-export ratio had exceeded 200%, net transfers had turned negative, and amid a foreign-exchange crisis an IMF program was initiated and debts owed to private and public creditors were rescheduled (tables 9.1 and 9.4).[7] Syria also stepped up its borrowings in the 1980s until the supply of funds dried out. Since, it has been running arrears including to multilateral institutions and it now conducts a large share of its international trade on a barter basis. Lebanon was not able to tap external resources.

Table 9.4
External debt (millions of current dollars and percentage)

	1973	1977	1982	1985	1989
Total external debt (percent from official sources)					
Egypt	2.1	12.2	28.8	40.2	48.8
Jordan	0.2	0.8	2.7	4.2	7.4
Syria	0.4	1.8	3.0	4.0	5.2
Lebanon	0	0	0.6	0.4	0.5
Total debt to export plus remittances					
Egypt	145	248	278	304	355
Jordan	52	64	86	134	245
Syria	66	118	102	155	243
Total debt service (paid) to exports plus remittances					
Egypt	34	12	26	24	22
Jordan	8	5	9	18	19
Syria	8	7	13	13	22

Memorandum: Debt work-outs

Egypt: Paris Club reschedulings in 1987, 1989, and 1991 (with debt reduction).
Jordan: Paris Club rescheduling in 1989.

Source: World Bank, WDT 1991.

In light of the constraints expected to prevail on the current account, increased GNP growth can result essentially only through improved domestic performance. This has two main elements: (1) improvements in the efficiency of both the public and private sectors, and (2) increasing the rate of capital formation through increases in national savings. Conceptually, efficiency improvements can be attained in several ways, including improvement in the management of the public sector parastatals, privatizations, price liberalization and decontrol, and fiscal reforms to increase the efficiency of revenue collection. Trade reforms are advocated to help attain the current account objectives without undue cuts in imports, to facilitate the movement of resources to the tradable sector and reduce the bias against exports, and generally to improve overall efficiency through greater impact of market forces on economic activity. Finally, to stimulate private savings and improve their allocation, financial and banking system reform are required.[8] But while sharp macroeconomic adjustment becomes inescapable in times of crisis, bold microeconomic reforms aiming at increased efficiency can and have been consistently delayed in favor of gradual and slow change, if any.

The Incentives to Reform

Most pressures for change in the region seem to come only on the heels of persistent budgetary and balance-of-payments crises, such as in Egypt (1977) and Turkey (1980), and more recently in Jordan, Algeria, and Iraq (Iraq embarked on a major privatization effort prior to the Gulf crisis). When less dramatic alternatives could be found, however, even if not more than short-term palliatives, reforms stalled. The typical reformist program must have appeared as a daunting task to economic decision makers in the Middle East, concerned as they were with delicate political balances and fragile economic structures.

Three types of arguments can be offered to explain the delays in macroeconomic adjustment and the gradualism of microeconomic reforms: (1) the inflexibility of an economic structure inherited from the boom years, (2) security concerns with the possibility of rising domestic instability, and (3) strategic considerations related to existing military tensions.

First, in the presence of rigidities in the economy, economic reforms were expected to produce large costs in the short term. In addition, the supply response was not expected to be strong enough to justify the political risk involved. In a sense, reforms were perceived as bad investments because of their low rate of return.[9] In principle, adjustment would lead to the closing of some lines of economic activity and the emergence of others as a result of changes in relative prices to reflect better actual scarcities and needs. But rigidities abounded in these economies weakened by the legacy of years of rentier state mentality, a prevalence of oligopolistic rather than competitive production, distorted factor markets, and productive structures protected from foreign competition. In such a context there is a large initial wealth loss because a substantial share of existing capital—both human and physical—must be retrained, converted, or simply scrapped to make room for the accumulation of more-adapted forms of capital. In addition, in the absence of perfect and undistorted factors markets, reconstruction does not start as soon as destruction takes place, leading to the (temporary) unemployment of the released factors of production. In Egypt, Jordan, and especially

Syria and Lebanon, domestic capital could not be expected to fully accommodate the needed new investments, especially because of the large risks linked to regional instability.[10] Furthermore, rising budget deficits and increased internal and external public debts do not augur well for future taxation and even expropriations—the so-called disincentive effect of a debt overhang. The long lags needed for the supply response to emerge are also increased by the lack of credibility of policy changes, which is linked to a difficult fiscal position, increasing indebtedness, and to regional instability. In such an environment the prospects of a further rise in already high levels of unemployment, with the attendant increase in popular discontent, deterred policies that would have led to bold changes in relative prices.

Second, adjustment policies are redistributive, and their implementation threatens the sociopolitical status quo. Devaluations generate distributional conflicts between the traded and nontraded sectors. Trade reforms oppose the interests of the import-competing sector against those of the export sector. The removal of price controls hurts some lines of business and benefits others. And to the extent that fiscal austerity is required, conflicts arise among socioeconomic groups that are affected differently by various taxes including the inflation tax, that have varying abilities to evade taxes, and that rely to different degrees on government subsidies, programs, and employment opportunities. While redistributions of income can conceptually take care of opposition when the policy measures increase economic efficiency and thus the overall output, such redistribution is in effect impossible to achieve in a satisfactory way when the reforms are implemented in a wholesale fashion and thus involve complex tradeoffs between several competing groups. It is quite likely that the frontline states, concerned first and foremost with security, could not "afford" the domestic instability that such wholesale redistributions would entail. Instead, reforms have tended to focus on one sector at a time, and compensations were granted carefully so as to diffuse as much as possible the resulting political opposition.[11]

Third, domestic instability in the Middle East had some aspects of a public good (or rather of a public bad), since instability in one country can affect the geopolitical posture of a whole coalition of states. When it became clear that ongoing policies could not be sustained for long without major economic reforms, governments typically chose not to reverse course but instead to continue in the same track with the (usually self-fulfilling) expectation of being saved—for a while—by new flows from their strategic allies. In this respect the scarcity of strong adjustment lending programs by the international financial institutions to the frontline states is closely related to security requirements, which did not permit the partial loss of sovereignty that is necessary to enforce conditional lending.

Reforms to Date

The necessity to reduce public sector deficits posed some serious dilemmas. Ultimately, expenditures were hit mostly because the capacity to raise revenues was severely constrained by an inability to broaden the tax base and institutional weaknesses in revenue collection.[12] This was partly the result of the deterioration of fiscal controls during the boom years, but also a reflection of the strength of the informal economy. Although subsidies have been reduced over time, the capacity to do so was limited both by the need to maintain essential services and the desire to continue programs benefiting powerful interest groups. Some governments continued to run substantial budget deficits, thus absorbing a significant amount of savings from the private sector (Egypt, Lebanon, Jordan), but the budget deficit tended to decline in other countries after they instituted stabilization programs (Israel in 1985 and Syria in 1986). Recently deficits have widened again throughout the region.

The reduction in the public sector deficits was accompanied in all cases by steep reductions in investment expenditures. This was partly the result of direct cuts in public investment, but reduction in private investment also occurred indirectly as a consequence of the impact of efforts to finance the public sector deficit. In Egypt, Syria, and Jordan investment in 1989 was at least 10% of GDP below its 1980 level (table 9.5).

Attempts to finance the budget deficit domestically have led to large distortions in the domestic financial markets. Large monetization of the deficit has also led to increasing inflation (30% in Egypt and Jordan by 1989) and to the development of parallel market activities when price controls were instituted in order to repress inflation (Egypt, Syria). In addition, governments borrowed heavily from the banking sector at rates that are regulated rather than market determined (Jordan, Egypt, Syria). This often has encouraged the development of an unofficial curb market, thus reducing the tax base. It has also prompted in some countries the creation of foreign-currency

Table 9.5
Saving and investment as a share of GDP, selected periods, 1973–89 (in percent).

	1973–76	1977–81	1982–85	1986–89
Savings				
Egypt	10.7	15.7	15.4	8.5
Jordan	na	na	−10.0	−2.5
Syria	13.5	9.8	11.5	11.7
Israel	7.0	9.7	11.0	10.9
Investment				
Egypt	14.4	30.1	28.2	19.2
Jordan	na	na	30.7	20.5
Syria	23.2	27.8	24.0	14.5
Israel	28.2	23.0	20.2	16.7

Sources: World tables, World Bank 1991.

deposit accounts in order to reduce capital flight and to attract workers' remittances (Israel, Egypt), thus reducing the effectiveness of the seigniorage tax. Governments' attempts to keep borrowing costs down also have had adverse effects on private saving. In Egypt private saving plummeted to 8% of GDP in 1987–88, down from 15%–18% in the early 1980s (table 9.5).

The degree of external adjustment undertaken depended on the size of the external shock, and on the amount of financing including debt rescheduling when available. But financing constraints and the inability to raise exports in the short run have led to increased quantitative restrictions on imports, with adverse effects on growth. Few Arab countries were successful in building a strong nontraditional export base, mainly because of the high cost of capital. But the recent (pre–Gulf war) growth of manufactures exports in Egypt and Jordan suggests that export-led growth can work in a peaceful environment (Wilson 1988).

Depreciation was resisted and usually undertaken only when reserves were nearly depleted. This occurred for Egypt in 1987 and for Jordan and Syria in 1988. In addition to the transitional costs involved in shifting resources to tradables in order to effect the payments in foreign exchange, devaluations usually resulted in a deterioration of the budget because in Egypt, Jordan, and Syria the public sector derives a large share of its revenue from the nontraded goods sectors, while it must transfer resources to its external creditors in foreign exchange. This posed a further challenge for accomplishing the already substantial fiscal adjustments that needed to be implemented. Finally, devaluations have hurt the domestic financial sector, which has net obligations in foreign exchange and a large share of its assets invested in the nontraded goods sector. As happened in Israel after the 1985 stabilization plan, this will require a costly recapitalization of the banking sector in Egypt and in Jordan.

Microeconomic reforms to increase efficiency by removing price controls did not always work as expected because of a lack of competition.[13] But the gradual removal of price ceilings in agriculture ultimately increased production markedly in Egypt and Syria. And the process of deregulation started in Jordan after 1988 with the removal of price, interest rate, and foreign-exchange controls and a liberalization of investment, looked promising before the Gulf war and may have increased the resilience of the economy and its ability to cope with the present crisis. On the other hand, the liberalization of the foreign investment codes did not have a sizable effect in Syria, while the effects in Egypt were mixed.

Debt restructuring was helpful in dealing with the adjustment problems in Egypt and Jordan. The recent debt forgiveness granted to Egypt by the Paris Club, which is partly conditional on strong adjustment measures, could help facilitate the adjustment process (although the implied reduction in the macroimbalances may also reduce the need for microeconomic reforms).[14]

The Peace Process and New Economic Challenges

While peace will create an environment that is conducive to substantial long-term benefits, only countries that are able to adjust their policies to the new realities will manage to reap large benefits. By reducing external risks and allowing for cooperative and regional responses to common problems, peace will also alter the terms of some old tradeoffs, increasing the attractiveness of specific reforms, and in some cases, the costs of not undertaking them. Finally, by reducing the security bias against conditionality, peace will also allow for the emergence of programs with a stronger and more credible conditionality content.

This section examines four areas where peace is likely to offer new challenges: reductions in military spending; strengthening of civil society and of the private sector; the possibility for stronger conditionality attached to external inflows; and increased regional cooperation, especially in water management.

Military Expenditures

Reduction in tensions and a stable security arrangement in the region imply that there may well be a peace dividend arising from a reduction in military expenditures. In principle, a security arrangement accompanied by an arms nonproliferation treaty, will allow countries to reduce defense expenditures without harming their national security.

The order of magnitude of arms expenditures is large by any measure. Between 1977 and 1987, SIPRI estimates the cumulative military expenditures of all the countries of the Middle East to be approximately $615 billion. As a share of GNP, military expenditures in the region averaged 17% between 1978 and 1985. At least seven countries in the region (Iraq, Israel, Oman, Saudi Arabia, Syria, Yemen PDR, and Egypt) devoted resources worth over 10% of their GNP to military expenditures (table 9.6). In contrast, military expenditures as a percentage of GNP in the NATO member countries averaged far less for the same period. Between 1978 and 1988, countries in the Middle East imported over $176 billion (1988 dollars) in arms, averaging about $17 billion per year, which represents 15% of total imports for that period. This also represents nearly 40% of all arms imports in the world (McNamara 1991). The largest importers have been Iraq, Saudi Arabia, Iran, Syria, Israel, and Egypt, in that order.

The advent of more stable security relationships, especially if reinforced by an arms nonproliferation treaty, will reduce the amount of resources needed for national security. It is not unrealistic to expect that, in the medium term, the frontline states can redirect as much as 10% of their GNP each year toward more productive sectors. The potential benefits of cutbacks in the defense budget will accrue over time as human resources will move into more productive activities. How large might these benefits be? In the past, military expenditures were partially allocated as investment, and this has had a positive effect on growth, especially in Egypt and Israel. But it seems fair to assume that in a postwar environment, such investment will not be as profitable. Domestic demand (i.e., valuation of) for military ser-

Table 9.6
Military expenditures in the Middle East, 1978–1986 (as a percentage of gross domestic product)

	1978	1979	1980	1981	1982	1983	1984	1985	1986	1978–86 average
Egypt	24	15	11	12	11	10	6	—	12	
Israel	26	30	28	26	24	26	29	21	21	26
Jordan	16	18	14	14	14	14	13	14	15	14
Syria	15	16	17	15	16	15	17	17	18	16
Iraq	8	7	6	13	23	34	51	57	—	25
Oman	28	21	20	21	21	23	23	21	28	22
Sudan										
Yemen	8	24	17	21	25	18	15	13	—	18
Iran	10	24	15	11	12	11	10	6	—	12
Kuwait	4	3	4	5	6	7	7	8	—	5
U.A.E.	5	6	6	7	7	7	7	8	—	6
SA	17	21	17	15	17	20	21	22	—	19
Average (unweighted)	15	18	15	15	16	18	19	18	—	17

Source: SIPRI, Yearbook, 1989.

vices will go down, and military exports are also likely to go down. A quick and rather conservative estimate reveals that the total net effect of a reduction in military spending of 10 percentage points of GNP lies between 0.7 and 1.7 percentage points in GNP growth. The net effect may be far larger if other elements are taken into consideration, in particular the fact that military expenditures have a large dose of import content.[15]

In the short term, however, adjustment costs are likely to predominate. Governments will be sensitive to the idea of releasing large numbers of conscripts rapidly. The number of men under arms as a percent of the total labor force averages 6% for the region, with a high of 18% and 15% for Iraq and Syria, respectively. There are further costs involved in the short term, as that portion of the economy that depended on large armies will feel the effects of any drastic reduction in local expenditures.

Strengthening the Private Sector

A postpeace environment could help speed the development of the private sector, which will add dynamism to the frontline state economies. Reduced regional instability, if coupled with domestic political and economic stability, can dramatically increase the willingness of domestic entrepreneurs to invest their skills, time, and capital in new ventures. Such a scenario requires the adoption by governments of reforms that create the economic space, stabilize the macroeconomic situation, and release the necessary factors of production. We argue below that the governments' incentives for change will be positively affected by three factors: (1) governments will need to rely increasingly on domestic rather than external savings and on tax rather that aid revenues; (2) because of reduced military tensions, they can "afford" more of the short-term negative effects of reforms from a security point of view; and, (3) they can expect a stronger supply response to bold reforms than in the past.

In the aftermath of the Gulf crisis and the easing of the old East-West tensions, geopolitically motivated aid is likely to continue to decrease.[16] The Gulf countries have become materially poorer.[17] They are also less likely to rely on their neighbors to insure their security needs. For both reasons the tendency to reduce their aid budget will remain, at least in the medium run. The West does not need to compete with the Soviet Union, and it relies less than in the past on stability in the Middle East to protect the oil routes. And competition for scarce resources has been increased by the demands for capital from the reforming countries of Eastern Europe and the emerging economies in Latin America. It is thus unlikely that much private money can be attracted before economic reforms are deepened and social stability is reinforced. The Gulf investors—who have some measure of comparative advantage at investing in the Arab world—will not flood the Egyptian, Syrian, Lebanese, or Jordanian markets before expropriation risk is reduced. While a peaceful resolution of the Palestine issue will certainly help, economic reforms that enhance the return on capital, create growth opportunities, and enhance civil society in general represent the only credible commitment that these states can make as a guarantee against expropriation.

The need to increase domestic savings will also become more pressing. This will create additional incentives for more-efficient financial markets and institutions. Besides the question of total savings, the economies of the Middle East have also witnessed large amounts of capital flight and a large underground economy. For example, recorded worker remittances to Egypt seem to have been strongly correlated not only with regional instability (negatively), but also with the expected differential between domestic return on assets and international returns (Kibbe 1991). The scope for diverting remittances from the unofficial to the official economy seems sizable if domestic interest rates and exchange rates were liberalized.[18]

More generally, governments will need a more-efficient domestic economy to rely on in order to finance necessary public expenditures. Such concerns will be facilitated by a reduction in security requirements. For example, over time governments may safely withdraw from several sectors of economic activity that were considered strategic during the confrontation years, including utilities, transportation, energy, communications, and heavy industry. Some of these sectors might have to be discontinued when they do not encompass any comparative advantages, but many others will be picked up by the emerging private sector. In this respect the recent rise of high-tech small business that has sustained much of the recent growth especially in Israel, but also in Jordan, Lebanon, and Egypt is encouraging. It is not clear how Arab business will react to the lifting of the Arab boycott on Israel, as such a measure (while optimal from an economic perspective) will increase competition for Arab producers and governments will be under pressure to continue protection, if not through a boycott than perhaps through other means.

In sum, given the prospects generated by a reduction in regional instability, the benefits generated by a performing and stable domestic economy become more attractive, increasing the incentives for bolder economic reforms. But a crucial element in such scenarios is the preservation of domestic stability. The reduction in regional instability, if accompanied by rising domestic instability, will reduce the incentives for private investment, increase the costs involved in adjustment policies, dilute the credibility of announced policy changes, and generally, reduce the will to reform.

Conditional Lending

Often in the past, reforms with large returns in the medium term have not been attractive and have not been undertaken because of the degree of austerity expected in the short term. Adjustment lending to smooth these costs makes a lot of economic sense, rendering a reform program that is profitable at the world interest rate an attractive investment opportunity. The problem with external finance, however, is that the new loans can also be used to delay adjustment. In fact, the incentives to do so are large in times of scarcity, which is when drastic reforms are typically needed. For this reason external loans are scarce when they are needed most. Conditional lending resolves this time inconsistency problem by allowing the best not to become the enemy of the good. In this sense, conditionality—when it can be made effective and credible—is in the own interest of the borrower.[19]

During the confrontation years economic conditionality was strongly resisted in the Arab world.[20] The enforcement of conditionality requires close monitoring by the lending institution. Those institutions themselves are subject to political pressures by their major shareholders, which may have had different strategic orientation than the frontline states. In any event, in addition to the inflexibility issue the risks related to the temporary loss of sovereignty were perceived to be too costly and dangerous to be acceptable. From this point of view the reduction of regional instability and the reduction in the security threats will allow greater involvement of the international financial institutions. The challenge for policymakers will be to seek external support to help smooth the pains of transition for those that will lose, especially the poor, and at the same time to elicit support from the domestic constituencies that stand to gain from a change in the economic incentive structures relative to the current status quo.

Water Management

A sustainable water strategy will require costly investments and possibly difficult social choices in the short term, but the long-term benefits are tremendous given the stark alternatives. Political and economic stability in the region will depend increasingly on water availability. The population in the region is expected to double in the next forty years, with increases of at least 40%–50% in population by the year 2000. Water shortages due to these pressures are acute. At least ten of the countries in the region are presently under what is termed *water stress,* and over half exhibit *absolute water scarcity,* which means that the ratio of population to water exceeds minimum standards (measured as one thousand persons to one cubic meter of water). Today, Algeria, Jordan, Israel, Palestine, Saudi Arabia, Syria, Tunisia, and Yemen suffer from water scarcity, and Egypt will join the list by the year 2000 (table 9.7).

For usable water resources to increase, the development of regional and local projects (pipeline, water reclamation and desalination plants, better environmental protection) is crucial. Major sources of water encompass several countries. Israel, Jordan, and Syria share the Jordan and Yarmuk rivers, and Israel and Lebanon share the Litani and Hasbani rivers.[21] In the past, projects to enhance the available water and to increase its supply have not been undertaken because of risks of damage during wartime, heightened free-riding incentives that encourage decapitalization rather than investment in maintenance, conservation, and reclamation,[22] and the impossibility of undertaking projects encompassing countries at war with each other. Peace will allow for such costly projects by encouraging a cooperative approach and by reducing investment risk.

But scarce water resources also need to be rationed efficiently, both across countries and within each country. This cannot be achieved without a proper pricing policy, one that takes into account the regional component inherent in water supply and demand. In the absence of regional agreements (and improper pricing schemes), each country has had incentives to use as much water as possible without

Table 9.7
Water availability in Middle East and North Africa

	Persons/Mm^3/Yr	
	1984	2000
Front Line:		
Egypt	882	1097
Jordan	3500	5818
Lebanon	—	—
Syria	2293	3238
Israel	—	—
Other		
Algeria	1320	1818
Iraq	188	254
Morocco	808	993
Oman	704	985
Saudi Arabia	6250	9000
Tunisia	1713	2168
Yemen	5267	7253

Measures of water scarcity in persons per million meters cubed per year.
100–500 = water management problems
500–1000 = water stress
1000 = water scarcity

Source: World Bank (EMENA study) 1991, p. 4.

considerations for its alternative value in other countries. Such a strategy is clearly unsustainable, and the challenge that arises with peace is to redress the situation.

Supporting Economic Reforms in the Service of Peace

The economic challenges that face decision makers in the Middle East are changing. In the context of a peace process, economic growth and increased regional integration become more of a possibility. Reconstruction can be contemplated in Lebanon and in Palestine. Bold economic reforms become feasible in Syria and Egypt. And renewed private investments become attractive in Jordan and Israel. But lack of resources—exacerbated by the Gulf war—makes the needed economic changes less attractive and credible. This in turn reduces the speed of convergence of the peace process. In this section we discuss two initiatives that would support peace and growth in the Middle East: a stabilization of labor movements within the region, and increased availability of conditional loans, perhaps by a new regional development bank.

Stabilizing Regional Labor Flows

The crisis in the Gulf, with the attendant movement in populations, reduced dramatically the level of remittances, as Iraq, Kuwait, and Saudi Arabia expelled several million Arab workers. In both Yemen and in Egypt, 1 million are returning; in Jordan 300,000; in Lebanon 260,000; and in the Sudan 300,000.[23] Even though the governments of Syria and Egypt have been largely compensated for the loss of remittances arising from the conflict, simply making up the difference by increasing official development assistance is at best a short-term palliative and will not have the same qualitative effect on the economy. Labor remittances generally accrue directly to millions of migrants, often tenant farmers or landless peasants, and their economic effects are quite different from those of capital flows that occur at the intergovernmental level (Chaudhry 1989).

Labor movements served as the principal means for wealth redistribution in the region, from the oil-rich labor-importing countries to the oil-poor labor-exporting countries. The resulting capital inflows have been substantial (table 9.8), especially for Jordan, Egypt, and Lebanon. Egypt's (official) remittances have risen from $123 million in 1973 to over $4.2 billion in 1989. This represented about 17% of GDP and 41% of exports in 1989. Jordan's remittances rose from $55.4 million to over $1.2 billion in 1984 (about 50% of GDP), declining to about $600 million by 1989. Remittances also represent a sizable share of GNP in Syria and Lebanon.[24]

A resumption of labor flows is an important element to any future security arrangement. More restrictive immigration policies in the region, possibly because of the Gulf crisis, would sour the relations between Arab countries and endanger the very security that restrictive policies are intended to safeguard in the first place. The second possibility, of greater mobility, will not only alleviate demographic pressures and strengthen civil society and entrepreneurship throughout the region, but also will reduce markedly the scope of the external imbalances, especially in Jordan, Egypt, and Lebanon. Finally, labor mobility has a positive externality on capital flowing from oil-rich countries toward labor exporters. The labor-exporting country is less

Table 9.8
Unrequited transfers 1973–89, selected subperiods (billions of current dollars and percentage)

	1973–76	1977–81	1982–85	1986–89
Unrequited transfers (cumulative)				
Egypt	1.7	10.2	13.4	14.1
Jordan	0.7	3.0	3.7	3.2
Syria	0.2	3.0	1.4	1.2
Lebanon	na	na	na	na
Average unrequited transfers to GNP (percent)				
Egypt	4.1	11.5	12.1	11.5
Jordan	18.6	22.9	24.5	17.1
Syria	8.1	5.4	2.3	1.3
Total average financing plus unrequited transfers to GNP (percent)				
Egypt	21.6	25.1	21.7	19.4
Jordan	58.4	61.6	50.3	37.6
Syria	10.9	18.1	7.7	3.7
Lebanon	2.0	6.8	4.1	4.9

Memorandum: Oil revenues (dollar billion current)

	1973	1975	1980	1982	1984	1985	1986	1987	1988	1989
Egypt			2.0	2.1	1.9	2.0	1.1			
Syria			1.3	1.0	0.9	0.8	0.4			
OPEC			213	143	102	90	53			

Sources: IFS, table 1, and OPEC Annual Reports.

likely to expropriate or in any other way treat unfavorably investments from countries that host their expatriate labor. This dependence reduces foreign investment risk.

It is important to consider the policies of the Arab labor-importing countries, such as Saudi Arabia and Kuwait; will the present post-Gulf policy of favoring non-Arab labor over Arab continue? The resolution of the Palestinian issue and the emergence of a stable security regime can contribute to reducing the perceived need for "fortress states" in the region. A reversal by these two countries of their recent labor-importing policies will in itself contribute to reduced regional tension and a more stable regional environment.

Reforms, Domestic Stability, and External Financing

Increased regional stability is a necessary, but not a sufficient, condition for a reduction in total risk. Liberalization and economic reforms bring their own sources of instability. Unemployment—not to speak of underemployment—is high in Egypt (20%), Jordan (30%), and Israel (10%), as well as in Syria and Lebanon. And the reduction of the threat of war, while stabilizing international relations, may at the same time call for political adjustment. It may also create unrealistic expectations of an immediate and large peace dividend, making it difficult to convince public opinion of the need for austerity before growth can resume on a more sustainable path. For all these reasons, economic reforms may continue to be delayed out of fear of popular explosions.

Thus, while in the long run the chances are high that peace will be followed by the expansion of new sectors of economic activity, the dual need for economic and political adjustment that is likely to arise in a postpeace situation may initiate a period of domestic instability in many of the countries of the region. The difficulties involved in the transition period should not be underestimated, especially in countries where the state lacks the strong legitimacy that democracy grants. While this has been well understood in Jordan and Egypt where the state has recently moved toward a system of greater representation, the need for external finance (and in the cases of Jordan and Syria, of debt reduction) to smooth the cost of reconstruction and the transitory pains associated with economic adjustment must also be dealt with. In this context the recent debt reduction granted to Egypt by its Paris Club creditors will only help if it is accompanied by sufficient liquidity support.

In the absence of external support the peace process may come to a halt. Besides the nationalistic feelings, the continuation of a situation of instability must surely have its own constituency; the particular pattern of capital flows to the Arab frontline state and to Israel, and the structure of government expenditures based on war economics, have generated substantial rents and created strong interest groups that have not been supportive of radical changes.[25] In the absence of attractive alternatives, internal decay would accelerate the emergence of centrifugal forces in the multiethnic countries (Lebanon, Syria, and Iraq), and the development of delinquent economies specialized int he production of drugs, smuggling, and the management of illegal immigration.

This possibility and the real chance for economic growth in a peaceful environment militate for increased conditional finance to support reconstruction and the peace process in the Middle East.

While precise estimates of needs are difficult to project in the absence of detailed studies, a total of $10 to $15 billion a year for all of the frontline states during the next five years seems a reasonable approximation. While this amount of resources is too large for any single donor, it is not too far from the actual amount of resources that flow to the area. The key for effective conditionality, however, is to develop sufficient coordination between donors and to credibly commit large resources if reforms proceed. Because the task at hand is monumental, it would make sense to entrust such a role to a new regional development bank for the Middle East. Such a bank might be the best means for ensuring coordination between donors. It is expected that funding for such a bank would come mostly from the Arab Gulf states, with contributions from the United States, Japan, and European countries. Bringing international financial institutions into the bank in some manner reduces the chances that such a bank becomes overpoliticized and as a consequence cannot credibly enforce conditionality; on the other hand, the driving concept behind the bank is that it is regional, and its success depends to a large extent on the involvement of governments in the region. Furthermore, existing international financial institutions do not have the capacity to take on such a massive regional project alone, although small-scale precedents exist. The regional bank's success will depend on striking the right balance between regional and international participation and ensuring donor coordination.

Concluding Remarks

What are the growth prospects in the region if economic reforms are pursued? If we exclude Egypt, the prospects seem mildly favorable. Comparative advantages are embodied in a well-educated labor force, Mediterranean ingenuity and entrepreneurship, and Israeli technology. Pooled together, these would bring some prosperity. The relatively small and urban population of this subregion can provide a natural eastern expansion for Europe. Increasing productivity in agriculture and the expansion of trade and banking activities would sustain growth. But it is the provision of cultural services and of region-specific high-tech goods (Arabic software, arid-land irrigation, solar energy, water desalination) that remains the major potential engine of growth. The prospects for such a path of strong long-term growth depend on the existence of a large Arab market, which Egypt can provide, given the size of markets in the Arab inland and the Gulf. Indeed, Egypt offers enormous opportunities in the medium and long run. With a population more than double that of any other country in the Arab world, it represents a major prize for regional cooperation, allying the comparative advantage of the Arabs in the mobilization of capital and the command of "culture" with that of the Israelis in technologies. If it manages to "open up," Egypt could become the manufacturing center of the region. Whether sustainable growth can be initiated in Egypt is, in this sense, an important regional issue. The alternative is that the Suez Canal may instead become a north/south divide and a renewed source of instability for the whole region. As in the previously socialist countries of Eastern Europe, the task of reforming the economic incentives in Egypt and in the region without creating too much popular dissatisfaction remains a challenging and risky task.

Notes

1. For a good review of the political circumstances see, for example, Corm 1990.

2. See, for example, Chaudhry 1989, Beblawi and Luciani 1989, and Richards and Waterbury 1990.

3. For example, Galil Amin, a keen observer of the reforms in Egypt, writes, "if the state perceives that it is easier to increase its income from outside sources than from domestic sources, its interest in sound and efficient economic growth rapidly wanes" (Beblawi and Luciani 1989, p. 16).

4. For example, in Egypt the state instituted a set of policies designed to provide a minimum living standard for its population, including rent controls, subsidized food distribution, and free education and health care, in addition to a wide array of public services at low cost.

5. In Egypt the shock was smoothed by the opening of Iraq. In the early 1980s, over one million Egyptians emigrated to Iraq.

6. See, for example, Fischer 1986 and Corden 1989.

7. The fund program included price increases, and this touched off rioting that exposed the fragility of Jordan's domestic stability. King Hussein moved quickly to diffuse the tensions: the government was replaced, and elections for a new parliament were held in late 1989. The elections established Islamic fundamentalist groups as the largest opposition group.

8. For a good exposition of a typical program of adjustment, see El-Naggar 1987.

9. In addition, reforms are less attractive when the implied cash flow effects are valued using a large discount factor to account for the intertemporal tradeoffs involved. Such "impatience" can be associated with the decision makers' preference for domestic stability in the short run.

10. While no estimates are available, capital flight is believed to be widespread throughout the Middle East. Domestic capital flies to both international-safe havens as well as to the underground economy. On the latter see Choucri 1986.

11. For a fascinating account of Egypt's experience with "stealth" reforms, see Sadowski 1991a.

12. In Egypt government expenditures were reduced from a peak of 63% of GDP in 1982 to their current level of about 43% of GDP and over the same period, they dropped from 45% to 25% in Syria.

13. For example, when Egypt removed price controls on some fruits and vegetables consumer prices rose, but not producer prices. The difference was pocketed by the monopoly that controlled the distribution of such products in Cairo (Sadowski 1991a).

14. The external debt situation in Jordan is explosive again in the aftermath of the Gulf crisis. In Jordan, and possibly in Syria, there is a need for further initiatives to reduce the overhang of debt and to allow for a normal resumption of market activity.

15. Assume that military investment is unprofitable in this new world order and consequently that a 10% reduction in military spending affects output marginally. For the sake of comparison, assume that the associated military investment drops by 3% of GDP leading to a drop in growth of 0.3% (using a marginal return on investment of 10%). Assume a marginal return on new investment of 20%. If the whole 10% goes to investment, growth will increase by 2% (1.4% net). Even if half goes into investment, growth increases by 1% (0.7% net).

16. Such predictions have often proven wrong. Egypt received about $4.5 billion and Syria about $3 billion in foreign loans and grants in the aftermath of the Gulf crisis. In addition, Egypt has had half of its official debts reduced by the Paris Club.

17. See, for example, Sadowski 1991b.

18. In Egypt total remittances are thought to be much larger than those that flow to the official economy, perhaps by a factor of two or three.

19. The bad reputation of conditionality in some developing countries and the controversies it has generated is probably more related to its content than to its nature. A priori, disagreements about the content of needed policy measures can be resolved by a careful assessment of the prevailing economic conditions and the use of income smoothing and income redistribution policies. It remains that once a conditional loan is disbursed, it may

be in the short-term interest of the borrower to deviate from the conditions, or to use the provider of the conditionality as a scapegoat for domestic dissatisfaction.

20. For example, the World Bank did not make any adjustment loans to frontline states in the Middle East until 1989, although they were all classified as countries with a clear need for adjustment (World Bank 1990).

21. In addition, the Nile, the only source of water in Egypt, is shared with Ethiopia and Sudan; Turkey, Syria, and Iraq share the Tigris and Euphrates rivers; most of North Africa, including Algeria, Tunisia, Libya, and Egypt, utilizes water from the same regional groundwater aquifer.

22. The low priority given to water management and maintenance of water systems has also resulted in underutilized capacity, low recovery, and inefficient distribution. But as the situation worsens, annual investments in water resources have grown recently and represent currently between 2% to 4% of GNP in most countries in the region.

23. More recently some new markets have been opening, in particular for Egyptian workers in Libya.

24. During the period 1982–89, the frontline states benefited from workers' remittances totaling approximately $41 billion.

25. But perhaps the situation has recently improved in that capital flows in the absence of peace are likely to be lower than in the past.

References

Beblawi, H., and G. Luciani. *The Rentier State: Essays in the Political Economy of the Arab Countries.* London: Croon Helm, 1989.

Chaudhry, Kiren Aziz "The Price of Wealth: Business and State in Labor Remittance and Oil Economies." *International Organization* 43:1, Winter 1989.

Choucri, Nazli. "Hidden Economy: A New View of Workers Remittances in the Arab World." *World Development* 14: 1986.

Corden, Max. "Macroeconomic Adjustment in Developing Countries." *World Bank Research Observer,* no. 1, Jan. 1989.

Corm, Georges. *Le Proche orient eclate.* Collection Folio. 1990.

El-Naggar, Said. *Adjustment Policies and Development Strategies in the Arab World.* Washington, D.C.: International Monetary Fund, 1987.

Fischer, Stanley. "Issues in Medium Term Macroeconomic Adjustment." *World Bank Research Observer,* no. 2, July 1986.

International Monetary Fund (1990), *International Financial Statistics Yearbook,* Washington, D.C.

Kibbe, Jamal. "Workers Remittances in Egypt." Mimeograph, 1991, Georgetown University.

McNamara, Robert. "The Post Cold War World and its Implications for Military Expenditures in the Developing Countries." Working Paper 1991, *World Bank Economic Review.*

Nowels, Larry, and Jonathan Sandford. "Arab Economic Aid: Donors and Recipients, 1973–89." Congressional Research Service, June 1991.

Richards, Alan, and John Waterbury. *A Political Economy of the Middle East.* Boulder: Westview Press, 1990.

Sadowski, Yehya. *Political Vegetables.* Washington, D.C.: Brookings Institution, 1991a.

———. "Power, Poverty, and Petrodollars." *Middle East Reports,* no. 170, May 1991b.

SIPRI. *Yearbook.* 1989.

Summers, Robert, and Alan Heston. "The Penn World Tables (Mark 5): An Expanded Set of International Comparison, 1950–1988." *Quarterly Journal of Economics* 106 May 1991, issue 2.

van den Boogaerde, Pierre. "The Composition and Distribution of Financial Assistance from Arab Countries and Arab Regional Institutions." IMF Working Paper WP/90/67. Washington, D.C.: International Monetary Fund, July 1990.

Wilson, Rodney. "Jordan's Trade: Past Performances and Future Prospects." *International Journal of Middle East Studies* 20, 1988.

World Bank. *The World Debt Tables,* various issues.

World Bank. "Adjustment Lending Policies for Sustainable Growth." *Policy and Research Series,* no. 14, 1990.

World Bank. *The World Tables,* 1991.

World Bank. *World Development Report,* 1991.

World Bank. "Water Resources Management Study." EMENA Issues Paper, Jan. 1991, p. 4.

Comments

John Waterbury

The two chapters share a fundamental premise: that peace is to be judged in terms of its impact on the economic adjustment process underway in several of the countries of the Middle East region. I am sure none of the authors would want to claim that that is the only significance of peace in the region, but given their mandate within the division of labor of the conference it is upon that they have focused. Unsurprisingly both chapters conclude that a peace settlement in the Arab-Israeli arena would have a major positive impact on the adjustment process. Both chapters see this emerging from a substantial peace dividend, estimated by Diwan and Papandreou at 10% of GDP per annum for several of the most heavily armed states, and by El-Naggar and El-Erian at $30 billion per year in aggregate if the most heavily armed states reduced their outlays on armaments to average levels for the rest of the world. Finally, Diwan and Papandreou in particular see a strong possibility that peace would promote regional economic integration with resulting positive returns to regional economies. I want to elaborate on and criticize some of these assumptions.

The notion of a peace dividend becomes crucial to the two analyses because there is no other obvious positive effect that the end of hostilities would bring to bear upon the economic adjustment process. The estimates of the dividend's potential magnitude in the two chapters are very generous and glass over problems in measurement and probability. The evidence on the real domestic resource costs of large military establishments in the Middle East is not at all clear. Military hardware has often come on concessional terms (or through outright grants), and even then is frequently never paid for. It is thus not clear what magnitude of real domestic resources could be reallocated to productive, civilian purposes were peace to break out.

A more important consideration is that regional arms levels and races are by no means solely determined by the Arab-Israeli theater. Egypt is concerned by threats emerging from its Nilotic hinterland and from Libya, and Turkey by Greece and whatever may transpire in Armenia, Georgia, Azerbaijan, Iraq, Iran, and Syria. It seems inconceivable to me that a post-Saddam Iraq could be required to remain relatively defenseless in the face of heavily armed and traditionally hostile neighbors in Iran, Turkey, Saudi Arabia, and Syria. The united Yemens are likely to try to bolster their military in step with Saudi Arabia's growing acquisitions. The only way in which a major peace divided could be realized would be through a regionwide build-down of strategic, chemical, and nuclear weapons.

Such a development is not very likely. On the positive side, the end of the cold war and the dissolution of the Soviet Union may stem part of the flow of arms to the region. On the other hand, Soviet successor states may want to sell of hardware and technical expertise for hard currency, and Western, particularly U.S., arms exporters will continue to push hard to capitalize on the technologies tested in the Gulf war. With U.S. trade balances continuing negative, arms exporters will find plenty of domestic political support for their cause.

We should also not lose sight of the fact that not a single head of state, nor the head of the PLO, changed as a result of the Gulf war. The entire cast of characters that produced the war is still there to deal with its aftermath, and it brings with it the baggage and habits of a status quo that did not include formal peace. It is not at all clear that any of these leaders sees distinct advantages to peace as opposed to the status quo. It is probably the Palestinians of the West Bank and Gaza who have the biggest stake in change.

Neither chapter paid much attention to once-and-for-all payoffs for a peace settlement. I think that were a formal settlement to be reached, there might be substantial compensatory rewards doled out to the main actors as was the case after the Camp David accords. These might take the form of funding regional water development projects and programs to stimulate economic growth in the occupied territories or to absorb Soviet Jews. Such payoffs could in turn attract new private investment in domains related to the projects, but for any of this to have a lasting positive impact will require that adjustment and liberalization programs be carried forward resolutely. Both chapters mentioned the possibility of a Middle East development bank but did not deal sufficiently with the issue of (1) the sources and magnitude of funds for the bank, and (2) the conditions under which it would lend. The pressure from countries of the region for concessional lending will be enormous, and if they are heeded the results will be the same as the wasted decade of the oil boom (1973–82).

The last point I wish to address is regional integration. As a result of the Gulf war it may be farther off than ever. Even the states of North Africa, which had made some progress in this direction, may fall away from one another if the Islamic front takes power in Algeria. The kinds of interdependencies that real integration would entail seem more threatening than ever to the leaders of the region. One need only think of the expulsions of Palestinians from Kuwait or Yemen is from Saudi Arabia or Egyptians from Iraq, or Turkey's closing down of the oil pipeline from Iraq to grasp the risks involved. Israel, we hear, is not interested in Turkey's proposal for a peace pipeline to bring fresh water to Jordan, the West Bank, and Israel proper, because nothing short of direct sovereignty over its water sources will any longer suffice.

These kinds of fears will not soon go away. In the interim the donor community could play a very useful role in helping "rationalize" the use of water in the region. My proposition is simple. If the region is facing severe water constraints, they are the result of agricultural use. Many parts of the Middle East may not enjoy comparative advantage in agricultural production. Moreover, the invocation of food security by many states to justify continued use of scarce water is bogus, because the region is already and will remain heavily dependent upon agricultural imports (Turkey being an exception). Many countries, from Israel to Egypt, could ease their water constraints by reorganizing their agricultural sectors and crop mixes, but to do so would require a great deal of patient coaxing coupled with the best agronomic and economic advice available. Reducing the saliency of water resources in the calculus of national security among Middle Eastern countries could help solidify a peace were one ever to be negotiated.

III

The Transition to Peace

10

The Future of Economic Development of the West Bank and Gaza and Their Economic Relations with Israel and Jordan

Ephraim Ahiram

Preface

For almost forty-three years the economic growth and development of the West Bank and Gaza (WB/G) have been distorted; for political reasons normal economic relations with their neighbors were denied. Since the 1948 war and until the occupation in 1967, the territories had to adhere to the Arab trade boycott against Israel, and the WB was simultaneously discriminated against by Jordan in development in comparison with the East Bank. Since the occupation by Israel in 1967, trade with Israel was restored but was dictated by all kinds of prohibitions and regulations. Also, the Arab boycott was now applied to the territories. Economic development of WB/G was prevented by these measures. The restrictions on trade and development became intensified during the four years of *intifada,* as the Palestinians introduced their own boycott on Israeli products, which were retaliated by the tightening of Israeli restrictions concerning the import of WB/G products, in particular the agricultural ones. The result was that Israel's exports to WB/G declined from 1987 to 1988 by 30% and the export of WB/G to Israel was reduced from 1987 to 1988 by 44%. In addition, a considerable reduction occurred in labor services input from WB/G in Israel, due to strikes and threats on the Palestinian side and extensive curfews and other restrictions by Israel on labor movement from the territories.

In 1989–91 an apparent restoration of trade in goods and labor services was gradually redressed. Jordan and the Gulf states intensified their embargo on WB/G products, in particular agricultural ones, since the formal separation of the West Bank initiated by Jordan in August 1988, and even more so since the occupation of Kuwait by Iraq in August 1990 and the Palestinian stance on the issue. The West

Bank also was gravely hurt by the 40%–50% devaluation of the Jordanian dinar and the discontinuance or reduction of the transfer of remittances of hundreds of thousands of Palestinians working in the Gulf and in other Arab countries.

From the beginning of the 1980s the increase in the standard of living in the territories leveled off and then decreased dramatically following the onset of the *intifada,* reducing the GNP per capita by 25% initially, then by 50–60% by 1991. The hardship that the WB/G population is now experiencing calls for immediate remedies. These cannot await the outcome of peace negotiations, which will most likely be of a protracted nature. The immediate remedies may in themselves make a positive contribution to the peace negotiations. These talks may yield an oft spoken of transitional period in which it would be possible to introduce further economic normalization in the economic relations between Israel, WB/G, and Jordan, as well as further economic recovery and nascent growth and development in the territories.

Finally, once the permanent political solution for the territories and the frame of the economic relations between WB/G, Israel, and Jordan are agreed upon, it may become possible to give these relationships concrete substance and seriously further the economic buildup of the WB/G.

According to the above-mentioned junctions of economic normalization, three stages of change to be introduced shall be proposed in this chapter.

The First Stage—Immediate Remedies

In this stage measures should be introduced to revert the economic situation, as far as the Palestinians, Israel, and Jordan are concerned, to about the pre-*intifada* status. To reach this goal would require the following steps.

- Sanctions introduced during the *Intifada* should be abolished. This would require the Palestinians not to boycott Israeli products and the Israelis to end the embargo on WB/G agricultural products like grapes and plums, which existed already prior to the *intifada.* Israel should also abolish discrimination against Palestinian farmers, such as denying them subsidies paid to Israeli farmers, as has been the case with poultry, milk, and dairy products. These subsidies have anyhow been considerably reduced in the past four years, so that their total abolition or alternatively, their payment to Palestinian farmers, too, would not make much of an inroad in the Israeli budget. Any prohibition of imports of agricultural products between WB/G and Israel should be made only on the bona fide grounds of preventing the spreading of contagious diseases of vegetables, plants, fruits, livestock, and poultry.

• Limitations on any kind of business licensing should be abolished, except in cases in which they would be required of the Israelis too, e.g., because of their potentially unfavorable impact on ecology. In particular the issue whether an enterprise has the potential to become a rival to an Israeli one should not be taken into consideration.

• Free movement of labor, as took place more or less prior to the *intifada*, should be renewed, as both sides should give up any disturbances to this movement.

• There should be no limitations on the import and export of Jordanian dinars to and from the territories. Other currencies should enjoy the same status in the territories as in Israel.

• At the least, Jordan should revert to the trade policy it practiced prior to the break of relations with the West Bank in August 1988.

• The oil-rich Gulf states should also return to their policies concerning agricultural imports from the territories.

• The Gulf states should also allow transfer of remittances to relatives of Palestinian workers, as was customary prior to the restrictions introduced in the last years of the 1980s. These are the main issues to be settled between WB/G, Israel, and Jordan in order to return to the economic relations and standards of living prevalent prior to the *intifada* and the Gulf tension and war period. However, in addition to the above steps it would be desirable, even during the pretransitional period, to make further advance toward economic recovery and normalization. The main additional improvements should be:

• Abolition of restrictions on the influx of investment capital as long as it is designated for investment purposes proper, excluding projects that may constitute a security danger to Israel. There should be no more restrictions on the influx of capital because of its source. As long as it is not directly involved, Israel should cease its policy of judging the appropriateness of any investment. Neither should Israel restrict investments on account of their intended purpose, be they economic, social, or infrastructional.

• Establishment of appropriate Palestinian financial institutions should be encouraged.

The Second Stage—The Transitional Period

There are many possible scenarios for a transitional period: transition during a period of negotiations toward a permanent solution; a period in which the territories should be prepared for the permanent solution that has already been decided upon, be it an independent Palestinian state, federation or confederation with Jordan, or autonomy within the state of Israel. The various scenarios may also determine what kind of economy may be appropriate for the economy of WB/G and its economic relations with Israel and Jordan. The envisaged length of the transitional period also may be an important determinant in this respect.

In order not to engage in a lot of detailed differences between a number of scenarios, it will be preferred in this chapter to dwell on one scenario (within the context of continued Israeli occupation of the territories during the transition period). In this scenario there will be free movement of trade, labor, and capital between Israel and the territories and considerable movement toward the same freedoms with Jordan, and considerable economic self-rule while adhering to basic Israeli economic arrangements such as customs due, monetary policy including exchange rates, et cetera.

In addition, an initial push should be encouraged toward economic buildup based also on refugee rehabilitation and on undisturbed influx of capital (which under these circumstances will probably be rather moderate). It will also be assumed that those economic steps proposed for the first stage will have already been implemented, or will be so in the second stage.

The main change in the second stage is the construction of a framework in which the Palestinians would take over most of the economic and social policy-making and its implementation.

• All the civil functions that at present are performed in WB/G by Israeli officials should be transferred to Palestinian teams. For coordination with the relevant Israeli civil authorities, every team should be appointed one Israeli liaison officer in the relevant Israeli office. However, except for matters concerned with security, the Palestinian teams will be invested with all the authority that de facto is now in the hands of Israeli ministers.

• The annual budget (income and expenditures) of the territories should be prepared by a Palestinian team. The only prerogative Israel should still keep in this respect is the determination of the maximum size of the annual budget deficit in cooperation with the Palestinian budgetary team.

• Economic policy disagreements between Palestinian and Israeli civil authorities should be brought before a joint Palestinian-Israeli committee for decision.

• A Palestinian team of experts should be given the task of drawing up an economic plan for the entire transitional period. A tripartite committee of Palestinians, Israelis, and representatives of the World Bank should discuss and revise the plan if necessary.

• According to the plan the requested foreign assistance and private investment requirements should be established. If it would turn out that the envisaged financial means cannot be expected to materialize, the plan will have to be adjusted accordingly.

• The Jordanian dinar and the Israeli NIS should remain the sole legal tender in the territories. Monetary policy, including foreign-exchange policy, should remain in the hands of the Bank of Israel. If during the transitional period peace agreements with Arab states should be reached, their currencies will have to be given the status of legal foreign currencies in the territories as well as in Israel.

• Within this administrative framework most of the present economic-related problems, such as trade and business licensing, and trade with OECD and East European countries, should be solved.

• Jordan should lift its sanctions against WB/G by abolishing all quantitative restrictions on exports from WB/G, exports of firms established during the occupation, and on goods that contain Israeli raw material and equipment imported by Israel. In addition, Jordan should stop luring firms (by threats or otherwise) from the West Bank to Jordan. Jordan should also encourage banks active in Jordan to strengthen the financial setup in the WB/G.

• During the transitional period it may become possible to further the rehabilitation of in-camp refugees in WB/G. However, one should be aware that during this period it may still be difficult to arrange comprehensive rehabilitation for several reasons: unwillingness of the Arab states and of the Palestinians to prematurely liquidate what, by the Arab states, is considered to be one of the major political assets in their struggle with Israel; reluctance by the refugees to give up their official status as refugees, which provides them with some advantages; the difficulty of finding capitalists to invest in a region that is still considered unstable; and, last but not least, the apprehension of the Israeli authorities that a major involvement by international agencies and foreign countries, in particular Arab ones, may liquidate almost completely Israel's authorities' impact on economic and even political issues in the territories. However, in spite of these obstacles, it may still be feasible to start to rehabilitate on a small scale. This start may include comprehensive planning of rehabilitation on a grander scale.

In order to make rehabilitation possible, the following efforts will have to be made:

• Several hundred million dollars of aid and investment will have to be secured. This may be obtained from international agencies such as the World Bank, various organizations for refugee aid, the EEC, the United States, Canada, and Japan, and the oil-rich Arab countries.

• Israeli goodwill to support this effort will have to be obtained.

• The UNRWA will have to be convinced that it should prolong the refugee status until the permanent solution for the territories will be agreed upon and implemented, and perhaps even one to two years thereafter, for those refugees who will be rehabilitated. The rehabilitation should include proper housing and infrastructure inside or outside the refugee camps and provision, as far as is possible, of jobs within the territories by establishing new enterprises and general infrastructure facilities.

The Third Stage—The Permanent Solution

Political Obstacles and Intrinsic Constraints

There are several possible scenarios for the permanent political solution, of which the main ones are autonomy within the state of Israel, confederation or federation with Jordan, and an independent Palestinian state.

If it is the will of the three peoples to have close economic relations, the economic impact in all three scenarios can be very similar. However, if this does not exist, then only in the autonomy scenario will the economic relations between Israel and the territories be necessarily very close, while the relationship with Jordan is not predictable. In the other two scenarios—confederation/federation—with Jordan, or an independent Palestinian state, the closeness of the relationships may run the whole spectrum. In the stages prior to the permanent one, the main attention should be focused on the removal of political obstacles to economic relations and developments. However, one can be assured that in all the permanent solution scenarios, WB/G's intrinsic or natural endowment constraints to economic growth and development will be more binding than the political ones. The main intrinsic constraints of WB/G are the smallness of the economy and population, the geographic position, the extreme scarcity of natural resources, and certain scarcities in human capital resources. There is not much that can be done about the immediate scarcity of natural resources, except perhaps to intensify the search for oil. The lack of water will certainly constitute a major bone of contention in the peace negotiations, but whatever the outcome, water in this region will remain scarce and dear (until cheap technologies for desalination are developed). Therefore water will not be able to contribute much to the economic development of the area. Human capital resources from abroad may become partly available in the short run, in particular from the Palestinian Diaspora; in the long run the educational system will have to be thoroughly overhauled.

Of these constraints the main intrinsic one to development will be the smallness of the economy of the territories. Therefore the strategy for economic growth and development will have to be molded with this major shortcoming in mind—the future Palestinian economy will depend to a considerable degree on its ability to export.

The Main Goals of a Strategy for Development of WB/G

The development of the WB/G must be based on an overall strategy of economic development and economic goals. The three primary goals for a Palestinian entity can be identified as follows:

(a) Sustained economic growth, which should lead to a radical improvement of the derelict infrastructure and to a gradual increase in the standard of living of the population, that had a 1987 (pre-*intifada*) annual per capita GNP of $2,130 in the WB and $1,470 in Gaza.

(b) Domestic absorption of a large proportion of the 105,000 workers from the territories employed in Israel, as well as most of the net annual addition to the labor force of 10,000 workers. To these may be added in the wake of modernization many more thousands expelled annually from economic branches (in particular agriculture) in which disguised unemployment still prevails. Further need to absorb workers in the economy may result from the immigration of returnees from the Palestinian Diaspora.

(c) A reasonably balanced balance of payments.

These goals of growth and worker absorption may be effectively achieved mainly by a large-scale process of industrialization. Agricultural production may expand, even considerably, if additional water resources can be made available, but such a process is inevitably linked to modernization of agriculture, which would result in a decline in the number of workers engaged in this branch, and in all circumstances water will remain an expensive production input.

Construction, in particular housing, will most probably employ an increasing part of the labor force. But this will be a passing phenomenon, and the impact of construction on the balance of payments may be wholly negative: increasing imports while contributing little, if anything, to exports. Because of lack of relevant natural resources except for those needed in the production of cement, most raw materials will have to be imported as well as a large part of the finished products. In addition, as the West Bank and Gaza are net importers of most of the necessary construction products, a very large part of salaries and profits would be spent on imports, too. At the same time, housing is not usually exported except if sold to rich foreigners.

In a self-governing entity it is also reasonable to expect that the public sector and welfare services will expand considerably. Experience in newly established countries in the Middle East provides evidence that there is grave danger in overexpanding and overmanning these services, which then become a heavy and lasting burden on the government budget and thereby on the whole economy. The temptation for Palestine to tread the same line will be very great because the public sector appears the easiest one, and the cheapest in which to establish jobs in the short run. This trend may be even more tempting in the Palestinian case because of the large numbers of high school graduates without specific skills. The proportion of the population with this kind of education is much larger in the WB/G than in other countries that are in the same range of income per capita. While such employment could be an easy way to achieve the second goal—domestic employment of the labor force—it would not make a contribution to economic development, and would even prevent it to a large degree.

There is only one economic branch—besides industry—that could make an important contribution to the export and to the economic development of Palestine, and this is tourism. Because Palestine features a considerable number of places holy to the three monotheistic religions, enjoys a climate attractive to Arabs from many countries in the Middle East, and is also regarded among many in the Palestinian Diaspora as their homeland, tourism could become, in peacetime, a major pillar of the Palestinian economy, contributing to its three most important goals. While the major generator of sustained economic development in Palestine will have to be the industrial branch, many industries could be established to cater to the anticipated large influx of tourists.

A Strategy of Industrial Development in the WB/G

Export Orientation versus Import Substitution Strategy in WB/G

A small domestic market cannot provide the necessary economic environment for the production of a large variety of goods. Even goods for which domestic demand may be large enough to justify relatively large-scale efficient production would require no more than one single firm or factory in a specific industrial branch to enjoy economies of large scale. The monopoly or oligopoly thus created may nullify, to say the least, any gain resulting from large-scale production processes. Therefore a small economy usually has to import large quantities of goods. To finance this, it must develop exports. If the economy concentrates on production for the domestic market, most probably by preventing competition from abroad with the help of tariff and nontariff measures, the country's production will become qualitatively inferior and therefore unable to compete in international markets.

The almost inevitable conclusion is that in order to grow and develop economically and to raise the standards of living, the main anchor for a strategy of development of Palestine in the long run will be the development of exportable goods. In this case the ongoing debate on import substitution versus export promotion as a long-term strategy is simply not relevant. The case for making the Palestinian economy export oriented seems obvious. However, it is important to dwell on this subject because of the tendencies developing among Palestinians since the outset of the *intifada,* and to a degree, even before. Self-sufficiency (which is used as a synonym for autarchy) has become almost the official dogma of the *intifada.* Though this dogma advances immediate political goals, it may in the long run prove fatal to the economic development of the Palestinian entity in times of peace. The reason is that in the interim, economic interest groups may become entrenched in economic advantages that they acquire and will therefore work as pressure groups to prevent change in the status quo, to the detriment of the Palestinian economy. This could also lead to dangerous social unrest. Such pressure groups are usually very effective because they have the means to endear themselves to the political leadership and thus acquire considerable wealth and privileges, thanks to economic legislation that supposedly furthers the self-sufficiency of the economy.

If such legislation is passed due to the pressure of interest groups, it may also generate other interest groups that agitate in the opposite direction. But once legislation has been passed in order to further nationalistic, religious, or other ideologies, it becomes extremely difficult to get rid of; the whole debate moves into the realm of the irrational.

For all these reasons, despite the international evidence that in order for small countries to prosper, their strategy must be export oriented, there are numerous difficulties in the path of developing such an economy. This will be especially true for an entity with so little industrial experience in relatively large and technologically advanced enterprises. It is very difficult to develop an export-oriented industry without having previous experience in industrial production for domestic use, through which the elementary handling of the industrial production process and management can be acquired.

In addition, export markets, especially in the countries of the Organization for Economic Cooperation and Development (OECD), are notoriously "spoiled": the standards of quality and consistency that they require are very high, delivery times must be adhered to, marketing methods are very different from those prevailing domestically, and information about the competitors' capabilities and intentions is difficult to come by. Thus, there exists an apparent paradox in the approach to development in general, and industry in particular, of an export-oriented strategy: an import substitution path is feasible as a start toward economic growth but leads to a cul-de-sac; the export-oriented strategy is not feasible at the start (in particular, if exportable natural resources are scarce) but is the best long-term strategy if a critical industrial mass and experience already exist. Therefore the challenge should be to achieve reasonable dovetailing of the two strategies: import substitution and export orientation, avoiding the pitfalls inherent in each approach. A brief outline of such a dovetailing strategy for development as applied to the case of the WB/G is presented in the following paragraphs.

The Rehabilitation of Refugees to Generate General and Industrial Development

As is well known, a large number of Palestinian refugees live in the territories: 250,000 in Gaza, where they constitute 44% of the Palestinian population, and 95,000 in the WB, where they are 10% of the population. Most live in extremely primitive conditions. One of the first tasks of a sovereign Palestinian entity will be the rehabilitation of these refugees. This is first of all a grave humanitarian issue, which may also have far-reaching political consequences. If no major effort is made for the rehabilitation of these unfortunate people, they will continue to be the powder keg of the Middle East, and out of their misery will spread terrorism and unrest throughout this area and far beyond. (It may turn out that the number of refugees will be increased by returnees from Lebanon and elsewhere, but by how much it is impossible to estimate. We shall refrain from taking them into account because of the difficulty in estimating their numbers, and also because they will not change the principles of our analysis, but only the magnitude of the problem.)

In the interest of promoting stability, it is likely that the international community—the OECD countries and the rich Arab oil states, as well as international institutions such as the World Bank and the International Monetary Fund—will be willing to contribute generously to this cause with aid and easy loans. Very rough estimates put the capital needed for housing, establishment of working places, and the construction of infrastructure at $10–$15 billion to be spent over a period of about ten years, or about $1–$1.5 billion, on the average, per annum. Part of this investment, in particular the establishment of working places and infrastructure, may be made on a purely commercial basis by the private sector in the above-mentioned countries and in the territories themselves. Such a magnitude of investment, in particular in infrastructure—electricity and water supply, telecommunications, industrial parks, roads, schools, hospitals and clinics, and public buildings—will benefit not only the refugees but also the population at large. If the capital in fact becomes available on reasonable terms, the refugees will not constitute an economic burden on the Palestinian entity at all, but rather will become its greatest economic asset.

Such an influx of capital will enable in the first years almost a doubling of aggregate demand. Not only the magnitude of the increased demand will be of significance but also its composition, which will include an exceptionally high component of capital goods. In the territories it will be possible to produce economically only some of the goods demanded; the rest will have to be imported. It is not within the scope of this chapter to detail which products can be produced in the territories. But we shall point out, as illustrations, prospective candidates for domestic production. These products are chosen based on two criteria: the magnitude of anticipated domestic demand and the exportability of the goods in the future, in particular to Arab countries. While eventual profitability should be the main criterion, this cannot even be assessed at this stage.

Housing and construction will be the first area affected in a massive way, through the building of homes for refugees and large infrastructure construction, such as the deep-sea port in Gaza, road and rail connections between the WB/G and probably Jordan, roads in general, and industrial parks. For such purposes alone, hundreds of workshops and small-to-medium-size enterprises (measured by the territories' standards) can be established:

(a) a cement factory

(b) prefabricated house factories to supply housing to the poor and lower middle classes and for industrial parks and schools

(c) factories to produce bathroom and kitchen accessories, such as bathtubs, showers, sinks, toilets, faucets, water and sewage pipes for home installation, etc.

(d) factories and workshops for furniture for homes, schools, offices, and hotels

Manufacture will also be required of various components for infrastructure:

(e) electricity and telephone poles

(f) pipes for water and sewage conductors

(g) various small-scale transformers and generators

(h) numerous metal and plastic products connected with the infrastructure construction and various spare parts for machines

These are only a few examples of the kind of products whose profitability should be studied.

In order to prevent some of the pitfalls of import substitution projects mentioned above, a few suggestions follow on how to go about the establishment of such enterprises. Contractors of large projects, such as the Gaza port or the telephone exchanges, should be required in their contracts to help establish some of the relevant factories in the territories, and to buy their products if they are competitive in terms of quality and cost. Likewise, such contractors should be asked to provide vocational training for local workers who will administer and maintain the project upon completion. Such products will also be exportable.

In this way, refugee rehabilitation can become the generator of industrial development. In fact, the rehabilitation will provide a unique opportunity—which is not likely to recur—for the establishment of a solid foundation for sustained industrial development and economic growth in the territories.

So far these suggestions envisage an export industry developing on the basis of an industry created in response to domestic demand. However, this domestic demand and therefore also the industry based on it, will be in part of a temporary nature, through it will be an excellent training ground for further industrial development. Such further development will of necessity be mainly export oriented, as domestic demand will become of marginal importance.

The main imponderables in the problem of what kind of industry has a chance to succeed in the export markets are twofold: which markets have the best prospects for absorbing products produced in the territories, and which of the territories' products will be almost exclusively for export? Both of these questions are dependent on the time horizon: In the long run, it may be expected that more markets will open up to Palestinian products, and as a function of time, the range of products and the extent of value added in the Palestinian products will increase.

Prospective Export Markets for Palestinian Products

In principle there are six major prospective markets for Palestinian goods: the rich Arab oil countries, other Arab countries, Israel, the less developed countries (LDCs), Eastern Europe, and Western Europe.

The rich Arab countries are a natural major target for industrial products and for services. Their proximity should be regarded as a considerable advantage. Although the competition for the oil-rich Arab market is fierce and the market has shrunk considerably in the second half of the 1980s, it still amounts to about $30–$40 billion, mainly of civilian goods. Thus capturing even 2%–3% of this market (constituting 40%–60% of the territories' GDP) could mean a breakthrough for the Palestinian economy. Furthermore, cooperation in the production of industrial and agricultural products between the WB/G and Israel could very much expand the range of exportable products from Palestine to the Arab countries. Knowledge of the Arab language, culture, life-style, and particularly of the very special traditions of doing business and the many contacts that the Palestinians have acquired through their Diaspora and otherwise, should give them a competitive edge over other, non-Arab countries.

The second potential export market, the poor Arab countries, is probably much less promising, because they are already producing so much of what the Palestinians may be expected to produce, and the labor costs there may be lower. Again cooperation with Israel could provide the Palestinians with an extension of the export range in products in which they would not have to face competition with local Arab products in these countries.

The new developments in Eastern European countries may raise justifiable hopes of their becoming an important market for the Palestinian exports. This statement rests on several a priori considerations: the Eastern European market is less particular than the Western world and the rich Arab countries and Israel. Therefore, in the beginning stages of industrial and agricultural exports it may be easier for the Palestinian goods to satisfy the Eastern European markets. It is also well known that the East Europeans have great difficulties in paying in convertible currencies for their imports. This may work in favor of the Palestinians because they could make barter deals much more easily than the Western countries or Israel; for example, by importing heavy electrical equipment in return for their exports.

The Western European market may prove very difficult for Palestinian industrial exports, because of the high demand in quality and standardization. This market may become even more difficult after 1992. The primary exception to this may be the traditional cottage industry products.

With the development of industrial and agricultural know-how, of appropriate marketing methods, and the establishment of more sophisticated industries, the Palestinians may also become competent competitors in the Western markets. But this is a lengthy process. The oft-cited successes of Singapore, Hong Kong, South Korea (and to some extent also Israel) were not achieved overnight; they were rather the results of effort over a protracted period of time.

The last but not least important prospective market for Palestinian exports is Israel. Although the occupied territories achieved a considerable success in their exports to Israel (about $300 million in 1987) it would certainly have been much greater if the economic system had not been rigged against the Palestinians, as already mentioned. The considerable quantity of exports to Israel, which was realized despite the lengths to which Israel went in order to prevent the developing of exports from the territories to Israel, are the best witnesses that the exports to Israel may be increased considerably if the artificial barriers are removed. Such exports to Israel may also generate additional exports from Israel to Palestine. Any further economic agreement between Israel and the Palestinians should include clauses of preferential treatment for the Palestinian entities' exports and imports, which in fact will mean a temporary discrimination in favor of the Palestinians by the countries importing from WB/G and exporting to them.

Israelis and Palestinians will have to find ways to cooperate in spite of deep-seated resentments. Both parties will have to consider not only the losses they may suffer due to deeds of the other side but also the gains that cooperation may offer. Israel will have to realize that opening its markets to Palestinian food, textiles, footwear, metalworks, and other products may meet with compensation in the export of equipment and know-how for these very industries to the Palestinians, and by establishing joint ventures for marketing, a variety of jointly produced goods in the large Arab markets.

Some industries have been proved inefficient in the latest economic upheavals in Israel, and the Israeli economy in general has outgrown them and may be better off without them; at the same time these industries can provide an important stage in the development of an industrial structure for the Palestinians. Israel should not fear Palestinian competition, as long as it maintains its ability to innovate and to keep pace with technological innovation. By way of parallel, Japan may feel uncomfortable with South Korean competition, and is even gradually losing to it some of its more prestigious industrial branches, but it is successful in new ventures and in breaking new horizons. Israel should be more worried about being flooded by cheap imports dumped through the WB/G by third countries. This problem can only be efficiently prevented by coordination of economic policies with Palestine.

The Palestinians on the other hand should be aware that quick industrial development may be achieved to a large extent through cooperation with Israel. The very proximity of Israel and the similar experiences that Israel has had in industrialization may be more relevant to the Palestinian needs than the alternatives: assistance by far-away countries with less relevant experience than Israel has, or the import of almost all products from abroad.

Therefore it may be argued that the most important determinant for economic cooperation between Israel and Palestine will be the development of awareness by both parties that there is much more to be gained than lost through cooperation. This will create a modicum of interdependence, but that is the road many countries, and most of the developed ones, took—successfully—after the Second World War. Israel for its part will have to learn to think of the territories as a state and not as a corner shop in competition with the one on the next street. The main factor in advancing economic cooperation between Israel and Palestine will be their willingness to pursue the cooperation.

Conclusions

The main conclusion of this paper is that for the development of the Palestinian economy a strategy of dovetailing should be applied: first establishing industries producing goods for the domestic market, the aggregate domestic demand for which will be increased by a large capital inflow. Most of these industries should be established with the intention of their eventually producing goods for export, and not just for domestic use. This dual purpose—for domestic and export markets—will facilitate the dovetailing strategy, as the Palestinian entrepreneurs and laborers will be able, under the umbrella of the domestic market, to gain experience in producing export quality products and marketing them in foreign countries. The second stage will be the establishment of almost purely export-oriented industries.

The beginning stage of this strategy carries with it certain dangers, in particular that the domestic production will be quarantined—that is, cut off from the outside world, by heavy subsidization, establishment of monopolies, tariff and nontariff barriers, and similar measures. This should be prevented and arrangements with friendly prospective markets should be made, such as time-limited reduction in tariff, exemption from nontariff, and similar measures, which the importing country will also be allowed to abolish.

Also of major interest should be the attempt to lure foreign companies to invest, on a commercial basis, in the industrial development of Palestine. This could be most helpful in establishing profit-seeking industries, keeping product quality standards high, and facilitating the marketing of products in other than the domestic market.

To achieve this the large Palestinian and Arab Diasporas should be recruited.

Cooperation with Israel may enlarge the range of exportable goods and facilitate the development process.

Some Casual Reflections of the Economic Framework in WB/G, and the Economic Relationships between the Three Entities—Israel, WB/G, and Jordan—Following a Permanent Solution of the Arab-Israeli Conflict

Following any of the three permanent solutions, the 105,000 workers from WB/G in Israel would continue to work there for a considerable period of time. Therefore it would be important for WB/G to insist on the continuation of free movement of labor. As has been explained, WB/G will have a lasting interest in increasing its exports, which of course can best be achieved within a relationship of at least a customs union. Therefore WB/G should be interested in such a union with Israel and Jordan and would be most likely to seek a close economic relationship with the EEC as well as a trade agreement with the United States on the lines of the Israeli–U.S. agreement.

In the case that the permanent solution will be autonomy status for the territories as part of Israel, the economic setup of WB/G would be similar to that outlined in the second stage. Any remaining regulation of the Arab boycott by Jordan and other Arab countries concerning the territories as well as Israel will have to be lifted.

In the case of an independent Palestinian state or a confederation with Jordan, economic relations with Israel may turn out to be less close, though a customs union or even an economic union (on the lines of the 1992 EEC envisaged relations) with Israel could still be worked out. In any case WB/G would most probably seek close economic relations with the EEC, which would most likely be granted and in one way or another would also yield close economic relations with Israel. With Jordan the relations are likely to be closer than in the autonomy solution.

In any of these solutions it would probably be advisable that Israel, and perhaps also Jordan and the Arab Gulf countries, grant preferential treatment to WB/G exports and subsidize exports to WB/G (e.g., petroleum) for a limited number and quantity of products and a limited period of time. Thereby the handling of the preferential treatment would be in the hands of those extending it.

Appendix: The State of Industry in the WB/G

The state of industry is poor by any standards. In the West Bank the industrial branch comprises about 8% of the GDP and in Gaza 14% (mining and industry). (In Gaza this probably includes some Israeli industries.) Most of the industrial establishments are small by any standard: the number of workers, capital investment per worker, production. In fact, most are actually workshops rather than factories, employing fewer than five workers; only some 5% of all laborers in industry in the West Bank are employed by the half dozen relatively large establishments that have more than one hundred workers. In Gaza the situation is even worse. Efficiency in the West Bank is very low; the 17% of the working population employed there produce only 8% of GDP; in Gaza 18% of the employed product 14% of GDP. The industrial branch is mainly based on traditional industries such as processing foods, soap making, textiles, handicrafts, and quarrying.

Despite this generally sorry picture of the industrial branch, there exist a few islands of efficiency and modernization. The main food industry—olive oil production— is also one of the two main industrial branches that has undergone a thorough modernization process in the past fifteen years, including major capital investment in state-of-the-art equipment. The other branch that has modernized and made large capital investments is quarrying. Both of these industrial branches are also large exporters of their products to the east of the Jordan river; large quantities of cut quarry stone are also exported to Israel.

In the traditional food processing branch of industry there are also two relatively large, long-established firms, one producing samneh (a kind of margarine), and another producing chocolates and sweets. Both export much of their product to Jordan and east of it.

The other traditional industries have made, at the best, slow progress in their production processes. There are, however, a few relatively new firms, especially in the plastic industry and in pharmaceuticals, paper products (which have made probably the largest inroad of all Palestinian products into the Israeli market), detergents, agricultural appliances, and soft drinks. A few of these firms have been established since the occupation. Some use reasonably modern and effective equipment. To the best of my knowledge, none of the traditional or new firms is engaged in research and development activities. Most of the industries are in the West Bank. In Gaza, it should be mentioned, there are several firms engaged in assembling electronic and electrical appliances.

11 Palestinian-Israeli Economic Relations: Is Cooperation Possible?

Hisham Awartani

Economic cooperation among all countries in the Middle East, including Israel, has become one of the central components of the international order envisaged for the region in the wake of the Gulf war. Economic stability and growth are certainly high priorities against the background of poverty, famine, and extreme inequality, which has long characterized many countries in the region. Of course there have been many reasons for the economic predicament of some countries, but the prolonged state of war between Arab countries and Israel is certainly a major factor. So it is not surprising to see that all countries in the region perceive economic cooperation as a valuable outcome for a peaceful settlement to their endemic conflict with Israel.

The economic rewards following peace between Israel and its Arab neighbors are easy to envisage, although difficult to quantify. These gains relate mainly to expected cuts in military expenditure, improved investment climate, gains accruing to free trade, and the enormous potential for joint ventures. Many economists suspect, however, that some of these changes will proceed at a slower pace than anticipated. They point in particular to the reluctance of some countries in the region to introduce abrupt and substantial cuts in military spending.

The prospects of economic cooperation between Israel and Palestinians in the West Bank and Gaza Strip are particularly difficult to identify and evaluate because of the ambiguity regarding the future of relations between the two feuding sides. The forthcoming analysis views prospects of economic cooperation between Israelis and Palestinians under the following political assumptions:

1. The West Bank and Gaza Strip will continue to constitute one political entity, despite geographical separation. While under occu-

pation the two territories are often referred to as the "occupied Palestinian territories." Another name may have to be suggested for the autonomy period, which is viewed by many as a period of transition to independence. For the sake of this chapter, Palestine is used to denote a geopolitical entity comprising the West Bank and Gaza Strip, before and after independence.

2. Admittedly, the transition from a political scenario of occupation to one of total independence will undergo stages during which the evolving Palestinian entity will not assume total sovereignty. Yet, it is still assumed that Palestinians will seek sovereignty over their economic resources and policies even during preindependence period.

3. The Palestinian leadership will not resort to closing borders with Israel under any foreseeable political scenario. On the other hand the degree of openness of Israeli-palestinian borders will be contingent on the nature of relations negotiated between authorities in both sides.

The Background

Economic connections between Palestinians in the West Bank and Gaza Strip and Israel have occupied a central position on the spectrum of their relations during the past twenty-four years. Given a background of conflicting claims and aspirations, economic policy has reflected the divergent interests of the two areas. Instead of playing a pacifying role, economic issues have aggravated differences and further separated Israelis and Palestinians.

No Israeli government has ever formulated a well-defined economic policy relevant to the territories occupied in June 1967. Nevertheless it is abundantly clear that whatever policies were implemented in the territories were consistently weighed in the light of their bearing on Israeli interests, economic or otherwise. And in every case where there had been a conflict of interest among Israel and its Palestinian neighbors, it was Israel's interests that came first. As a consequence of premeditated manipulation, Israeli authorities have gone a long way toward achieving a wide range of ambitious colonial and exploitative objectives. A partial list of Israel's thick track record includes the following:

- Around 65% of all West Bank land area and 50% of Gaza Strip are under Israeli control.

• Israel exploits around 80% of all usable water resources available in the territories.

• Israel was able to absorb around 40% of all Palestinian labor force in the territories at wage levels and conditions considerably lower than those of Israelis. Although the employment of Palestinians from the territories in Israel turned out to be an important form of "cooperation" that served the interests of both sides, this relation was structured to give priority to Israeli interests.

• By deliberate manipulation of bilateral trade, the occupied territories were transformed into a backyard captive market with which Israel enjoys a huge surplus.

• The two major productive sectors, agriculture and industry, have lost much of their relative weight, so much so that their combined share in the territories' GNP dropped below that of wage earnings from Israel.

• Because of a severely retarded economic base, the domestic labor absorptive capacity was sharply undermined, hence stimulating a massive exodus of educated Palestinian workers.

Until 1987 it was not always easy to draw attention to existing anomalies in the economic relations between Israel and the occupied territories. But the eruption of the Palestinian uprising provided a stark reminder of the injustices that characterized Israel's rule of another people. And during the five years since then, evidence has accrued on the high priority of restructuring relations between the two feuding neighbors. It is of course true that the crux of the whole dispute is political. But under the seemingly political surface there lie profound conflicting economic interests that tend to perpetuate the more volatile political and national aspects of the conflict.

Areas of Complementarity

Economic gains to peace between Palestine and Israel will accrue to cooperation in areas of common interest to both sides, in addition to gains derived through other peace-related means. One of the key determinants to the level of cooperation is the scope and magnitude of complementarity that exists or may exist between cooperating partners. This poses the basic question of identifying and evaluating the prospects of complementarity between Israel and its Palestinian neighbors.

Areas of complementarity cannot be fully ascertained at this point, as entrepreneurs from both sides will always come up with new ideas and opportunities for cooperation involving some degree of complementarity. It is possible, however, to envisage complementarity and cooperation in the free flow of labor and capital; more prudent and efficient exploiting of common water resources; and construction of common infrastructure. Obviously, each of these areas is worth detailed investigation and objective evaluation. This chapter, however, is only addressed at identifying and evaluating the prospects of cooperation and complementarity in five sectors that are of special prominence to the Palestinians and Israelis, namely trade, agriculture, industry, water, and tourism.

Trade

Trade between Israel and the occupied Palestinian territories commenced shortly after the onset of occupation in 1967. It has proceeded vigorously both in commodities and services. Trade in services comprises numerous areas, such as banking, insurance, technical expertise, health, and communication. But the main form of service trade is that of labor commuting across the green line.

Immediately following occupation, local markets of the West Bank and Gaza Strip were unconditionally opened to Israeli industrial and agricultural products. The flow of produce from those territories to Israel, on the other hand, has been governed by stiff regulations that are laid down in light of Israel's own interests. Industrial goods of Palestinian origin are in principle permitted entry, subject to compliance with prescribed labeling and hygienic regulations. The entry of farm produce to Israel is contingent on obtaining special permits from relevant (Israeli) marketing boards. In an effort to safeguard their delicate price stabilization scheme, those boards permit the entry of Palestinian produce at the lowest scale, and only when that is needed to alleviate occasional shortages in local supply. Under no circumstances, however, is this form of trade permitted to undermine the interests of Israeli growers.

Inequitable bilateral terms of trade between Israel and the occupied territories have given rise to a typically colonial subjugation of Palestine's economy to that of Israel. As one might very well expect,

Table 11.1
Summary of external commodity trade*—1987 (U.S.$ millions)

	Israel	Other countries	Total
Imports—total	961.2	90.0	1051.2
Agricultural**	114.4	15.8	130.2
Industrial	683.4	80.6	764.0
Exports—total	303.7	93.3	397.0
Agricultural**	30.4	44.8	75.2
Industrial	244.2	58.9	303.1
Balance	(−)657.5	3.3	(−)654.2

*Does not include trade with East Jerusalem (population around 138,000, i.e., 14% of West Bank and Gaza).
**Commodity breakdown is for 1986, as no detailed data are available for 1987.

Sources: Statistical Abstract of Israel, 1990, p. 717. Judea, Samaria, and Gaza Area Statistics, 1987(3), p. 6.

Israel's lopsided policies in regard to the territories' industrial and agricultural sectors have precipitated large gains. Israeli exports to the West Bank and Gaza grew steadily until they hit a record of U.S. $961 million in 1987, which adds up to 91% of the territories' total imports. By contrast, the West Bank and Gaza exports to Israel amounted in the same year to $304 million. This leaves Israel with a substantial surplus in its commodity trade with the territories, amounting in 1987 to $657 million (see table 11.1. In addition to being a major market, especially for certain goods, the territories provide Israeli exporters with the distinctive advantages of operating in a captive market that is rigidly sealed against competing trade, and with which they incur negligible transportation costs.

Commodity breakdown of trade for 1986 shows that 86% of all Israeli exports to the territories are classified as industrial, and only 14% are agricultural (see table 11.1).

Trade in labor services constitutes one of the fundamental facets of relations between Israel and the occupied territories. Ever since the early years of occupation, Israel has become a venue for around 35%–40% of the labor force in the territories. The economic and social implications to this phenomenon are too complex to be evaluated in this chapter, yet it is important to illustrate the impact of this form of cooperation on the balance of trade between the two sides. Based on Israeli statistical data, wage earnings received by Palestinians in the West Bank and Gaza Strip amounted in 1987 to approximately U.S. $466 million, i.e., 18.7% of the territories, GNP for that year (Statistical Abstract of Israel, 1991, p. 736).

Bilateral trade between the territories and Israel was severely restructured in the wake of the Palestinian uprising. The National Command of the *intifada* imposed a strict boycott on all Israeli goods that can be substituted by local produce. Moreover the purchasing power of Palestinian residents was severely curtailed as a result of numerous adverse developments. Consequently, imports from Israel dropped markedly during the *intifada,* possibly by around one-third of their 1987 level.

Cooperation (or confrontation) between Palestinians and Israelis in the area of trade bears differently on the two major productive sectors, agriculture and industry. Relations in each sector will be evaluated separately.

Agriculture

Agriculture plays a unique role in the economic, social, and political life of both Jews and Palestinians. For many decades before and after the establishment of Israel, Jews attached a high value for the "return" to land as being a major conduit to settling on what they perceive as "Erets Israel." Not surprisingly, Palestinians also conceive of agriculture in a para-economic way. Agriculture is the primary user of land and water resources, both of which lie at the heart of the Palestinian-Israeli conflict. The role of agriculture as a source of food supply is also of vital significance to Palestinians. Attaining a reasonable degree of "sufficiency" is important to reduce vulnerability to pressures.

Excessive politicization of agriculture may have its own justifying rationale for both peoples, yet Palestinian and Israeli authorities should be fully aware of the economic implications to their agricultural policies. Given the unabated thrust toward more free international trade on one hand and soaring consumer prices on the other hand, sustaining nonviable farming patterns in Israel or Palestine does not serve the long-term interests of either country. It is therefore imperative that Palestinians and Israelis reexamine their agricultural policies on more solid grounds with a vision of attaining greater efficiency. Bilateral cooperation is an effective way of achieving this objective.

Notwithstanding its complex noneconomic ramifications, the economic setting of agriculture differs markedly on both sides of the green line. This is vividly illustrated, for instance, by sharp differences in agriculture's contribution in gross domestic product (for 1987: 5% in Israel vs. 26% in the territories), share of labor force (5.2% vs. 22%), and share in total exports (7.5% vs. 28%).

Palestinian agriculture has been subject to far-reaching transformations during the occupation period. Among the most significant of these were changes in the labor market, technological transfer, and capitalization shortages. But transformations in external agricultural trade played a particularly significant role in shaping Palestinian agriculture. The following is a brief exposition of trading relations with Arab countries and Israel.

Agricultural Trade with Arab Countries

The flow of Palestinian farm product to Jordan and neighboring Arab countries suffers from transformations originating from political adversities, marked growth in domestic production in Jordan and the Gulf states, exorbitant trucking costs across the bridges, and competition with producers accorded generous subsidies. On top of all these "comparative disadvantages," Palestinian growers are often confronted with arbitrary protectionist regulations that are clearly addressed to obstruct the entry of Palestinian produce.

The aforementioned transformations have reflected in a substantial way on the volume of Palestinian agricultural produce shipped to Jordan and neighboring Arab countries, which dropped from over 200,000 tons per year during 1975–84 to only 42,000 tons in 1989.[1]

Agricultural Trade with Israel

Competition between Palestinian and Israeli producers in markets on either side of the green line has never been equitable. In addition to direct regulatory discrimination aimed at establishing nearly one-way traffic in agricultural trade, Israeli producers enjoy the additional advantages of lavish subsidies and access to a highly developed system of supportive services. Inequitable competition has thus accorded Israel a lucrative surplus on its agricultural trade with the territories, amounting in 1986 to $84 million.[2]

Despite official restrictions, however, Palestinian growers and traders have been able to channel significant quantities of their produce into Israeli markets. This applies to such major products as cucumbers, grapes, and citrus. Given their numerous comparative disadvantages, the Palestinians' apparent competitiveness is worth special notice.

Cooperation Prospects

Contrary to the current confrontational nature of agricultural trade between Palestinians and Israelis, there is abundant room for complementarity and cooperation in this sector. Past experience has clearly demonstrated that Palestinian producers are in principle able to raise their productivity to levels comparable or close to those of Israelis. This applies in particular to certain market-oriented patterns of farming, such as vegetables produced in greenhouses. The technological gap can be narrowed further should the level of supportive institutions available to Palestinian producers and traders be adequately upgraded.

Palestinian growers enjoy important comparative advantages vis-à-vis their Israeli counterparts. Most important, they operate at relatively much lower labor costs, and this assumes critical significance in the economics of labor-intensive production patterns, such as vegetable production.

The comparative advantage of Palestinians in regard to labor comprises two components. First, wage levels are considerably lower than those in Israel, and they are likely to stay like that for a long time. Second, and probably more important, Palestinian farm families resort to mobilizing plenty of labor input that has low or no opportunity cost (women, children, old family members, and the spare time of the family workers). With such a cost advantage they can go a long way in competing with Israelis.

Palestinian producers seem to enjoy also a cost advantage relating to irrigation water. A recent study has revealed that water pumped from artesian wells in the territories is about 20% cheaper than that of Mekorot.[3] The gap may become greater if Palestinians are able to rehabilitate their wells. It is important to note in this connection that farmers in the territories buy water at its actual cost, whereas Israeli farmers have enjoyed for many years heavy subsidies on the price of water, amounting in 1987 to 50% of its delivery price.[4]

The foregoing analysis demonstrates that Palestinians can expand their agriculture in those subsectors where they have a cost advantage, should they be permitted free access to Israeli markets. But the gains for liberalized agricultural trade are also significant on the

Israeli side. Evidently, Israelis will reap the benefits of buying cheaper products, an advantage that bears on every family in Israel.

There are other less visible but equally important benefits accruing to Israel. Palestinians may find it more plausible to take advantage of the extremely well-developed marketing infrastructure in Israel. Hence it is more likely that they will channel the bulk of their farm exports through Israeli intermediaries. Palestinians may also find it more viable to channel their surplus produce to Israeli agroindustrial firms, instead of establishing small and possibly nonviable units of their own. Furthermore, by relying more heavily on Palestinian producers for fresh produce, both for meeting domestic and export needs, Israelis will succeed in sharply cutting their demand for irrigation water. This will help alleviate the presently alarming shortage of water in Israel. If viewed in a long-term perspective, it is then clear that liberalized agricultural trade between Israel and the occupied Palestinian territories would be profoundly rewarding for both sides.

Industry

Unlike agriculture, industry does not play a significant role in the economy of the occupied Palestinian territories. Its contribution to the territories' GDP amounted in 1989 to 7.5%, and its share of the employed labor force was 15.9%.[5] In addition to being noticeably low fraction of GDP, these ratios point to a relatively low productivity. The bulk of existing industrial firms consists of household service or artisan workshops, operated and financed mainly by their owners. A recent survey of West Bank industries has revealed that 88% of all firms that employ fewer than eight workers, and 67% of firms that employ eight workers or more, are owned by individuals.[6] Around 93% of all industrial firms in the occupied territories employ ten workers or fewer.[7] The average total size of investment for firms that employ fewer than eight workers is U.S. $16,200, and for those that employ eight or more workers it is U.S. $192,000 per firm.[8] Counting on the size of investment per worker, this adds up to U.S. $4,418 and U.S. $10,168, respectively.

Problems and Constraints

The relatively minor role of industry in the territories' economy is attributed in part to some inherent and deep-rooted constraints that date back for many years prior to the onset of Israeli occupation. Such obstacles include the marked scarcity of local raw materials; domestic markets too small to sustain viable local industries; and chronic deficiency of skilled manpower, despite one of the highest rates of education in the world. The ratio of workers with above high school education amounted to around 15% in "large" firms and 9% in "small" firms.[9] The ratio of workers who have had industrial education was particularly low, estimated for both categories of firms at about 6%. Another obstacle is the chronic and severe shortage of capital resources in the West Bank and Gaza.

The onset of Israeli occupation precipitated additional impediments bearing on Palestinian industry. The scarcity of credit facilities has assumed greater significance following the total closure of all local banking facilities, and the failure of Israeli banks to play a real role in the area of credit. Furthermore, Palestinian industrialists were confronted with rigid restrictive policies in regard to licensing of new industries. Israeli authorities have consistently manipulated their licensing policies in light of their economic interests, often rejecting applications for industries that may compete with Israeli firms. They have also regularly and freely used their licensing authority in the context of their carrot-and-stick policies of administering local residents.

In addition to all previous factors, the stunting of the Palestinian industrial sector was an unavoidable outcome of the subtle restrictions imposed on the entry of manufactured goods into Israeli markets. Palestinian manufacturers are required to comply with elaborate labeling and hygienic regulations, which often seem to be specifically designed to serve as tacit hurdles, clearly aimed at serving Israeli manufacturers. For instance, labels on all Palestinian-manufactured items should indicate in sufficiently large script the origin of those products so that Israeli consumers are alerted to their origin before deciding to buy them. In sheer contrast, Israeli manufacturers exercise total freedom in identifying the country of origin on the labels of their exported products, as that may best serve their interests.

Inequitable trading relations between Israeli and Palestinian manufacturers have been further aggravated by the tremendous gap in the level of infrastructural and other supportive services available to industrialists on both sides of the "green line." Israeli firms have access to a wide range of easy credit facilities, concessional tax structure, infrastructural subsidies, highly sophisticated research facilities, and an elaborate and highly efficient marketing system. Palestinian firms on the other hand are categorically denied all such privileges and, in contrast, they have had to cope with numerous restrictive policies. Under such circumstances, the emergence of full-fledged industrial firms was rendered extremely difficult.

Despite stagnation in most industrial branches, a pronounced growth was noticed during the occupation period in some subsectors where local firms were able to enter into subcontractual arrangements with Israeli firms. This was most evident in labor-intensive industries, such as the sewing branch. During its early stages, this process entailed a narrow margin of real value added, and it amounted basically to one other way of mobilizing unskilled and semiskilled Palestinian labor into the Israeli economy.

In addition to damage ensuing to Israeli policies, the territories' industrial sector was significantly hurt (probably more than agriculture) by Arab regulations relative to the entry of industrial products into Jordanian markets. As a consequence of prohibitive regulations imposed on the flow of raw materials and manufactured goods across the bridges, industrial exports have been confined to a few products that, for reasons specific to each, were able to bypass existing constraints (e.g., stones, marble, margarine, and soap). The total value of industrial exports across the bridges amounted in 1986 to $35.7 million, which accounted for 35.5% of total exports to and through Jordan.[10]

Post-Intifada Developments

The Palestinian industrial sector has undergone profound transformations following the outbreak of the uprising in December 1987. In direct response to the boycott declared on substitutable Israeli products, occupation authorities escalated their regulatory restrictions relative to the entry of Palestinian products. The damage was further aggravated by numerous "security" measures that were targeted to quell the *intifada*. Many such measures had direct economic bearing, such as curfews and roadblocks, but the most vicious of them was resorting to exorbitant tax policies that are of clearly punitive nature.

After a turbulent period of around one year during which many firms went out of business, the majority of industrial firms in the occupied territories have succeeded in surviving Israeli sanctions. Following the shock of the first year after the uprising, most industrial firms have managed to take advantage of the massive protection generated as a consequence of the boycott policies enforced by the uprising command.

Industrial Growth during the Intifada—Costs and Benefits

Industrial growth during the *intifada* is tangibly felt along such indicators as wider range of products produced, larger volume of output and sales, and higher profits earned by industrialists. What is more difficult to quantify, however, is the net ultimate impact of industrial growth on local communities at the macro level.

Certainly, there has been a pronounced rise in the size of the labor force employed in industry. Likewise, there has been a positive impact on the territories' GDP and balance of trade. Palestinian industrialists have also acquired much greater technical and managerial expertise in operating their firms. These successes are manifest in many branches; among the best known are those in the areas of textiles, shoes, and processed food.

Despite the apparent successes, however, growth in Palestinian industry during the *intifada* years poses basic questions relative to the future of this sector, and the prospects of cooperation with Israel. In particular, the following two developments cause serious concern:

1. Locally manufactured products suffer a real problem of quality, both in terms of uniformity and overall quality level. Quality deficiencies, deliberate or not, are being easily passed on to consumers because of the total absence of quality control regulations and institutions.

2. Upon comparing price levels with similar Israeli products, many researchers and consumers suspect that prices of local products are probably higher than justified by a situation of free trade. Consequently, price levels in many industries might have been noticeably lower had Israeli and foreign products been permitted free entry to local markets.

The negative features outlined above justify raising the major question of how real and how stable is the industrial growth that has emerged during the *intifada* years. There are deep fears that many firms might collapse once they are forced to compete in a free market.

Cooperation Prospects

Palestinians and Israelis have very strong motives to promote fairly large industrial sectors, mainly as a safeguard for unemployment hazards and balance of trade deficits. On the other hand the authorities on both sides should presumably have profound interest in optimizing the allocation of their scarce resources and satisfying consumer demand of quality products at sufficiently low prices. A fundamental prerogative for achieving these basic objectives is permitting an advanced degree of free foreign trade.

Industrialists on both sides of the green line will inevitably have to compete in domestic markets, because this serves the long-term interests of Palestinians and Israelis. And if competition is to serve its purpose, Israel should lift those restrictive policies that have been instituted since the onset of occupation. Likewise, Palestinians will be required to abolish the boycott measures they instituted on Israeli products since the outbreak of the *intifada*. Promoting local industries can still be pursued by resorting to means that do not obstruct the Palestinian commitment to free trade.

There remains the fundamental question of identifying the areas in which Palestinian industrialists have enough comparative advantages to compete with or complement Israeli industrial firms. Given the present discrepancies in technical expertise, funding resources, and level of supportive infrastructure, Palestinian firms can compete with Israelis only in those few subsectors where they may enjoy distinct comparative advantages. Such advantages may evolve as a result of the following attributes:

1. The availability of some raw materials in abundant quantities and of good quality and at competitive prices is a classical case for a viable local industry. A prominent example is the relative abundance of building stones and marble. Local industries based on these materials enjoy an important comparative advantage arising from the difficulty and high cost of transporting them as uncut rocks. With the abundant supply of high-quality stones and marble in several parts of the West Bank, this subsector is likely to grow at high rates, since a peaceful settlement is expected to result in sharply rising demand on the construction sector in the Palestinian entity, Israel, and Jordan. Obviously, Israel has a deep interest in procuring building stones and marble from its Palestinian neighbors.

2. The cost differential of labor provides another solid advantage for some Palestinian industries. It is true that wage levels in the territories have risen tangibly during the occupation period, but if one accounts for direct wages and other fringe benefits, then wage levels in the territories are still equivalent to no more than one-third of those earned by comparable Israeli workers. The ultimate impact

of wage differentials on the final cost of the product is proportional to the relative weight of labor cost in the production process. Hence, the impact of this advantage will be greater in labor-intensive industries.

There are numerous cases of manufacturing industries that have taken advantage of the relatively cheap labor in the territories. Prominent examples include textiles and shoes. Israeli interests are likely to be well served when consumers are offered cheaper shoes and clothes, and when Israeli exporting firms acquire greater competitive potential in foreign markets by selling some products that are partly or wholly manufactured by a relatively cheap labor force.

3. The proximity of markets and manufacturing firms in both Israel and the occupied Palestinian territories is conducive to a mutually remunerative advantage. Manufacturers on both sides of the green line will enjoy a transportation cost advantage when competing with products imported from more distant countries. Again, this constitutes an important strategic catalyst to "creating" trade between the two neighboring economies.

4. Handicraft industries can play a considerably more significant role in the bilateral economic relations between Israel and the Palestinians in the occupied territories. The range of industries that go under this category is long, and it includes a wide variety of tourist products (those made of wood, mother of pearl, glass, copper, ceramics), rugs, and traditional dresses. The comparative advantage of Palestinian manufacturers in most of these industries incorporates a combination of indigenous forms of technical expertise and cheap labor.

The above-mentioned examples of comparative advantages indicate that the benefits accruing to the expansion in certain Palestinian industries are likely to reflect positively on both Israeli and Palestinian economies. However, the consequences on the Israeli economy go much beyond those identified above. Palestinian industrialists in the West Bank and Gaza will have to depend on Israeli sources for much of their equipment and machinery, production inputs, several infrastructural services, and advanced technical know-how. Besides, it is possible that while the process of peacemaking is underway, businessmen on both sides will engage more vigorously in joint ventures involving industrial activities in which either side has a comparative advantage. Israelis may not regret leaving some industries for their Palestinian neighbors while they continuously look for higher technology industries.

Tourism

Tourism in the West Bank witnessed rapid growth prior to the onset of Israeli occupation in June 1967. This was facilitated by the complementary nature of tourism between both parts of Jordan, west and east banks. Tourists found it particularly attractive to be able to visit within one country such a combination of sites as the Petra and Jerash in the East Bank, and the unique collection of religious sites in the West Bank. Not surprisingly, the number of tourists grew during 1960–66 by nearly five times, from 132,000 to 617,000.[11] Furthermore, revenue from tourism was consistently higher than commodity exports of Jordan for nearly the entire period of 1960–66.[12] Tourism was estimated to have contributed around 14% of the West Bank's GDP in 1966.[13]

Like in the West Bank, tourism in Israel grew fairly rapidly during the 1950s and 1960s. For instance, the number of rooms in tourist hotels rose from 6,501 in 1958 to 13,091 in 1968.[14] Tourism was motivated until then by the desire to express political solidarity with the Jewish state. The flow of Christian tourists grew only modestly, mainly because Israel did not emerge from the 1948 war with a relatively great share of the religious shrines in Mandatory Palestine. Furthermore, Israel did not develop until then the facilities necessary for leisure tourism.

Tourism in the occupied territories and Israel has been subject to far-reaching consequences in the wake of Israeli occupation. Most important, traffic between the east and west banks of Jordan was drastically obstructed after it had been completely free. By contrast, Israelis and foreign tourists in Israel have been permitted unconditional entry into the territories across the green line after nearly two decades of closed borders. This has accorded Israel the unprecedented opportunity of launching vigorous marketing campaigns, this time promoting itself as the "Holy Land." Israel's tourism potential grew further following the signing of the Camp David accords. Israeli and foreign tourists visiting Israel were permitted entry into Egypt through two border points, hence giving Israel another comparative advantage.

The rapid growth in Israel's tourism sector since 1967 is manifest in many indicators. The number of tourists visiting Israel rose from 114,000 in 1960 to a record of 1,379,000 in 1987. Hotel rooms rose from 6,501 in 1960 to 32,028 in 1987.[15] In 1990, foreign currency earnings from tourism amounted to U.S. $1,080 million—which was equivalent to 11% of Israel's total exports. The overall contribution of tourism in Israel's GNP during the same year was estimated at 3.8%.

Unlike that in Israel, tourism in the West Bank and Gaza stagnated markedly during the occupation period. It is true that the number of tourists visiting both territories had probably continued to rise, yet they were handicapped by numerous problems and constraints. Most important, Palestinian tourism firms and institutions were denied access to financial resources, marketing campaigns, training and manpower development facilities, and proper planning by a Palestinian sovereign authority. In addition to all that, Palestinian tourism institutions were often confronted with numerous restrictive regulations that were clearly discriminatory.

The impact of all these problems and constraints on Palestinian tourism was disastrous. This is evidenced, for instance, by a noticeable decline in the number of hotels and the bed capacity in West Bank hotels. Not counting Jerusalem, the number of West Bank hotels dropped during 1970–87 from twenty-nine to eighteen, the number of beds from 868 to 807, and the number of person-nights from 84,590 to 39,272.[16] A similar drop occurred in all other supportive infrastructure, which continued to lag far behind that of Israel.

The tourism industry was hit very hard following the outbreak of the Palestinian uprising. This was expected in light of the excessive sensitivity of this sector to political unrest and security hazards. Compared with 1987, the number of tourists visiting Israel declined by 15% in 1988 and by 14.7% in 1989.[17] The consequences on Palestinian tourism, however, were much worse. Tourists have become considerably more concerned for their safety in East Jerusalem and Bethlehem, as well as in other parts of the occupied territories. For obvious discriminatory purposes, such fears were over exaggerated by Israeli authorities.

As a result of all these adverse transformations, the tourism sector in the West Bank has nearly collapsed during the past four years. This was abundantly clear in regard to the hotel industry, where bed occupancy averaged on a year-round basis at about 15%,[18] which is much below the minimum required for break-even volume of business. Similarly, there has been a severe recession in the tourism-oriented cottage industries, which have occupied for a long time a significant role in the economies of Bethlehem and Jerusalem.

Cooperation Prospects

Tourism is the economic sector that reflects the highest degree of complementarity between the occupied territories and Israel. The two entities constitute a wealth of tourism attractions that qualify them for a leading position in international tourism. The West Bank is probably the richest country in the world with respect to religious shrines dear to followers of the three great religions: Christianity, Judaism, and Islam. While the potential for promoting tourism to Judaic and Christian locations is fairly well exploited, much more could be done to promote the inflow of Moslem tourists to the second-most-sacred country for them.

In addition to religion-based tourism, the occupied territories and Israel are endowed with a very rich inventory of historic sites that are of prime tourist value. Leisure and weather-based tourism is important in both entities. Health-related tourism occupies increasing importance in Israel, and it certainly has a great potential in the West Bank.

Economic planners in Palestine and Israel are fully aware of the great potential tourism offers to their countries. Palestinians foresee tourism as one of the major components of their economy, especially with regard to its share in GNP and as a source of foreign earnings. Many of them are even hopeful that tourism will be easier to expand than agriculture and industry. Israeli economists and policymakers cherish similar hopes. Many of them realize that opening the borders of the Holy Land to Moslem tourists will entail substantial spin-offs on Israeli tourism and other economic sectors. In addition, vigorous tourism with Arab and Islamic countries will provide further momentum to peaceful relations between Israel and its long-time adversaries.

The areas of cooperation in tourism are easier to identify than those for other sectors. Much could be done with regard to joint planning for this sector. There is a vast potential for reaping economies of scale, hence improving the level of services accorded to tourists and thereby strengthening the competitiveness of both countries in the international tourism market. However, cooperation in tourism, unlike that in bilateral trade and labor, is contingent on a fairly advanced degree of normalization between the two sides, something that has to come up late during the peace process.

Water

Exploiting common water resources is probably the most important area of potential cooperation or confrontation between Israel and its Palestinian neighbors. So far, water relations have been completely unilateral, that is, characterized by total Israeli domination and uncontrolled exploitation of joint resources. In pursuance of old aspirations Israel has consolidated its control on all water resources in Palestine, and even on some resources lying in neighboring Arab countries.

The record of Israeli restrictions and barriers aimed at controlling proper access of Palestinians to their water resources is fairly substantial and it includes the following:

1. Israel instituted a combination of security and political obstacles that resulted in denying Palestinians of their share in the Jordan River Basin, despite being one of its main riparians. According to the Johnston Plan. Jordan (east and west banks) was allocated 720 million cubic meters.[19]

2. Palestinians are not permitted more than minimal use of their underground water supply. The drilling of new wells for irrigation purposes is strictly prohibited, and existing wells are confined to rigid quotas.

3. Israeli wells lying on both sides of the green line and connected to the same aquifers tapped by Palestinians are operated at a dangerous scale. According to Israeli sources, for instance, Israeli wells connected to the Yarqon-Tanninim aquifer pump 320 million cubic meters per year, as against 20 million cubic meters pumped by Palestinian wells connected to the same aquifer.[20] Similar anomalies exist in all other joint aquifers. Excessive overpumping has resulted in a marked decline in the water table and a serious deterioration in the quality of underground water.

Overpumping is one of the major practical manifestations for Israel's lavish water policies. The four-decades-old Israeli commitment to subsidizing irrigation water and growing low-value crops lies at the root of the present crisis. However, exploiting neighbors' water resources is not the answer to Israel's problems.

Table 11.2
Comparative water consumption estimates–1989 (in million cubic meters, unless specified otherwise)

	W. Bank	G. Strip	Total	Israel	Jordan
Total consumption	117	99	216	1840	733
Agriculture	84	70	154	1238	535
Domestic	28	27	55	495	164
Industry	5	2	7	107	34
Avg. population (1,000)	905	720	1625	4560	3091
Per capita (m^3):					
Overall	129	137	133	404	237
Domestic	30	37	34	108	53
Irrigated area					
Total (1,000 donums)	97	100	207	2142	506
% of cultivated area	5.5	58	10.4	49.4	16.4

Sources: 1. Statistical Abstract of Israel, 1990, pp. 3, 8.
2. M. Bilbaisi and M. Bani Hani, Water Resources in Jordan, Proceedings of the Conference on Water Resources in the Arab World, Jordan University, 1989, p. 77.
3. Y. Abu Maile, The Water Problem in Gaza, 1990, p. 4.
4. Departments of Agriculture in the West Bank and Gaza.

The Consequences of Domination

Israel's restrictive and exploitative domination of water resources in the occupied Palestinian territories has gravely affected on the social and economic underpinnings of the Palestinian society. The most visible consequence is the considerably lower per capita consumption in the territories vis-à-vis Israel (and Jordan).

The data in table 11.2 indicate that per capita domestic consumption in the occupied territories amounts to 33% that of Israel, and that the ratio of area under irrigation is about one-fifth that of Israel. Consumption levels are also considerably lower than in Jordan. The impact of these shortages on Palestinians' quality of life and the productive potential of their agriculture is certainly grave.

Cooperation Prospects

Despite their high emotions on the subject of water, cooperation between Israelis and Palestinians and other neighboring riparians is an absolute necessity and not a wishful priority. By contrast, it is dangerously unfair to permit any country in the region to solve its problems at the cost of its neighbors, who in turn may suffer from similar or worse shortages.

The Israeli fervent call for regional cooperation on water is abundantly visible, and it is evidenced by a multitude of political statements and economic studies. But what strikes attention is the reluctance of most Israelis, including some with "dovish" political views, too engage in fair negotiations with the Palestinians on the allocation of joint water resources. The underlying goal for Israel's water policies, it seems, is to create such profound tangible realities that the recourse to major changes becomes unrealistic. Lacking any legal alibi for taking another people's water, some Israeli strategy experts, like Zeav Schiff, explain that on account of "security" needs.[21] Others argue that Israel has acquired de facto ownership rights on account of having used its partners' water for so long. Both arguments can be seriously contested.

Israeli water experts are fully aware of the alarming size of the water crisis that confronts Palestinians in the West Bank and Gaza. Israeli estimates of the demand for water in the territories by the end of the century are forecast by a Palestinian economist at 403 million cubic meters,[22] and at 290–475 million cubic meters by an Israeli water expert.[23] Yet, despite admitting the Palestinians' sore need for additional water resources, senior Israeli experts and officials foresee the solution of this problem only in seeking water from "external sources, such as the Nile, the Litani and the Yarmuk rivers, singly or in combination."[24]

It is of course realistic and highly desired to foresee an advanced degree of regional cooperation in exploiting available water resources. And within this context water might be drawn from external sources. But this is no alternative to giving the Palestinians their fair share of existing resources. And in light of entrenched Israeli water misuses. Palestinians may agree to a gradual restoration of their rights in order to allow Israelis an reasonable adjustment period.

Relinquishing the Palestinians' water rights may look on the surface as a painful and unneeded concession. Viewed from a long-term perspective, however, this need not be the case. There are important justifications to a fair Israeli stand on the water conflict with the Palestinians, other than conforming with international legitimacy and diffusing a major source for their conflict with the Palestinians.

For instance, it is difficult to see how Israel is likely to settle its water disputes with its other neighbors without giving the Palestinians their fair share. Furthermore, if Israel continues to defy international legitimacy on the Palestinians' water rights, it may risk being sanctioned by aid-donor governments and international organizations. International pressure may in fact take forms that are difficult to foresee at the present.

An unavoidable element in the Israeli-Palestinian water conflict is its potential implications for relations between Israel and its neighbors. It is always important to remember that the water conflict lay at the root of most Israeli-Arab wars in the past. Given the excessive vulnerability of water projects and the proliferation of military power within militant fringe groups, it is then easy to see how water disputes may trigger more military confrontations rather than facilitate peace. Should confrontation on water escalate to such destructive levels, one will find it difficult to apportion blame between those who took another people's water and those who resorted to sabotage in order to restore what they perceive as their legitimate rights.

Is Cooperation Possible?

The vast majority of Palestinian and Israeli economists, irrespective of their political denominations, seem to agree that economic cooperation between both sides is not only possible but is imperative for fulfilling long-term economic and legitimate national aspirations. Yet, there are some asymmetries in the gains to cooperation. On the Israeli side, there is the question of whether gains accruing to equitable cooperation are greater than those earned in the context of exploitative subordination. Many economists, including some Israelis, have provided a positive answer to this question.[25] In any case, there are only few Israelis who cherish serious hopes of structuring their relations with the Palestinians on colonial grounds, irrespective of the magnitude of accruing material gains.

The other aspect to asymmetry is that relating to relative gains accruing to cooperating partners. Again, it is likely that the smaller partner, namely Palestine, will benefit relatively more by cooperating with Israel. But this may not be the case if benefits are viewed from a broader and longer term perspective. The dividends to Israel for economic cooperation may take less immediate but very substantive forms. Expenditure on defense will eventually be sharply reduced. With a share of about 27% of the Israeli budget, any cut in the defense budget to levels comparable with other conflict-ridden regions will result in tremendous positive consequences for the Israeli economy.

An important dividend for Israel is paving the way for substantive cooperation with its Arab neighbors. Irrespective of the ups and downs in its relations with the Palestinian leadership, it is very unlikely that any Arab regime will agree to relaxing its boycott of Israel, let alone normalizing relations with it, before it reconciles its conflict with the Palestinians. The Egyptian stand on many aspects of its relations with Israel provides a vivid example on what other Arab countries might do in the future. If, on the other hand, Israel succeeds in gaining admission into the Arab world, and into those Moslem countries that are sensitive to the Palestinian question, then the gains accruing to Israel will be enormous.

On top of the gains identified above, by embarking on a course of cooperation, Israel will evade the rising cost of subjugating another people, which may reach unexpected levels in the future. Palestinians are rapidly learning how to solicit support for their economic grievances from governments and organizations that command heavy weight relative to Israel's economy. The growing pressure exerted on Israel by the European community on account of economic injustices inflicted on the Palestinians is indicative of what Israel may have to expect from other "friends" whom they have thus far taken for granted.

Moving from Subordination to Cooperation

Economic reasoning has not been the only underlying motive for Israel's policies bearing on the economies of the occupied Palestinian territories. In addition to those major nationalistic ambitions outlined earlier, Israeli economic policies were heavily influenced by pressure groups with profound vested interests (e.g., farmers' unions, marketing boards, and certain firms). Furthermore, Israel's reluctance to structure its economic relations with the Palestinians on equal grounds is partially rooted in the way Israelis have become accustomed to dealing with the Palestinians for nearly a quarter of a century. Until now, most Israeli leaders and a great many Israelis have dealt with the Palestinians as unwelcome tenants on "Eretz Israel," and not as people who are striving for their rights.

In light of these deep-rooted inhibitions, it seems too optimistic to expect that Israel will agree to engaging in equitable cooperation with the Palestinians in the near future. A shift in the Israeli stand is contingent on two major transformations. First, Israeli authorities should come to realize that by continued subjugation of another people they might forgo substantial economic gains. Second, Israelis should feel in a tangible way that injustices inflicted on their Palestinian neighbors, economic or otherwise, may entail a heavy economic cost. The recent confrontation between the U.S. administration and the Israeli government on the linking of loan guarantees with Israeli settlement policies in the territories is a vivid example of other future linkages.

Obstacles to cooperation will emanate as well from the Palestinian side, not only on economic grounds. In fact, it is possible that some Palestinian economic sectors will have more to gain from cooperation with Israel than with some neighboring economies. Yet full-fledged cooperation involves moving to a state of normalization that can only be accepted in the context of a political settlement. Until then the forms of cooperation that Palestinians are likely to accept are those deemed so vital that they warrant the implicit political cost (such as employment in Israel and the restructuring of bilateral trade). The least accepted form of cooperation, on the other hand, is that of joint ventures, since it symbolizes an advanced and premature state of normalization.

To conclude, the pace and nature of economic cooperation between Palestinians and Israelis will have to follow decisions made by politicians and not by economists. But entrepreneurs and economists on both sides are anxious to join forces in building a more prosperous Middle East.

Notes

1. *Agricultural Statistical Bulletin,* Nablus: An-Najah University, 1989, p. 10.

2. *Judea, Samaria and Gaza Area Statistics,* Jerusalem: Central Bureau of Statistics, 1987 (3), p. 6.

3. Hisham Awartani, *Artesian Wells in the Occupied Palestinian Territories,* Jerusalem: Palestinian Hydrological Group, 1991, p. 48.

4. David Kahan, *Agricultural and Water Resources in the West Bank and Gaza (1967–1987),* Jerusalem: The West Bank Data Base Project, 1988, p. 50.

5. *Statistical Abstract of Israel,* 1991, p. 717, 731.

6. Abu Shoker et al., *Industrialization in the West Bank,* Nablus: An-Najah University, p. 56.

7. *Statistical Abstract of Israel,* 1991, Jerusalem: Central Bureau of Statistics, p. 746.

8. Abu Shoker et al., op. cit., p. 80.

9. Abu Shoker et al., op. cit., p. 94.

10. *Judea, Samaria and Gaza Area Statistics,* 1987 (3), p. 11.

11. Hanna Odeh, *Economic Development of Jordan 1954–1971,* Amman: Jordan Development Board, 1972, Appendix 6, 11.

12. *Statistical Yearbook 1966,* Amman: Department of Statistics, vol. 17, p. 50.

13. Jamil Hilal, *West Bank Economical and Social Structure 1948–1974,* Beirut: PLO Research Center, 1975, p. 160.

14. *Statistical Abstract of Israel,* 1980, p. 11.

15. *Statistical Abstract of Israel,* 1990, p. 5 and 9.

16. *Statistical Abstract of Israel,* 1989, p. 742.

17. *Statistical Abstract of Israel,* 1990, p. 164.

18. From interviews with board members of the Arab Hotel Association.

19. Thomas Naff and Ruth Matson, *Water in the Middle East: Conflict or Cooperation?,* Boulder: Westview Press, 1984, p. 42.

20. David Kahan, op. cit., p. 21.

21. Zeav Schiff, *Israel's Minimal Security Requirements in Negotiations with the Palestinians,* Washington, D.C.: Washington Institute for Near East Policy, 1989.

22. Hisham Awartani, *A Projection of the Demand for Water in the West Bank and Gaza Strip 1990–2000,* Nablus: An-Najah University, 1991, p. 29.

23. E. Kally and A. Tal, *Economic Cooperation and Middle East Peace,* London: Weidenfeld and Nicolson, 1989, p. 76.

24. Ibid., p. 80.

25. Simcha Bahiri, *Peaceful Separation or Enforced Unity,* Tel Aviv: International Center for Peace in the Middle East, 1984.

12 Some Basic Problems of the Economic Relationships between Israel, and the West Bank, and Gaza

Ephraim Kleiman

This chapter tries to identify what are bound to be the main problems of the economic relationships between whatever political entity that may come into being in the West Bank and Gaza, and Israel, and to outline some possible solutions.[1] No particular assumptions are made about the character of this entity, beyond that both territories will be part of it. As will be shown, the basic problems remain the same for the whole gamut of possible political solutions, from full independence, through some federative association with Jordan, down to full annexation by Israel, though the range of feasible or probable solutions does, of course, vary. It is further assumed that all parties involved will be acting purely out of (economic or political) self-interest, and not out of any altruistic goodwill or concession, as the term cooperation, used sometimes in this context, might suggest.

Because the economic relationships between the territories and Israel are bound to affect the territories to a much greater degree than Israel, the chapter focuses on developments in the former. The Israeli aspect will be brought into the discussion mainly when it reflects on their economies. But being written by an Israeli, this chapter inevitably presents "a view from Israel," though by no means an (official) Israeli view. The previous chapter dealt with the same problems, as seen from the West Bank and Gaza. A comparison of the views from both sides may go a long way to delineate the common ground of the debate.

Underlying the present discussion are national income, balance of payments, and employment data. The only body able to collect such statistics in the territories since 1967 is the Israel Central Bureau of Statistics (C.B.S.). The bureau's professional integrity guarantees that the data published by it have not been tampered with for political reasons. Nonprofessional considerations, however, may dictate which data are collected and with what frequency, and their territorial classification. Thus, for example, no population census has been taken in the West Bank and Gaza for more than two decades, and East Jerusalem is treated as part of Israel. For lack of alternative data, the last practice will be also mostly followed here.[2] The Israeli settlements in the territories are treated throughout as part of the Israeli economy.

No amount of professional integrity can ensure all data to be of the same quality. Thus, for example because of difficulties in monitoring the trade flow between Israel and the territories, the reliability of the data on its commodity structure seems to be much poorer than of those on labor force characteristics.[3]

In the case of the West Bank, the interpretation of national accounts data is complicated by the cyclical behavior of its olive crop. This often varies in a proportion of five to one between alternate years, and on occasion, as in 1988, even of twenty to one! In such a bumper crop year, olives account for over one-third of all agricultural output in what is predominantly still a farming economy. Their cyclicity caused GDP to fluctuate by as much as 20% between successive poor and good crop years.[4] Neutralizing the statistical effects of these fluctuations restricts comparisons to cyclically matched periods of years.

For the period before the 1967 war the compendium of Jordanian data prepared, at the time, by the Israel Economic Planning Authority has still to be superseded; a reconstruction of separate national accounts estimates for the West Bank has also been prepared by the Jordan Department of Statistics.[5] Practically no statistical information seems to be available on the economy of Gaza in those years.

The Conditions of Economic Viability

The question is sometimes raised, whether a political entity comprising an area as small as the West Bank and Gaza can be economically viable. This presumably refers not just to the ability to support the machinery and trappings of government, but to sustaining a standard of living that meets peoples' expectations. An operational definition of when such a standard is satisfactory may be difficult to determine, though the absence of net emigration is a good candidate. In the present context it may suffice if we regard a severe fall in incomes, or possibly even their stagnation over time, as inconsistent with viability.

With economic viability viewed thus as related to the level of income, there is no empirical evidence of it being negatively associated with size: Even if we ignore the oil economies, tiny Monaco and relatively small Switzerland are among the world's richest countries, while gigantic China and India are among the poorest. The popular view of small countries as economically unviable reflects an implicit assumption regarding their inability to take advantage of specialization in production to the same extent as large ones do. But the degree of specialization that large countries attain within their own borders can be achieved also by small ones through the medium of international exchange. Viability thus has to do not with size per se, but with autarky. The smaller the economy, the more closely it has to be integrated in larger markets to achieve a given degree of viability.

The effects of such an integration on the economy, and by implication also the potential ones of a retreat from it, are amply illustrated by developments in the West Bank and Gaza in the wake of their occupation by Israel. No data are available on economic growth in Gaza in earlier years, and those cited sometimes for the West Bank seem contradicted by the high rates of emigration experienced at the time.[6] As the emigration figures refer to a period before the rise in oil revenues and the construction boom in Jordan greatly increased its pull, they imply economic growth in the West Bank to have been very slow, both absolutely and in comparison with the growth experienced in later years. But once the immediate crippling effects of the 1967 war were overcome, the economy of these territories began to benefit from the access to the larger Israeli market, from which it had been isolated until then.

Table 12.1 presents growth figures for the West Bank and Gaza, taken as a whole, between 1969 and 1987, the last year before the outbreak of the *intifada*. The last two subperiods of the table overlap because of the aforementioned necessity, in view of the olive crop cyclicity, to restrict comparisons to even-numbered year periods. As can be seen from the left-hand panel of the table, the per capita gross national product of the territories grew very rapidly in the first decade or so covered by the table, at a rate much exceeding that experienced by the Israeli economy in the same period. As is well known, a considerable portion of this growth represented the remuneration of West Bank and Gaza labor, employed in Israel in growing numbers

Table 12.1
Growth of per capita product, 1969–1986 (percent per annum)

	GNP			GDP		
	West Bank and Gaza (1)	Israel (2)	Difference (3)	West Bank and Gaza (4)	Israel (5)	Difference (6)
1969–72	19.5	7.9	*11.6*	11.9	7.9	*4.0*
1973–76	5.4	0.8	*4.4*	5.6	1.2	*4.4*
1977–80	5.0	1.0	*4.0*	4.5	1.1	*3.4*
1981–84	−0.9	0.6	*−1.5*	−1.6	0.6	*−2.2*
1985–86	3.3	2.6	*0.7*	5.5	2.0	*3.5*
1986–87	5.8	2.9	*2.9*	4.1	2.8	*1.3*

Sources: GDP rates of growth for the West Bank and Gaza, at constant 1986 prices, C.B.S., "National Accounts of Judea, Samaria and Gaza Area," *Special Series no. 818*, Tables 9 and 16, as revised in "National Accounts of Judea, Samaria and Gaza Area, 1983–1989," *Statistics*, XIX, 1989–1990 (February 1991), pp. 8–32 (and unpublished C.B.S. revisions for earlier years); see also C.B.S., *Statistical Abstract of Israel, 1991*, Table 27.6. GNP growth rates derived by multiplying the GDP figures by the GNP/GDP ratio at current prices, obtained from the same table. Population growth rates calculated from midyear population figures, C.B.S., *Statistical Abstract of Israel, 1991*, Table 27.1. Rates of growth for Israel similarly calculated from loc. cit., Table 6.1.

from 1968 onward. In particular, the growth of GNP was nearly double that of the domestic product in the first subperiod covered by the table. But as can be seen from its right-hand panel, domestic economic activity was by no means stagnant. In fact, its growth lagged only little behind that of GNP in the following periods, and GDP per capita nearly doubled between 1969 and 1980.

The political and social conditions in the territories did not favor much indigenous growth. As their economies have become highly dependent on Israel, their growth may have been expected to closely mirror the Israeli one. But, as can be seen from the third row of each panel of table 12.1, until about 1980 the economic growth rate of the West Bank and Gaza greatly exceeded that of Israel. The excess of the former over the latter rate was the outcome of the economic integration process that took place in those years. Integration was due to the partial removal of the until then insurmountable barriers to the movement of goods and factors of production. The resultant pressures toward price unification could be expected to set relative prices close to those obtained in the much larger and richer Israeli economy. In the case of movements of factors of production, it is the price of the relatively abundant factor of production in the territories, labor, that should have risen (and that of the relatively scarce one, capital, that should have fallen). Consequently, integration may have been expected to raise the overall level of the product of the territories, and to raise it there relatively more than in Israel.[7]

In fact, the combined per capita GNP of the territories rose from 13.8% of the Israeli one in 1970 to 22.7% in 1986. A similar rise—from 12.4% to 21.4%—occurred in the GDP ratio of the West Bank (but not in Gaza, where it remained constant), showing the decrease in the income differential between it and Israel not to have been the result just of work in the latter. A retreat from integration may be expected to reverse this process.

Flows of Goods and Factor Services

A movement toward the equalization of prices across the integrated market requires some movement of either or both factors of production and goods. Table 12.2 summarizes the main economic flows that took place between the West Bank and Gaza, and Israel in 1986. The data shown there underline both the high share of Israel in their external transactions, and the importance of these transactions to their economies. It can be seen that of the combined labor force of the two territories, more than one-third was employed in Israel, the wages earned there amounting to nearly one-fourth of their GNP. Israel purchased also nearly three-fourths of their exports, equivalent to about 14% of GNP. At least some of these exports consist of high-value-added goods, such as fruit and vegetables and quarry products. Estimating this value added at, say, one-half that of exports and adding it to the wages earned in Israel, we may say that about one-third of the combined GNP of the West Bank and Gaza was due directly to the sale of goods and factor services to Israel. Of the imports purchased with the proceeds, no less than 90% came from (or, as will be argued later, in part only *via*) Israel. It can also be seen that the importance of these flows was much greater for the smaller and more labor-intensive Gaza than for the West Bank.

It may be noted that missing from table 12.2 are movements of capital, which perhaps may have been expected to have occurred between Israel and the West Bank and Gaza. This is so both because

Table 12.2
Main economic flows between the West Bank and Gaza, and Israel, 1986

	West Bank	Gaza Strip	Total terr.	Israel[a,b]
Employment in Israel ('000)	51	43	94	94
As percent of total employment	*31*	*46*	*36*	*7*
Factor incomes from Israel[b] (NIS millions)	385	341	726	726
As percent of total imports	*50*	*60*	*54*	*5*
As percent of GNP	*17*	*41*	*24*	*2*
Exports to Israel ($ mill.)[c]	156	119	275	275
As percent of total exports	*65*	*85*	*72*	*3*
As percent of GNP	*11*	*21*	*14*	*1*
Imports to Israel ($ mill.)[c]	451	347	798	798
As percent of total exports	*88*	*92*	*90*	*10*
As percent of GNP	*31*	*62*	*39*	*3*
GNP (NIS millions)	2,211	836	3,047	42,070
GDP (NIS millions)	1,826	495	2,321	43,711

a. East Jerusalem included in Israel. The percentages for Israel relate to the obverse phenomena: e.g., exports to Israel from the territories amount to 3% of Israel's total.
b. From National Accounts data.
c. Goods only, exclusive of trade in services.
Sources: C.B.S., *Statistical Abstract of Israel, 1988*, Tables XXVII/22 and XII/10; XXVII/12 and VII/2; XXVII/7 and VI/1; and XXVII/21 and XII/18 (unrevised data).

of the unavailability of data and because, by all indicators, any such flows that took place were negligible.[8]

In contrast to the great dependence of the territories on Israel, the last column of table 12.2 shows the flows between them to have been of much smaller importance for the latter. The great disparity in economic size expresses itself in the same flow of labor services, which accounted for over one-third of all the labor force of the territories, amounting to only 7% of all employment in Israel in 1986; and all purchases of goods and factor services from the West Bank and Gaza amounted to just 3% of Israel's GNP that year. Even as a percent of all imports, imports from Israel to the West Bank and Gaza, were nine times more important in the territories than in Israel.

The data contained in tables 12.1 and 12.2 suggest, first of all, that the immediate costs to the territories of severing all their economic relationships with Israel could be prohibitively high. It is difficult to envisage the circumstances under which an alternative to them could emerge, at least not in the foreseeable future. Provided the necessary capital becomes available, exports of goods could, in principle, take the place of the present export of labor services to Israel. It is also true that, as will be shown later, some of the exports now sold to Israel could in the longer run find alternative markets, and the same could be true, albeit on an even smaller scale, of labor services. (Only some, because no similarly close distanced markets are available for either.) But on the other hand no account has been taken here of the multiplier effects of the incomes thus presently generated, or of the technology transfers and the externality effects resultant from the close association with Israel.[9] Hence the importance of the magnitudes that these flows, as well as that of capital, will assume in the future.

Second, these data also point out the asymmetry in the importance to the territories and to Israel of the flows between them. This suggests that Israel's interest in their continuation will stem mainly from a political consideration, the maintenance of political stability along its borders by means of economic prosperity.

The Flow of Labor Services

The exports of labor services from the territories to Israel are the result of the much lower income and wage levels, and of the poorer employment opportunities, in the former. Despite the rapid GDP growth after 1967, commented upon earlier, the growth of the demand for labor in the territories lagged far behind that of its supply. In this respect the past two decades were a continuation of the two that preceded them. Neither the Jordanian government, in the case of the West Bank, nor the Egyptian government with respect to the Gaza Strip, made any serious attempt to develop the Palestinian territories under their respective rule. The former, because for political (and possibly also security) reasons it preferred to do so in the East Bank of the kingdom;[10] the latter because it considered the strip a burden thrust upon it, and not an integral part of its own, in any case resource-short, country. The result was large-scale emigration, especially of the residents of the West Bank who, as citizens of Jordan, not only could move freely to the East Bank, but also found it relatively easy to hold jobs in other Middle Eastern countries. It has been estimated that emigration offset about 70% of the natural increase in the West Bank in the years 1952–67.[11]

Israeli occupation constituted a break with the previous period in that, *inter alia,* it offered an opportunity for exporting labor services without emigrating, either temporarily or permanently: surveys conducted in the past have shown that nearly nine-tenths of all West Bank residents employed in Israel, and three-fourths of those of Gaza, commute to work daily.[12] The resultant flow can thus be regarded as a case of border trade, except that its magnitude, relative to employment in the territories themselves, is of an order uncommon in such trade.[13]

The reliance on work as commuting *Gastarbeiter* in Israel has the advantage of releasing the territories from the need to mobilize the capital resources that would be needed for their employment there, without carrying with it the social and political price of emigration. It does, however, also expose them to some risks and is not free of certain drawbacks, even if we ignore matters of national pride. The most obvious, especially in view of recent events, is political risk. Having a high proportion of their labor force employed outside their borders may make the West Bank and Gaza highly vulnerable to the threat of the host countries to expel or restrict it, in an attempt to bring pressure upon, or punish, the territories, often at a low cost to themselves. Insofar as this is the case, it can severely impair their economic viability. This was vividly illustrated during the 1990–91 Gulf crisis with the expulsion of Palestinians working in Kuwait in retaliation for the PLO's political support of Iraq, and Israel's suspension of the entry of workers from the territories during the war itself. The continued large-scale reliance on work in Israel may, therefore, be politically unacceptable to a Palestinian entity as perpetuating this vulnerability, even after a comprehensive settlement of the Israeli-Palestinian conflict has been reached.

The employment pattern usually observed when labor flows from lower to higher income countries makes the West Bank and Gaza also highly vulnerable to fluctuations in a small number of industrial activities in Israel. As can be seen in the first line of table 4.3, nearly half of all the residents of these territories working in Israel in 1987 were employed in construction. Of all industries this perhaps is generally the most volatile one, as the demand for housing seems to be highly income and interest rate elastic. In Israel it is also highly

Table 12.3
The industry structure of employment in Israel and share in total employment, by industry—Workers from the West Bank and Gaza, 1987 (percent)

Share in	Agricul-ture	Con-struc-tion	Manufac-turing	Other	Total
Employed in Israel	14.5	45.6	18.1	21.8	100.0
Share in territories' labor	5.7	17.9	7.1	8.5	39.2
Share in industry in Israel	18.0	42.3	5.7	2.5	7.2

Source: C.B.S., *Statistical Abstract of Israel 1990*, Tables 12.9 and 27.21.

sensitive to fluctuations in immigration. Work in Israel may thus transmit this volatility to the economies of the territories, magnifying it in the process: With 18% of all the gainfully employed residents of the West Bank and Gaza, the Israeli construction industry is their largest provider of employment; and the wages earned in construction in Israel contributed at least 14% of their combined GNP in 1987, exceeding the contribution of domestic agriculture in a poor olive crop year.[14]

A further drawback of employment in Israel is the restricted range of occupations to which workers from the West Bank and Gaza are admitted. No more than 5% of those working in Israel are employed in white-collar jobs, most of them probably in East Jerusalem. Whether due to the unsuitability of the human capital acquired in the territories, to security restrictions, to insiders fending off outsiders in the labor market, or to outright discrimination, this range is not likely to expand significantly in the foreseeable future. In the territories themselves, on the other hand, the share of white-collar jobs is more than six times as high. A reallocation of labor, away from Israel and toward an expanded domestic economy, could thus improve the utilization of their human resources by upgrading the employment profile of the labor force (as well as by drawing back into it some presently discouraged workers).

But if the export of labor services was to be suddenly discontinued today, new employment would have to be generated in the West Bank and Gaza at the rate of one new job for each two jobs presently held there. With the natural increase in the working-age population also taken into account, the number of jobs available would have to double within five years. Given the investment gestation period, it is difficult to imagine how this could be achieved even if the required investment funds were freely available. Thus, the Palestinian entity may be able, at most, to aim at gradually phasing out labor exports to Israel.

It may have to be prepared to phase them out also because of changing attitudes on the other side. What made work in Israel possible was the demand of certain Israeli employers for the cheap, unskilled labor the territories could provide, and the Israeli authorities' hope of buying quiet there in exchange for economic prosperity. These motives may no longer be valid: The role of the slowdown in economic growth in the decade preceding the *intifada* (observable in table 12.1) among the factors leading to its outbreak, especially in Gaza, has yet to be evaluated.[15] But the uprising did prove that work in Israel was of only limited effectiveness in ensuring quiescence in the territories. In particular it did not prevent acts of individual terror against civilians in Israel itself. As these were facilitated by the free access to work in Israel, the vehement reaction they provoked from the Israeli public included the growing demand that such access be curtailed or even denied altogether.

The total closure of the territories during the Gulf war, on the other hand, has shown that the fears—common to all guest-worker-employing countries—of their withdrawal leading to the collapse of some essential services, were greatly exaggerated. Even the increased demand for housing due to the Soviet immigration was satisfied, as may have been expected, by recourse to prefabrication, and by the growing entry of both new immigrants and temporary guest workers from abroad into the industry.[16] The recent restoration of civic travel rights in Eastern Europe will make such substitution even easier in the future. (It remains to be seen whether Israel will be ready to live with the social problems that the large-scale presence of a resident foreign work force would pose.)

The movement of labor from the West Bank and Gaza to Israel in the future will be probably more strictly regulated than it was prior to 1991. In an attempt to contain the frictions resulting from the overlap of ethnic and class tensions, Israel may restrict both the number of workers admitted from the territories and their movement within its borders, along the lines of the restrictions already enforced with respect to residents of the Gaza Strip. Any Palestinian entity that will come into being in the West Bank and Gaza will have to negotiate with Israel over the volume of the labor flow, the rules governing the travel of their residents in Israel, and the conditions of their employment there. Indeed, these questions are important enough to merit their inclusion in the provisions of any negotiated settlement of the conflict.

Capital Movements

The economic pressures resulting from the integration of the West Bank and Gaza economies with that of Israel could have been accommodated, in principle, also in the absence of labor movements. Thus, the labor flow from the territories into Israel could conceivably have been substituted by a flow of labor-intensive goods in the same direction. It could also have been substituted by a flow of capital in the opposite direction, from Israel into the West Bank and Gaza. This would have brought the machinery to the workers, instead of bringing the workers to the machinery. If, as has been argued here, both sides will have an interest in reducing the labor flow between them, maintaining integration's gains will require these other flows to assume a greater importance than they had in the past.

The absence of virtually any private Israeli investments in the West Bank and Gaza is explained first and foremost by the uncertainty stemming from their unclear political status, which inhibited also third parties, as well as the territories' own residents, from investing there. (Though we may assume that, unlike the latter, they would not have been subject to the restrictive policies that the Israeli military authorities adopted with respect to industrial development, partly to protect Israeli firms from competition.) Furthermore, Israel did not extend to the territories the extensive system of subsidies and tax concessions it offers investors. In view of the ease with which labor could be imported from the territories, this preferential treatment of investment in Israel proper sufficed to turn the alternative of investing in them into an unprofitable one. In the extreme case of the industrial park set up at the Erez checkpoint, just outside the Gaza Strip, Israeli entrepreneurs could have the best of both worlds, by locating their plants at the closest point to their labor supply that would leave them eligible for capital subsidies. Subcontracting, prompted by the availability of trapped female labor in the territories, required little fixed capital.

The available statistics provide no estimates of short-term capital movements between Israel and the territories. To judge by anecdotal evidence, commercial short-run credit used to be extended fairly freely on both sides.[17] Assuming it to have been of one month's duration, the net credit extended by Israel to the territories amounted to one-twelfth of its trade surplus with them, averaging $40 million in the period 1983–87.[18] But only in two of the five years preceding the *intifada* the annual change in the sum outstanding could have reached the order of $10 million. And a considerable part, if not all, of this flow may have been offset by changes in the holdings of Israeli currency and of deposits in the Israeli banks that used to operate in the territories, and in the wages owed to their residents by Israeli employers, insofar as these were not paid daily.

Institutional capital flows, on the other hand, seem to have gone in the opposite direction. Long-run investments, mainly in the infrastructure, by the Israeli Civil (i.e., military) Administration in the territories were on the whole financed out of revenues collected in the West Bank and Gaza themselves. The sums involved were, in any case, very small: The total public sector investment in the territories averaged $60 million in the five years ending in 1987. Much of that represented investment by local authorities, financed by transfers from abroad, mainly from oil-producing Arab countries.

The customs duties and value-added tax (VAT) collected on imports to the territories from and through Israel can only be guessed at. We tried to estimate them on the extreme assumptions that all imports into the territories were liable to VAT, and that they embody an outside import component of between one-half and three-fourths, liable also to the average custom duty. The revenues from both sources, net of those collected by the Civil Administration on exports to Israel—which under sovereign trade relations would have accrued to the latter—could have amounted then to as much as $150 million in 1986, and to $180 million in 1987.[19] If we assume that the existing deficit in the budget of the Civil Administration is equal to that part of its outlays used to ensure Israel's rule there, rather than to finance services to the inhabitants, the above revenues constitute a flow of tribute capital from the territories into Israel.

Incidentally, this outflow does not reduce the resources at the disposal of the territories, as currently estimated. Under the accepted national accounting procedures, the import surplus deducted from total expenditures to arrive at the GDP estimate is valued at prices already incorporating taxes leveled on them abroad. Had it not been for them, the product of the territories would have been higher than presently estimated. Insofar as these sums increased with time, because of either tax hikes or the rise in net imports, the "true" rates of economic growth in the territories exceeded those shown in table 12.1.

Finally, there were also the social security payments withheld from the earnings of residents of the West Bank and Gaza employed in Israel under work permits. Net of pensions and compensations paid out of them, these payments constitute a long-run investment of the territories in Israel. The net flow on this account amounted to between $25 and $30 million in 1987.[20] The income tax deducted at source from wages earned in Israel raises the question of the economy to which taxes of guest work are supposed to accrue, and is referred to briefly later.

Whatever relationships evolve between the Palestinian entity and Israel, no large-scale flow of capital from Israel to the West Bank and Gaza can be expected in the foreseeable future. Realizing the need to expand production in the territories if employment in Israel is to be curtailed, the Israeli authorities have recently reversed their former policy of discouraging investment in any plant that could pose a competitive threat to an Israeli producer. But it cannot be expected that the Israeli government, given its own pressing capital needs, will go as far as to divert investment funds to the territories. Under a favorable political atmosphere, however, private Israeli investors may start to invest there, especially if the subsidization of investment within Israel itself is discontinued as part of a general liberalization process.

On the other hand the establishment of a Palestinian political entity in the West Bank and Gaza may eliminate the present flow of institutional funds from them into Israel. This requires, first of all, that the view is rejected of indirect taxes accruing to the authorities of the place of purchase (and not of residence), as is the case, for example, in the United States. The sums involved may have some importance for the public finances of the territories, especially if they will include also the income tax presently withheld in Israel from wages earned there under work permits. But they are minuscule and insignificant in terms of their capital requirements.

Merchandise Trade

Irrespective of where the capital required to create employment opportunities in the West Bank and Gaza will come from, the flow of labor services from them to Israel can be ultimately substituted only by trade, that is, by exports of presumably labor-intensive goods. As can be seen from table 12.2, providing all but one-tenth of their imports and taking close to three-fourths of their exports, Israel came close to completely monopolizing the trade of the territories by 1986. Hence the importance of the direction in which the trade relationships between them may be expected to develop.

The present, almost total dependence of the West Bank and Gaza on trade with or via Israel is the result of the opening up of trade between them for the first time since 1948, and of the customs union imposed on them at the same time, in place of their previous ones with Jordan and Egypt, respectively. It thus reflects both trade creation and trade diversion. Both the Palestinian entity and Israel will wish to avoid any new trade alignment that would adversely affect the results of trade creation, as well as (to the partner considered) beneficial effects of trade diversion. The positive factors behind the growth of imports from Israel were negligible transportation costs, and the absence of customs duties on their passing into the territories. Insofar as these factors made increased specialization and exchange possible, they generated new trade. But even some of the trade diversion caused by them could have been beneficial to both sides, to the extent the Israeli goods were more cheaply acquired or transported than those hitherto imported from the rest of the world.

A negative factor causing trade diversion was the imposition of the Israeli customs tariffs on imports from the rest of the world. These were generally much higher than those applied earlier. Thus, for example, the average duty on manufactured goods imported into the West Bank rose more than fourfold almost overnight in 1967.[21] Raising the price of imports from the rest of the world, but not from Israel, the higher tariff can be expected to have resulted in their being substituted by Israeli goods. (By the same token, this also should have encouraged the substitution of such imports by domestic production in the West Bank and Gaza. But in view of the very narrow industrial base there, the practical effects, if any, must have been negligible.)

On the export side, the dominant development was the newly

Table 12.4
Distribution of trade in merchandise (percent)

	Imports			Exports		
	West Bank		Gaza	West Bank		Gaza
	1966	1986	1986	1966	1986	1986
Jordan	18	2	—	46	35	13
Israel	—	88	92	—	65	85
Others	82	10	8	54	—	2
Total	100	100	100	100	100	100

Sources: Israel Economic Planning Authority, *An Economic Survey of the West Bank*, July 1967, chap. C; C.B.S., *Statistical Abstract of Israel, 1990*, Table 27.11

gained access to the Israeli market, even if restricted by export quotas imposed to protect Israeli agriculture, or marking and quality standards requirements on consumer goods. As exports from the West Bank, at least, continued to enter Jordan duty free (though, as in the case of Israel, subject to certain restrictions), the trade diversion effects on exports may be expected to have been small, relatively to those on imports.

Table 12.4 shows the shares of Israel, Jordan, and the rest of the world in the trade of the territories. These refer only to the trade in merchandise, which constituted, however, as much as 90% of their combined exports, and 80% of their imports, in recent years. Anecdotal evidence suggests that a considerable amount of imports from third countries to the West Bank and Gaza is purchased not directly, but through Israeli importers (often serving as the exporters' authorized agents in Israel), so that the present data overestimate Israel's true share in their trade. (Similar evidence also suggests that many of the reported exports to Jordan are destined, in fact, to markets beyond it, mainly in the Gulf countries.) From the Israeli point of view, this is equivalent to saying that exports to the territories have a lower value added than the rest.[22] To the extent that this is, in fact, the case, the following analysis overstates the effects of Israel's rule in the territories on the country structure of their trade.

The data on this structure are shown separately for the West Bank and Gaza to enable a comparison with the pre-1967 estimates available for the former. It can be seen that Israel completely crowded out both Jordan and the rest of the world as supplier of the West Bank's imports. It has also taken over the role of the rest of the world as a market for the West Bank's products, but only marginally that of Jordan. This differential effect on imports an on exports was due in part to exports from the West Bank continuing to enter Jordan free of duty, but imports from Jordan being now subject to the Israeli tariff. It also reflected the restricted supply of export goods in Jordan, suggested by Jordan's share in them being much lower than in imports already in 1966.

Any analysis of the trade figures of the territories has to be qualified by the relatively low reliability of the data on their trade with Israel. In the words of their own compilers, these data are only "a gross evaluation based on sample enumeration of movement[s] of goods through the main transit points."[23] The difficulty of monitoring such movements stems from the nature of the, relatively to the size of the country, long land borders and the, for most of the time, virtually free traffic across them. But it was also precisely this nature of the border between the territories and Israel, and the short distances involved, that made their opening to the movement of goods across them so trade creative.

Table 12.5 presents the ratios of imports and exports to income and to GDP, respectively, in the West Bank and Gaza by four-year periods. To neutralize fluctuations caused by the olive crop cycle already referred to above, the figures shown here are the averages of the ratios in the even (i.e., large olive crop) years of each period.[24] This makes it possible to compare them to the only available pre-1967 figures, those of the trade ratios of the West Bank in 1966. Generally speaking, it may be expected that as income levels rise, so does the variety of goods demanded. In the absence of governmental import substitution encouraging policies, the import-to-income ration will also rise then. Because of the role played by wages earned in Israel and by transfers from the rest of the world, GDP is not a good measure of income in the present case. Hence the alternative ratio shown in the table, that of imports to the sum total of all three income sources.

It can be seen that the West Bank's overall income import component rose little after 1966, indicating that imports grew only slightly more rapidly than income under the conditions of the forced customs union with Israel.[25] Had the pre-1967 trade conditions prevailed, any increase in imports because of economic growth would have had to

Table 12.5
Ratio of merchandise trade to income (percent)

	West Bank[a]		Gaza	
	Exports to GDP	Imports to NI[b]	Exports to GDP	Imports to NI[b]
1966	8.1	34.5	(21.2)[c]	(36.0)[c]
1968–71	26.7	36.2	27.8	40.0
1972–75	23.0	33.9	39.9	52.7
1976–79	26.3	36.2	55.4	58.8
1980–84	25.1	38.0	61.4	57.0
1985–87	21.2	35.2	37.9	56.2

a. The data for the West Bank are arithmetic averages of the ratios in the even years of each period.
b. "Disposable National Income," equal to GNP plus payments to factors of production and transfers from abroad.
c. In the absence of any pre-1967 data for Gaza, the figures shown in parentheses are those for 1968.
Sources: Merchandise trade data in U.S. dollars—C.B.S. "National Accounts of Judea, Samaria and Gaza Area 1968–1986," *Special Series no. 818*, Tables 30 and 41, and *Statistical Abstract of Israel No. 40*, Table XXVII/11; Exchange rates—Bank of Israel, *Foreign Currency Exchange Rates in Israel 1948–1985*, Jerusalem 1986, Part A, Table 4, and *Statistical Abstract no. 40*, table IX/13. GDP and National disposable income data—C.B.S., unpublished revised data.

come from sources other than Israel. From the point of view of the West Bank (though not from that of Israel), the growth of Israel's share in its imports thus represents trade diversion, except insofar as the economic growth of the West Bank itself may be ascribed to trade with Israel. Furthermore, to the extent that this trade diversion has been due not to the higher Israeli customs tariffs now applying to the territories but to lower transportation and transaction costs, it has benefited rather than harmed the West Bank.

The growth of exports can be expected to parallel the import-income relationship, in being positively associated with changes in the incomes of a country's trade partners. In the case of a small economy, it may be argued also that the growth of exports may depend, on the supply side, on the growth of the country's productive capacity, that is, its GDP. But as table 12.5 indicates, the export to GDP ration in the West Bank rose sharply as a result of the opening of the former hermetically closed border with Israel to trade. The data show this rise to have taken place in the years immediately following the establishment of trade, the ratio remaining fairly constant until the beginning of the 1980s and declining after that. Nevertheless, even then it was still two-and-a-half to more than three times higher than in 1966. As the growth of exports from the West Bank also outstripped both the rise in imports to Jordan and the growth of world trade as a whole, we may ascribe it to the demand of the Israeli market.[26] Thus, unlike in the case of imports, viewed from the West Bank, Israel's high share of the West Bank's exports seems to represent trade creation rather than its diversion from other destinations.

For lack of any pre-1967 data for Gaza, the earliest year with which comparisons can be made there is 1968, by which time, to judge by developments in the West Bank, a considerable change in the trade ratios had already taken place. Nevertheless, unlike in the West Bank, the ratio of imports to income in Gaza is seen to have risen quite sharply, suggesting a considerable trade creation effect. On the conservative assumption that all trade creation that occurred since 1967 is represented by the difference between the current import ratio and its level in 1968, it would account for over one-third of present imports. On the same assumption, nearly one-half of Gaza's present exports can be ascribed to trade creation, their growth, relative to the corresponding income measure, outstripping that of imports.

Gaza was almost completely cut off from Jordan before 1967, the only trade routes between them then being either the costly sea route via the Suez Canal or a tortuous land and sea link via Sinai. Thus, the total absence of imports from Jordan into Gaza, shown in table 12.4, seems to perpetuate the pre-1967 pattern. Israel's almost complete monopolization of Gaza's imports, shown there, reflects considerable diversion from other supply sources, probably mainly Egypt. This could amount to as much as half of the strip's present import volume (Israel's share—92%—of the nearly two-thirds of imports that, on our above extreme assumption, cannot be ascribed to trade creation.) By the same token, however, Jordan's present share in Gaza's exports, shown in table 12.4, should be viewed as representing either trade creation or the beneficial effects of trade diversion, because of the reduction in transportation costs with the opening of a short land route via the Jordan bridges.

As can be seen from table 12.5, the trade ratios started to decline in the early or mid-1980s. Though other influences may also have been at work, this suggests that, as may have been expected, no further trade creation took place once the market integration process played itself out.

Alternative Regimes—Free Trade

What, in view of the above analysis, are the alternative trade alignments available to the future Palestinian entity, and their implications for the future trade flows between it and Israel?[27] As will be shown below, such an entity's choice of trade regimes will be heavily circumscribed by those adopted by its close neighbors, the Hashemite Kingdom of Jordan and Israel in particular. For reasons that have become apparent in the preceding sections, we may rule out a retrogression to the pre-1967 total absence of trade relationship between the territories and Israel. The question of trade relationships with Israel thus becomes one of the customs tariff policies that the Palestinian entity will opt for.

Consider first the implications and the feasibility of its adopting a perfect free trade regime, both with respect to the world at large and with respect to Israel. This would not affect the status of imports from Israel, which are already admitted free of duty into the territories. But by reducing the cost of competing imports from other sources, presently kept out by the Israeli customs tariff (as well as by nontariff barriers), a free-trade policy would greatly reduce Israel's role as supplier of imports to the West Bank and Gaza. They also would be further reduced by the increased opportunities of importing from other countries directly, rather than through Israel. Nevertheless, having the advantage of significantly lower transportation costs, Israel could possibly continue to serve as the main single source of their imports.

Free trade will also remove the protection from competition from sources other than Israel, which domestic producers in the territories enjoy under the Israeli tariff. In view of the present limited scope of industrial production there, the effects of any ensuing decline in it may seem to be of relatively little importance. But if income levels are not to decline, it will have to be compensated for by expanded exports. For these, as for its exports in general, the Palestinian entity will be heavily dependent on the policies pursued by its trade partners.

So far we have completely ignored the potential reaction of the

Palestinian entity's main trade partners, Israel and Jordan, to its policies. Suppose, perhaps rather optimistically, that both Israel and Jordan will be ready to remove all the administrative barriers or restrictions on importation from the West Bank and Gaza presently in force.[28] The removal or relaxation of the present requirement of a Jordanian import component in manufactured goods imported into Jordan from the territories, and of their originating in plants established before 1967, can be expected to be, on the whole, trade creating. So would be also the removal of the existing restrictions on the entry of manufactures from them to Israel. Both steps would encourage the expansion of production for export in the territories, and raise their total trade volume. The removal or relaxation of the restrictions on agricultural imports from the West Bank and Gaza to Israel, on the other hand, could be expected to be mainly trade diverting: Given the soil and water limitations in the territories, any increase in exports of farm produce to Israel would have to come not out of expanded production, but out of a shift in sales, from across the Jordan to the nearer, more lucrative Israeli market.

Further trade diversion, away from both Israel and Jordan, as well as some trade creation, would result from eased access to larger markets outside the region, such as the granting to the entity of a preferential status by the EEC. The removal of the obstacles put up by the Israeli administration on exports to third parties would have a similar, albeit quantitatively much smaller, effect. However, because of the border-trade situation, Israel could be expected even then to continue to constitute the largest market for exports from the West Bank and Gaza.

The last conclusion will be especially true if, as suggested above, the flow of labor services from the territories into Israel comes to be restricted in the future. Such restrictions will make certain economic activities no longer profitable in Israel, at least at the margin. But there will still be a demand for their product at the previous prices. This demand could then be satisfied by exports from the territories, for example, of construction carpentry work or of certain items of clothing.

However, this abstracts from the interests of both Israel and Jordan. As long as these two countries continue to maintain some protective tariff toward the world at large, they might be unwilling to see it circumvented by an indiscriminate free entry of goods from the new entity, upholding a free-trade policy. In principle, these countries could solve the problem by administratively excluding imports from the territories originating elsewhere, or by subjecting them to their respective tariff schedules. (The former policy is, in fact, already pursued by Jordan with respect to goods originating in Israel.) In practice, however, both such an exclusion and differential tariffs are difficult to enforce, and both invite evasion and smuggling. For as long as the Jordan River will continue to constitute Israel's security frontier, smuggling opportunities across it into (the kingdom of) Jordan will be heavily restricted. But, because of its long land border with the territories, the West Bank in particular, smuggling into Israel will be much more difficult to prevent. Israel might, therefore, be expected to pressure the Palestinian entity into forgoing free trade policy in favor of a customs tariff on imports from the rest of the world, similar to its own one.

The Palestinian entity may thus have to choose between accepting this demand or having to face the tariff and other barriers through which Israel protects its producers, especially in agriculture, from competition from abroad. In the former case the West Bank and Gaza will find themselves locked in a customs union with Israel, presumably more equitable but basically not different from the present one. Unlike in the present situation, they may then find themselves no longer enjoying duty-free, even if quantitatively restricted, access to the markets east of the Jordan, so that their dependence on Israel for their exports may actually increase. In the latter case they will find themselves deprived of some part of their markets in Israel, where even the border-trade conditions will be unable to compensate for the tariff. Furthermore, with the West Bank and Gaza no longer joined to Israel in some sort of a currency union, it would make good second-best sense for Israel to subsidize exports to them much in the same way in which it subsidizes exports in general. This would reduce the negative effect of a free-trade policy on the territories' imports from Israel, further increasing the imbalance in their trade with it.

Alternative Regimes—Protectionism

As is often true with new political entities (Israel itself is a case in point), the Palestinian entity may opt for a highly protective tariff policy, both with respect to the world at large and with respect to Israel. Such a policy will, of course, be trade destructive, as by making imports more expensive it will encourage their substitution by domestic production, this indeed being the reason behind its adoption.

The imposition on imports from Israel of the same tariff as on the rest of them would affect their *relative* competitiveness in precisely the same manner as the abolition of tariffs on all imports: The trade regime presently in effect in the West Bank and Gaza discriminates in favor of imports from Israel, which enter them free of the duties to which imports from the rest of the world are subjected. A free-trade regime would put an end to this preferential treatment by equalizing the entry conditions of imports from the rest of the world with those now reserved to imports from Israel. A uniform protectionist regime, on the other hand, would do so by subjecting imports from Israel to the same hurdles that face imports from the rest of the world. Thus, both policies would divert trade from Israel toward in the former case now cheaper, or in the latter one no longer more expensive, sources. The two would differ, however, in their effect on the total volume of trade: A free-trade regime would result in an expansion of the territories' trade with other countries, exceeding the contraction of their trade with Israel. Under a protectionist policy, however, the expansion of trade with other countries would fall short of the contraction of their trade with Israel. Because of the income effect of overall higher customs duties, the decline of the territories' trade with Israel may be expected to be larger under the protectionist, than under the free-trade, regime.

Israel and Jordan will not be compelled in this case to impose a tariff on imports from the Palestinian entity, as they were—to buttress their own protectionist regimes—in the case of it following the free-trade option. But popular sentiment ("they tax us, let's tax them") not necessarily being good economics, Israel would probably retaliate by imposing a tariff on its imports from the West Bank and Gaza. Unless the consideration of maintaining political stability in the territories prevails, or else the general tariff imposed by the Palestinian entity and presumably also the retaliatory one, is fairly low, the effects on its economy will be even more severe than in the corresponding case under a free-trade regime. A low tariff, however, would raise problems similar to those raised by free trade, insofar as circumventing Israeli customs is concerned.

Noneconomic considerations might also tempt the Palestinian entity to impose a discriminatory tariff against imports from Israel.

Trade with Israel would then decrease more sharply than under either the free-trade or the uniformally protective tariff regimes. This, however, would be most certainly interpreted in Israel as a continuation of the Arab boycott, an expression of the Arab states' hostility toward Israel. Israel's retaliation in this case, therefore, can be considered unavoidable and would not be restricted to merchandise trade. It is difficult to think of any trade relationships that could fully compensate for the loss of the Israeli markets for both exports and labor—which, as has been shown, gave rise to nearly 40% of the combined GNP of the territories in the mid-1980s.

Alternatively the Palestinian entity may enter a customs union with Jordan. With the removal of the present restrictions on exports to the East Bank, some rise in them may be expected insofar as markets for the West Bank and Gaza's exports exist there. In the case of agriculture these exports would probably come at the expense of exports to Israel, and could compensate for the probable increased enforcement of restrictions on marketing them there, in the absence of free trade between Israel and Jordan. In manufacturing, on the other hand, the main export opportunities to the East Bank may be in industries other than those exporting nowadays to Israel, and also may be far less extensive. It should also be kept in mind that such a customs union will expose the economies of the West Bank and of Gaza to duty-free competition from Jordan's East Bank. As has been mentioned earlier, the availability of importables there, and the consequent competition potential, is probably much smaller than in Israel. But unlike competition from the latter, which inhibited the establishment of new industries, increased imports from the East Bank would compete with those already operating in the territories.

Whether under these circumstances the West Bank and Gaza will continue to purchase much of their imports from Israel, and be able to continue to export there, depends on the general tariff regime that their customs union with Jordan will adopt and its discriminatory or preferential treatment of Israel. Furthermore, insofar as exports from the territories to Jordan are marketed to the east of it, their continuation and possible expansion will depend on the trade policies of other Arab countries, especially Iraq and the Gulf states. In the absence of a comprehensive peace settlement between the Arab countries and Israel, trade agreements between the Palestinian entity and Israel might adversely affect these policies, even if the Israeli-Palestinian conflict is satisfactorily settled.

Finally, we may wish to consider the possibility, often raised in discussions of a political settlement, of a tripartite customs union consisting of Israel, Jordan, and the new Palestinian entity. From the point of view of the latter, this would allow it the benefits of a customs union with Israel without losing its present duty-free access to the Jordanian market. Being equivalent to the removal of all barriers to trade with its two neighbors, this would be a marked improvement on the present situation. On the other hand, however, it would also expose the West Bank and Gaza to competition from the East Bank and, probably more damaging, to being crowded out in the Jordanian market by competition from Israel. From the point of view of Jordan, such a union will have all the benefits and drawbacks of a customs union with the Palestinian entity, plus all the consequences of raising its tariffs to the Israeli level.[29]

It should be emphasized that the problems surveyed in the last two sections do not stem only from the protectionist policies pursued by Israel, and to a lesser extent by Jordan, and from the high probability, to judge by the experience of other new entities, that such policies will be adopted also by any Palestinian entity that will come into being in the West Bank and Gaza. If this was, indeed, the case, the whole problem of trade relationship between this entity and Israel might have ultimately found its solution in the present general world movement toward trade liberalization. For the present purpose, however, all indirect taxation, the VAT in particular, raises problems similar to that posed by customs tariffs.

Admittedly, VAT does not in general discriminate between imports from different sources, or between them and domestic production. But unless it is levied at the same rate in both Israel and the territories, goods will be attracted from the low-rate to the high-rate country, seriously impairing the latter's tax system. The border tax adjustment necessary to prevent this requires the existence of tax borders, creating a new impediment to the free flow of goods.

Some Further Remarks

This chapter has raised some questions regarding the future economic relationships between any political entity that may evolve in the West Bank and Gaza, and Israel. The problems surveyed here are those relating to the flow of goods and of factors of production. The remaining problems, to which attention must be paid, can be broadly divided into three main groups: One is the allocation of national property rights over regional economic and strategic resources, first and foremost water. Another is the exploitation of potential externalities in the provision of such services as transportation, port facilities, power generation, etcetera. Finally, there is a plethora of mainly technical questions arising from the solutions to the basic problems surveyed here. Thus, no attention was given in this chapter, for example, to questions of currency. But these will not be solved on their own, being dependent to a great extent on the trade regimes chosen. (The present situation in the West Bank, with two legal tenders—the NIS and the JD—and counting in the U.S. $, three currencies, suggests the unconventional character of some of the potential solutions.)

Two main morals may be drawn from the chapter. The first is that of the high price small economic units have to pay for a given measure of autarky. Much has been made of the so-called increased economic self-reliance in the territories since the outbreak of the *intifada*. Much of this, in practice, took the form of cottage industries, or of the expansion of farming activities, which ultimately boil down to disguised unemployment in agriculture. While these enterprises may have been good for morale, and helped to mitigate the economic hardships of the past few years, they cannot substitute for external economic relationships, such as evolved in the two decades preceding them between the West Bank and Gaza, and Israel.

The other, perhaps no more palatable conclusion, is that a closer economic relationship with the outside world, not to mention economic integration with some part of it, entails some abdication of economic sovereignty. As we have seen, the choice, for example, of a trade regime for the future Palestinian entity will depend to a great extent on decisions made by its neighbors, and may necessitate the adoption of the customs tariff of one or another of them. As the experience of the EEC indicates, this means some restriction of political sovereignty as well.

Notes

This chapter draws heavily on some of my earlier papers on the subject, in particular "The Economic Interdependence of the West Bank, the Gaza Strip, and Israel," in E. Denter and J. Klein (eds.), *Economic Aspects of a Political Settlement In the Middle East*, Amsterdam, VU University Press, 1991, pp. 31–

42; "The Future of Palestinian-Arab and Israeli Economic Relationships," *Truman Institute Working Paper Series No. 1;* "The Flow of Labor Services from the West-Bank and Gaza to Israel," paper presented at a workshop on Labor Markets and Labor Mobility in the Middle East, Institute for Social and Economic Policy in the Middle East, Kennedy School of Government, September 26–27, 1991. For comments and advice, not always heeded, I am grateful to my colleagues, Nadav Halevi and Ruth Klinov, and to the organizers and participants of the conference.

1. As is usually the case when two peoples contend for the same bit of geography, the names by which places are known tend themselves to become contended, and their choices comes to be regarded as expressing a political opinion. These susceptibilities are ignored here, and we shall refer indiscriminately to the (kingdom of Jordan's) West Bank, (the biblical) Judea and Samaria, and the (alternatively occupied or administered) territories.

2. Changing political attitudes find an expression in the vicissitudes of the title under which the statistical data for these regions are published by the Israeli Central Bureau of Statistics (C.B.S.): Known first as the *Monthly Statistics of the Administered Territories,* it changed successively into the *Administered Territories Statistics Quarterly* and the *Judea, Samaria and Gaza Area Statistics Quarterly,* becoming presently the *Judea, Samaria and Gaza Area Statistics.* For the sake of space considerations, we shall refer to it throughout simply as *Statistics.*

3. In an attempt to constantly improve its estimates, the bureau occasionally revises some of the definitions used in deriving them. This sometimes raises questions of comparability with the data for earlier years, especially as insofar as such revisions are carried back, they are not always easily accessible. Data sources published at different times therefore may be at some variance with each other. But these differences are, on the whole, small and do not in general tend to affect the qualitative conclusions.

4. Value added in agriculture contributed between 20% and 40% of the West Bank's GDP (depending, not surprisingly, on the olive crop). See C.B.S., "National Accounts in Judea, Samaria and Gaza Area, 1968–1986," *Special Series no. 818,* table 13. As oil extraction is a major industrial activity in the West Bank, manufacturing product is also affected. In the period 1969–86 as a whole, GDP varied by 0.5% for each 10% change in the olive crop, with a correlation coefficient of 0.83. For data on the olive crop, see ibid., table 32. Superimposed on the basic biennial cycle are also some longer, five-or-six-year cycles, as well as random causes. The same cyclicity is also evident in the East Bank; see the Economist Intelligence Unit, "Annual Supplement, 1991," *Quarterly Economic Review—Syria, Jordan.* The Israeli olive crop does not quite conform to the above pattern, suggesting that irrigation and other differences in cultivation are also involved.

5. See, respectively, Israel Economic Planning Authority, *An Economic Survey of the West Bank,* Jerusalem, July 1967 (in Hebrew), and Jordan Department of Statistics, *The Contribution of the West Bank in Jordan's Economy,* Amman,

1969 (in Arabic) as quoted in F. A. Gharaibeh, *The Economics of the West Bank and Gaza Strip,* Westview Press, Boulder, Colorado, 1985, p. 5. The latter estimates put the share of the West Bank at some 3%–4% higher than the former ones. It is to be regretted that, perhaps because of the language in which the *Survey* was published, no West Bank or Jordanian economist has attempted a critical evaluation of the manner in which its authors disaggregated the all-Jordan data by its East and West Banks, and vice versa for the Jordanian estimates.

6. One source cited estimated GDP in the West Bank to have grown at 8.2% per annum between 1960 and 1966. See E. Tuma, "The Economics of Occupation in Palestine since 1948 and the Cost of Non-Cooperation," in G. Fishelson, ed., *Economic Cooperation in the Middle East,* Westview Press, Boulder, 1989. For emigration, see the section on the flow of labor services.

7. Generally speaking, the gains from trade are due to the reallocation of production toward the more efficient producers in the combined market. But the way these gains will be shared by the trade partners depends also on the changes in the relative factor prices in the two economies. In the present case, where trade in factor services played a dominant role, they operated, as explained in the text, in favor of the territories.

8. The capital that did move between has actually gone in a direction opposite to the expected one. See also the section on capital movements.

9. As has been sometimes argued, any technology acquired or learned from Israel could also be acquired from other sources. But the fact remains that, in agriculture at least, this did not happen, suggesting the importance of the demonstration effect. The main externalities, so far, occurred probably in tourism.

10. Though the West Bank accounted then for just over one-third of Jordan's GDP, and an even larger share of its population, it was allotted only one-tenth of the government's development fund in 1966. See Israel Planning Authority, op. cit., table XI–1. The West Bank's share of all investment in the 1960s was roughly proportional to its share in GDP. But most private investments were in housing, not in the direct expansion of productive capacity. See ibid., table IX–4; also A. Mansour, "The West Bank Economy: 1948–1984," in G. Abed, ed., *The Palestinian Economy,* Routledge, London, 1988, pp. 71–99; and E. Kanovsky, *The Economy of Jordan,* University Publishing Projects, Tel-Aviv, 1976, chap. 1.

11. See S. A. Gabriel and E. F. Sabatello, "Palestinian Migration from the West Bank and Gaza: Economic and Demographic Analyses," *Economic Development and Cultural Change,* vol. 34, 1986, pp. 245–62. Also, Israel Economic Planning Authority, op. cit., p. II–8. Mansour's estimate of a 0.54% annual population growth rate suggests emigration to have been even higher; loc. cit., pp. 71–72. But the source he cites seems to have overestimated the population of the West Bank at the time of its incorporation in Jordan.

12. See C.B.S., "Persons Employed of Judea, Samaria and the Gaza Area

Working in Israel, 1981," *Judea, Samaria and Gaza Area Statistics Quarterly* 12 (1983), table 2. Comparisons with earlier surveys show this ratio to have been fairly stable over time.

13. Though in terms of geographic distance, and certainly in those of commuting time, this represented only a return to the pre-1948 pattern, when "many workers from the West Bank were employed in the coastal cities and other industrial centers in Northern Palestine," and similarly for Gaza. See Gharaibeh, op. cit., p. 1.

14. The contribution of wages earned in the Israeli construction industry to the GNP of the territories has been estimated on the conservative assumption that the industry's share of wages earned by workers from the territories in Israel was the same as in the number of persons employed. Because of the cyclicity of the olive crop in the West Bank, referred to earlier, the contribution of agriculture to the combined GNP of the territories fluctuated between as much as 22% in 1986, which was a super bumper year, and 13% in 1987.

15. But see Z. Schiff and E. Yaari, *The Intifada,* Schoken, Tel-Aviv, 1990 (in Hebrew), pp. 75–83 [ref. to English edition].

16. These developments were consistent with a forecast made early in 1990 of the expected response of the Israeli economy to a curtailment of the flow of labor services from the West Bank and Gaza.

17. Such evidence came to light when this credit was no longer extended, as a result of difficulties in collecting the debts outstanding after the outbreak of the *intifada.*

18. We assume here that similar credit was extended by West Bank and Gaza exporters to their Israeli clients, hence the use of the trade surplus as the basis of our calculation.

19. In assessing the economic effects on the Israeli economy of the first year of the *intifada,* the Bank of Israel implicitly assumed the value-added share in exports to the territories to have been roughly half that in exports as a whole; see Bank of Israel, *Annual Report 1988,* Jerusalem 1989, chap. 6, p. 153 (Hebrew version). The latter share is estimated at 50% to 60%.

20. Calculated assuming social insurance equivalent payments, net of pensions and compensations, of 20%, shared in equal parts by employers and employees. The range cited in the text corresponds to the share of the employees being calculated under alternative assumptions: for the actual wages earned by permit holders, as reported by the Ministry of Labor, and for a share proportionate to their share in employment of all wages estimated to have been earned by workers from the territories. Despite some changes introduced since then, the only published enumeration of the various components of these payments is still that of A. Bregman, *Economic Growth in the Administered Areas, 1968–1973,* Jerusalem, Bank of Israel Research Department, 1975, table III–7.

21. From the average Jordanian one of 17% in 1966 to the nearly 80% Israeli one in 1967. See Israel Economic Planning Authority, op. cit., p. C–28, and M. Michaely, *Foreign Trade Regimes and Economic Development: Israel,* N.B.E.R. Special Conference series on Foreign Trade Regimes and Economic Development, vol. 3, New York, Columbia University Press, 1975, table 3–4.

22. Thus, for example, the Bank of Israel's estimate of the effect on Israel's GDP of the decline in exports to the territories as a result of the *intifada* implied a value-added share only about one-half as high as in exports in general. See Bank of Israel, *Annual Report 1988,* chap. 6.

23. C.B.S., "National Accounts of Judea, Samaria and the Gaza Area, 1968–1986," *Special Series no. 818,* Jerusalem, Jan. 1988, p. xxv.

24. The olive crop cycle affects the trade ratios by raising output, thereby raising the GDP figures in (the large crop) even years, and by raising the export of olive oil, thereby raising total export figures in the (following) odd years. Both effects operate to raise the trade ratios in odd years and lower them in even ones. Because imports are sensitive to incomes, and therefore to the sale of the oil, they exhibit a similar periodicity.

25. The present data might underestimate the rise of income's import component since 1966, as the estimates for that year were inclusive of East Jerusalem with a presumably higher income and a higher import propensity than of the mainly rural rest of the West Bank.

26. The dollar value of the West Bank's exports, unadjusted for changes in the purchasing power of the U.S. dollar, grew by 12.7% per annum between 1968 and 1986. Similarly valued, Jordan's imports grew by only 7.9% per annum between 1970 and 1986. (Valued at constant, end-of-period prices, the annual rate of the West Bank's export growth amounts to 7.8% in this period.) See C.B.S., "National Accounts of Judea, Samaria and Gaza Area, 1968–1986," *Special Series no. 818,* Jerusalem 1988, tables 30 and 12, respectively; See World Bank, *World Tables 1991,* table 20.

27. Much of the ground covered in the following sections has already been discussed along similar lines in Gharaibeh, op. cit.

28. See, for example, Ephraim Ahiram, "Obstacles to Economic Development of the West Bank and Gaza," Paper presented at a Seminar on Economic Cooperation in the Middle East, at the Kennedy School Government, 5–7 Sept. 1989; also Antoine Mansour, loc. cit., p. 90.

29. We have assumed here throughout that, Israel being economically the senior partner in any of the alignments discussed here, it is the Israeli tariff level to which the other ones will have to adjust themselves.

Comments

Sulayman S. Al-Qudsi

The authors of the chapters on the transition to peace bring out some insightful and controversial issues. Ephraim Kleiman's basic thesis is of continued integration of the West Bank and Gaza (WBGS) into the Israeli economy. However, the benefits of such integration to the territories are questionable on several grounds, not the least of which is Kleiman's choice of data points. That is, the starting and ending data points do not represent "normal" or "average" years for WBGS economy, and the conclusions sought are therefore not robust. Moreover, I doubt the evidence he presents would convince a nonbeliever.

First, dependency of WBGS on Israel did not develop as a result of free choices of Palestinian consumers and producers. Instead in many ways it was a forced dependency. The model Kleiman employs assumes that the "market fundamentals" are operating in the case of Israel and WBGS economies. Reality is very far from this nice textbook assumption. For example, Israel's agriculture and manufacturing (as well as services and trade) were granted a substantial amount of credit at negative real interest rates from the public purse for both exports and domestic consumption (Bruno and Meridor 1991). In contrast, the concurrent Israeli policies toward WBGS distorted the productive capability of the territories and created "productivity anemia."

Second, Palestinian dependence on employment and income-generation sources in Israel has subjected the domestic WBGS economy to vacillations in economic performance and has deprived citizens of command over their livelihood.

Third, there is the issue of the preexistence of a wage gap between Palestinian and Israeli workers. Palestinians working in Israel earn 30%–40% the wage of Israeli workers (Tuma 1989). While some of this difference may be explained by differences in productivity-enhancing factors, one cannot help but think that a substantial portion of the difference reflects discrimination against Palestinian workers. In other countries wage-parity between natives and immigrants is usually observed after the lapse of a few years following the arrival of migrants (Chiswick 1980; Borjas 1987).

Fourth, as a result of Israel's punitive economic measures and its continued demographic strangulation of Palestinians through a stepped up settlement program, educated Palestinians have been unemployed, expelled, or driven to emigrate. Furthermore, emigration of Palestinians tends to be sex and age specific. Between 1967 and 1986, 67% of Palestinian emigrants from the West Bank and 80% from Gaza were males, 69% and 58% of whom (in WB and GS, respectively) were cohorts in their productive years, that is, between the ages of 21 and 35 (Gabriel and Sabatello 1986).

Finally, a forward-looking approach to the dynamics of Israeli and Palestinian populations reveals the imperative of breaking the future from historical trends. Specifically, the Palestinian histogram is flat based with 47% of the population in the age group 0–15. Their number is about 600,000 (Statistical Abstract of Israel 1972–90). Allowing for lower female participation rates, this implies that within a decade the Israeli economy must either (1) integrate approximately 500,000 new Palestinian entrants into the labor market by providing skill-enhancing education/training opportunities and productive employment, or (2) stunt their human resource development potential by extending the historical "maldevelopment" path into the future and by employing them in subservient, unskilled occupations. Kleiman notes in his chapter that no more than 5% of Palestinians working in Israel are in white-collar jobs, and 95% are in blue-collar, low-skill jobs. What has emerged therefore is an "ethnic" distribution of employment.

A third scenario is to make the utilization of future Palestinian cohorts vacillate with the cyclical movements in the Israeli economy, for example, construction sector cycles, which would worsen the already high unemployment and underemployment profile.

The rapidly changing Israeli demographic and human capital profiles enhance the chances of occurrence of scenarios (2) and (3) above. The Israeli government is projecting that more than 1 million Soviet immigrants would arrive within the next five to six years, which would constitute a 20% increase in domestic population and in fact equal half the total number of all immigrants into Israel during the country's first four decades of existence (Clawson and Rosen 1991). The new arrivals constitute a "brainpower machine" for the Israeli economy as they are extremely well educated and trained. In fact, upon assimilating them, Israel is expected to double its value of human capital (Avishai 1991). Given these prospective developments, why should the Israelis "bother" about enhancing the Palestinian human capital?

Ephraim Ahiram delineates a development strategy for WBGS whose core is the industrial and trade sectors. The author is correct in choosing the term *industrial activities:* for a Palestinian manufacturing activity to succeed it must follow a niche strategy, that is, developing small, specialized niches in which Palestinian firms create a competitive advantage in certain industrial activities on the basis of initially low cost but subsequently high quality. Although the discussion is detailed and illuminating, the linkages among sectors need to be evaluated more systematically and quantitatively. For instance, (1) policymakers in WBGS need to understand the relationships between selected industrial activities and trade and exchange-rate policies; (2) the financial sector of WBGS is currently deeply repressed because of structural factors, policy mandates, and measures. It needs to be liberalized and activated by gradually relinquishing restrictive measures and allowing Palestinian, Arab, and Israeli banks and financial intermediaries to open branches in a temporal and planned manner; and (3) finally and more ominously, the author neglects altogether the interaction between the industrial/economic strategy and manpower development strategy.

From the Israeli perspective, cooperation between Palestinians and Israelis facilitates the marketing of jointly produced products because it provides Israel with access to land and a bridge to Arab, LDCs, and Western markets and eliminates the Arab boycott.

Ahiram's paper falls short of probing into the following issues: (1) the incentives that would attract particularly Arab oil countries to join a Palestinian/Israeli cooperation scheme once a Palestinian entity, state, or confederation with Jordan is achieved; and (2) tentative estimates of the time span of each stage until the ultimate and durable peace is established.

Hisham Awartani's paper starts with a discussion of the anomalies and costs that the Israeli occupation inflicted upon the WBGS, but the bulk of it addresses the cooperation prospects between Palestinians and Israelis. The arguments, however, tend to be more impressionistic than analytic. For instance, cooperation in the industrial sector is deemed beneficial but the author does not indicate why and which activities are likely candidates, and who will produce what in which location using whose capital/technology and what the probable market outlets are.

I concur with the author that tourism has significant potential for growth once permanent peace arrives. For one thing, the demand for tourism is income elastic; for another the traffic could accelerate for visits of religious shrines once pilgrims' safety is ensured. Joint Israeli-Palestinian ventures could be developed to upgrade existing tourist facilities. This assumes that territorial disputes are resolved and that land would be bid away from current uses (housing?) into tourist attractions. The chapter, while interesting, is in need of an overall perspective that ties the sectors' analytics together. Moreover, by focusing on the Israeli-Palestinian sides only, Awartani (like Ahiram) left out the potential role of Arab countries.

Continued conflict between Palestinians and Israelis represents a process of disorder: the destruction of human lives and goods and services for no evident want-satisfying purpose. Often, the process has been driven by "passions" rather than "interests." Ultimate peace, by contrast, would save human and physical capital; invigorate foreign direct investment by reducing uncertainty; and offer a chance for a balanced development in Israel and WBGS.

In the interim Israel should start the process of confidence building by allowing Palestinian financial, law, health, education, commercial, and manufacturing institutions to function normally. As argued by Ibrahim Dakkak at the conference, the Palestinians should be allowed to have their autonomous data collection agency, which would be valuable for providing data and independent research for planning the postpeace WBGS economy.

There was some support at the conference for an import-substitution strategy. Such a strategy is likely to be distortive for agriculture and produce bias against the export-growth potential of WBGS and to provoke reciprocity by the Israeli and Jordanian economies. In contrast I suggest that openness and efficiency combined with a reasonable degree of self-reliance ought to be the norm: WBGS should also pursue a temporal human resource development path and specialize in high-value-added small industrial niches. Palestinians stand to learn tremendously from their "brothers" and "cousins" across their shared borders.

References

Avishai, B. 1991. "Israel's Future: Brainpower, High Tech, and Peace." *Harvard Business Review* Nov.–Dec.: 50–64.

Borjas, G. 1987. "Self-Selection and the Earnings of Immigrants." *American Economic Review* 77 (4): 531–53.

Bruno, M., and L. Meridor. 1991. "The Costly Transition from Stabilization to Sustainable Growth: Israel's Case." In M. Bruno, S. Fischer, E. Helpman, and N. Liviatan, *Lessons of Economic Stabilization and Its Aftermath.* Cambridge, Mass.: MIT Press.

Central Bureau of Statistics. 1972–90. *Statistical Abstract of Israel,* Annual Publications nos. 23–41.

Chiswick, B. 1980. "An Analysis of the Economic Progress and Impact of Immigrants." Final Report of the U.S. Department of Labor.

Clawson, P., and H. Rosen. 1991. *The Economic Consequences of Peace for Israel, the Palestinians, and Jordan.* The Washington Institute.

Gabriel, S., and F. Sabatello (1986). "Palestinian Migration from the West Bank and Gaza: Economic and Demographic Analysis." *Economic Development and Cultural Change,* 34: 2, p. 245–262.

Tuma, E. (1989). "The Economics of Occupation in Palestine since 1948 and the Costs of Noncooperation." in G. Fischelson ed. *Economic Cooperation in the Middle East.* Westview Press, Boulder, CO.

IV Panel Discussion

On the Political Economy of Peace in the Middle East

Zein Mayassi

The present various chapters, prepared by Arab and Israeli economists within the framework of a two-year seminar on the "Economics of Peace in the Middle East," map out a vast *potential* of economic benefits for a region that has had more than its share of conflict and suffering. Most of the papers also spell out the conditions under which such a potential may be realized.

More specifically, the papers indicate that in order for the substantial gains to be achieved, two *types* of conditions must be fulfilled: the first having to do with the specific character of the political settlement, and the other with internal adjustments individual countries would have to undertake (mainly in the form of structural economic reforms) to help exploit new opportunities created by peace. The second set of conditions has to do with the design of appropriate economic policies and is amply discussed by several of the authors; I will therefore focus my remarks on the first.

Several of the chapters emphasize that an essential condition for the economic benefits of peace to become even potentially realizable is that "the resolution of the conflict must entail a real, durable, and comprehensive peace," as El-Naggar and El-Erian put it.

The chapters, restricted as they are to the purely economic meaning and consequences of this statement, do not spell out its *political* content. But if the statement is to mean anything at all, it must surely mean that the envisaged peace must entail at least three operational principles, namely the full implementation of relevant U.N. Security Council resolutions calling for the withdrawal of Israel from the Palestinian and Syrian territories occupied in the course of the 1967 war and from South Lebanon, the negotiation of peace agreements providing for secure and recognized borders and for normalization between Israel and its Arab neighbors, and the full cooperation of Israel in an internationally supervised interim arrangement for the occupied Palestinian territories (including Jerusalem) leading to the establishment of a Palestinian state to be confederated with Jordan. Needless to say, mutually agreed adjustments of pre-1967 boundaries may be called for and ought to be allowed. The essential requirement is the removal of the consequences of war that have remained obstacles to peace. This would clear the path for entering further agreements on economic, diplomatic, and strategic issues leading to a durable and comprehensive peace in the region.

It is simply inconceivable that the Arab states, much less the Palestinians, would proceed to sign a peace agreement that entailed continued Israeli occupation of Arab territories. To proceed beyond that to normalize relations in such a circumstance would be patently fanciful.

It is also important to take note of the Palestinian component of the envisaged settlement, universally viewed as the very core of the Arab-Israeli conflict. Any settlement that does not deal fairly and adequately with the national political rights of the Palestinians will not stand the test of time even if such a settlement were to be somehow squeezed out of the current discussions. For as has often been stated, Israel may succeed in negotiating limited agreements with its Arab neighbors (à la Camp David), but it is only the Palestinians who can legitimize *comprehensive* peaceful settlement and thereby make it durable.

The *economic* implications of the requirement for a genuine and comprehensive peace are no less compelling. A limited agreement between Israel and the Arabs that leaves key issues unresolved (e.g., Palestinian self-determination) will be correctly viewed as a mere truce in an extended conflict. Most, perhaps all, of the economic benefits discussed in the papers would therefore not materialize. In the shadow of an ever-present potential for the outbreak of hostilities, no peace dividend from reduced military spending can be assumed, nor will direct foreign investment or expanded tourism materialize. More important, under the ever-present threat of a possible return to armed conflict inherent in a limited agreement, governments will not be inclined to undertake the internal economic and political reforms essential for an effective exploitation of the opportunities of peace. Handoussa and Shafik clearly demonstrate this crucial point in the case of Egypt where, despite the Camp David accords, economic interaction with Israel has remained minuscule because of the limited nature of the agreement and the accompanying tension and violence that have continued to afflict the region.

It is interesting to note that the Arab economists in the group of authors stress the comprehensive and durable nature of the envisaged peace, whereas the Israeli economists remain distinctly more tentative on this point. Indeed, Halevi gives reasons why Israel would need to maintain its military strength (presumably including the atomic bombs, missiles, sizable armed forces, etc.) even *after* a peace agreement had been concluded. Such a posture is self-defeating and could only undermine the credibility and hence the sustainability of a peace agreement. For a fully armed Israel could always induce the temptation, on the part of one or more of the Arab states, to seek to match Israel's armed strength, thereby bringing about the whole vicious cycle of threat of war and possibly armed conflict into the region.

But suppose a genuine and comprehensive peaceful settlement were to be ultimately achieved, what would be the economic consequences?

Before one answers the question it is perhaps worth reminding oneself that the attainment of such an objective (assuming it is at all possible) requires several years (perhaps longer) of arduous negotiations marked by delays, suspensions, and possible breakdowns. It is interesting that not many of the authors address explicitly this transitional period and its economic implications. Two such authors do (Ahiram and Halevi). The latter especially, pointing out the enormous structural changes now taking place in the Israeli economy as a result of the massive immigration of Soviet Jews, reminds us that by the time a peace agreement is finally reached the Israeli economy and society will be radically different from what they are now. This notion carries ominous implications to the occupied territories if it also means that Israel's drive to colonize the West Bank and the Gaza Strip would be permitted to proceed unchecked during this period.

But assuming this does not happen and negotiations proceed rather smoothly and soon toward agreement (a development not easy to envisage), and assuming the agreement entails measures for normalization of economic relations between Israel and its Arab neighbors, then of course the economic benefits would be immense. These would arise not only from the reallocation of resources previously dedicated to defense toward more productive uses, but also from augmented trade and investment flows, revived tourism, as well as regional cooperation on infrastructure, energy, and the environment. The chapters describe fully these salutory effects for individual countries and for the region as a whole.

One final point needs to be made concerning the development strategy and economic orientation of the future Palestinian state. Although the papers discuss several possibilities, there is in fact little choice in the matter. Given its narrow resource base, its small size, and its relative state of underdevelopment (in large part as a result of more than two decades of occupation), the future Palestinian state must by necessity adopt fairly open and liberal policies on currency and trade and must orient its development strategy toward the export markets. This will not be easy, but it is not unrealistic either.

Given the expected availability of considerable external financial resources, the high levels of skills and education of the Palestinian labor force, the proven entrepreneurship of its professionals, and chances of success may be judged good. Such a state would also attract human and financial capital from the Palestinian Diaspora, which in light of its performance in other countries could make a considerable difference to the economic prospects of the new state.

In terms of the future state's relationship with its neighbors, there is little doubt that once an initial period of adjustment is traversed, some form of economic union, at least with Jordan and Israel, would have to evolve. This of course, like all the other good things that are held in promise following a settlement, depends first and foremost on achieving a "real, comprehensive, and durable peace" in the region as a whole.

Comment

Michael Bruno

I would like to start by stating my bias with respect to the subject of this conference: when talking about peace I consider the subject first and foremost as an Israeli and not as an economist. For our generation and that of our parents and our children, war and peace have been very real and vivid matters that go much beyond economic considerations. A real peace is worth paying for.

I am not sure whether the net economic benefits of peace are all that clear. My own country enjoyed very fast economic growth during 1948–73, even though a state of belligerency prevailed between the surrounding Arab states and Israel. Israel's profound economic crisis during 1973–85 had relatively little to do with its military situation, and although Israel incurred substantial defense expenditures in those years the defense burden was not the major reason for the crisis. Governments, such as Israel's during much of the 1970s and up until 1985, can mess up the economy and fail to reform it for a variety of reasons. It could equally well happen in peacetime, so it is not peace by itself that will help economic progress. Moreover, governments (though I do not think any Israeli government ever did that) may use war and belligerency to attract the public's attention away from internal economic and social problems.

Will peace bring about a substantial cut in defense expenditures? I doubt whether this would happen in Israel's case in the first few years because of the smallness of the country, the length of its borders, and the territorial risks that it would have to take. The tradeoff would be to invest more, for a while, in expensive early warning signals.

There would, of course, also be some economic advantages to the peace process, quite apart from the redirection of social and political concerns. Countries' risk rating in the eyes of foreign investors very much depend on the geo-political factor. If it were not for regional instability, Israel's relative rating on an international scale would have been considerably enhanced, commensurate with its excellent record as a sound borrower and its improved macroeconomic policy performance in recent years.

What I found missing in this conference was a much greater emphasis on the reverse causality going from economics to the peace process. Rather than talk about the long-run implications of peace for the economy we should concentrate more on economics as a servant or as a *vehicle* for furthering the peace process.

I agree with the argument mentioned here that the timing of the *intifada* was in no small measure connected with the worsening of the economic conditions in the West Bank and Gaza. Consider for a moment Israel's policy options in 1967–68. Economic developments in the territories proceeded very fast after the end of the Six Day war, in large part due to the liberal approach to trade across the Jordan, the promotion of agricultural extension services, etcetera. Israel made two mistakes, however. One way to rely on free movement of labor into Israel as a substitute for investment in economic activity in the territories (I thought at the time that letting labor move in freely was also detrimental to Israel's long run interests). The other mistake was to believe that while 'waiting for the phone call' (from Jordan), Israel could remain the 'benevolent occupier' without accompanying its liberal economic policy with promotion of political self-expression. The fact is that neither the phone-call nor local political emancipation ever took place. Rising economic welfare, however, kept the area relative stable for quite a long time.

There are numerous confidence-building measures that could be taken as first steps towards better understanding on an inter-country basis. Joint tourist packages, joint environmental protection of the Red Sea, joint arid-zone research and development projects are some of the examples. On the side of developing sounder and healthier economic relationships between the Palestinians and Israelis, one should be talking about trade liberalization between Israel and the West Bank and Gaza, monetary and banking arrangements, promotion of capital inflow for physical investment in the territories, and steps to liquidate refugee camps in Gaza.

My final comment relates to what I believe has to distinguish a professional meeting like this one at Harvard University in Cambridge, Massachusetts, from the peace talks in Madrid, Washington, or any other capital. To be constructive, participants of a conference like this one should not appear here as if they were being transmitted on a loudspeaker to their political home audiences. At times, during the discussion in this conference, I was not sure whether these in fact were the ground rules. Let us leave the political negotiations to the legitimate political representatives of the various sides and try to concentrate here on what economists can contribute on a professional level to the promotion of the peace process.

Comments

Hani Abu-Jabarah

Important Issues Discussed and Highlighted by the Workshop

The workshop must be commended for its attempt to identify the economic consequences of peace in the Middle East. The thesis developed in this workshop is clear: from an economic viewpoint, every country involved in the Arab-Israeli conflict will benefit from peace, though in varying degrees. The conference participants have clearly shown that once peace arrives, the need for military spending will subside. Normalization of diplomatic and political relations among the countries of the region, it is hoped, will lead to the normalization of economic relationships. A larger volume of trade, slowly but surely, will start to flow among the countries of the region, especially among those countries that were not trading with each other before peace was achieved. Freer movements of labor and capital will ensue as well.

The workshop succeeded in providing the framework that led participants to realize independently that the economies of the countries of the Middle East complement each other. Some countries, such as Egypt and Jordan, are labor abundant. Other countries, such as the Gulf states, are capital abundant. Still another country, Israel, is relatively advanced in technology. When peace prevails, the region will have an opportunity to better utilize its factors of production. The returns of this development will be shared by all nations in the region.

Another achievement of the workshop is the implied recognition of all participants that no solution to the conflict would have any chance of success unless it takes into consideration the economic needs and aspirations of all of the peoples involved, including the

Palestinians. The conference scored points when it emphasized the importance of equitable and even-handed treatment of all nations in the Middle East.

Finally, I believe that the most important achievement of this conference was the understanding it so successfully advanced: that peace will entail some sacrifices in the short run from all countries involved in the conflict. But surely in the long run peace will bear economic dividends to be distributed among all nations of the region.

Important Issues Ignored by the Workshop

Although we are gratified to see that the conference dealt in a profound way with some burning economic issues, we should recognize that it overlooked other important topics. For instance, the workshop did not specify a possible set of assumed conditions for a peace agreement between Israel and the Arab states. This is important because the outcome of a peaceful settlement will have a bearing on economic relationships in the region.

I must cite at least one example to demonstrate the importance of mapping out the framework of a peace treaty before embarking on a detailed analytical exercise on the economic implications of peace. A peace based on a completely independent Palestinian state will result in a certain set of economic relationships that differ fundamentally from those arising from a Palestinian entity that enjoys only limited power over economic decisions. Another possibility is that the Palestinian entity will enter into a form of economic unity with Jordan. A different possible outcome of peace is the establishment of a kind of an economic coordination between Palestine, Jordan, and Israel. The point here is that a set of assumptions on which peace will be established will lead to different economic relationships.

Another issue not directly covered is the impact of peace on democracy in the Middle East. No rational person would argue against the hypothesis that there is a direct and positive relationship between democracy and economic choices. In the past few decades, we have seen that certain leaders in the Middle East, without consulting their fellow citizens, chose to transform their economies from basically free enterprise systems to centrally planned economies. This transformation has been effected under the pretext that these countries should marshal all of their resources for battle with the enemy. An independent and objective observer of the Middle East would conclude that democracy, in the sense of the right of people to freely express their choices, did not advance much in certain countries of the region. One excuse given by some political leaders for not advancing democracy is the external threat posed by the enemy. The implication here is that democracy and confrontation with the enemy are two mutually exclusive phenomena. Once peace prevails, this excuse will no longer be valid. The pressure on political leaders to yield to popular demands for democratization will be strong. This aspect of the post-peace era was overlooked by the workshop, perhaps because it is highly sensitive. But I can assure you that the people of the Middle East will cherish democracy as the most precious fruit of peace.

A third aspect that should have been subjected to some sort of analytical study in this workshop is the effects of peace at the subsector level. Labor, manufacturing, agriculture, water resources, capital flows, health care, and financial institutions are only a few examples of the subsectors that need to be thoroughly analyzed under a peace setting. The conference dealt with the consequences of peace on a macro level. This was a necessary step for advancing the analysis of the consequences of peace on a sectoral level. To be sure, some papers touched on certain subsectors. But this was not accomplished in a way that helps to answer the questions that may be asked by policymakers. Decisionmakers are anxious to know how peace will specifically affect every sector of their economies.

A Few Suggestions for the Future

Having mentioned the positive outcomes of the workshop and the issues that were overlooked by the conference, I would like to suggest a few topics to be addressed by the institute in the near future.

First, it seems that all indications point to the fact that a Palestinian entity will be created as a result of a peaceful settlement. It is believed that this entity will pass through two stages. The first stage will be transitional and of limited duration, perhaps three to five years.

In the second stage, the final shape of the Palestinian entity will emerge. I believe that the economic relationships and institutions of the final entity will depend on those of the transitional stage. Therefore, a comprehensive study of the economics of the transitional stage of the would-be Palestinian entity must be initiated without delay. An advantage of conducting such a project would be the development of a viable economic framework for such an entity before it comes into existence. It will be too late to start thinking about the economics (macro and micro) of the Palestinian entity after its creation. The suggested study should be designed at the subsectoral level. Moreover, the study has a better chance of being appreciated by the policymakers of the Middle East if it starts by spelling out the basic assumptions on which the Palestinian entity would be founded. Its relationships with the economies of both Jordan and Israel must be realistically assumed if such a project is going to gain any credibility.

Another topic that was not emphasized by the workshop is regional economic integration. In the post-peace era, the countries of the region will surely appreciate the fruits of economic stability and cooperation. As a matter of fact, however, to be a key player in world affairs, a country must be economically strong. Further, to reap the benefits of economic development, production processes must be competitive. This is better achieved by large economic entities, in which integration will result in better resource allocation and utilization. Once peace takes place, the countries of the Middle East will realize the advantages of economic integration. If not out of desire, the countries of the region will seek economic integration out of need. Only a comprehensive study would explore the reality of this dream: the economic integration of the countries of the region in a peaceful Middle East. This endeavor must encompass the Gulf states in addition to the countries directly involved in the Arab-Israeli dispute. The proximity of the Gulf states to the area of the conflict and their role as the largest market in the Middle East for foreign labor, make their exclusion from any study of the region's economic integration unrealistic.

Perhaps the first step of a workshop on the outcome of peace should have been the construction of a model for the process of decisionmaking in the Middle East. Before a scholar engages in qualitative and quantitative analyses of the possible economic outcomes of peace, he or she should logically pose the following question: How do policy- and decisionmakers of the Middle East arrive at their decisions? What variables to they take into consideration when they contemplate an economic issue? Unless researchers on the consequences of peace profoundly comprehends the behavioral aspects of Middle East policymakers, their conclusions may be academic and theoretical. The workshop did not give this dimension the attention it deserves.

Finally, I must close my comments by emphasizing the fact that my observations are by no means intended to imply that the issues covered in the conference were irrelevant or unimportant. Nor should it be assumed that the quality of the papers and their discussions were of compromising standards. On the contrary, I believe that they will prove to be of great help to peace—the commodity that we, the Middle Easterners, are longing for.

Contributors

Hani M. Abu-Jabarah has worked with the Cairo-Amman Bank in Jordan since 1990. Between 1972 and 1990, he was on the faculty of the School of Economics and Administrative Sciences at the University of Jordan. His research interest lies in the areas of economic development, the economics of taxation, auditing and accounting, and research methodology. He holds a Ph.D. in accounting, finance, and international economics from the University of Wisconsin-Madison.

Ephraim Ahiram is a research fellow at the Davis and Truman Institute and lecturer of economics, focusing on Middle Eastern countries and Israel, at the Hebrew University. He received his Ph.D. from the London School of Economics. Ahiram has served as a colonel in the Israeli military in the capacity of head of economic affairs in the military administration of the West Bank.

Sulayman S. Al-Qudsi has been a visiting associate professor at the University of California-Davis since 1989. He also works as an associate energy specialist at the California Energy Commission. He has written extensively on several aspects of the economies of the Middle East. He has worked at the Kuwait Institute for Scientific Research and Kuwait University.

Hisham Awartani is a professor of economics at An-Najah National University in the West Bank, where he is involved with academic and policy-oriented research relevant to the occupied Palestinian territories. He is the author of numerous papers and reports on the Palestinian economy, and has just completed a reference book on *The Economy of the Occupied Palestinian Territories, 1967–1990*.

Amer Bisat is an economist in the International Monetary Fund's European Department. His research interests focus on financial sector development. His contribution to this volume was written while he was at Columbia University. He has worked at the World Bank. He holds a degree from the American University of Beirut and a Ph.D. from Columbia University.

Michael Bruno began teaching at the Hebrew University in Jerusalem in the 1960s, becoming a professor there in 1970. In 1975–76 and 1984–85 he served as an economic advisor to the Israeli Minister of Finance. He was governor of the Bank of Israel from 1986 to 1991. He has been president of the Econometric Society and is currently president of the International Economic Association. His main research interests include development and international and monetary economics.

Ishac Diwan is a senior economist in the Middle East and North Africa Regional Office of the World Bank. Previously he was an assistant professor of finance at New York University. His research interests and publications include international finance, international trade, and macroeconomics of structural adjustment. He received his Ph.D. in economics from the University of California-Berkeley.

Mohamed A. El-Erian is division chief in the Middle Eastern Department of the International Monetary Fund. He is a graduate of Cambridge University and received his master's and doctorate degrees in economics from Oxford University. He has written about international financial and economic issues for several publications.

Said El-Naggar is a professor emeritus at Cairo University. He has held various positions in international organizations, including executive director at The World Bank representing Arab countries, director of the United Nations Economic and Social Affairs in the Middle East, and deputy director of research at UNCTAD. He has written extensively on international economic issues.

Stanley Fischer is the Elizabeth and James Killian Professor and director of the world economy laboratory in the department of economics at the Massachusetts Institute of Technology. He has served as Vice President of Development Economics and Chief Economist at The World Bank; and held consulting appointments with the State Department, The World Bank, the International Monetary Fund, and the Bank of Israel. Professor Fischer is a Fellow the Econometric Society and the American Academy of Arts and Sciences, a Guggenheim Fellow, and a Research Associate of the National Bureau of Economic Research. He took the B.S. and M.S. in economics at the London School of Economics and obtained his Ph.D. in economics at MIT.

Nadav Halevi is currently the Aron and Michael Chilewich Professor of International Trade at Hebrew University of Jerusalem. He received his Ph.D. in economics from Columbia University and has been a member of the Hebrew University department of economics since 1960.

Osama A. Hamed is a member of the department of finance at Temple University in Philadelphia. He worked from 1988 to 1989 as a senior economist at the National Bank of Kuwait, where he did research on a number of Middle Eastern economies. His present research concerns international labor migration, the business cycle, and foreign exchange regimes. He holds a Ph.D. in economics from the University of California-Los Angeles.

Mohamad L. Hammour is an assistant professor of economics at Columbia University. He was educated at Stanford University and the Massachusetts Institute of Technology, from which he received his Ph.D. in 1989. He conducts research in the area of macroeconomics.

Heba Handoussa is vice provost and professor of economics at the American University in Cairo. She also works as an advisor to the Minister of Industry in Egypt and has served as a consultant to the Egyptian government and to The World Bank. Previously she served as chair of the department of economics and political science at the American University. She has a Ph.D. from the University of London and has written widely on public enterprises, industrial strategy, employment issues, and macroeconomic policy in Egypt.

Rizkallah Hilan is the former economic advisor to Syrian Prime Minister Kassem. He is a professor emeritus at Damascus University and a former lecturer at Aleppo University.

Ephraim Kleiman is a professor of economics at the Hebrew University of Jerusalem. Born in Poland in 1931, he grew up in Tel Aviv, where his family settled before World War II. After serving with the Israeli Defense Forces in the 1948 war, he studied economics in Jerusalem and at the London School of Economics, where he received his doctorate. He has held visiting appointments at the Universities of Pennsylvania and Illinois, the Australian National University, the Stockholm Institute for International Studies, and the International Monetary Fund.

Zein Mayassi is the chairman of K & M Properties Limited, a real estate, engineering, and construction company in London. He is a member of the Palestinian National Council as well as a member of the Board of Trustees of the Palestinian Students' Fund and the Welfare Association. He obtained a bachelor of science degree in civil engineering from the American University of Beirut.

Howard Pack is a professor of city and regional planning, economics, and public policy and management at the University of Pennsylvania and director of the program in international development and appropriate technology. He has been a research associate of the Falk Institute for Economic Research in Israel and the department of economics of the Hebrew University, as well as a consultant to The World Bank, the U.S. Agency for International Development, the Interamerican Development Bank, and other international aid agencies. He holds a Ph.D. in economics from the Massachusetts Institute of Technology.

Nicholas Papandreou earned his B.A. at Yale University and his Ph.D. in economics at Princeton University. After serving in the Greek air force, he taught at the School for Public Administration in Athens and at the University of the Aegean. He served as a consultant to The World Bank, where he worked on issues of industry and finance in North Africa and the Middle East. He has published articles on labor markets, soft budgets, the effects of price controls, and the economic costs of the tensions between Greece and Turkey. He is completing a book on culture and politics in Greek society.

Gustav Ranis is the Frank Altschul Professor of International Economics at Yale University. He served as director of the Economic

Growth Center at Yale from 1967 to 1975. He has been a consultant to The World Bank, the U.S. Agency for International Development, the United Nations Development Program, and the Ford and Rockefeller Foundations, among others. He sits on the advisory boards of several Third World research institutions. He has written several articles and books on theoretical and policy-related issues of development.

Dani Rodrik is currently a professor of economics and international affairs at Columbia University in New York. A native of Turkey, he received his Ph.D. in economics from Princeton University and subsequently was an associate professor at Harvard University. He was a National Fellow at the Hoover Institute, Stanford University, during the period when work for this book was undertaken. He specializes in international economics and development.

Radwan Ali Shaban is an assistant professor of economics at the Georgia Institute of Technology. He has been an assistant professor of economics at the University of Pennsylvania and a researcher at the Kuwait Institute for Scientific Research. His research interests are in development economics with a focus on rural markets and applied microeconomics. He earned a Ph.D. in economics from Stanford University.

Nemat Shafik is an economist at The World Bank, where she has worked in various economic research and consultant capacities since 1988. She also holds an adjunct professorship in economics at Georgetown University. She has served as an economic policy analyst, evaluation officer, and consultant for the U.S. Agency for International Development. She received her doctorate in economics from St. Anthony's College at Oxford University.

Elias H. Tuma is professor of economics at the University of California-Davis. A Palestinian Arab from Israel, in the United States since 1955, Tuma has kept in close touch with events in the Middle East, especially with regard to the Arab-Israeli conflict. He has been a consultant to the United Nations and FAO concerning problems of development in the region. He has written several books and many articles relating to the Middle East. For the last five years he has published a monthly forum, *Another Viewpoint,* which centers around the Arab-Israeli conflict and other Middle Eastern issues.

William G. Tyler is currently the lead economist for the Middle East Department of The World Bank. Before joining The World Bank in 1982, he was on the economics faculty of the University of Florida and the director of the Center of International Economic and Business Studies. He has been a professor at the Getulio Vargas Foundation in Rio de Janeiro, a senior fellow at Kiel University, an economic advisor in the Brazilian Planning Secretariat, and a visiting professor at Uppsala University.

John Waterbury is the William Stewart Tod Professor of Politics and International Affairs at Princeton University. His research and teaching interests are comparative government, the politics of development, and Middle East politics. He is the author of several books and articles about the political and economic aspects of the Middle East. He has been a Guggenheim Fellow, a visiting member at the Institute for Advanced Study, and has had grants from the Ford, Rockefeller, and Pew Foundations. He earned a Ph.D. in political science at Columbia University.

Index